BAD MODERNISMS

DUKE UNIVERSITY PRESS   DURHAM & LONDON 2006

BAD
MODERNISMS

Douglas Mao & Rebecca L. Walkowitz, editors

Contents

Acknowledgments

The editors take pleasure in thanking the Humanities Center, the Literature Program, and the Department of English at Harvard University for sponsoring the "Bad Modernisms" conference, which helped to launch this volume. Warm thanks also to Matthew Bremer, who designed the beautiful poster for that event. In the making of *Bad Modernisms*, we are grateful to Marjorie Garber, Barbara Johnson, Joseph Litvak, Henry S. Turner, Evelyn Schwarz, and Chip Wass for their intellectual generosity and warm support from the beginning and to the anonymous readers for Duke University Press, who made the book better at the end. Finally, our thanks to Taryn Okuma, Sara Phillips, and Christopher Schmitt, who assisted us with the preparation of the manuscript, and to Ken Wissoker, Courtney Berger, Kate Lothman, and Katharine Baker who welcomed and nurtured the volume at Duke.

Douglas Mao and Rebecca L. Walkowitz

Introduction: Modernisms Bad and New

The essays in this volume take up a range of artifacts from poetry and manifestos to philosophy and movie musicals; in so doing, they both exemplify and interrogate the so-called new modernist studies or new modernisms. To be sure, this critical project, whose emergence has coincided with a powerful revival of modernist sensibilities in architecture, design, poetry, and other arts, has not been formulated in any strict or polemical sense by its practitioners. Rather, the new modernisms seem to have arisen from diverse quarters; to have found a stimulus in a new journal (*Modernism/Modernity*); to have come into focus as the title of a conference (the inaugural meeting of the Modernist Studies Association); and thereafter to have been certified as a coherent trend by a prominent article in the *Chronicle of Higher Education*. It is clear, nonetheless, that the rubric encompasses at least two significant enterprises: one that reconsiders the definitions, locations, and producers of "modernism" and another that applies new approaches and methodologies to "modernist" works.

In its definitional aspect, the new modernist studies has extended the designation "modernist" beyond such familiar figures as Eliot, Pound, Joyce, and Woolf (to take the subfield of literature in English, central to this volume) and embraced less widely known women writers, authors of mass cultural fiction, makers of the Harlem Renaissance, artists from outside Great Britain and the United States, and other cultural producers hitherto seen as neglecting or resisting modernist innovation. Some contemporary scholars have even chosen to apply "modernist" yet more globally—to, say, all writing published in the first half of the twentieth century—thereby transforming the term from an evaluative and stylistic designation to a neutral and temporal one, and thus economically countering the implication that a few experimental works were somehow the only ones authentically representative of their age (as in the familiar sequence Romantic-Victorian-Modernist-Postmodernist). The essays in this volume do not replace the qualitative sense of the term with the chronological, however, so much as they ask what happens when the two collide. What effects of synergy or friction result when the many, sometimes contradictory, criteria of high modernism are tested against less evidently experimental texts by principal figures; against principal works by less well known or non-European artists; against texts that seem neither to be art nor to be about art, such as erotic novels, popular films, spy thrillers, melodrama, and ethnography?

On the side of approaches, the new modernist studies has moved toward a pluralism or fusion of theoretical commitments, as well as a heightened attention to continuities and intersections across the boundaries of artistic media, to collaborations and influences across national and linguistic borders, and (especially) to the relationship between individual works of art and the larger cultures in which they emerged. This direction resonates with developments occurring throughout the humanities in recent years, of course, but it seems to accrue particular influence in the orbit of modernism, because early-twentieth-century writers were themselves so preoccupied with border crossings such as cosmopolitanism, synesthesia, racial masquerade, collage, and translation. In *Bad Modernisms*, this new variousness of approach is represented by, for example, a comparative reading of European and African American dandyisms, an approach to Filipino American modernism in the context of anti-colonialism, treatments of popular and political works alongside aesthetic treatises and canonical novels, and the commingling of values and techniques from fields such as queer theory, cultural history, cinema studies, anthropology, and literary criticism.

Thus the new modernisms; but why *bad* modernisms?

Since "modernism" first became a leading topic of critical disquisition, in the cold war writing of figures like Clement Greenberg, Harry Levin, and Irving Howe, a persistent assumption has been that badness is at once the essence and the Achilles heel of modernist art. The idea that there might be something good about bad artistic behavior did not originate with modernism, but no kind of art, so the early retrospectives suggested, has been more dependent upon a refractory relation between itself and dominant aesthetic values, between itself and its audience, between itself and the bourgeoisie, between itself and capitalism, between itself and mass culture, between itself and society in general. In 1967, for example, Howe led off his list of modernism's signal features by observing that its writers and artists form "a kind of permanent . . . opposition, . . . an *avant-garde* marked by aggressive defensiveness, extreme self-consciousness, prophetic inclination and the stigmata of alienation."[1] According to Lionel Trilling in 1965, any "historian of the literature of the modern age" would "take virtually for granted the adversary intention, the actually subversive intention, that characterizes modern writing" and "perceive its clear purpose of detaching the reader from the habits of thought and feeling that the larger culture imposes."[2] In their 1976 survey *Modernism: A Guide to European Literature 1890–1930*, Malcolm Bradbury and James McFarlane named as key elements of modernist style "shock, the violation of expected continuities, the element of de-creation and crisis," and ventured that if "Modernism is our art," this could be because "it is the one art that responds to the scenario of our chaos."[3]

In offering these generalizations, these critics were drawing upon a century of instigations by artists and reactions from audiences in which bad manners were bound up with bad times, bad feelings, and a radical destabilizing of the criteria by which a work of art's goodness or badness could be judged. The history of the modernist affront — whose influential purveyors included Baudelaire, Marinetti, and Schoenberg, and whose celebrated events included the New York Armory Show of 1913, the debut of *Le sacre du printemps* the same year, and the obscenity trials of *Ulysses* in 1921 and 1933 — was shaped by an antagonism to certain all-too-positive elements judged characteristic of works achieving more immediate public acceptance. These elements included uncritical endorsement of traditional forms, uplifting sentiments and happy endings, complacency about the course of world events, approbation of the social order, and the view that instrumentality and moral legibility were distinguishing features of worthwhile art.

Whether they used the term "modernism" or not, early-twentieth-century analysts of the new art noted not only its rejection of such positives but also how this mode of social criticism could look more like voluble disdain than visible address. In their 1927 *Survey of Modernist Poetry*, for example, Laura Riding and Robert Graves tried to show that modern poetry's apparent withdrawal from the "plain reader" owed much more to that reader's timid conventionality (and appetite for "Spiritual Elevation") than to any willful obscurantism practiced by poets; in 1931's *Axel's Castle*, to take another instance, Edmund Wilson saw both richness and danger in innovative British and French writers' increasing scorn for popular language and sentiments.[4] In the middle third of the century, Greenberg and Theodor W. Adorno authored especially influential versions of the idea that the new art most engaged society when it seemed most to turn away. Greenberg, who did more to consolidate a theory of modernism in the visual arts than any other critic, credited the avant-garde with the crucial insight that art could only find "new and adequate cultural forms for the expression of [bourgeois] society" by fixing on problems intrinsic to each artistic medium (the flatness of the canvas in painting, for example) and thus rejecting both society's "ideological division and its refusal to permit the arts to be their own justification."[5] Adorno, meanwhile, drew on the dissonances of modern music and the bleak austerities of modern writing to argue that art's meaningful protest against the way things are lay in resistance not merely to pleasing representations but to virtually all obvious social content.

To this day, no other name for a field of cultural production evokes quite the constellation of negativity, risk of aesthetic failure, and bad behavior that "modernism" does. But a profound peril lurked in this involvement with badness: it left modernism's program vulnerable to incoherence once its work achieved wide acceptance as good. And indeed the early retrospectives of modernism confirmed themselves *as* retrospective by marking how modernism's impulses had withered under the sun of esteem. In his 1960 "What Was Modernism?," for example, Levin began by reading the name of a new apartment building in New York (The Picasso) as symptomatic of was-ness, then went on to remark the relative weakness of contemporary literary production in comparison to that of the modernism whose features he was cataloguing. Seven years later, Howe noted that the avant-garde was "no longer allowed the integrity of opposition or the coziness of sectarianism; it must either watch helplessly its gradual absorption into the surrounding culture or try to preserve its distinctiveness by continually raising the ante of sensation and shock—itself a course leading perversely to its growing popularity with the bourgeois audience."[6] By 1981, Robert

4

Hughes could declare in *The Shock of the New*, a survey of modern visual art, that the "age of the New, like that of Pericles, ha[d] entered history." Though the "bourgeoisie, butt and nominal enemy of the *avant-garde*, was also its main audience," he observed, it had through much of the century remained roughly "a generation behind the art." Around 1970, however, "the middle-class audience finally enfolded every aspect of 'advanced' art in its embrace, so that the newness of a work of art was one of the conditions of its acceptability."[7]

Some critics have descried some good in this domestication of the once-bad. Trilling saw meaningful benefits in adversarial culture's reconciliation with the middle class through universities and museums; Levin found a compensation for the lassitude of art after modernism in the thought that he and his contemporaries could "so effortlessly enjoy those gains secured by the pangs of our forerunners";[8] and some later critics (such as Ricardo Quinones in *Mapping Literary Modernism*, 1985) have stressed still more heavily the sheer good of the existence of modernism's masterpieces. But many, above all those writing from a broadly Marxist orientation in the 1980s and beyond, have argued that the sapping of subversive energies deprived modernism of its meaning, either as a force in new artmaking or as a body of past works to which one might turn. Denouncing the avant-garde's loss of connection to political radicalism, Andreas Huyssen wrote caustically in *After the Great Divide* (1986), "Like a parasitic growth, conformism has all but obliterated the iconoclastic and subversive thrust of the historical avantgarde of the first three or four decades of this century."[9] In "When Was Modernism?" (1987), Raymond Williams charged that modernism gets confined to a "highly selective field . . . in an act of pure ideology" when formerly "marginal or rejected artists become classics of organized teaching and of travelling exhibitions in the great galleries of the metropolitan cities."[10] Dating the death of modernism closer to the fall of the Berlin Wall, T. J. Clark has wondered more recently whether there can be any "modernism without the practical possibility of an end to capitalism existing, in whatever monstrous or pitiful form."[11] And Fredric Jameson has insisted on a radical difference between the Greenberg generation, which nullified critique by providing institutional sanction, and the early-twentieth-century artists who, in Jameson's view, knew "no identifiable public" and "came into a world without models . . . without any pre-existing social role to fill."[12]

A number of critics have even defined "modernism" in opposition to "the avant-garde," aligning the former with a "passive stance" of cozy relationship to the status quo, the latter with a mission of "actively attacking the institution of art."[13] By the end of the century, certainly, "modernism" could be used in a way that "avant-garde" could not: to suggest a persistent orthodoxy rather than a deliberate challenge. In the visual arts, this turn was impelled partly by the rise of commercial and museum apparatuses that promoted modernism's absolute value. In architecture, it was abetted by the sheer proliferation of built examples of the "International style" and associated modernist modes. In literature, it was assisted by demonstrations — from T. S. Eliot, the New Critics, and their heirs — of how modernism was not at war against but rather continuous with tradition. And in all of these arts, as well as music, dance, theater, and film, it was thoroughly supported by a university culture that first transmitted modernist values as twentieth-century standards and later promoted the view that "postmodernism" was the energizing refutation of the complacencies for which modernism had come to stand. An eloquent encapsulation of the reversal from bad outsider to far-too-good insider is offered by Susan Stanford Friedman, who begins her 2001 reflection on the ambiguities of the term "modernism" with a pair of sketches. The first is that of the graduate student she was in 1965, for whom modernism "was rebellion. Modernism was 'make it new.' Modernism was resistance, rupture. . . . Modernism was the antidote to the poison of tradition." The second is that of her own students thirty years later, who found their own antidote to tradition in postmodernism and for whom "Modernism was elitism. Modernism was the Establishment. 'High Culture' lifting it skirts against the taint of the 'low,' the masses, the popular."[14]

Yet modernism, as we noted at the outset, seems suddenly to be enjoying a new life. In the sphere of the arts themselves, this may be in part because postmodernism has revealed itself to be at least as subject to cooptation; in postmodern architecture, especially, the line between irony or pastiche and mere recycling of comfortingly familiar forms has proven perilously thin. But across fields, "modernism" seems again to be naming something that can surprise and challenge, if not indeed profoundly unsettle. This is the hope that Marjorie Perloff voices for poetry, at least: in her critical manifesto *Twenty-First-Century Modernism: The "New" Poetics*, she proposes that since "the aesthetic of early modernism" represented by early Eliot, Stein, Duchamp, and Khlebnikov "has provided the seeds of the materialist poetic which is increasingly our own," the present might be the moment at which the "radical and utopian aspirations" of "first-stage modernism" could forcefully revive.[15] New directions in the study of modernism, meanwhile, have included efforts to recover oppositional stances occluded by institutional enshrinement and to scrutinize more closely how, in Marianne Thormählen's words, the "periodizing, characterizing, and valorizing" functions of the term "modernism" have shaped discussions of early-twentieth-century art.[16]

Even as recent scholarship has sought to bring forgotten badness to light, however, it has also questioned whether modernism's earliest incarnations were really as bad as all that. Crucial in this regard has been the thought that modernism's original professions of daring or disdain can themselves be seen as marketing strategies — how, far from opposing commerce in some absolute fashion, the modernist "work of art invites and solicits its commodification, but does so in such a way that it becomes a commodity of a special sort, one that is temporarily exempted from the exigencies of immediate consumption prevalent within the larger cultural economy, and instead is integrated into a different economic circuit of patronage, collecting, speculation, and investment."[17] Lawrence Rainey's *Institutions of Modernism* (1998), from which this quote is drawn, is only one of a number of recent studies of the economics and promotion of modernism; others include Michael FitzGerald's *Making Modernism: Picasso and the Creation of the Market for Twentieth-Century Art* (1995), Joyce Wexler's *Who Paid for Modernism?* (1997), Thomas Crow's *Modern Art in the Common Culture* (1998), and the collections *Modernist Writers and the Marketplace* and *Marketing Modernisms* (both 1996). These investigations have been complemented by a vast inquiry into exchanges between high modernism and popular culture, from Jennifer Wicke's *Advertising Fictions* (1988) to Thomas Strychacz's *Modernism, Mass Culture, and Professionalism* (1993) and beyond.

The old story in which heroic modernist outsiders assault a complacent bourgeoisie has also been complicated by the observation that there were numerous ways of being outside in the early twentieth century — many of which invited a marginalization far more enduring that that briefly experienced by Picasso or Eliot. In their 1986 collection *The Female Imagination and the Modernist Aesthetic*, Sandra Gilbert and Susan Gubar suggested that "in their problematic relationship to the tradition of authority, as well as to the authority of tradition, women writers" could be seen as "the major precursors of all 20th-century modernists, the *avant garde* of the *avant garde*," and feminist criticism has since shown how modernism was shaped by a host of exclusions and embattlements pertaining to gender.[18] The effort here has been not only to recover the central role in modernism of female artists, publishers, patrons, and critics (as in Shari Benstock's groundbreaking *Women of the Left Bank* from 1986, or Bonnie Kime Scott's *Gender of Modernism* anthology from 1990, or Bridget Elliott and Jo-Ann Wallace's collaboration, *Women Artists and Writers: Modernist (im)positionings* from 1994) but also to show how integral to modernism's development were phenomena such as women's growing economic independence and the predominantly female audience for genres legible as "bad" by middlebrow and modernist alike (as in Gilbert and Gubar's *No Man's Land*, 1988, or Suzanne Clark's *Sentimental Modernism*, 1991, or Ellie M. Hisama's *Gendering Musical Modernism*, 2001). Nor has inquiry focused on gender been the only source of complications to the heroic-outsider narrative; also crucial have been studies of exclusions and exchanges across boundaries of politics (as in Cary Nelson's *Repression and Recovery*, 1989), race (as in Houston A. Baker Jr.'s *Modernism and the Harlem Renaissance*, 1987), and sexuality (as in Colleen Lamos's *Deviant Modernism*, 1998).

For some, modernism's claims to a virtuous badness are most seriously compromised by its appearance as a dominant cultural mode in imperial centers at the very height of imperialism. In a 1990 essay, for example, Stephen Slemon declares that modernism must be seen not simply as a "radically vanguardist and anti-bourgeois movement" but rather in terms of a "wholesale appropriation and refiguration of non-Western artistic and cultural practices by a society utterly committed to the preservation of its traditional prerogatives for gender, race and class privilege," indeed as a movement whose militant version is "colonialism itself."[19] Other critics, however, have stressed the ways in which the "periphery" appropriated modernism. In their 2000 collection *Modernism and Empire*, for example, Howard J. Booth and Nigel Rigby point out that for "key figures in . . . what came to be called post-colonial studies — one thinks, for example, of

Chinua Achebe and Edward Said—modernist literature was at once the near-contemporary established great literature of their early maturity and the father to be slain and overcome."[20] In *Writing in Limbo: Modernism and Caribbean Literature* (1992), Simon Gikandi explores how modernism's vocabularies could be creolized in anti-colonialist directions. In *The Experimental Arabic Novel* (2001), Stefan G. Meyer shows how texts taking inspiration from the innovations of Euro-American literary modernism emerged in Lebanon and Egypt in the 1950s and 1960s. In the collection *Alternative Modernities* (2001), Dilip Parameshwar Gaonkar, drawing on Charles Taylor, discusses a "creative adaptation," where peoples " 'make' themselves modern, as opposed to being 'made' modern by alien and impersonal forces, and where they give themselves an identity and a destiny."[21]

Still others have challenged the assumption that modernism was ever essentially a creature of the Western European metropole. In the introduction to their 1999 collection *Modernism and Its Margins* (1999), for example, Anthony L. Geist and José B. Monléon observe that "modernism's reversal of the artistic priorities at the turn of the century provided the periphery with a certain authority. . . . Thus . . . within the Hispanic world—and the margins of the margin—it is with Rubén Darío's modernism that the ex-Spanish colonies manage for the first time to 'conquer' and influence Spain's cultural landscape." Nor does the example of Darío and company's *modernismo*, whose relationship to "modernism" remains a subject of vigorous debate, stand alone. As Geist and Monléon point out, "the invention of new communication technologies and the increasing globalization of capital following World War I" meant that "the avant-garde movements appeared simultaneously in the margins and the center. No longer can one speak of culture 'arriving late' to the far-flung removes of the empire."[22] In an essay in the same collection, George Yúdice recalls that the "international character" of modernism encompassed not just "French, Germans, English, Russians, Swiss, and so forth" but also "Africans, African Americans, Brazilians, Chileans, Peruvians, Jamaicans, Martinicans, Senegalese, Turks, Greeks, and others who . . . participated either in Paris or at home."[23]

One way to describe the trajectory of writing about "modernism" over the last half century, then, would be to say that it has disclosed in more and more striking ways how badness is relative and contextual. What reads in one frame as the purest oppositionality may appear in another as an intra-group squabble reinforcing all manner of tacit unanimities; what seems from one perspective the most spirited defiance of rules may be shown to require the retention or amplification of other strictures performing their own kind of gate keeping. Yet it would be wrong to conclude that recent efforts to broaden the embrace of "modernism" are no more than prescriptive and historically foundationless reaching after inclusivity. On the contrary, the achievement of recent scholarship has been a richer, more accurate history, one that sees how problems and qualities said to distinguish modernist art informed other spheres of life, and how exchanges among many modernisms — as the new locution goes — helped to shape culture in the early twentieth century. *Bad Modernisms* contributes to this project by working outward from a general base in English-language literature (and back again, and outward again) to styles of dress, philosophical treatises, Hollywood backbiting, popular fiction, anthropological field work, advertising campaigns, and other realms of life and art the extent of whose interconnection is perhaps just beginning to be appreciated.

The subject of the volume's first essay, Walter Pater, has long been emblematic of one problem in defining modernism — that of setting its temporal boundaries. For some, putting this late-nineteenth-century writer under the modernist rubric is an inadmissible stretch; for many others (including W. B. Yeats, who in 1936 placed a sentence from Pater's prose commentary on the Mona Lisa, now broken up into lines of poetry, at the front of the *Oxford Book of Modern Verse*), Pater was the veritable fountainhead of the modern in English-language writing. In "Forced Exile: Walter Pater's Queer Modernism," Heather Love takes a new approach to Pater's possibly inadequate modernness, historicizing "badness" to investigate the vocabulary of refusal and recoil with which Pater addresses changes in the taxonomy of sexuality. For Love, one of the lessons to be drawn from Pater is that effective forms of action, perhaps especially in the orbit of queer politics, may need to incorporate rather than disavow the hitherto inassimilable bads of abjection and failure. The next essay, Martin Puchner's "The Aftershocks of *Blast*," takes up the productivity of regression in a different way, placing the strident, anti-revolutionary broadsides authored by Wyndham Lewis in 1914–15 within a tradition of "manifesto modernism." Reading the self-consciously English *Blast* against Continental exempla such as Marx and Engels's *Communist Manifesto* and Marinetti's *First Futurist Manifesto*, Puchner argues that *Blast* positions itself as a sort of homeopathic remedy, taking on the form of the manifesto in order to oppose the will to immediate and radical change that manifestos embody. Adopting the avant-garde's form in order to undermine its program, Lewis produces a "rear-guard modernism"—a defending, distancing, and redirecting that seeks to transcend both the dutiful moralizing of political revolutionaries and the bad or "naughty" morality of soi-disant decadents.

From abjection and defensiveness, the volume shifts to other fertile negatives: nonsense and cliché. Michael LeMahieu argues that Ludwig Wittgenstein's *Tractatus* dramatizes the tension between a positivist understanding of modernity and an anti-positivist aesthetic modernism, via a rhetoric of "feelings" that disorients the language of both logic and art. What Puchner argues of Lewis, LeMahieu argues of Wittgenstein: that he uses the tools of modernism in order to criticize modernism, and, in so doing, suggests why a constitutive aspect of modernism lay in a strong self-negation under which critique teeters always on the edge of nonsense. In "The Romance of Cliché," which follows, Laura Frost confronts the rhetoric of modernist originality with modes of erotic representation shared by high modernist and popular fiction from the interwar years. Noting that D. H. Lawrence appropriates elements of sexual fantasy from E. M. Hull's best-seller *The Sheik*—in spite of the latter's denigration both by Lawrence himself and by pro-Lawrence critics like F. R. and Q. D. Leavis—Frost points out that formulas designed to produce pleasure in Hull's female readers are deployed to anti-erotic, moral ends in Lawrence. The derivativeness and earnestness often imputed to popular fiction thus prove to emerge more strongly in a modernist appropriation of popular clichés.

As Rebecca L. Walkowitz notes in the volume's fifth essay, Virginia Woolf too was charged with lack of seriousness by the Leavises (as well as other critics), though where Hull was faulted for clichés, Woolf was damned for evasion and quietism. Reading Woolf's fiction in the context of cosmopolitanism and social theories of dissent, however, Walkowitz argues that Woolf's indirectness constituted a strategic response to the rigidities of national culture and wartime patriotism. By refusing to conform to political or aesthetic expectations of goodness—that is, by indulging in what some took as a highly indecorous decorousness—Woolf resisted versions of generalization and literalism that supported what she believed to be worst about her society: imperial triumphalism, heroic masculinity, and sexism. In this effort, Walkowitz proposes, Woolf suggests that the modernist critique of evasion must involve the willingness to cultivate it. Walkowitz's concern with modernist and anti-modernist ways of reading is then echoed in Sianne Ngai's essay, which reveals what viewers might gain by interpreting Josef von Sternberg's film *Blonde Venus* in an "amodernist" or "bad-modernist" fashion, a fashion that would privilege plot over style or story over medium. Proposing that *Blonde Venus*, starring the German actress Marlene Dietrich, is both a tribute to and parody of the life of the African American cabaret star Josephine Baker (known as "the Black Venus"), Ngai remarks the difficulty of deciding whether the "inverted" imitation of Baker is theft or flattery. She speculates that the film's ambiguities in this regard result from a problem inherent in homage and dramatically exacerbated here by matters of race, nationality, emigration, and celebrity: that any praise effectively arrogates to itself the *right* to praise, and in this exerts a control over its object as unshakeable as it is abstract.

Monica Miller continues this discussion of race, performance, emulation, and critique in "The Black Dandy." Extending Jessica Feldman's suggestion that the dandy might be a "sign" for modernism, Miller examines how the early-twentieth-century African American dandy stood at the intersection of prior black sartorial and theatrical performances, black optimism about the unprecedented urban community that was Harlem, and white fears and desires concerning the future of black culture. Miller's analysis thus encounters the badness of modernism in two senses, one pertaining to the inevitable inability of the dandy figure to bear the burden of "uplift" with which it was charged, the other (which evokes LeMahieu and others on modernism's self-negation) pertaining to an inevitable heterogeneity or syncretism that makes modernism feel ever different from or not quite itself, always in oscillation between a cultural authenticity that can be exposed as artifice and an artifice legible as authenticity.

The next essays continue two themes taken up in earlier pieces: the relationship between modernism and regression (Love, Puchner, LeMahieu, Frost, and Walkowitz) and the elaboration of identity through contrast with racial or ethnic others (Frost, Ngai, Walkowitz, and Miller). In "A Shaman in Common," Douglas Mao shows that Wyndham Lewis and W. H. Auden both used anthropological accounts of a homosexual Siberian shaman to refine a vision of liberalism's ideal citizen as a licensed transgressor. Bringing their constructions of this figure of good badness together with their treatments of interwar politics and of relations between intellectuals and masses, Mao argues that Auden and Lewis were united by belief in certain of liberalism's core features, though they disavowed the liberal label and are remembered as belonging to more radical (and opposing) political camps. Joshua Miller, meanwhile, turns to the transpacific modernism of the Filipino American writer Carlos Bulosan to illustrate how a text's modernism can result less from a will to unsettle aesthetic norms than from a rejection of colonialist political strategies. Reading Bulosan's 1944 short story collection *The Laughter of My Father* in conjunction with Ralph Ellison's 1952 *Invisible Man*, Miller notes that audience appreciation of a text's "subversive" elements will vary with cultural—and commercial—context (the edge of Bulosan's anger seems to have been missed, for example, by American audiences). But Miller also shows that some strategies of subversion, such as the laughter in Bulosan's narratives, can bespeak affinities across historical and geographical divides.

Like Joshua Miller's essay, the volume's final two entries ask whether and how modernism persisted past the decades most often said to mark its height or peak (1910s, 1920s, 1930s). Lisa Fluet's essay, "Hit-Man Modernism," first, considers how modernist indicia meet anxieties about social change in a genre not usually associated with high culture. Pivoting her reading on Graham Greene's *A Gun for Sale*, but weaving in numerous other examples of early- and late-twentieth-century pulp fiction, Fluet argues that the figure of the contract killer links two apparently opposite social elements: on the one hand, a highly individual expertise evocative of modernism at its most Olympian; on the other, the vast welfare state whose offers of security can seem predicated on the sacrifice of individual freedom. Fluet shows that the contract killer points both ways because he is frequently a version of the "scholarship boy," a young man who rises to uneasy professionalism from humble origins and becomes an object of feminine middle-class solicitude. In Fluet's analysis, both the killer (who does not quite love society but recognizes a difficult bond to it) and the woman (who does not quite love the killer but recognizes difficult bonds to him and to the society that made him) suggest how social responsibility can be predicated on the feeling that one is *not* feeling what one should.

In Fluet's telling, this predication offers a partial answer to Raymond Williams's lament that modernist iconography has been appropriated by the critique-neutralizing forces of the administered world. And this leads directly into the volume's concluding essay, wherein Jesse Matz re-evaluates the argument that impressionistic techniques crucial to modernism mutated into a "distraction" effect deployed to bad ends in advertising and other manipulative mass cultural forms. Rather than attempting to exculpate modernism by denying this connection, Matz pursues Jonathan Crary's claim that the same forces attempting to harness distraction also produced the forms of modern attention against which distraction strains. He then goes on to consider how a number of figures from the history of impressionism understood the dialectic of attention and distraction, and how some readers of contemporary culture have pointed to progressive possibilities this dialecticized impression might hold.

The essays of this collection thus form a chain in which each speaks to the one that precedes and the one that follows, even as the overall sequence adheres to a rough chronology of the artifacts discussed. As the foregoing outline may indicate, however, the essays also group in other ways around various senses of "bad modernisms." For one thing, all the contributors take on what we have already seen to be modernism's most notorious way of going bad: its alleged surrender of resistance and transgression (aptly described by Jennifer Wicke as "our critical *bêtes blanches* these days") to sanctification and success.[24] Walkowitz and Love, for example, complicate what we might too easily dismiss as quietism; Matz and Fluet locate positive possibilities in failures of feeling and attention; LeMahieu discusses how a performance of the limits of knowledge might constitute a critique of a dominant worldview. Many of our contributors also examine bad behavior toward mainstream institutions or prevailing aesthetic standards: here one might cite Puchner on the manifesto as a kind of anti-institutional institution, Mao on the role of dissent in the liberal polity, Monica Miller on the balancing act of the black dandy, and key moments in Joshua Miller, Walkowitz, and Love. Another recurrent topic, finally, is how these forms of badness relate to "bad modernism" in the sense of work deemed inferior or inadequate *as* modernism. Fluet and Monica Miller speak to this question; so does Frost, writing on the disavowed appropriation of a mass-cultural motif; so does Ngai, positing anti-modernist ways of reading a quasi-modernist film; so does Joshua Miller, revisiting a book admired for a non-modernist serenity its author did not intend.

The last-mentioned essay may turn most vividly on a problem in reception, but in fact all the contributions to *Bad Modernisms* concern moments in which a work or performance has been misjudged or misunderstood. Purporting to set right prior misprisions is, of course, the very bread and butter of scholarly production in our time, but a little reflection will reveal that something more than this routine maneuver is at work here. In each of the cases laid out by our contributors, a failure of apprehension seems fundamental to the very interest of the work; in each, the way in which the artifact was bad according to somebody (or was good in the wrong way) tells us something about its possible meaning or value for us. And if this point strengthens the connection between modernism and badness in a general way, it illuminates more specifically the significance — among modern*isms* in all their diversity — of that invitation to misunderstanding that we call "difficulty." Leonard Diepeveen has recently argued that the difficulty enshrined as the dominant criterion for valid modernist (and postmodern) art is "not a property of the difficult work at hand, but a reading protocol that is radically affect-based";[25] expanding the focus slightly, we might say that difficulty can also come into view retrospectively, as the quality of something that seems not to have yielded all its secrets to prior readers or viewers, whether or not we delude ourselves into thinking it will yield everything to us.

From here, we might be led to one more possible reason for modernism's recent comeback. In 1960, Levin wrote that "[s]tupidity has decidedly not been the forte of the Modernists," that "they were preoccupied with the minds of their characters, and . . . make serious demands upon the minds of their readers."[26] What Levin does not quite say is something that almost always goes not-quite-said in summaries of modernism — perhaps because it seems so obvious, perhaps because it exposes too painfully how "modernism" is entangled with scarcely admissible antipathies belonging to intellectuals as a class. This point is that encounters with "difficult" artifacts or performances, whatever elation or frustration they may otherwise engender, hold always a capacity to hearten inasmuch as they seem to confirm how intelligence, complexity, and curiosity have been alive in the world (and draw life again from just such confrontations between perplexed audience and elusive object). Could it be, then, that the new-old appeal of modernism lies partly in a consolation of this sort, emerging from its very negatives? If so, we will not be surprised to find modernism holding special allure in times when the future of thinking seems uncertain, when anti-intellectualism seems ascendant, when resistance to all but the simplest positions and solutions has arrogated to itself the mantle of the good.

Notes

1. Irving Howe, "Introduction: The Idea of the Modern," in *Literary Modernism*, ed. Irving Howe (Greenwich, Conn.: Fawcett, 1967), 23–24.
2. Lionel Trilling, *Beyond Culture: Essays on Literature and Learning* (New York: Viking, 1965), iv.
3. Malcolm Bradbury and James McFarlane, "The Name and Nature of Modernism," in *Modernism: A Guide to European Literature 1890–1930*, ed. Malcolm Bradbury and James McFarlane, reprint ed. (London: Penguin, 1991), 24, 27.
4. Laura Riding and Robert Graves, *A Survey of Modernist Poetry* (London: William Heinemann, 1929), 9, 191.
5. Clement Greenberg, *The Collected Essays and Criticism*, vol. 1 (Chicago: University of Chicago Press, 1986), 28.
6. Howe, "Introduction," 24.
7. Robert Hughes, *The Shock of the New* (New York: Knopf, 1981), 375, 367–68.
8. Harry Levin, "What Was Modernism?" *Massachusetts Review* 1, no. 4(August 1960): 613.
9. Andreas Huyssen, *After the Great Divide: Modernism, Mass Culture, Postmodernism* (Bloomington: Indiana University Press, 1986), 3–4.
10. Raymond Williams, *The Politics of Modernism: Against the New Conformists*, reprint ed. (London: Verso, 1996), 34.
11. T. J. Clark, *Farewell to an Idea: Episodes from a History of Modernism* (New Haven, Conn.: Yale University Press, 1999), 9.
12. Fredric Jameson, *A Singular Modernity: Essay on the Ontology of the Present* (London: Verso, 2002), 199.
13. Jochen Schulte-Sasse, foreword to *Theory of the Avant-Garde* by Peter Bürger, trans. Michael Shaw (Minneapolis: University of Minnesota Press, 1984), xxxvi.

14. Susan Stanford Friedman, "Definitional Excursions: The Meanings of *Modern/Modernity/Modernism*," *Modernism/Modernity* 8, no. 3 (September 2001): 493–94.

15. Marjorie Perloff, *Twenty-First-Century Modernism: The "New" Poetics* (Malden, Mass.: Blackwell, 2002), 3.

16. The useful triad of gerundives comes from Marianne Thormählen's introduction to *Rethinking Modernism*, ed. Marianne Thormählen (Houndmills: Palgrave Macmillan, 2003),3.

17. Lawrence Rainey, *Institutions of Modernism: Literary Elites and Public Culture* (New Haven, Conn.: Yale University Press, 1998), 3.

18. Sandra Gilbert and Susan Gubar, introduction to *The Female Imagination and the Modernist Aesthetic*, ed. Sandra Gilbert and Susan Gubar (New York: Gordon and Breach, 1986), 1.

19. Stephen Slemon, "Modernism's Last Post," in *Past the Last Post*, ed. Ian Adam and Helen Tiffin (Calgary: University of Calgary Press, 1990), 1.

20. Howard J. Booth and Nigel Rigby, introduction to *Modernism and Empire*, ed. Howard J. Booth and Nigel Rigby (Manchester: Manchester University Press, 2000), 1.

21. Dilip Parameshwar Gaonkar, "On Alternative Modernities," in *Alternative Modernities*, ed. Dilip Parameshwar Gaonkar (Durham, N.C.: Duke University Press, 2001), 18.

22. Anthony L. Geist and José B. Monléon, "Introduction: Modernism and Its Margins: Rescripting Hispanic Modernism," in *Modernism and Its Margins: Reinscribing Cultural Modernity from Spain and Latin America*, ed. Anthony L. Geist and José B. Monléon (New York: Garland, 1999), xxi, xxx.

23. George Yúdice, "Rethinking the Theory of the Avant-Garde from the Periphery," in *Modernism and Its Margins*, 59.

24. Jennifer Wicke, "Appreciation, Depreciation: Modernism's Speculative Bubble," *Modernism/Modernity* 8, no. 3 (September 2001): 400.

25. Leonard Diepeveen, *The Difficulties of Modernism* (New York: Routledge, 2003), 244.

26. Levin, "What Was Modernism?," 627.

Heather K. Love

Forced Exile: Walter Pater's

Queer Modernism

to be weak is miserable,
Doing or suffering . . .
Paradise Lost (1.157–58)

In thinking about *bad modernism*, it may be useful to recall that it was modernism itself that gave *bad* a good name. Being bad has always meant crossing the line, turning away from what is accepted and familiar, heading out for the unknown; but it was only with modernism that the value of such transgression underwent a sharp reversal. Certainly, we may say that the Romantics inaugurated the possibility that bad could be good, that revolt could be a moral duty rather than a moral failing. But it was modernism that gave currency to the idea that going to the limits might be essential to the recreation of the world. From Baudelaire's Satanism to Marx's "poetry of the future" to Nietzsche's "transvaluation of all values," modernists sought to wreck the old world in order to make room for the new. They viewed the world of their predecessors as so corrupt and oppressive that it practically begged for destruction; they prescribed, in the words of D. H. Lawrence, "surgery—or a bomb." Although it made up only a fraction of the aesthetic production in the period, this "heroic" version of modernism has been most consistently identified with modernism itself. The academy has welcomed many of modernism's most notorious bombsquads, making a place not only for the Men of 1914, but also for Futurists, Dadaists, and Surrealists. Over the course of the twentieth century, this version of modernism has prevailed to such an extent that innovation and the break with authority now look like core values.

It is a mark of modernism's profound success, in other words, that "we moderns" tend to think that making good depends on a willingness to do bad. As a result, it is difficult to say what we might mean by *bad modernism*. If we are considering making a break with the orthodoxies of modernism, resistance may be futile: iconoclasm is what modernism is all about. If we hope, instead, to identify and claim a subaltern current or deviant strain of modernism, we are once again in trouble. Such modernism would not really be bad modernism: it would just be modernism. Again, we might interpret *bad modernism* as a dissident form of modernist scholarship; however, in an academic context that values transgression or, at the very least, novelty, modernism that is not a little bit bad does not get much play. Given the modernist transvaluation of values, it is difficult to imagine a bad modernism that would not seem anything but just fine.

In his book on the modernist work of art, *Untwisting the Serpent*, Daniel Albright characterizes modernism as an art of extremity. He writes, "Much of the strangeness, the stridency, the exhilaration of Modernist art can be explained by [its] strong thrust toward the verges of aesthetic experience: after certain nineteenth-century artists had established a remarkably safe, intimate center where the artist and audience could dwell, the twentieth century reaches out to the freakish circumference of art."[1] Albright describes the extremist impulse in modernism as a desire to cross boundaries, to set off from the center of culture toward its outer limits. What is crucial in such a definition, however, is the different valence of exile for those escaping from the center and for those who find themselves already positioned on the "freakish circumference." The meaning of modernist transgression — of crossing the line — depends to a great extent on which way you are headed: it is one thing to light out for the Territory, and something different, after all, to live there.

Recently, critics have begun to rethink this image of modernism as a "drive to the margins" by situating aesthetic modernism within a broader geographical and cultural framework. The ascendancy of American and European high modernism has been challenged by recent work that explores black and white modernism, non-elite cultural production in the period, the gender of modernism, and the global dimensions of modernity.[2]

While it is possible to understand the transgressive aspect of modernism as an escape from the crumbling center of culture (the "white flight" model), the early twentieth century was also an era of new social possibilities for a range of marginal or dominated subjects. If the prevailing image of modernism remains the drive to the margins, it is in part because modernism itself is still defined from the center; recent work on alternative cultures of modernity has not been integrated into an understanding of the period as marked by traffic *between* the center and the margins. The exemplary modernist gesture of self-exile is at some distance from the experience of "forced exile" — whether through migration or marginalization — which is one of the most widespread and characteristic effects of modernization. If one has not departed under one's own steam, being on the margins looks less like heroic sacrifice and more like *amor fati*. Such a modernism cannot easily be recuperated as good: in recording the experience of forced exile, it undermines the heroism of modernist transgression, revealing the uneven terrain of twentieth-century modernity.

As important as it is to attend to the real differences between "dominant" and "marginal" modernisms, it is also important to remember how difficult it can be, in any given case, to tell the difference. Consider the example of James Joyce, who in a certain light looks to be a perfect representative of dominant modernism. Joyce's position is significantly complicated by his status as a subject of British colonial rule. In the case of Joyce's decision to leave Ireland, it would be difficult to say whether this exile was forced or chosen. Stephen Daedalus's embrace of Lucifer as his role model in *A Portrait of the Artist as a Young Man* is perhaps the most iconic gesture of modernist transgression. Stephen is modernism's proudest exile: he takes the rebel angel's motto — "*non serviam*: I will not serve" — as the cornerstone of his aesthetic and moral program. "I will not serve that in which I no longer believe, whether it call itself my home, my fatherland, or my church: and I will try to express myself in some mode of life or art as freely as I can and as wholly as I can, using for my defense the only arms I allow myself to use, silence, exile, and cunning."[3] In the conventional account of divine history, voiced in the novel by the pastor at a school retreat, exile is figured as the punishment for Lucifer's rebellion; in following Lucifer, Stephen embraces exile as the very means of his rebellion. Stephen's decision to betray the sacred trinity of family, God, and nation is one of the defining moments of modernism. In this by-now familiar narrative, the proud exiles of Joyce's generation abandoned the bankrupt certainty of their fathers' world in order to construct new modes of life and art: they betrayed the old world in order to forge a new one.

While modernism may have destroyed the old world, it's not clear that it successfully created a new one. In this sense, Lucifer is an apt emblem of high modernism: his stand against God is both courageous and doomed from the start. Milton offers the paradigmatic account of the tragic rebellion of the most beautiful of angels. He draws attention to the intimate link between defiance and abjection at the beginning of *Paradise Lost*, when we find Satan "vanquish'd, rolling in the fiery gulf" (1.52). In these opening lines, Milton constantly juxtaposes Satan's continued defiance with his utter misery, as he describes him "prone on the flood" (1.195), raising his head above the waves to speechify against God. This constant underlining of the contrast between Satan's condition and his rhetoric is to emphasize the continuity between them: Milton suggests that it is because Satan is feeling so bad that he is talking so big.

We hear a similar quaver in Stephen's voice when he tells his friend Cranly that he is willing to bear damnation. The irony of Stephen's pledging himself to eternal solitude as he "thrills" to Cranly's touch is not lost on the reader (269), who hears the imminent disappointment in this oath of defiance. Stephen's namesake Daedalus captures the ambivalence of modernist transgression: he is at once heroic artificer — the architect of the labyrinth — and at the same time a failed creator and an involuntary exile. I think we can trace the underside of modern Satanism in the word "apostasy," derived from the Greek *apostasia*: "to stand off, withdraw" (OED). Given God's absolute power, the angels can do nothing but "stand back" from Him. As a form of aesthetic and moral apostasy, modernism joins the image of revolt to the image of abject failure. While Stephen claims to fly in the face of God, his act of apostasy is an act of refusal, a step backward rather than a lurch forward.

In his article "Salt Peanuts: Sound and Sense in African/American Oral/ Musical Creativity," Clyde Taylor offers a version of modernism that resonates with this Satanic version of rebellion. Treating the relation between black and white modernism, Taylor suggests that we think of all modernism as a response to the experience of alienation and exclusion.

[A]ll people in extreme situations are either experimenters or passive victims. African experimenters in America differ from the experimenters of Western creativity only in having less choice whether or not to try something new. The displaced Africans shared the same motivations for experimentation and for indifference to faithful representation of the world ordered by Western rationalist intelligence as those which drove Picasso, Stravinksy, and Ezra Pound. In both the African American oral tradition and the art movements we call modernist, we find a driving search for forms of spiritual and human expression that could withstand the alienation of modern industrial culture and its inclination to transform human relations into commodity relations.[4]

Taylor traces modernist innovation as a response to victimization and sees continuity between the kinds of experiments undertaken in dominant cultures and those undertaken in vernacular ones. The only difference is that "African experimenters in America" have had less choice than "the experimenters of Western creativity [about] whether or not to try something new." Drawing a link between the experience of black Americans and of high modernists, he suggests that in the early twentieth century both groups found themselves on the margins; setting the heroics of modernist innovation side-by-side with the experience of victimization, he draws out the strain of failure that runs through all modernism. Such a framework offers a usefully rich account of "dominant" modernism, of "marginal" modernism, and of the many modernisms ranged along this spectrum. Yet there are crucial differences between a generalized sense of alienation and structural forms of domination.[5] A rethinking of bad modernism — of modernism gone bad — along Taylor's lines also demands a new attention to the specific forms of exclusion faced by early-twentieth-century subjects.

We might begin to think through such exclusions by considering the history of the word *bad*. According to the OED, *bad* originally derives from the Middle English *bad-de*, a variation on the Old English term *bæddel* ('homo utriusque generis, hermaphrodita') and its "derivative *bædling* 'effeminate fellow, womanish man,' applied contemptuously." Webster's Unabridged Dictionary links the term further to *bædan*, to defile. This term finds its origin in an experience of social domination, in the stigmatizing force of the insult ("*bædling* . . . applied contemptuously"). With the performative force of any slur, *bad* constitutes the other as abject, marginal, and degraded simply through the act of naming. It is possible to trace the aftereffects of this origin in a range of meanings over the last several centuries: these meanings range from more neutral definitions of *bad* as "lacking good qualities" to stronger characterizations such as unpleasant, unhealthy, deficient, downcast, corrupt, decayed, false, pernicious, morally depraved, and evil.

This longer etymological history of bad runs parallel to the history of the word *queer*, which also has its origin as a term of abuse for sexual and gender outsiders. This playground slur underwent a change in its fortunes when in the late 1980s it was recuperated as the name for a rebel strand of lesbian and gay politics. At the end of *Bodies That Matter*, Judith Butler discusses the history of the term *queer*, asking "How is it that a term that signaled degradation has been turned . . . to signify a new and affirmative set of meanings? . . . Is this a reversal that retains and reiterates the abjected history of the term? When the term has been used as a paralyzing slur, as the mundane interpellation of pathologized sexuality, it has produced the user of the term as the emblem and vehicle of normalization. . . . If the term is now subject to a reappropriation, what are the conditions and limits of that significant reversal?" Butler considers the challenges of turning *queer* to good effect, given its "constitutive history of injury."[6] Butler's reflections here are indebted to Michel Foucault's discussion of "'reverse' discourse" in *The History of Sexuality*, in which he traces the origins of modern homosexual identity to the legal and medical literature of the late nineteenth century. Foucault's account of this history is marked by ambivalence, as he points out that the claim for the "legitimacy" of homosexuality was made "in the same vocabulary, using the same categories by which it was medically disqualified."[7] Both Foucault and Butler suggest that turning a negative category into a positive one cannot be done cleanly: modern homosexuality is bound up with modern regimes of categorization, discipline, and stigma.[8] In the context of *bad modernism*, we might ask whether the reclaiming of *bad* is a reversal "that retains and reiterates the abjected history of the term." As in the case of *queer*, the modernist affirmation of this term is haunted by its history as an instrument of shame.

If modernism in general can be said to have deployed a certain inversion of good and evil, the specific turn in the meaning of the word *bad* seems to have been an invention of black American vernacular speech. While the OED names a whole range of bad meanings of *bad*, from deficient to corrupt to evil, its one positive meaning ("Possessing an abundance of favourable qualities; of a musical performance or player: going to the limits of free improvisation; of a lover: extravagantly loving") is traced to "*Jazz* and *Black English*." The OED locates the first positive use of *bad* in the Harlem novel *The Walls of Jericho* (1928) ("This crack army o' Joshua's . . . walk around, blowin' horns. . . . The way they blow on them is too bad."). *The Random House Historical Dictionary of American Slang* traces a slightly earlier usage ("Ellington's jazzique is just too bad," 1927) and a much earlier black dialect usage in the work of the American humorist George Ade ("a pohk chop 'at's bad to eat," 1897). Geneva Smitherman traces this use of "good" bad to the Mandinka language, and specifically to the phrase "*a ka nyi ko-jugu*" ("It is good badly"), suggesting that the black dialect inversion of *bad* was an African retention.[9] This outtake from the history of *bad* points toward a bad modernism speaking in the vernacular, and speaking back to a history of victimization. The reversal of bad in an African American context is perhaps most visible as an example of reverse discourse in the reclaiming of the term "bad nigger," which originated as strictly a term of abuse but emerged later as a name for proud resistance. Classic figures of the "bad nigger" such as Jack Johnson and Stagolee embody the ambivalence of the Satanic ideal; their good badness is marked by a long history of social exile.[10]

It is striking that "bad" seems, from the beginning, to have been caught up with the fate of social exiles.[11] And while I would not want to conflate the situation of medieval hermaphrodites with that of black Americans at the turn of the twentieth century, it is nonetheless true that the word *bad* is haunted by a history of social domination. This bad or ruined history of *bad* may help us to rethink the image of modernist rebellion as heroic resistance and to bring out the strain of failure in all modernism.

In this essay I consider the bad modernism of the late-nineteenth-century critic and novelist Walter Pater, exploring his aesthetics of failure specifically in relation to his experience of bearing a marginalized sexual identity. Pater has proved difficult to classify in several ways. Understood alternately as a late Victorian, a decadent aesthete, and an early modernist, Pater resists easy situating within traditional literary periods. His most significant work, *Studies in the History of the Renaissance* (1873), looks backward to exemplary moments in the history of Western culture, celebrating the coming together of the Greek and the Christian spirit in the Renaissance. Pater's turn toward the past aims to transform the present and the future; he explored these moments in an effort to ignite a similar moment of cultural revolution in the present. He drew on the past in part to break with it; his thoroughgoing critique of religious, moral, and social tradition is legible as modernist. Pater's social position is equally difficult to classify. In one sense, we can see him as situated within the inner sanctum of traditional English culture, especially if we understand Oxford's Brasenose College (where Pater was a don) as answering to that description. However, he was also positioned at the "freakish circumference" of culture. Pater's distance from norms of gender and sexual behavior meant for him a kind of internal exile; his position of educational and national privilege could be maintained only by fending off the constant threat of exposure. While Pater avoided the fate of the most famous martyr to homosexual persecution (he died in 1894, less than a year before Oscar Wilde's trial), his position at Oxford was seriously undermined by rumors of an affair with an undergraduate, William Money Hardinge.[12]

A "queer" Pater has emerged in recent criticism, as several critics have explored the relation between his status as a sexual outsider and his aesthetics. While these critics have attended most fully to the effects of secrecy and concealment in Pater's work, here I am interested in particular in drawing out Pater's investment in failure and in victimization. We might read all of Pater's writings as dedicated to the figure of the victim: in this sense, he cultivates a modernist aesthetic based not on violent transgression but rather on refusal and passivity. Such a form of shrinking resistance may seem at odds with the protocols of modernist rebellion, and it has often been read as a sign of Pater's aestheticist withdrawal from the field of the social. I suggest recasting his aesthetics of failure as a complex response to a particular historical experience of exclusion. Pater's own situation was paradoxical; he participated in older, private forms of homosexual sub-cultural life at the same time that he witnessed the birth of homosexuality as a modern category of identity. In this sense, I think it is possible to understand Pater as doubly displaced, inhabiting a threatened position as someone with secrets to keep and as someone whose particular form of secrecy was fast becoming superannuated. Living through this moment of profound historical transformation and of displacement, Pater imagined a world in which time was suspended.

Pater's break with the future and with the hard and fast revolutionism of the modernists has made him the cause of some embarrassment. He has been closely linked to the ills of aestheticism: political quietism, withdrawal from the world, hermeticism, nostalgia, a slack relativism, and the elevation of beauty above justice. I want to suggest that what has been seen as a lack of political commitment might be better understood as Pater's failure to approximate the norms of modernist political subjectivity. I read withdrawal in Pater not as a refusal of politics but rather as a politics of refusal; I propose that we understand his shrinking politics as a specifically queer response to the experience of social exclusion. The key practices of such a politics — secrecy, the vaporization of the self, ascesis, and temporal delay — depart significantly from the modernist protocols of political intervention. Nonetheless, I argue that we should understand such practices as constituting an alternative form of politics — one consonant with the experience of marginalized subjects.

Pater begins the famous conclusion to *The Renaissance* with an epigraph from Heraclitus ("All things are in motion and nothing at rest") and a gloss on this citation. He writes, "To regard all things and principles of things as inconstant modes of fashion has more and more become the tendency of modern thought. Let us begin with that which is without — our physical life. Fix upon it in one of its more exquisite intervals, the moment, for instance, of delicious recoil from the flood of water in summer heat."[13] The profound anonymity of Pater's writing is in evidence here as he moves from an infinitive construction ("To regard . . .") to a generalizing use of the first-person plural ("Let us begin . . .") to a moment of narration that is introduced by an invocation to the reader ("Fix upon . . .") and then moves to a complete vaporization of the subject.

The agentless action that Pater describes ("the moment of delicious recoil from the flood of water in summer heat") recalls the dynamic that Eve Kosofsky Sedgwick identifies, in her work on Henry James, as "queer performativity." For Sedgwick, this term describes a combination of reticence and virtuosic stylistic performance; she traces this dynamic to the experience of queer childhood, with its combination of alienation, extreme self-consciousness, and lots of time for reading. Sedgwick draws on Silvan Tomkins's description of shame as "interrupted interest" in order to describe queer performativity as a gesture of approach followed by a blushing withdrawal. This dual movement of solicitation and self-effacement occurs throughout Pater's writing. In his approach to the reader, Pater somehow manages to be both forward and shrinking, both suggestive and withdrawn. What is striking in the passage quoted above in particular is the way that Pater identifies the movement of recoil as the most delicious moment: this investment in recoil is matched rhetorically by the delicious secreting of the subject in the text.

Throughout his writing, Pater evinces a fascination with the disappearing subject. In his first published essay, "Diaphaneitè," delivered as a lecture to the "Old Mortality Society" at Oxford in July 1864, Pater offers a breathtakingly abstract account of a particular "type of character," that "crosses rather than follows the main currents of the world's life."[14] He writes,

> There are some unworldly types of character which the world is able to estimate. It recognizes certain moral types, or categories, and regards whatever falls within them as having a right to exist. The saint, the artist, even the speculative thinker, out of the world's order as they are, yet work, so far as they work at all, in and by means of the main current of the world's energy. Often it gives them late, or scanty, or mistaken acknowledgement; still it has room for them in its scheme of life, a place made ready for them in its affections. . . . There is another type of character, which is not broad and general, precious above all to the artist. . . . It crosses rather than follows the main current of the world's life. The world has no sense fine enough for those evanescent shades, which fill up the blanks between contrasted types of character. . . . For this nature there is no place ready in its affections. This colourless, unclassified purity of life it can neither use for its service, nor contemplate as an ideal. (154)

In his description of this crystal character, Pater describes a figure even less welcome in the world than unworldly, yet recognizable, historical actors like the saint, the artist, and the speculative thinker. Pater sketches a character without characteristics; nothing positive attaches to this figure, who is defined solely by his imperceptibility and his state of permanent exile. This figure occupies the blanks between recognizable social forms and between other people. This colorless character is not solid enough to be the object of antipathy or aggression; so complete is the world's refusal of him that his only response is to evanesce, to become transparent.

Such diaphanous types appear throughout Pater's work. They populate in particular the world of *The Renaissance*. Pater imagines the Renaissance through a series of extended reveries on the lives of a range of historical and fictional characters. The book spans a period that extends from the twelfth to the eighteenth centuries and includes nearly all major movements in Western aesthetics and philosophy. This world is populated by characters or types who are indecisive, shrinking, transparent.[15] The beautiful passivity of these figures is enabled by the quality of suspended animation that characterizes this era. As Pater describes it, the Renaissance is a realm free from surveillance and from the necessity of taking sides: "[W]ithin the enchanted region of the Renaissance, one need not be forever on one's guard. Here there are no fixed parties, no exclusions" (17). In a world without warfare, warriors are not needed: one is freed up to imagine a realm populated exclusively by crystal characters. In *The Renaissance*, Pater creates a world that appears as the "counterimage" of the paranoid world of the late nineteenth century. Many of the central descriptions of this world are taken from a lexicon of homosexual secrecy: this language of suggestion indexes the diffuseness and suggestibility of male homoerotic subcultures on the eve of the invention of the homosexual.

In his article "Pater's Sadness," Jacques Khalip suggests that transparency in Pater is "allied . . . to a need for defensiveness," and he explicitly links Pater's embrace of anonymity to his experience bearing a marginalized sexual subjectivity. In a discussion of ascesis in Pater's work, Khalip writes, "We suffer because of our lack of knowing, but for Pater, the willful suffering that accompanies ascesis, or his kind of renunciation, is a far better gesture than the arrogant effort to extend and insinuate oneself over other persons and things."[16] Khalip understands Pater's withdrawal as a way of diminishing his epistemological hold over the world, a refusal to dominate. In Pater's case, such a willed act of self-overcoming can often have the air of a forced march. Khalip writes, "That sadness characterizes and vivifies a sense of absence is made clear in the way that certain habitual failures to attend both in and to the social world register the effect of various coercive routines of concealment" (147). Out of this experience of marginalization, Pater imagines an ideal type or character "whose first act of descent is a death, a self depleted by the simultaneous disappearance of the fields of sociality which are available for its self-realization" (141). In this sense, we may understand the moment of ascesis in Pater not only as a withdrawal of the subject from the world but also as a withdrawal of the world from the subject.

In her account of Pater's historical romance *Marius the Epicurean*, Maureen Moran writes that Pater draws attention to "the value of the excluded and the victimized".[17] This emphasis on the "heroic importance of the marginalized" is legible not only as a strategy for redefining Victorian manliness but also a way of registering a particular experience of exclusion. In "Diaphaneitè," Pater describes the redemptive significance of his basement type:

> Over and over again the world has been surprised by the heroism, the insight, the passion, of this clear crystal nature. Poetry and poetical history have dreamed of a crisis, where it must needs be that some human victim be sent down into the grave. These are they whom in its profound emotion humanity might choose to send. (157–58)

Pater's "clear crystal character" is defined not only by his transparency but also by his status as victim. Heroism, insight, and passion are here all bound up in an experience of martyrdom, even scapegoating, as this figure is sent to the grave by all humanity.

Pater offers a specific image of the victim as hero in a story borrowed from Heine's *Gods in Exile*, reproduced in a chapter on Pico della Mirandola in *The Renaissance*. Heine's tale recounts the twilight existence of the Greek gods after the triumph of Christianity: rather than disappearing with the coming of Christianity, the pagan gods go into hiding, live their lives out in disguise, drinking beer instead of nectar. Pater cites Heine: "Let me briefly remind the reader . . . how the gods of the older world, at the time of the definite triumph of Christianity, that is, in the third century, fell into painful embarrassments, which greatly resembled certain tragical situations in their earlier life. They now found themselves beset by the same troublesome necessities to which they had once before been exposed during the primitive ages. . . . Unfortunate gods! They had then to take flight ignominiously, and hide themselves among us here on earth, under all sorts of disguises" (21).

Pater is particularly concerned with the fate of Apollo, the god of light, who fell under suspicion "on account of his beautiful singing." A spiritual tribunal ensues, during which Apollo confesses his true identity "on the rack." Condemned to death, Apollo makes a last request: "[B]efore his execution he begged that he might be suffered to play once more upon the lyre, and to sing a song. And he played so touchingly, and sang with such magic, and was withal so beautiful in form and feature, that all the women wept and many of them were so deeply impressed that they shortly afterwards fell sick" (21).

On the one hand this is a story of the triumph of the villagers, who force Apollo's confession before executing him. The story narrates the victory of the confessors, who not only discover Apollo but torture and bury him.[18] Still, the villagers are not content to let him lie in the grave but dig him up to make sure that he is dead. The narrative continues: "Some time afterwards the people wished to drag him from the grave again, that a stake might be driven through his body, in the belief that he had been a vampire, and that the sick women would by this means recover. But they found the grave empty" (21).

Heine's story demonstrates the strategic value of disappearance under a regime in which vigilance takes the form of identification and surveillance. The gods in Heine's story are already in disguise, but this strategy of camouflage (or "fitting in") does not prove to be adequate. Apollo's most effective form of resistance is through sacrifice—his death at the hands of his torturers. It is only when he is dead that he is finally able to disappear completely, absenting himself from the grave they have made for him. Before disappearing completely, Apollo reveals himself in a performance that infects the locals with its beauty. We might understand Pater's own aestheticist practice in a similar vein; like Apollo, he "kills us softly" with his gorgeous prose before fading out altogether.

In his conclusion to *The Renaissance*, Pater writes: "Well, we are all condamnés, as Victor Hugo says: we are all under sentence of death, but with a sort of indefinite reprieve." In this vision of a universal death sentence, we can read an allegory of Pater's historical position. His experience of displacement seems to lead not only to a politics of camouflage and disappearance but also to a politics of deferral. His investment in this story of the gods lingering on after they have been dispossessed is legible in terms of the lingering on of queer figures as the new era of homosexual identity approached. According to Khalip, Pater's crystal figures indicate the possibility of a transformed future without ever moving toward that future. In describing this figure in Pater's work, Khalip writes, "The crystal character is imbued with a type of visionary beauty specific to his (or its) diaphanous description, but this transparent, recuperative alien, most himself when he is not himself, can only remind us of the process of liberation he is meant to perform, without ever actually accomplishing it" (148).

The power of this figure for Pater is represented in terms of latency, potential, and delay. He writes, "Those who prosecute revolution have to violate again and again the instinct of reverence. That is inevitable, since after all progress is a kind of violence. But in this nature revolutionism is softened, harmonized, subdued as by a distance. It is the revolutionism of one who has slept a hundred years" (158). In such passages, Pater gestures toward an underworld politics that draws on the potential that gathers beneath and behind the visible social world. Rather than violent revolution, Pater recommends sleep. He does not rise up against the onset of modernity. Instead, he responds to it with a weak refusal: he quails at its approach.

In his chapter on Botticelli in *The Renaissance*, Pater traces a "middle world" in which "men take no side in great conflicts, and decide no great conflicts, and make great refusals" (36). Pater specifically contrasts Botticelli's attitude toward these melancholy figures to Dante's: "what Dante scorns alike of heaven and hell, Botticelli accepts." The explicit reference here, as Paul Tucker notes, is to Dante's consigning of "the neutral angels, together with the historical figures guilty of futility and indecision," to the Vestibule of Hell.[19] These indecisive, neutral angels are the subject of Pater's luminous essay on Botticelli. Taking his cue from a poem by Matteo Palmieri, Pater describes a "fantasy" that "represented the human race as an incarnation of those angels who, in the revolt of Lucifer, were neither for Jehovah nor for His enemies" (35). In this alternative genealogy, Pater suggests that humanity itself is the residue or trace of a failed or weak apostasy. Like their heavenly forebears, these human figures "take no side in great conflicts, and decide no great causes, and make great refusals" (36). Their

Forced Exile

gesture of apostasy is not an act of heroic revolution; rather, they take an almost imperceptible step back from God. They are marked by loss of an indeterminate nature, a sweet melancholy that infuses each gesture and look. This melancholy is intimately tied to their refusal to act, as Pater writes that these figures are "saddened perpetually by the great things from which they shrink" (36).

Pater never names these "great things" from which Botticelli's sad angels shrink, but we might read his description of the world they inhabit as an allegory for spaces for male-male intimacy before the advent of modern homosexuality. The "queerness" of Botticelli's figures is suggested by several of the "traits" that Pater ascribes to them—wistfulness, a peculiar beauty, the air of victimization and underground existence that marks them —but also by the particular quality of their exile, which is described here as both a spatial and a temporal displacement. In tracing the celestial genealogy of these figures, Pater writes,

> True or false, the story interprets much of the peculiar sentiment with which he infuses his profane and sacred subjects, comely, and in a certain sense like angels, but with a sense of displacement or loss about them— the wistfulness of exiles, conscious of a passion and energy greater than any known issue of them explains, which runs through all his varied work with a sentiment of ineffable melancholy. (36)

The sense of loss about these figures seems to be a result of their alienation from dominant social structures: with only vaporous, insubstantial parents and no "known issue," these figures fall outside structures of kinship. Their place is not in the home; but they don't seem to belong in the closet either. Rather, Pater seems to propose here an epistemology of the vestibule, as he imagines a community of subjects defined through indecision and delay. This liminal, semi-public space allows for a beautiful deferral, and, one assumes, for the emergence of alternative forms of sociability. As attractive as this world is, the air of melancholy that infuses it serves as a reminder that this dwelling place is not freely chosen. One ends up there by failing to choose.

The spatial displacement of these figures is matched by a temporal displacement: they fall outside the home, but also outside of the linear narratives and ordered temporalities of blood kinship. These figures are outside time, suspended in an endless present of indecision. While we might think of the strange beauty of these figures as an effect of their resistance to age, they are also beautiful because they are "out of it," at a distance from the pulsions of anticipation. Pater explicitly describes the refusal of the future as beautiful in a passage on Greek sculpture in his essay on Winkelmann:

> [I]n the best Greek sculpture, the archaic immobility has been stirred, its forms are in motion; but it is a motion ever kept in reserve, and very seldom committed to any definite action. Endless are the attitudes of Greek sculpture, exquisite as is the intervention of the Greeks in this direction, the actions or situations it permits are simple and few. There is no Greek Madonna; the goddesses are always childless. The actions selected are those which would be without significance, except in a divine person—binding on a sandal, or preparing for the bath. When a more complex and significant action is permitted, it is most often represented as just finished, so that eager expectancy is excluded. (139)

The beauty of these figures is specifically tied for Pater to their lack of expectancy and to their timeless embodiment of "motion in repose." The minute gestures of the statues invoke a timeless present, imaging forth a heaven in which nothing—or nothing of significance—ever happens. To be beautiful in Pater's view is to expect nothing, least of all a child. It is significant that reproduction itself is signaled as the culprit for linear history itself: the birth of a child is defined as the "great event" which demands the breaking up of immobility into a grasping expectancy.[20]

Despite Pater's equation of beauty with childlessness, he focuses on a mother in his chapter on Botticelli: the essay centers on that shy and shrinking figure, the Madonna of the Magnificat. For Pater, however, this figure is compelling precisely for the "great refusals" of which she is capable. Not only does this peevish mother seem the victim of an unwanted pregnancy, she also refuses the historical facts of the coming of Christ and of her own deification. Through her impassivity and melancholy Botticelli's Madonna signals her weak protest; in the end, like Apollo, she is subject to a forced confession. Pater writes,

> For with Botticelli she too, though she holds in her hands the "Desire of all nations," is one of those who are neither for Jehovah nor for His ene-

mies; and her choice is on her face. The white light on it is cast up hard and cheerless from below, as when snow lies upon the ground, and the children look up with surprise at the strange whiteness of the ceiling. Her trouble is in the very caress of the mysterious child, whose gaze is always far from her, and who has already that sweet look of devotion which men have never been able altogether to love, and which still makes the born saint an object almost of suspicion to his earthly brethren. Once, indeed, he guides her hand to transcribe in a book the words of her exaltation, the *Ave*, and the *Magnificat*, and the *Gaude Maria*, and the young angels, glad to rouse her for a moment from her dejection, are eager to hold the inkhorn and to support the book. But the pen almost drops from her hand, and the high cold words have no meaning for her, and her true children are those others, among whom, in her rude home, the intolerable honor came to her. (37)

The great event that Pater describes in his account of this painting is the birth of Christ, whose divinity casts a shadow over those who receive him. I understand this passage as a melancholic meditation on the inevitability of historical change. Pater's Madonna seems burdened by her knowledge of the profound difference that Christ's birth will make. Pater suggests that Mary is saddened in particular by the inevitability of her own deification as a result of having borne the Son of God. As he describes the infant Christ guiding his mother's hand to trace out the words of the Marian Liturgy, Pater imagines that the Virgin was exalted against her will.

I want to suggest that we might read this passage as an allegory of Pater's resistance to his own future exaltation. The "intolerable honor" that came to him was the onset of late-nineteenth-century modernity, and with it the birth of homosexuality as a newly public and newly recognizable social identity. Pater was situated on the verge of a new era of possibility for queer subjects, and his ambivalence about this historical development is palpable: his choice is on his face. In this image of the Madonna, Pater produces another image of the forced confession, reminiscent of Apollo's singing before his execution. As in Heine's account of Apollo's final moments, being identified or named is described as tragic but it is at the same time a moment of glorification.

What is lost in such a moment of transformation is suggested by the opening words of the *Magnificat*, one of the prayers Pater's Madonna is forced to copy out. The words of the prayer record Mary's response to her cousin Elizabeth's praise ("Blest are you among women and blest is the fruit of your womb . . ."). The passage from Luke begins: "And Mary said: My soul proclaims the greatness of the Lord, and my spirit rejoices in God my Savior; because He has looked upon the humiliation of His servant. Yes, from now onwards, all generations will call me blessed." Mary embodies a profound contradiction: she is both God's humble servant and the Blessed Virgin, a kind of deity in her own right. What is unsettling to Pater about the moment of her glorification is that it entails the forgetting of her life of servitude. Once God looks on her humiliation, it is transformed into glory: as if magically, her shame is transmuted into pride. Pater seems to suggest that if such a deification means erasing the record of one's life on earth, it might be better to resist it. This passage resonates in surprising ways for those future generations, queer subjects forced to copy out the *Ave* and the *Magnificat* of contemporary gay and lesbian identity.

Tout s'efforce vers sa forme perdue . . .
André Gide, *Le traité du Narcisse*

Critics continue to disagree about the specific meaning of the Great Refusal in Dante's *Inferno*, arguing about whether the unnamed figure in the Vestibule of Hell is Celestine V, Boniface XIII, or Pontius Pilate. At the same time, the notion of the great refusal has been linked to a queer tradition of the refusal of reproduction and of the future. We might think, for instance, of the reworking of this passage from Dante in "*Che fece . . . il gran refuto*," by the Greek poet C. P. Cavafy:

> For some people the day comes
> when they have to declare the great Yes
> or the great No. It's clear at once who has the Yes
> ready within him, and saying it,
> he goes from honor to honor, strong in his conviction.
> He who refuses does not repent. Asked again,
> he'd still say no. Yet that no — the right no —
> drags him down all his life.[21]

Cavafy's poem suggests a model of queer subjectivity based on the experience of refusal, and on the failure to find the "great Yes" within. Cavafy suggests that this affirmation might be replaced by "the great No"—a form of refusal that, while linked to degradation, is nonetheless "right." Eve Sedgwick alludes to this poem in her introduction to *Performance and Performativity*, when she argues that performatives can work negatively as well as positively.[22] Recent work on queer performativity has focused on the importance in J. L. Austin's work of positive performatives; Sedgwick and Judith Butler have both drawn attention to the importance for Austin of the example of "I do," the great Yes of the wedding ceremony. In this context, we might understand Cavafy's refusal, his No, as the inverse of "I Do," a queer performative that is articulated in resistance to the heterosexual order.

Herbert Marcuse also takes up the idea of the great refusal in *Eros and Civilization*, when he contrasts the rational, reproductive order of sexuality (identified with the figure of Prometheus) with an alternative tradition of sexuality as pleasure and affirmation. Marcuse identifies this alternative tradition with two figures long associated with perverse desire, Orpheus and Narcissus. Prometheus, for Marcuse, defines the dominant image of the "culture-hero": "the trickster and (suffering) rebel against the gods, who creates culture at the price of perpetual pain. He symbolizes productiveness, the unceasing effort to master life; but, in his productivity, blessing and curse, progress and toil are inextricably intertwined."[23] The culture-making revolt of Prometheus is contrasted with the Orphic/Narcissistic revolt "against culture based on toil, domination, and renunciation" (164). While Prometheus is marked by suffering, his suffering is in the service of a higher aim: out of his rebellion and his work, he makes the future. Against the background of these dialectical struggles and reversals, Marcuse describes the powers of Orpheus and Narcissus as "the redemption of pleasure, the halt of time, the absorption of death; silence, sleep, night, paradise—the Nirvana pleasure not as death but as life" (164).

While Marcuse sees a great potential for liberation in the figures of Orpheus and Narcissus, he also describes the difficulty in translating these figures out of art and into politics. Describing the "order of gratification"—both aesthetic and sensual—that defines the Orphic/Narcissistic realm, he writes: "Static triumphs over dynamic; but it is a static that moves in its own fullness—a productivity that is sensuousness, play, and song. Any at-

Heather K. Love

tempt to elaborate the images thus conveyed must be self-defeating, because outside the language of art they change their meaning and merge with the connotations they received under the repressive reality principle" (164–65). In Marcuse's description of a dynamic stillness and a static productivity realized in song, we hear echoes of Pater's aesthetic ideal. But as in the case of Pater's basement types, his drowsy revolutionaries, one gets the feeling that Orpheus and Narcissus don't travel well. These are figures that are at home in the realm of art, but their interventions remain "isolated" and "unique" (209). In describing the contrast between the Promethean world and the Orphic/Narcissistic world, Marcuse recapitulates the contrast between a heroic bad modernism and a failed bad modernism:

> In contrast to the images of the Promethean culture-heroes, those of the Orphic and Narcissistic world are essentially unreal and unrealistic. They designate an "impossible" attitude and existence. The deeds of the culture-heroes also are "impossible," in that they are miraculous, incredible, superhuman. However, their objective and their "meaning" are not alien to the reality, on the contrary, they are useful. They promote and strengthen this reality; they do not explode it. But the Orphic-Narcissistic images do explode it; they do not convey a "mode of living"; they are committed to the underworld and to death. At best, they are poetic, something for the soul and the heart. But they do not teach any "message" — except perhaps the negative one that one cannot defeat death or forget and reject the call of life in the admiration of beauty. (165)

In contrast to the heroic, active rebellion of Prometheus, Orpheus and Narcissus are defined by their withdrawal from the world of the real — by their refusal to "participate." These queer figures protest "against the repressive order of procreative sexuality. The Orphic and Narcissistic Eros," writes Marcuse, "is the end to the negation of this order — the Great Refusal" (171). The problem, according to Marcuse, is how to make refusal count as anything more than refusal — or, how to make a revolt against productivity productive rather than simply negative. Like Pater's victim-heroes, Orpheus and Narcissus are pledged to the underworld: whatever their designs on the world, they do not see the light of day.

Pater himself has been understood entirely through the terms of the Orphic/Narcissistic tradition: his drowsy, shrinking form of revolution has been understood at once as a model of aesthetic subjectivity and as a political embarrassment. It is almost as if Cavafy were telling Pater's fortune in "*Che fece . . . il gran refuto*": Pater found his No—the right No, the most beautiful No—and it dragged him down all his life. In rethinking this legacy, however, I want to suggest that we might understand the Orphic/Narcissistic world not only as an aesthetic mode but also as a "mode of living"—as an alternative form of political subjectivity.

In his essay "The Commitment to Theory," Homi Bhabha writes:

> The language of critique is effective not because it forever keeps separate the terms of the master and the slave, the mercantilist and the Marxist, but to the extent to which it overcomes the given grounds of opposition and opens up a space of translation: a place of hybridity, figuratively speaking, where the construction of a political object that is new, neither the one nor the other, properly alienates our political expectations, and changes, as it must, the very forms of our recognition of the moment of politics.[24]

If we are to discover new political objects, I would argue, we need to rethink the structures and affects of political subjectivity and political expectation. Ordinarily, we are interested in a politics that would respond to the experience of the powerless, but we construct a model of politics that has nothing in common with the experience of powerlessness. The dominant model of political agency commits itself to activity and to strength and so seeks to distance itself from this legacy of weakness. The fear, of course, is that political consciousness that incorporates the "damage done" by social violence will be ineffectual and isolating. However, the streamlining of the political—of "proper" political subjectivities and affects—excludes many potential political subjects. In particular, it excludes those "unrecognizable" types who "cross rather than follow the main currents of the world's life."

We might think of the first volume of Foucault's *History of Sexuality* as another queer site for the articulation of a politics of refusal. In this project, Foucault aims to recast power as something other than a stark confrontation between the powerful and the powerless. Foucault's reframing of power is legible as an attempt to rethink strategies of resistance in response to shifting modes of domination. At the same time, we might understand Foucault's rethinking of power as clearing the way for alternative forms of political subjectivity. He writes, "Where there is power, there is resistance. . . . These points of resistance are present everywhere in the power network. Hence there is no single locus of great Refusal, no soul of revolt, source of all rebellions, or pure law of the revolutionary" (95–96). Foucault denies the concept that there is one great Refusal, suggesting instead that resistance is made up of an endless number of refusals, a "plurality of resistances, each of them a special case" (96). Given the history of queer refusal, we might read Foucault's theory of power as an attempt to make room for "special cases" — to create a politics for subjects who do not credibly embody the "pure law of the revolutionary."

The historical experience of shame and secrecy has left its imprint on queer subjectivity. The effects of this history are often understood simply as historical waste products, the shaming traces of internalized homophobia. However, instead of denying or trying to "get over" this past, queer subjects might begin to forge a politics that keeps faith with those who drew back and those whose names were forgotten. Those subjects don't wake up after a century haunting the underworld ready to plunge ahead into a glorious future. Engaging with and using the experience of ruination, failure, or badness as a resource is crucial to the construction of a model of political subjectivity that does not create a new set of exclusions. The example of Pater's shrinking resistance suggests that we need to rethink the heroics of rebellion and to begin to imagine a politics that incorporates a history of forced exile. Such a "homeopathic" approach to political subjectivity would incorporate rather than disavow the causes of social inequality. Given the "ruination" to which history's others are subject, we need to recognize and even affirm forms of ruined political subjectivity. We need a politics forged in the image of exile, of refusal, even of failure. Such a politics might offer, to quote that beautiful loser Nick Drake, "a troubled cure for a troubled mind."[25]

Notes

Thanks to Douglas Mao and Rebecca Walkowitz for their sensitive and engaged readings of this piece. I am also grateful to Andrew Gaedtke, David Kurnick, Mara Mills, Keja Valens, Michael Vazquez, and the Mods Group at the University of Pennsylvania for their feedback and support.

1. Daniel Albright, *Untwisting the Serpent: Modernism in Music, Literature, and Other Arts* (Chicago: University of Chicago Press, 2000), 30. Thanks to Doug Mao for this reference.

2. For a good general account of such recent work, see Rita Felski, "New Cultural Theories of Modernity," *Doing Time: Feminist Theory and Postmodern Culture* (New York: New York University Press, 2000), 55–76. A brief list of work in "alternative modernities" might include Arjun Appadurai, *Modernity at Large: Cultural Dimensions of Globalization* (Minneapolis: University of Minnesota Press, 1996); Homi Bhabha, *The Location of Culture* (London: Routledge, 1994); Dipesh Chakrabarty, *Provincializing Europe: Postcolonial Thought and Historical Difference* (Princeton, N.J.: Princeton University Press, 2000); Paul Gilroy, *The Black Atlantic: Modernity and Double Consciousness* (Cambridge, Mass.: Harvard University Press, 1993); Rita Felski, *The Gender of Modernity* (Cambridge, Mass.: Harvard University Press, 1995); Dilip Parameshwar Gaonkar, *Alternative Modernities* (Durham, N.C.: Duke University Press, 2001); Ranajit Guha, *History at the Limit of World-History* (New York: Columbia University Press, 2002); Timothy Mitchell, ed., *Questions of Modernity* (Minneapolis: University of Minnesota Press, 2000); Michael North, *The Dialectic of Modernism: Race, Language, and Twentieth-Century Literature* (New York: Oxford University Press, 1994); Gayatri Spivak, *A Critique of Postcolonial Reason: Toward a History of the Vanishing Present* (Cambridge, Mass.: Harvard University Press, 1999).

3. James Joyce, *A Portrait of the Artist as a Young Man* (New York: Penguin, 2003), 268–69.

4. Clyde Taylor, " 'Salt Peanuts': Sound and Sense in African/American Oral/Musical Creativity," *Callaloo* 5 (1982): 3.

5. If Taylor seems to minimize the difference between dominant and marginal modernisms, it is perhaps because he makes the criterion of activity so central. For Taylor, extreme situations make people into *either* active experimenters *or* into passive victims. In practice, however, it is often the case that extreme situations turn people into both experimenters *and* victims: being on the receiving end of social domination can make you bad and it can make you *bad*.

6. Judith Butler, "Critically Queer," *Bodies that Matter: On the Discursive Limits of "Sex"* (New York: Routledge, 1993), 223.

7. Michel Foucault, *The History of Sexuality*, vol. 1, trans. Robert Hurley (New York: Vintage, 1978), 101.

8. Such a confrontation with the mixed origin of homosexual identity has the status of a trauma in the discipline of lesbian, gay, and queer studies; the process of working through the fact of homosexuality's origin in social marginalization and modern disciplinary structures can never be finished, since homosexuality has no origin outside of this troubled history.

9. Geneva Smitherman, *Black Talk: Words and Phrases from the Hood to the Amen Corner* (Boston: Houghton Mifflin, 1994). The tracing of such early-twentieth-century "inventions" to African sources also significantly complicates the traditional means for "dating" modernity.

10. Cecil Brown discusses the Satanic legacy of the folk anti-hero Stagolee in his recent book *Stagolee Shot Billy* (Cambridge, Mass.: Harvard University Press, 2003). Tracing Stagolee's appearance in the art and literature of the twentieth century, Brown describes this figure as a "fallen angel" whose criminality and coldness register as social protest. For the "bad nigger," disregard for danger and death, extravagant displays of virility, and the ability to control women constitute a form of social protest; folk traditions such as the dozens "sum up," in Brown's words, "the mood of despairing rebellion" (202). While such swaggering masculine protest might seem miles away from the shuddering withdrawals discussed below, we might consider a link between Pater's crystal character and Stagolee's cool; both might be understood as alternative forms of masculinity that negotiate the loss of social power.

11. The difficulty of reading this history of "bad" is amplified by the politics of etymology at the turn of the century. The period from 1880 to 1920 is defined by systematic attempts to standardize the English language (the founding of the OED itself being the prime example of such a project) in order to rid it of elements of what George Bernard Shaw referred to as "quaint slavey lingo." George Bernard Shaw, "A Plea for Speech Nationalisation," cited in Michael North, *The Dialect of Modernism: Race, Language, and Twentieth-Century Literature* (Oxford: Oxford University Press, 1994), 12.

12. See Linda Dowling's discussion of the affair and its aftermath in *Hellenism and Homosexuality in Victorian England* (Ithaca, N.Y.: Cornell University Press, 1994), esp. 92–103. Dowling offers an account of the extreme swings of Pater's career in a reading of his violent allegory of suspicion and violence, "Apollo in Picardy." She writes: "All the painful burden of Pater's experience at Oxford presses into view here—the intoxicating education, the fiery friendship, the hopes for cultural regeneration and a more liberal way of life, followed by the cold incomprehension, the hatred, the stony exile" (140).

13. Walter Pater, *The Renaissance: Studies in Art and Poetry* (Oxford: Oxford University Press, 1998), 150.

14. Included in the Oxford edition of *The Renaissance*, 150.

15. The book is also addressed to such a number, "the few . . . the elect and peculiar people of the kingdom of sentiment" (10). For later twentieth-century examples of queer texts in search of kindred readers, see Christopher Nealon, *Foundlings: Lesbian and Gay Historical Emotion before Stonewall* (Durham, N.C.: Duke University Press, 2001).

16. Jacques Khalip, "Pater's Sadness," *Raritan* 20, no. 2 (Fall 2000): 5, 138.

17. Maureen Moran, "Pater's 'Great Change': Marius the Epicurean as Historical Conversion Romance" in *Walter Pater: Transparencies of Desire*, ed. Laurel Brake, Lesley Higgins, and Carolyn Williams (Greensboro, N.C.: Macmillan Heinemann ELT, 2002), 170–88.

18. It is significant that the onset of this new historical era in Heine's story is characterized by the technology of forced confession. Christian confession is crucial in the genealogy of modern sexual identity that Foucault traces in *The History of Sexuality*, vol. 1.

19. Paul Tucker, " 'Reanimate Greek': Pater and Ruskin on Botticelli," in Brake et al, eds., *Walter Pater*, 123. The passage from Dante reads:

> And some I knew among them; last of all
> I recognized the shadow of that soul
> who, in his cowardice, made the Great Denial.
>
> At once I understood for certain: these
> were of that retrograde and faithless crew
> hateful to God and to His enemies. (3.55–60)

The Inferno, trans. John Ciardi (New York: Penguin, 1954).

20. We might compare this image of a woman "expecting" to Pater's more positive image of expectation, invoked earlier in the Winckelmann essay—the image of "Memnon waiting for the day" (135). In the image of this stone Egyptian tower, Pater offers an image of pregnancy that is aesthetic rather than biological: the first rays of the sun draw from Memnon a song rather than a child.

21. The translation is by Edmund Keeley and Philip Sherrard, in *The Dark Crystal: An Anthology of Modern Greek Poetry* (Athens: Denise Harvey, 1981).

22. Eve Sedgwick and Andrew Parker, eds., *Performance and Performativity* (New York: Routledge, 1995). Thanks to David Kurnick for this reference.

23. Herbert Marcuse, *Eros and Civilization: A Philosophical Inquiry into Freud* (Boston: Beacon Press, 1966), 161.

24. Homi Bhabha, "The Commitment to Theory," *The Location of Culture* (London: Routledge, 1994), 25.

25. Nick Drake, "Time Has Told Me," from *Five Leaves Left* (London: Island Records, 1969).

Martin Puchner

The Aftershocks of *Blast*: Manifestos,

Satire, and the Rear-Guard of Modernism

Among the many bad British modernists, Wyndham Lewis stands out as the inventor of a particularly unsavory brand of modernism, an amalgam of racial hysteria, homophobic diatribes, fascist politics, and social resentment. With the possible exception of *Tarr*, his literary works have not become part of the high canon and have instead served for many critics as symptoms of everything that was wrong with modernism — without any of its redeeming qualities.[1] A temporary admirer of Hitler and agitator against "every institution of Western Democracy," Lewis perfected the arts of pushing people's buttons and of biting the hands that fed him.[2] He had a particular eye for the incipient canon of high modernist art, including Joyce, Stein, Hemingway, Eliot, Lawrence, and Proust, but he used this canon as target practice for his own reactive form of modernism, which he developed in opposition to almost everything connected with that term. Although Lewis himself had been an associate of Eliot, Pound, and Ford, a member of the Men of 1914, most of his later literary and political writings were violent indictments of this earlier modernism. It was as an attack dog that he excelled, in calling modernism names: paratactic diarrhea (Joyce); childish mannerism (Chaplin and Stein); and bohemian apes (Bloomsbury).

What motivated Lewis's vicious outbursts, crude satires, and repetitive tirades was an anxiety about and an obsession with the act of judging, with determining value both in the aesthetic and the political sense. His essays are littered with the terms "good" and "bad," and their idiosyncratic variants such as "goodtimism" and "badtimism," through which

Lewis responds to the apparent failures of collective judgment and engages in a project of re-valuation or trans-valuation. Nietzsche once observed, "through Wagner, modernity arrives at its most intimate language: it hides neither its good side nor its evil side . . . one has almost passed judgment on the value of modernity when one comes to terms with the good and the evil in Wagner."[3] Lewis represents a similar case for modernism. He is a seismograph of the politically, aesthetically, and morally charged debate about judgment and value that characterizes early-twentieth-century modernism.

That Lewis was a reactionary in the political sense is beyond doubt. The notion of reaction, however, can be developed further to capture the various contradictions that mark Lewis's works: his admiration for communism and his defense of the individual artist; his recommendation of fascism and his practice of satire; his simultaneous denunciations of modernism, the avant-garde, bohemia, and academic art. Without wanting to go back and without wanting to embrace some utopian future, the only attitude that was left for him was that of a defensive battle on all fronts, a reactive form of avant-garde, even a reaction *to and against* the various avant-gardes, what I will call a rear-guard action against every major force and movement of the time. The way I use the notion of a reactive avant-garde or rear-guard is distinct from mere nostalgia for a premodern world; it is not simply the tradition-bound conservatism of a T. S. Eliot, nor the religion-inflected modernity advocated by Catholics such as Charles Péguy (though Péguy did use the word *arrière-garde*). Rear-guardism, which culminates in Lewis but which includes a wider range of figures, is located within the field of advancement but is skeptical of its most extreme practitioners; rear-guardism seeks to correct and contain the avant-garde's excess without falling behind and losing touch with it entirely.[4] Caught between advancement and retreat, the rear-guard lacks room to move and thus engages in an endless and often disoriented back and forth, sideway maneuvers and feints, and often breaks off from the main corps to find itself alone and surrounded by enemies everywhere.

Rear-guardism crystallizes in the journal *Blast* (1914–15), a project conceived by Wyndham Lewis and Ezra Pound in response to continental modernism. In an important essay, Perry Anderson has argued that some notion of revolution constitutes the horizon of modernism.[5] This is nowhere more true than in the case of *Blast*, but nowhere is it more difficult to disentangle the different strands—political, social, aesthetic, ideological—held together by this one term. And yet, it is in reaction to this notion of the revolution that the rear-guard articulates itself most clearly: *Blast* embraces and reacts to a variety of revolutionary forms and forces, whether they take the shape of literary styles, artistic movements, social theories, or political projects. And since these revolutionary forms and forces are largely imported from the Continent, the formation of the rear-guard must be understood in geographic as much as in historical terms, by means of a geography of modernism and of modernity.

The Geography of the Modern

A phenomenon was observed which has been repeated in history more than once, namely, that the backward countries . . . reflected in their ideology the achievements of the advanced countries more brilliantly and strongly. In this way, German thought in the Eighteenth and Nineteenth Centuries reflected the economic achievements of England and the political achievements of France. In the same way, Futurism obtained its most brilliant expression, not in America and not in Germany, but in Italy and in Russia.[6]

Written in defense of the embattled Russian Futurists in 1924, these lines offer a broad view of European modernism around the October Revolution. Their writer, Leon Trotsky, is little concerned with such questions as aesthetic autonomy or the divisions between modernism and the avantgarde or high and low, basing his analysis instead on the geographic dichotomy between modernism and modernity. Russian and Italian Futurists are the most advanced artistic movements precisely because these two countries are torn between a still dominant traditional peasantry and small pockets of industrialization. Modernity and modernism, in other words, are not in sync, but operate through a geographic differential.[7] Trotsky's observation may rely on a questionable form of geographic determinism, but his geographic differential can still serve to pose the question of why British modernism would have to import the latest and most advanced form of revolutionary modernism, namely Futurism, from a country at the semi-periphery of industrialization such as Italy, of why British and Anglo-

American modernists, such as Lewis and Pound, would feel the need to turn to Italy in order to bring British modernism, as they would put it, up-to-date.

The Futurists reflected the ideology of the advanced industrial nations not just in their worship of machinery and production processes but by capturing the temporal ideology of modernity, namely, the value of the new for its own sake. Denouncing the past as such, heralding the future as such, Futurism did not merely articulate some specific moment of advancement, what would now be called the first machine age, but the very concept of advancement itself: propelling yourself forward into the future by breaking with the past, without looking back to it like Benjamin's horrified and outright anti-futurist angel. Marinetti writes: "For the moribund, the sick, the prisoners, the glorious past is perhaps a balsam for their ills because they are barred from the future. . . . But we no longer want to know anything of it, of the past, we the young and strong Futurists!"[8] Futurism values the future as such just as it denounces the past as such, without giving this past and this future a specific content. What Futurism recognized was the modernist temporality that looks at the present from some hypothetical vantage point of the future, what Koselleck has called the "future's past."[9]

This articulation of advancement and of futurist—modernist—time took the form of a specific genre: the manifesto. The manifesto is the genre of the break: it announces and produces a rupture in the historical continuum, guided by a belief in the value of the future and the impossibility of returning to the past—a Futurist genre even before the Futurists laid their hands on it. For this reason, the history and geography of the manifesto amounts to a history and geography of the future's past.

The paradigmatic manifesto of the nineteenth century was of course the *Communist Manifesto*, which turned the manifesto into a distinct genre. Its geography reveals a complex interplay of continental and British thought, published, as it was, in London, but in the exile German-language journal *Deutsch-Londoner Zeitung*. There were texts that called themselves manifestos earlier, going all the way back to the radical wing of the Puritan revolution in seventeenth-century England, but the title manifesto appeared only as one of several alternatives, such as declaration, petition, or letter, one of several ways of bringing the will of a collective into the open, making it known, public, and manifest ("manus festus" refers to something being tangible, reachable by the hand). It was only when Marx and Engels abandoned their previous plan of writing a catechism and decided to write a manifesto instead that the distinct features of the manifesto began to crystallize.

The manifesto not only had to be invented, it also had to gain recognition as a new genre, and this happened only after the *Communist Manifesto*, or simply the *Manifesto* as it came to be known, had become widely printed, translated, and distributed in the late nineteenth and early twentieth centuries. As Engels observed triumphantly, the geographic distribution of the *Manifesto* became an index of the spread not just of communism but of modernization and industrialization.[10] It was through this proliferation that the *Manifesto* was capable of shaping the manifesto's defining features: a list of collective demands; a historiography geared toward the future (in this case the crisis of capitalism that would allow for communism to emerge); the dedication to revolutionary intervention. Through Marx and Engels, the manifesto became the genre of the revolution and thus the genre most intimately connected to a future that would be brought about by some revolutionary break. Eric Hobsbawm has called modernity the product of the "dual revolution," the French revolution and the industrial revolution.[11] The *Manifesto* inherited these two revolutions and hoped to turn them into a final and third one.

Italian Futurism marks the crucial moment when the manifesto moved from the sphere of revolutionary politics to art. This move would soon have severe consequences for the system of art, infusing it with modes of rude political agitation, new forms of propaganda, and agitational rhetoric. Marinetti's *First Manifesto of Futurism* (1909) is not the earliest manifesto in the sphere of art—there is, for example, Jean Moréas's more polite, so-called *Symbolist Manifesto* two decades earlier—but it was Marinetti who grasped the central features of this revolutionary and futurist genre and elevated it to the central mode of expression for Futurism. In fact, most so-called manifestos, including Moréas's, did not actually bear that generic marker in their title, appearing instead as *Le Symbolisme, Le Naturisme*, and so on. All of these were programmatic texts to be sure, but they did not or could not explicitly indicate their adherence to the manifesto as a distinct genre. This also means that they did not embrace the paratactic enumerations, sloganizing compressions, ruthless violence, and revolutionary aspirations embedded in the political manifesto. Nor did they envision anything like a "first" manifesto, a properly foundational act that was then to be followed by a whole series of similar expressions.

It was only with Futurism then that the art manifesto would come into its own. As Marjorie Perloff has observed in her classic study *The Futurist Moment*, Futurism was founded not only by manifestos but also before any Futurist work of art had been created.[12] Indeed, manifestos, and not poems or plays, became Marinetti's most successful export product so that the *First Futurist Manifesto* was quickly translated and printed in the leading art journals and even daily newspapers across Europe. This rapid proliferation initiated what one might call the Futurism-effect: the artists in most European countries felt compelled to articulate their attitude toward this new movement and its remarkable new genre. For better or worse, no form or genre would have more influence on the following decades than the manifesto, shaping what Mary Ann Caws calls a century of isms.[13]

Too Many Manifestos

As the manifesto swept across other places located at the periphery of industrialization, such as Russia and Latin America, and soon entered more industrialized countries, such as Germany and England, there formed a chorus of artists, journalists, and politicians who noticed the rise and ramifications of this new genre with horror. The critics of the manifesto in all these countries aired their distress in one single cry: too many manifestos, not enough good works of art. The repetition of this cry in the early twentieth century is overwhelming, an index of the prominence of this new genre and also of the sense that it somehow threatened the value of the work of art. For the influence of the manifesto on the artwork, so the consensus had it, was not a good one. The manifesto violated almost all values associated with high modernism by privileging the explicit rather than implicit, easy slogans rather than complex structures, shrill ruptures rather than subtle epiphanies, direct address of the audience rather than unreliable narrators, political interventionism rather than aesthetic autonomy, and finally revolution rather than transcendence. Manifestos openly competed with advertising, propaganda, newspapers, and political speech, not with a reified canon of art; they were written for immediate consumption and maximal effect, not for arduous and contemplative reading and exegesis. That Futurism had been able to announce itself solely based on manifestos, rather than on the strength of its artworks, was perhaps the first indication that the manifesto somehow tended to eclipse or otherwise threaten the artwork. Even Trotsky attacked this tendency, writing that "great proletarian art is not produced by writing manifestos."[14] One might say that Trotsky should have known better than to bemoan the rise of this revolutionary genre since he was socialism's most avid writer of agitational manifestos and ended up co-authoring the "Manifesto for a Free Revolutionary Art" (1938) with Breton. But Trotsky's dedication to the political manifesto was the very reason that he turned against the art manifesto, for he sensed the rivalry between the avant-garde manifestos of Futurism and his own manifestos, which themselves purported to represent the avant-garde of revolutionary Europe. (The distinction between the artistic and the political manifesto here harks back to the double meaning of the political and the artistic avant-garde.[15])

In response to the sudden rise of the Futurist manifesto and the manifesto-craze inspired by it, there emerged an immense reaction to or backlash against the manifesto across Europe. From Trotsky to Artaud, and from German Expressionism to English Vorticism, a general unease with the manifesto prompted these diverse writers to stand up for what they called good art and denounce the manifesto, conversely, as being variously bad: bad theory, bad form, bad manners, and bad art.[16] What is striking about these diverse critics of the manifesto is that many of them were eventually drawn into the manifesto craze themselves—that they found that the most effective, polemical, and successful genre in which to voice these complaints was none other than the manifesto itself.[17]

Vorticism makes for a particularly good case study of this backlash against the manifesto and the ideological, aesthetic, and philosophical doctrines bound up with it, for it was through Marinetti himself that the manifesto entered Britain in 1914.[18] Marinetti's visit, extensively covered in the press, fit the pattern of many similar visits across Europe. He gave well-attended lectures, readings, and, unavoidably, co-authored an *English Futurist Manifesto*. The mistake he made, if indeed a mistake it was and not a cunning strategy for sowing dissent, was to print this manifesto on the stationery of the Rebel Art Centre.[19] The center's autonomy was jealously guarded by Lewis, who had set it up in competition with the Bloomsbury circle, from which he felt systematically excluded. Lewis, who was not going to let this laboriously acquired status be hijacked by his Italian competitor, prepared a series of defensive measures, many of them quite in keeping with the techniques of public disruption adopted by the Futurists. First, he gathered some friends and interrupted Marinetti's lecture at the Dore Galleries. Then, in the next *Observer* on June 14, he and his friends promptly explained their opposition to the man whom the European press liked to call "the caffeine of Europe": "We the undersigned . . . beg to dissociate ourselves from the 'futurist' manifesto which appeared in the pages of the *Observer* of Sunday, June 7th."[20] The reasons for this dissociation and disruption are various. One might emphasize the differences in style and aesthetic doctrine, with Futurism favoring dynamism and movement while Lewis was attached to a kind of modernist classicism based on distinct forms and stasis, despite the movement implied in the metaphor of the vortex. More recently, however, Laurence Rainey and Janet Lyon have emphasized that the confrontation between Lewis and Marinetti was less about aesthetics than about publicity.[21] It is this latter understanding that feeds into my argument, namely, that Marinetti's success in London, like his success everywhere else, was a carefully orchestrated publicity stunt that demonstrated, above all, the effectiveness of his primary advertising instrument: the manifesto.

Lewis did not leave it at attacking Marinetti. He began to realize that he could only stop Marinetti from winning followers in England by coming up with something like a continental avant-garde movement of his own, complete with a program, a journal, and, most importantly, a manifesto. The result was the coinage and foundation of Vorticism and *Blast*.

For both Pound and Lewis, *Blast* constituted a new use of the manifesto, but it also profited from their previous editorial experience. Their involvement with little magazines such as *The Little Review* and *The Dial* can be seen as first steps toward a continental-style, manifesto-driven journal such as *Blast*, even though these former had not been created for the benefit of one clearly defined ism or movement.[22] Closer to Futurism was the coinage, by Pound, of Imagism. However, his "A Few Don'ts by an Imagiste" falls short of being a full-blown manifesto: while the manifesto signals a claim to totality, toward the absolute, the cautious or coy "Few Don'ts" deliberately renounces any such grandiose aspiration. Pound's later "ABC's" and his "How To" texts may be somewhat less modest, but they likewise circumvent the manifesto by being modeled on another down-market genre, namely, the user's manual or introductory guide.[23] However, the elaborate humility of these titles—the texts themselves are quite confident—is without doubt calibrated toward the manifesto. They must be understood in the context of the authoritative and programmatic manifestos that had begun to circulate through newspapers, magazines, and flyers everywhere around Pound and with which, as Janet Lyon has argued, Pound had to struggle and compete.[24]

Pound's Imagism and Lewis's rivalry with Bloomsbury can be seen as first instances of the typical avant-garde narcissism of small difference, with each movement trying to distinguish itself from the next. This dynamic certainly was in full swing when they created *Blast*, which is marked by Trotsky's geographic differential since it is Lewis's and Pound's attempt to counter the advanced Italian Futurism with a British ism, to meet the Italian invader with a home-grown product.[25] But this national struggle, heightened by the nationalizing rhetoric on the eve of the Great War, was also and more importantly a generic struggle, a struggle about different modernisms, for *Blast* embraced the new avant-garde repertoire of manifestos and isms only with reservation. Pound's and Lewis's ambivalent attitudes toward the manifesto are visible in two areas: their fear that the influence of the manifesto would turn the artwork into nothing but bad propaganda; and the related suspicion that the manifesto's collective authorship would undermine the autonomy of the individual artist.

Given the fact that the manifesto was pressed upon Pound and Lewis by Marinetti, it is only natural that they would identify the manifesto's bad influence on the artwork with that movement and consequently accuse the Futurists of being "too much propagandists" (*Blast* 2 42) and not enough creators of great works of art. A similar attitude also determines the end of *Blast 1*, which culminates not with the call-to-arms typical of the manifesto, but with a word of caution, directed at the violent wing of the women's suffrage movement: "To Suffragettes. / A word of advice. / In destruction, as in other things, / stick to what you understand. / We make you a present of our votes. / Only leave works of art alone. / You might some day destroy a good picture by accident" (151). Underneath the patronizing tone

of this note we can perceive a thinly concealed fear about the relation between art and revolution, a fear about the value of the artwork.[26] Pound and
Lewis felt a certain amount of gratitude toward *The Egoist*, which had run
the ads for the first issue of *Blast*, and suffragism also represented one of
the British traditions of manifesto-driven agitation that Lewis and Pound
felt increasingly compelled to imitate.[27] But political struggles of emancipation are questions of "votes" and not of "art," and *Blast* here signals a
desire to keep the two, art and politics — and this also means art and manifesto — separate.[28] The fear that a single "good picture" might be destroyed
in the course of a revolutionary struggle responds to the actual destruction
of paintings by British suffragists, but it also testifies to the extent to which
Pound and Lewis sought to preserve the artwork by any means necessary.[29]
Manifesto art, manifesto modernism, the bad influence of the manifesto on
art — these are so many formulations of a problem Pound and Lewis identify
and that they seek to combat.

The association, however uneasy, between Vorticism and the women's
suffrage movement also offered an additional way in which Lewis and
Pound could distance themselves from Marinetti's hypermasculinist language. Lewis's satirical manifestos may not necessarily seem much more
attractive than Marinetti's, but they did recommend themselves in a relative
manner by their lesser degree of warmongering and a form of misogyny
that was certainly virulent but perhaps less ideologically founded and in-
grained. But while the Vorticists' dependence on women patrons, on magazines run by women, and on the tradition of women's suffrage writing made
a Marinetti-style machine-machismo impossible, this dependence also led
to the aggression visible in the defense of the artwork against suffragist politics. In other words, what the suffragists represent, for Lewis, is the intrusion
of politics, manifesto-driven politics, into art. This dependence made him
fixate on suffragists when it came to defending art against politics. What
Lewis's manifestos and their allegiance to the political cause of women's suffrage demonstrated was that Marinetti's combination of manifesto and misogyny was subject to revision. The subsequent history of various feminist
rewritings of the manifesto further elaborated, critiqued, and revised the
recurring misogyny of the manifesto (especially those feminist manifestos
subsequently analyzed by Janet Lyon), as did the more oblique negotiations
with this genre visible in such texts as Virginia Woolf's *Three Guineas*.

It is important to recognize that Lewis and Pound's defense of the goodness of art in the face of the manifesto was not simply an inheritance of turn-of-the-century aestheticism, as Peter Bürger might argue.[30] Neither Pound nor Lewis advocated anything like the religion of art; Lewis declared outright that "Art is not a religion," emphasizing that "there is nothing mysterious about Fine Arts. . . . The pretentions of art, I take it, do not point to anything beyond the thresholds of life."[31] Lewis's constant attempts to separate the frauds from the real artistic geniuses and his anxiety about the destruction of the aesthetic sphere sound similar to aestheticism, but for Lewis these obsessions have acquired a new function within the system of art.[32] They are no longer simply part of an aestheticist inversion of nature and art, truth and lies, nor do they respond to the nineteenth-century realist and reformist art. Rather, they are part of a reaction to a much more recent form of modernism and avant-garde art, whose putative attempt to merge art and life Lewis decidedly rejects: "art . . . is not a way of life."[33] Indeed, his most outrageous attacks are directed not at modernist art works but at the tendency to turn this art into a bohemian lifestyle; these culminate in his venomous satire of Bloomsbury, *The Apes of God*. Instead of indulging in either the aestheticist cult of art or the avant-garde cult of life, Lewis undertakes a rear-guard action against the manifesto and its assault on art, here represented in the figure of violent suffragettes who are greeted not with a call-to-arms but with a call to disarm.

It is in the course of this reaction that the question of value comes to the fore: something of value is under attack and must therefore be preserved. *Blast* is only the first step in a whole series of such reactions which would span Lewis's entire lifetime and which mark him, as Jameson has said of Lewis more generally, as the primary reactionary of British modernism.[34] The classification of Lewis's as a reactionary modernism can be transformed into the concept of the rear-guard, a term that captures the various generic, political, and aesthetic reactions and contradictions that shape the group of writers for which Lewis can be used as a stand-in.

Blast's rear-guard action against manifesto modernism is not just a defense of the value of the artwork but also a reaction to a second feature of the manifesto, namely, its role in creating collective movements. The declaration "Blast presents an art of individuals" (80) echoes the subtitle of *The Egoist*, which calls itself "An Individualist Review."[35] In keeping

The Aftershocks of *Blast*

with this individualist attitude, some contributors did not sign the Vorticist manifestos, for example Rebecca West, whose story "Indissoluble Matrimony" can be read as a send-up of the term Vorticism itself.[36] *The Egoist* had adopted this title from the anarchist Stirner, who had also been one of the targets of Marx and Engels's *Manifesto* and who therefore lent himself well as inspiration for an anti-Marxist journal. The individualism of *Blast*, however, is more ambivalent that that of *The Egoist*. *Blast* includes several manifestos that are devoted to promoting a collective name, Vorticism, and which are signed, in standard manifesto fashion, by a collective. *Blast* is not simply against collectives and manifestos, nor are its contradictions a sign that the editors could not agree about these matters. The heterogeneity of *Blast* must be understood as part of *Blast*'s ambivalent relation to manifesto modernism more generally. *Blast* was engaged in a reaction with and against these modes and formations, using a homeopathic method, if you will, of keeping the manifesto at bay.

Using a little bit of manifesto to immunize England from the grand manifesto onslaught was a tempting strategy, and it seems to have worked: manifestos did remain a relatively rare phenomenon in British modernism. But no matter how successful this immunization may have been, it implied that now some form of manifesto had entered the system of art in England, was exerting its influence, and therefore had to be contained. After *Blast*, it is no longer possible to write the history of British modernism without taking the manifesto into account. Ford's stylistic doctrines, Pound's pamphlets, Lewis's tirades, Bertrand Russell's political manifestos, T. S. Eliot's critical essays — these and many others are subgenres and forms that must compete with the manifesto.

Pound's and Lewis's conflicted use of the manifesto is visible in the tone and style of the manifestos themselves in *Blast*. Vorticist manifestos attack almost randomly long lists of individuals as well as "the post *office*," "aperitifs," "sport," and "humor" (13) and it is difficult to extract from them even a halfway consistent position. Sometimes these manifestos have been described as mere parodies, suggesting that they need not be taken seriously and were of little consequence. Two things are to be kept in mind here. First, it was only once the manifesto was recognized as an established genre that it could be opposed or embraced, but also quoted, parodied, and alluded to in a variety of ways. In fact, a playful use of the manifesto can be found in many of the continental avant-garde movements, such as Dadaism, which created masterpieces of what contemporaries referred to as "manifestant-ism."[37] Second, even though the "Vorticist Manifesto" is not, simply, serious, it nevertheless served a serious purpose, for it must be regarded as the first line of defense against Marinetti. Instead of parody, I propose the term "satire," a term Lewis would soon use to describe the particular aesthetic and political mixture that characterized his later work. As I will be showing later in this essay, satire emerges as the rear-guard style par excellence, a way of using and co-opting avant-garde strategies without subscribing to their aesthetic and political implications.

Even as it satirizes some aspects of the manifesto, *Blast* participates in the bad-mannered mode of speech that characterizes this genre. In particular two texts, called *Manifesto I* and *Manifesto II*, take to an extreme the manifesto's polarization between condemnation and praise, its staccato style of enumerating apodictic demands, hostility toward the audience, aggressively enlarged letters, and hypertrophic speech acts. *Blast* announces, for example, how centrally it is concerned with its impact on the public: "Blast sets out to be an avenue for all those vivid and violent ideas that could reach the Public in no other way."[38] The communication of such "violent" ideas to the public might seem to be aligned with a series of classical modernist techniques, such as rupture or suddenness;[39] but it is best described by a poetics of action as it was envisioned by Kenneth Burke and later by J. L. Austin, a poetics that culminates in two quintessentially performative speech acts, satirically exposed: cursing and blessing.[40] The "curse" and the "blessing" are extreme versions of speech acts whose utterance is coextensive with their effects. But even though the speech acts of *Blast* are infused with violent irony, they continue to participate in what they ironize, they continue to be deployed for the serious business of reacting to the continental avant-garde. Relying on the manifesto's performative and foundational power, Pound and Lewis tried to erect with it a bulwark called Vorticism for the paradoxical purpose of containing the influence of Marinetti's manifestos and manifesto-inspired practices. It is thus misleading to say either that Lewis and Pound simply made fun of the manifesto or that they simply took it seriously. They distanced themselves from manifestos but also used them, saw in them a source of much danger for art and yet felt compelled to adapt this genre to their own uses.

The Rear-Guard

Distancing, adapting, redirecting, containing—these terms point us to the various strategies of the rear-guard. The concept of the rear-guard includes more than simply an ambivalence about the (Futurist) manifesto, although such an ambivalence is one of its clearest symptoms. In addition, the concept of the rear-guard captures the questions of judgment and value, of good and bad, that are intertwined with the struggle surrounding the manifesto, and it includes the political and ideological assumptions and formations—socialist and fascist revolution; collective and individual leadership; political propaganda and art—behind that struggle. It is to these political dimensions of modernism, of the Futurist avant-garde and the Vorticist rear-guard, that we must turn in order to understand the ideological underpinnings of rear-guardism.

The political and ideological charge of the manifesto appears when we recognize how surprising the transition from the *Communist Manifesto* to the avant-garde manifesto really was, surprising because it implied also a transition from a genre firmly in the hands of socialism to a genre used by a protofascist such as Marinetti. The missing link here is Georges Sorel, a French syndicalist who attacked orthodox Marxism in general and the *Communist Manifesto* in particular for its theoretical constructions and dialectical speculations, urging workers to adopt a more violent plan for immediate action instead.[41] An anti-intellectual and anti-theoretical conception of action, engagement, and violence out of which the new will somehow be born—these are the philosophical and ideological supports for the avant-garde manifesto, reinforced by a misreading of Nietzsche. Marinetti, Mussolini, and Italian fascism more generally were deeply under the sway of Sorel—Sorel himself had lived just long enough to approve of Mussolini's March on Rome—and it was the syndicalist attack on Marxism that instigated them to turn the manifesto into a genre that was less theoretical, less intellectual, and more violent. While Marx's dialectics provides the theoretical frame for the *Communist Manifesto*, Sorel's violent action supplies the basis for the fascist and Futurist manifestos.

The transition, via Sorel, from the communist to the fascist manifesto, however, did not proceed without conflict. In fact, Sorel's own ambivalent position between socialism and fascism points to the ambivalence of the manifesto in the early twentieth century, to the multiple pressures that came to bear on this developing genre. Fascism, after all, saw itself as a bulwark against the "red threat," as a containment of a socialist revolution on all fronts, including the generic front of the manifesto. For this purpose, fascism had to either avoid the manifesto or make use of it, just as it made limited use of the revolution but with the goal of unhinging it from its socialist origin. These two options, avoiding manifestos or wresting them from socialism, are the different paths taken by Marinetti and Mussolini respectively. While Marinetti created a new action-based manifesto, Mussolini and other fascists bemoaned, as Hitler did in *Mein Kampf*, communism's advantage in the sphere of philosophy, although Hitler argued that the success of Marxism owed not "to the literary work of Marxist patriotic writers" but to "agitators."[42] Indeed, Hitler even mentions "Dadaistic 'experiences' " (353–54). In reaction, Hitler formulated a fascist alternative, based on the privileging of the publicly declaimed speech, the action-like qualities of the spoken word, over the textual manifesto.[43] Some fascist modernists followed suit, most clearly so Ezra Pound, whose rants on Radio Rome are case studies in agitational speech; in fact, Pound theorized a type of agitational declamation that would be a perfect synthesis of speech and action.[44]

It is through this same alternative of either evading the manifesto or of recreating it that we can better locate the rear-guardism of *Blast*, which chose a third way in between these two. Rather than embracing the manifesto as Marinetti's vanguard had done, Lewis and Pound tried to contain and reduce its influence, but unlike Mussolini's escape into action speech, they took an ambivalent attitude toward the manifesto, mistrusting it but using it nevertheless. This position of the rear-guard is reiterated in Lewis's later writings *The Art of Being Ruled* (1926) and *Time and Western Man* (1927), which supply the political underpinnings of rear-guardism.[45] On the one hand, Lewis recognizes the revolution as the inevitable horizon of modernity — "all serious politics today are revolutionary" (17) — and furthermore identifies the Bolshevik revolution as its paradigm: "I believe in the Soviet system. It has spectacularly broken with the past of Europe" (320).[46] In the same vein, Lewis quotes, often approvingly, from socialist theory, including Marx, Kautsky, Lenin, Shaw, and Russell, concluding from these studies that, "any revolution today must to some extent start from and be modeled on socialist practice. This applies to a fascist movement or putsch, as to anything else" (18).[47] On the other hand, Lewis searches for an alternative to Bolshevism based on some vague combination of Marinetti and Mussolini: "*Fascismo* is merely a spectacular marinettian flourish put on the tail, or, if you like, the head, of marxism. . . . And that is the sort of socialism that this essay would indicate as the most suitable for anglo-saxon countries or colonies" (321). Strikingly, this move from Bolshevism to fascism is facilitated by the same link, Sorel: the "key to all contemporary political thought," Lewis insists, is "George Sorel" (119). The *Blast* circle encountered Sorel through the translations of the theorist behind *Blast*, T. E. Hulme. Lewis's politics is everywhere determined by the very context from which the alternative—Mussolini or Marinetti—had emerged.

When it comes to defining what a fascist, Sorel-flavored revolution looks like, however, things get more complicated, for here Lewis is really doing his best to reduce the consequences of revolutionary modernity wherever he can. This containment takes the paradoxical form of what must be called "aristocratic" revolution: "Revolution . . . is not the work of the majority of people," he observes, but rather "a small number of inventive, creative men are responsible for the entire spectacular ferment of the modern world."[48] Still in awe of revolutionary modernity, the "ferment of the modern world," Lewis denies the most central elements of this ferment—the unleashing of social revolution, mass democracy, industrialization, and so on—and restricts the "true" revolution to some neatly confined aristocratic elite. Lewis declares impatiently that most people want to and need to be ruled, rather than be rulers of their own fate. This aristocratic revolution corresponds to his position of artistic individualism. Everywhere Lewis found himself confronted with what Ortega y Gasset called the *Revolt of the Masses*: mass democracy, mass war, mass revolution, collective art movements.[49] And everywhere he saw himself as the single and solitary bulwark against them.

This is a good place to return to the difference between Lewis's rearguardism and aestheticism. Like Lewis, most aestheticists from Mallarmé to Wilde positioned their refined works against the masses. For them, however, the masses meant first of all mass-circulating media such as serialized novels and journalism, masses in the sphere of publishing. For Lewis, however, the notion of the masses was charged differently, with everything from the Bolshevist revolution to the mass slaughter of the Great War. His opposition to the masses, therefore, was formed in reaction to early-twentieth-century masses, whom Lewis wanted to rule through the exceptional individual, the single artist, the ruler.

More indirect, perhaps, but more significant in our context, is another aspect of this political argument, namely, Lewis's cooling to a philosophy and poetics based on "action," which indeed resonates with the notion of re-action. As much as Lewis recognizes the necessity of the revolution, including Sorel's theory of action, he ends up trying to contain the consequences of both. While Marinetti, despite his political affinity for fascism, holds onto a progress and future-oriented avant-garde—Gramsci's true revolutionary—Lewis does everything to stop and block any such advance, to slow down and derail such progress. Just as Mussolini accepts the concept of revolution for the purpose of containing its effects, so Lewis adopts the genre of the revolution, the manifesto, to contain its consequences. This amounts to a properly rear-guard stance in the sphere of genre: accepting revolutionary modernism, using its modes of articulation, but to function as a drag, to slow it down and bring it to a halt.

Satire in the Extra-Moral Sense

Lewis's writings of the twenties and thirties elaborate and extend his rear-guard stance to literary criticism and to modernist aesthetics through a series of extremely expansive terms and theories. *Time and Western Man*, for example, takes on almost all the representatives of "good" modernism in the sense of the canonized "high" modernists, including Joyce, Stein, Pound, Eliot, Proust, D. H. Lawrence, and Hemingway.[50] The operative terms here are "time," the "time cult," and the "time mind," and the range of phenomena Lewis subsumes under this one category of time is large to the point of becoming meaningless: the obsession with memory in such novelists as Proust; Pound's "antiquarian and romantic tendencies" (38); Joyce's unending stream of words, "fluid material gushing of undisciplined life" (112); and a long list of other figures and styles. "Time mind" apparently refers not only to an obsession with memory but also to everything having to do with processes, transformations, instability, shapelessness, lack of formal discipline, and flux. This aesthetic aspect of the time mind is extended to an equally long list of philosophies, represented by such figures as Russell and Spengler, who themselves borrow from scientific theories of the unstable and the fluid, especially Darwin's evolutionism and Einstein's theory of relativity. The time mind is epitomized, however, by Bergson, whose notion of creative evolution revolves explicitly around such notions as relativity, subjectivity, flux, and memory. Here we begin to approach the true function of this convoluted text, namely, the fact that "time" really stands for the idea of progress or progressive time as it organizes modernity: "no doctrine, so much as the Time doctrine, lends itself to the purpose of the millennial politics of revolutionary human change, and endless 'Progress' " (422). Now, even Sorel and Mussolini are denounced as "*pur-sang* bergsonian" (201). The time mind, here, becomes something that extends from literary modernism to the temporality of modernity, modernity's own peculiar form of futurist, progressive millennialism.

What is more important than the arguments with which Lewis wants to make us believe that Stein and Spengler, Chaplin and Proust, Joyce and Russell, Einstein and Mussolini all have something in common is the very abstraction of the category "time" itself. It presents, I argue, a shield with which Lewis wants to contain the consequences of literary modernism and modernity. The notion of the rear-guard helps us understand the all-encompassing nature of the time mind, why Lewis would create a term of critique so general that it ends up including almost all of modernity and modernism at once. It is as a rear-guardist that Lewis thus captures the full front of modernity.

In a compelling argument, Tyrus Miller has described Lewis's critique of modernism as an instance of "late modernism."[51] I would like to take this notion of lateness or belatedness as one feature of what I call rear-guard, which is not only behind, deliberately in the back, but also occupies the role of a defensive aggression. This argument can be exemplified with reference to the notion of satire, which constitutes the center of Lewis's rear-guardism in the sphere of art.

After the paradoxical experiments of *Blast*, Lewis rethought his literary practice and formulated a full-blown literary program for rear-guard art in his *Men without Art* (1934). Here he posits, against the millennial-modernist paradigm, an anti-action art that goes by the name of satire and that reacts point for point to the formation of modernity, manifesto, and revolution: "we may describe this book as a defence of contemporary art" (13). Even though Lewis's so-called satires include some of the features generally associated with this genre — exposing grotesque aberrations; exaggerating flaws and features; projecting these stark portraits against a tacit understanding of the commonsensical and the normal — his satire is less an attempt to define a specific genre than a definition of art, or more specifically of rearguard art, as such. More important than Lewis's practice of satire is the way in which this program gathers all the different components of Lewis's rearguardism and makes them into one literary form. This defense-formation called satire is embedded in a host of expressions and formulations — and this brings us back to our initial question of the "bad" — surrounding the question of value judgment. Lewis sees aestheticism from Pater through Wilde to Gide as "three consecutive generations of moralists — or moralists gone wrong" (145). But moralism extends to more than just aestheticism; it includes what I have called manifesto modernism as well. Imagining a historian of the future, Lewis presents a literary history of a sequence of different moralisms, a naughty or "bad" one and a dutiful or good one:

> he [the historian of the future] will see the trial of Wilde as the grand finale of the "naughty" decade — then fourteen humdrum years of Socialist tract-writing — then war — and then more "naughtiness." He will perhaps meditate — "here was a people, moralist to the core, who only possessed two modes of expression, one childishly rebellious, the other dully dutiful!" (148).

Both aestheticism and the manifesto — or "tract-writing" — are moralizing, bound up in the endless oscillation between the "naughty" and the "dutiful," good and bad. At other times, Lewis would accuse Marxism of breeding an art so bad that he feels compelled to call it "anti-art." Particular values have shifted — "our *bad* has not been quite their *bad*" he observes at one point — but badness and moral value dominate both to the detriment of art itself.

Hence Lewis's desire to dissociate satire from value in the moral and political sense entirely. This is surely Lewis's most counterintuitive strategy, since the word "satire" is traditionally infused with implicit and explicit value judgments and morality. One essay, "Is Satire Real?," opens with the statement "that the moralist — in whatever disguise — can give us as much trouble as the politician — in whatever disguise — is certain" (107) and concludes with the observation "So today Satire can be judged good or bad upon no familiar or traditional pattern of ethical codification" (111). Satire, and with it modernist art, must become entirely divorced from the question of judgment and moral value, and become hard, objective, static, abstract, value free. Lewis proposes the term "metaphysical satire" (232) but one should call it more properly satire in the extra-moral sense. This metaphysical sphere of art beyond value (and Lewis thinks of this very explicitly in Nietzschean terms) is the last and final place of retreat from the chaos of moral "naughtiness" and political moralism, fascist and socialist revolutions, collective avant-gardes, and the influx of socialist tracts and manifestos. This notion of "beyond good and bad" returns late in *The Art of Being Ruled*, in a chapter called "Beyond Action and Reaction," in which Lewis defines his own aspiration, with an outright Nietzschean dash, as that of becoming "neither a 'good European' nor a 'bad European' — but, in short, a 'beyond-the-good-and-the-bad European' " (359). This metaphysical or beyond-good-and-bad position is the place from which he hopes to take on high modernism as much as manifesto modernism; satire, in other words, is a term that claims to have overcome what we might now call the "grand récit" of modernity.

Lewis is a limit case of modernism in part because he himself was so engaged with delimiting what we would identify as modernism and its influence, because he, as a late and rear-guard modernist, was primarily interested in modernism's limits. What is important is not the question whether he was right in drawing the limit where he did, but his very attempt to do so, to attack what we might call a good modernism and then go beyond it. To us, Lewis's satire may appear not a solution to the question of good and bad modernism but something altogether worse and beyond the pale, full of grotesque distortions, offensive clichés, racist portraits, patronizing characterizations, sexist obsessions, and tiresome repetitions. From this perspective, Vorticism can be seen as a first and early example of rear-guarding — but one not yet charged by Lewis's later reactionary politics and reactionary aesthetics. It is a transitional project, caught between avant-garde and modernism, and between the Continent and England. It was only in the aftermath of *Blast* that Lewis revealed the true political and aesthetic face of rear-guardism. In this later phase, in the attempt to overcome good and bad modernism, Lewis managed to create something ugly, a truly nasty modernism whose value might lie in the fact that it makes *Blast* seem, retrospectively, not all that bad.

Notes

1. One example is Fredric Jameson's *Fables of Aggression: Wyndham Lewis, the Modernist as Fascist* (Berkeley: University of California Press, 1979). Peter Bürger's *The Decline of Modernism* (Cambridge: Polity Press, 1992) also positions Lewis outside modernism proper.

2. Wyndham Lewis, *Men without Art*, ed. Seamus Cooney (Santa Rosa, Calif.: Black Sparrow Press, 1987), 191.

3. Friedrich Nietzsche, "Der Fall Wagner," *Richard Wagner in Bayreuth, Der Fall Wagner, Nietzsche contra Wagner* (Stuttgart: Reclam, 1991), 88.

4. The notion of a rear-guard is beginning to become operative in the discourse on modernism, for example in a collection, which includes a short version of the present essay, entitled *Les arrière-gardes au XXe siècle: L'autre face de la modernité esthétique*, edited by William Marx (Paris: Presses Universitaires de France, 2004).

5. Perry Anderson, "Modernism and Revolution," in *Marxism and the Interpretation of Culture*, ed. Cary Nelson and Lawrence Grossberg (Chicago: University of Chicago Press, 1988).

6. Leon Trotsky, *Literature and Revolution* (Ann Arbor: University of Michigan Press, 1960), 126–27.

7. One example is Fredric Jameson's recent *A Singular Modernity: Essay on the Ontology of the Present* (London: Verso, 2002).

8. F. T. Marinetti, "Fondazione e manifesto del Futurismo," in *Teoria e invenzione futurista*, ed. Luciano De Maria (Milano: Mondadori, 1968), 12. The translation is mine.

9. Reinhard Koselleck, *Vergangene Zukunft: Zur Semantic geschichtlicher Zeiten* (Frankfurt am Main: Suhrkamp, 1979).

10. Friedrich Engels, "Preface to the German Edition of 1883," in *Birth of the Communist Manifesto: With Full Text of the Manifesto, all Prefaces by Marx and Engels, Early drafts by Engels and other Supplementary Material*, ed. Dirk J. Struik (New York: International Publishers, 1971), 141. For the geographic distribution of the *Manifesto*, see Bert Andréas, *Le manifeste communiste de Marx et Engels; Histoire et bibliographie, 1848–1918* (Milan: Feltrinelli, 1963).

11. Eric J. Hobsbawn, *Age of Revolution: Europe 1789–1848* (London: Weidenfeld and Nicholson, 1962).

12. Marjorie Perloff, *The Futurist Moment: Avant-Garde, Avant-Guerre, and the Language of Rupture* (Chicago: University of Chicago Press, 1986).

13. *Manifesto: A Century of Isms*, ed. Mary Ann Caws (Lincoln: University of Nebraska Press, 2001).

14. *Literature and Revolution*, 209.

15. For a history of the term "avant-garde," see Matei Calinescu, *Five Faces of Modernity: Modernism Avant-Garde Decadence Kitsch Postmodernism* (Durham, N.C.: Duke University Press, 1987). Originally published by Indiana University Press, 1977.

16. In a letter from 1932, for example, Artaud expressed his frustration with manifestos, declaring "there are too many manifestos and not enough works of art. Too many theories and no actions." *Antonin Artaud: Œuvres Completes*, vol. 5 (Paris: Gallimard, 1956), 85.

17. Expressionism produced a number of veritable anti-manifesto manifestos, for example Kanehl's "Futurism: A Sober Manifesto," which criticizes the irresponsible exaggerations of the Futurists, and August Stech's ironic "A Call for a Manifestantism" (Aufruf zum Manifestantismus), which protests against the veritable explosion of manifestos after 1909. All references to these manifestos are taken from Wolfgang Asholt and Walter Fähnders, eds., *Manifeste und Proklamationen der europäischen Avantgarde (1919–1938)* (Stuttgart: Metzler, 1995).

18. Luca Somigli has detailed the gradual infiltration of Futurism into England before Marinetti's well known and also well publicized third visit in 1914. Luca Somigli, *Legitimizing the Artist: Manifesto Writing and European Modernism 1885–1915* (Toronto: University of Toronto Press, 2003).

19. Cf. David Kadlec, "Pound, BLAST, and Syndicalism," *ELH* 60, no. 2 (1993): 1015–31.

20. Quoted in Hugh Kenner, *Wyndham Lewis* (Norfolk, Conn.: New Directions, 1954), 62.

21. Lawrence Rainey has shown to what extent Marinetti's well-attended lectures and the attention accorded him by the London press put pressure on one of these dissidents — Ezra Pound, who was lecturing to small audiences about esoteric subjects such as Provençal poetry. Lawrence Rainey, *Institutions of Modernism: Literary Elites and Public Cultures* (New Haven, Conn.: Yale University Press, 1998), 11ff.

22. The manner in which *The Dial* tried to market itself as a general modernist journal, modeled on the *Mercure de France*, can be deduced from the correspondence between Pound and the editors of *The Dial*. See Walter Sutto, ed., *Pound, Thayer, Watson and "The Dial": A Story in Letters* (Gainesville: University of Florida Press, 1994), 94.

23. What Pound called the "Tenets of Imagiste Faith" was published in 1913. "A Few Don'ts" was first printed in *Poetry* 1, no. 6 (March 1913), and "Credo," as part of "Prolegomena," in *Poetry Review*, later *Poetry and Drama*, February 1912.

24. Janet Lyon, *Manifestoes: Provocations of the Modern* (Ithaca, N.Y.: Cornell University Press, 1999), 124ff.

25. Paul Peppis, *Literature, Politics, and the English Avant-Garde: Nation and Empire, 1909–1918* (Cambridge: Cambridge University Press, 2000).

26. In his study, Rainey also emphasizes the competition between Lewis and Marinetti, a competition between Pound's aristocratic modernism and Marinetti's populist propaganda. Vincent Sherry also points out the significance of European modernism for Pound and Lewis, in *Ezra Pound, Wyndham Lewis, and Radical Modernism* (Oxford: Oxford University Press, 1993).

27. For more details on women's suffrage agitation, see Mark S. Morrisson, *The Pub-*

lic Face of Modernism: Little Magazines, Audiences, and Reception, 1905–1920 (Madison: University of Wisconsin Press, 2001), 84ff.

28. Keith Tuma has demonstrated that *Blast* is directed against the academy, but not against the artwork as such; see "Wyndham Lewis, *Blast*, and Popular Culture," ELH (1987): 403–19.

29. David Kadlec has pointed out that the context of *Blast* was not only the Futurist manifestos but also the manifestos of suffragism and syndicalism; see "Pound, *Blast*, and Syndicalism," ELH 60 (1993): 1015–31.

30. In a distinction made by Bürger, Vorticism does not belong to the avant-garde, which he defines as the desire to attack art as such, but to modernism, which only seeks to distance itself from nineteenth-century or "academic" art. Upon closer examination, the strategies of *Blast* with respect to the continental avant-garde are much too contradictory to be classified according to Bürger's modernism/avant-garde scheme.

31. Lewis, *Men without Art*, 231.

32. Douglas Mao has argued that aestheticism is being recoded in modernism: "one of modernism's key moves in its own defense of poesy—one so far accorded surprisingly little attention by scholars—was to try to legitimate Nineties aestheticism by, in effect, rewriting it along the lines of mid-Victorian moral earnestness." *Solid Objects: Modernism and the Text of Production* (Princeton, N.J.: Princeton University Press, 1998), 38.

33. Lewis, *Men without Art*, 225.

34. Fredric Jameson, *Fables of Aggression*.

35. Cf. Janet Lyon's argument in *Manifestoes: Provocations of the Modern* (Ithaca, N.Y.: Cornell University Press, 1999) about Pound's struggle with the "we" of the manifesto (133ff).

36. The text features a deadly fight between husband and wife in a vortex of water only to reveal in the end that the wife survived this fight without difficulty; the vortex turns out to have been nothing but a splash. I would like to thank David Damrosch for his suggestions regarding this and other points pertaining to this essay.

37. Reed Way Dasenbrock observes the greater playfulness of Lewis's manifestos. See Reed Way Dasenbrock, *The Literary Vorticism of Ezra Pound and Wyndham Lewis: Towards the Condition of Painting* (Baltimore: Johns Hopkins University Press, 1985), 25.

38. *Blast 1*, ed. Wyndham Lewis, foreword by Bradford Morrow (Santa Rosa: Black Sparrow Press, 1997), 7.

39. See Karl Heinz Bohrer, *Suddenness: On the Moment of Aesthetic Appearance*, trans. Ruth Crowley (New York: Columbia University Press, 1994).

40. Kenneth Burke, *A Grammar of Motives* (Berkeley: University of California Press, [1954] 1969), 200ff.

41. Georges Sorel, *Reflections on Violence* (New York: B. W. Huebsch, 1914).

42. Adolf Hitler, *Mein Kampf* (New York: Reynal and Hitchcock, 1941), 708.

43. Hitler developed a theory of spoken propaganda based on Gustave Le Bon, while Mussolini and his followers envisioned a heightened form of action-speech. For fascist theorists and philosophers, see *A Primer of Italian Fascism*, ed. Jeffrey Schnapp (Lincoln: University of Nebraska Press, 2000).

44. Ezra Pound, *Jefferson and/or Mussolini: Fascism as I Have Seen It* (New York: Liveright, 1936).

45. *Time and Western Man*, ed. Paul Edwards (Santa Rosa, Calif.: Black Sparrow Press, 1993). Wyndham Lewis, *The Art of Being Ruled*, ed. Reed Way Dasenbrock (Santa Rosa, Calif.: Black Sparrow Press, 1989).

46. Lewis, *The Art of Being Ruled*.

47. Eliot retreated from the manifesto-driven revolutionary Futurism in several essays engaging with tradition, in particular *Tradition and the Individual Talent* (1919).

48. Wyndham Lewis, *Time and Western Man*, ed. Paul Edwards (Santa Rosa, Calif.: Black Sparrow Press, 1993), 120.

49. Ortega y Gasset, *The Revolt of the Masses* (Notre Dame, Ind.: University of Notre Dame Press, 1985).

50. In *Time and Western Man* Lewis backpedaled politically, admitting that he had sold liberal democracy short by his overenthusiastic embrace of fascism: "Since writing *The Art of Being Ruled* (1925) I have somewhat modified my view with regard to what I then called 'democracy.' I should express myself differently today. I feel that I slighted too much the notion of 'democracy' by using that term to mean too exclusively the present so-called democratic masses, hypnotized into a sort of hysterical imbecility by the mesmeric methods of Advertisement" (25).

51. Tyrus Miller, *Late Modernism: Politics, Fiction, and the Arts between the World Wars* (Berkeley: University of California Press, 1999), 19ff.

Michael LeMahieu

Nonsense Modernism: The Limits of Modernity and the Feelings of Philosophy in Wittgenstein's *Tractatus*

The negation of nonsense is nonsense.
Wittgenstein, letter to Frank Ramsey

Is the absence of feeling a feeling?
Wittgenstein, *Zettel*

At once elegant and opaque, the *Tractatus Logico-Philosophicus*, the only work Wittgenstein published during his lifetime, oscillates between logical propositions and enigmatic aphorisms, and the well-remarked difficulty of reconciling its rationalist properties with its mystical qualities continues to fascinate philosophers and literary critics alike.[1] In a 1919 letter to Ludwig von Ficker, editor of the journal *Der Brenner*, Wittgenstein describes his work as "strictly philosophical and, at the same time, literary."[2] The critical reception of the *Tractatus* reflects this split personality: commentators who focus on the logical propositions that constitute the bulk of the work tend to describe a foundationalist text that initiated the tradition of logical positivism; those who emphasize the text's concluding remarks on ethics, death, and the mystical tend to describe a work closer in spirit to Nietzsche or Heidegger, or even to modernist poets, than to Frege and Russell. And indeed, the text's singular combination of rational and mystical features parallels what Jürgen Habermas identifies as the contradictions of "the philosophical discourse of modernity," wherein attempts at logical self-legitimation conjure the need for an aesthetic, mystical, or religious supplement.[3]

This protean quality has, not surprisingly, given rise to conflicting assessments of Wittgenstein's relation to "modernism," a term that itself encompasses many competing, and at times contradictory, definitions. At first glance, however, the *Tractatus* may not appear "modernist" in any sense of the term. Wittgenstein positions his individual talent neither as a natural outgrowth of the Western philosophical tradition nor as an explicit break with it, stating in the Preface that "I do not wish to judge how far my efforts coincide with those of other philosophers. Indeed, what I have written here makes no claim to novelty in detail, and the reason why I give no sources is that it is a matter of indifference to me whether the thoughts that I have had have been anticipated by someone else" (*TLP* 3). In its unconcern for its philosophical predecessors, the text expresses no nostalgia for a world that has been lost, but in making no claim to "novelty," neither does it attempt to "make it new." Although Wittgenstein does acknowledge his indebtedness "to Frege's great works and to the writings of my good friend Mr Bertrand Russell" (*TLP* 3), and thus aligns himself with the modern revolution in logic and the linguistic turn in philosophy, of which the *Tractatus* would become the exemplar, such a pedigree alone hardly qualifies the text as modernist, even in strictly philosophical terms.

Nevertheless, scholars of literary modernism have displayed a burgeoning interest in Wittgenstein's work in the decade since Michael Fischer declared that "discussions of modernism usually omit Wittgenstein and discussions of Wittgenstein usually ignore modernism."[4] Composed during the First World War and appearing at the height of high modernism, the *Tractatus* should, it would seem, bear some relation to modernism, if only for the contingent reasons of historical circumstance; and, indeed, critics such as Michael North and Marjorie Perloff have recently placed the work within a modernist context. North focuses on the reception and translation of the text, situating it in that *annus mirabilis* that saw the publication of *Ulysses* and *The Waste Land*. For Perloff, the date of the book's publication is less significant than that of its inception — not 1922, but 1914 — as she provocatively reads the *Tractatus* as "a war book." North emphasizes the logical sections of the work, seeing the *Tractatus* as a continuation of Frege's and Russell's attempts "to formulate a method of communication unmediated by any particularity whatever."[5] Perloff, on the other hand, stresses the text's poetic qualities, arguing that its "recognition of a mystery that cannot be solved" places it alongside "the gnomic and aphoristic manifestos of Malevich or the meditative poems of Wallace Stevens rather than with the writing of *fin de siècle* Vienna, much less the Bloomsbury of G. E. Moore or Maynard Keynes."[6] Taken together, these two readings suggest that Wittgenstein's treatise might be a text that advances the project of philosophical modernity even as it offers a "modernist" critique of that very project.

This essay seeks to locate those aspects of the *Tractatus* that allow one to read it as a document of either philosophical modernity or literary modernism, to identify the criteria according to which one might favor one reading or the other, and to examine the consequences of making—or not making—such a choice. My argument does not, therefore, attempt to adjudicate the competing definitions of "modernism" that North's and Perloff's readings respectively imply, nor to stipulate a correct one. I argue instead that Wittgenstein refuses to reconcile the competing modernist perspectives that his text exemplifies. In this respect, his description of the work as "strictly philosophical and, at the same time, literary" serves as an allegory of reading the *Tractatus*. Wittgenstein presents these two aspects as contiguous but not conjugated according to a logic of subordination: because philosophy does not subsume literature, nor literature philosophy, the text is, strictly speaking, both at the same time. This uncompromising simultaneity manifests itself in the text's figures of feelings, which waver between logic and psychology, necessity and contingency, sense and nonsense. In the end, Wittgenstein's refusal to provide the criteria by which one would definitively determine the standing of these figures in the text, and consequently make either a *philosophical* or *aesthetic* judgment as to the "modernist" standing of the *Tractatus*, is not, as Habermas would have it, tantamount to a mystical retreat from modernity. Rather, this refusal underwrites Wittgenstein's conception of ethical judgment as never circumscribed and always incomplete.

Wittgenstein's "Nonsense Experiment"

In his essay "Modernity—An Incomplete Project," Habermas adopts Max Weber's definition of cultural modernity as "the separation of the substantive reason expressed in religion and metaphysics into three autonomous spheres . . . science, morality, and art."[7] Cultural modernity seeks to develop these spheres "according to their inner logic" in order "to utilize this accumulation of specialized culture for the enrichment of everyday life" (103). Thus epistemology, ethics, and aesthetics can enjoy a relative autonomy from each other and from the *Lebenswelt* even as they harmoniously contribute to a praxis of everyday life. No small prize; and also not surprising, then, that Habermas claims that the "project of modernity has not yet been fulfilled" (107). Rather than redeeming the promise of modernity, aesthetic modernism has, he laments, negated it, sundering the aesthetic sphere from everyday life and withdrawing "into the untouchableness of complete autonomy" (104). This "modernist transformation," as Habermas refers to it, has provoked in turn a series of "surrealist" efforts to "force a reconciliation of art and life," undertakings that have ultimately proved to be so many "nonsense experiments" (105). Habermas argues that the "disillusionment" that results from these failures has "come to serve as a pretense for conservative positions," an excuse to withdraw from the project of modernity altogether (107). He classifies the advocates of these positions according to a typology of anti-modernist "young conservatives," pre-modernist "old conservatives," and post-modernist "neoconservatives." Among this last group, he includes "the early Wittgenstein" (108).

I begin with Habermas's argument not only because it misrepresents, to my mind, "the early Wittgenstein" but also because it allows one to see the "badness" of Wittgenstein's modernism. As opposed to Habermas's vision of a "good" modernism that would complete the project of modernity and fulfill its promise, Wittgenstein's modernism negates that project by presenting competing modernist perspectives that it refuses to reconcile. Wittgenstein thus engages in precisely the effort that Habermas laments, but, I will argue, for reasons entirely different from those Habermas adumbrates.

In another respect, however, one might say that Habermas insightfully, if unintentionally, describes the project of "the early Wittgenstein," for the

Tractatus is in fact a sort of "nonsense experiment." Indeed, in the text's penultimate remark, Wittgenstein describes the work as such: "My propositions serve as elucidations in the following way: anyone who understands me eventually recognizes them as nonsensical, when he has used them — as steps — to climb up beyond them. (He must, so to speak, throw away the ladder after he has climbed up it.) He must transcend these propositions, and then he will see the world aright." (*TLP* 6.54). This remark, and the text's famous conclusion that immediately follows it — "What we cannot speak about we must pass over in silence" (*TLP* 7) — constitute for Habermas a two-step of mysticism and quietism, as his multiple allusions to the *Tractatus* indicate. Take, for example, his comparison of Heidegger with "the early Wittgenstein": "[Heidegger] makes use of metaphysical concepts for purposes of a critique of metaphysics, as a ladder he casts away once he has mounted the rungs. Once on the heights, however, the late Heidegger does not, as did the early Wittgenstein, withdraw into the mystic's silent intuition."[8] Although it is perhaps odd that, when placed alongside Heidegger, it is Wittgenstein who emerges as the "mystic," Habermas's comparison is otherwise apt. For just as Heidegger makes use of the concepts of metaphysics in order to develop his critique of metaphysics, so too Wittgenstein adopts the perspective of the modern world view in order to perform an immanent critique of that worldview. Wittgenstein's characterization of his own propositions as nonsense forms part of this strategy, but, *pace* Habermas, it is less reclusive than recursive, and ultimately, less mystical than ethical. In order to see why Wittgenstein deals in nonsense, and why his conception of ethics demands that he do so, it is first necessary to see how he develops a certain method in response to what he considers the "illusion" of the modern worldview.

Because Wittgenstein's writings display relatively little interest in the problems of modernity that captivated many early-twentieth-century thinkers, it is all the more remarkable to find in the midst of the ideas on propositional form and logical operators that fill his early notebooks — those that he composed during the war and that would provide the raw material for the *Tractatus* — an observation dated May 6, 1916, concerning the typical worldview of modern people: "At bottom the whole *Weltanschauung* of the moderns [*der Modernen*] involves the illusion that the so-called laws of nature are explanations of natural phenomena."[9] Wittgenstein preserves this remark in the *Tractatus*, couching it within a larger discussion of empirical fact and logical necessity:

6.3631 [Induction], however, has no logical justification but only a psychological one. It is clear that there are no grounds for believing that the simplest eventuality will in fact be realized.

6.36311 It is an hypothesis that the sun will rise tomorrow: and this means that we do not *know* whether it will rise.

6.37 There is no compulsion making one thing happen because another has happened. The only necessity that exists is logical necessity.

6.371 The whole modern worldview [*Weltanschauung*] is founded on the illusion that the so-called laws of nature are explanations of natural phenomena.[10]

6.372 Thus people today stop at the laws of nature, treating them as something inviolable, just as God and Fate were treated in past ages.
And in fact both are right and both are wrong: though the view of the ancients is clearer in so far as they have a clear and acknowledged terminus, while the modern system tries to make it look as if everything were explained.

For Wittgenstein, a veneration of (pseudo-)scientific discourse constitutes a defining feature of modernity.[11] The modern worldview naturalizes the divine, substituting the irrefragable laws of nature for the binding word of God. To be sure, Wittgenstein's remarks in this section of the *Tractatus* hardly amount to a coherent argument, let alone a complete theory, concerning the relationship between inference, necessity, and explanation.[12] To worry the finer points of these matters is, however, to miss Wittgenstein's larger point about the "illusion," or "delusion" [*Täuschung*], of the modern *Weltanschauung*, which elides the difference between empirical generalizations and logical necessities, thereby making it "look as if *everything* were explained," or, as an earlier version of the remark puts it, "as if everything had a foundation."[13]

"Explanations," Wittgenstein would announce years later, "come to an end somewhere," and rather than expanding the purview of the modern *Weltanschauung* by means of his philosophy, he attempts to limit what he perceives as its excesses, to reveal the terminus that it fails to acknowledge.[14] This effort manifests itself in what Wittgenstein's commentators typically describe as his rejection of "psychologism," a doctrine that reduces linguistic processes to mental processes, holding that the meaning of a word can be explained by virtue of the intentional content associated with it.[15] Wittgenstein makes scattered and largely dismissive references to psychology throughout the *Tractatus*. In addition to characterizing induction as a procedure which "has no logical justification but only a psychological one," Wittgenstein sets aside the idea of the will as a question "of interest only to psychology" (*TLP* 6.423) and makes a blanket reference to "the superficial psychology of the present day" (*TLP* 5.5421). Despite the denigrating tone of these remarks, he remains apprehensive of the "risk" that psychological considerations present to the integrity of his logical investigations: "Does not my study of sign-language [*Zeichensprache*] correspond to the study of thought-processes, which philosophers used to consider so essential to the philosophy of logic? Only in most cases they got entangled in unessential psychological investigations, and with my method too there is an analogous risk" (*TLP* 4.1121). The success of Wittgenstein's effort to reveal the limits of the modern worldview thus rests on his ability to delimit in the first instance the "unessential psychological investigations" that threaten to corrupt his method.

Wittgenstein recognizes, however, that his critique must unfold within the terms of the modern *Weltanschauung*. He acknowledges, somewhat reluctantly, that he is implicated in the worldview that he seeks to unsettle, and he thus entertains no delusions of ushering in a postmodernity that would supplant or surpass modernity — Habermas's characterization of "the early Wittgenstein" notwithstanding. In the foreword to the 1930 manuscript *Philosophical Remarks*, Wittgenstein clearly situates his antagonism toward modernity within a modern context: "This book is written for such men as are in sympathy with its spirit. This spirit is different from the one which informs the vast stream of European and American civilization in which all of us stand."[16] But logical as well as historical factors restrict his methodology: because the modern worldview acknowledges no limits to its discursive reach, there is no metalanguage that would escape its discourse, and consequently no external perspective from which he could conduct his critique. As Wittgenstein would later put the point, in a move that invites a further comparison with Heidegger, "I cannot use language to get outside language."[17]

In response to these methodological constraints, Wittgenstein sets out to delimit language from within language, to perform an immanent critique rather than a transcendental one. However, as one sees in his introduction of the aims of the *Tractatus*, this solution is beset with its own problems:

> Thus the aim of the book is to draw a limit to thought, or rather — not to thought, but to the expression of thoughts: for in order to be able to draw a limit to thought, we should have to find both sides of the limits thinkable (i.e. we should have to be able to think what cannot be thought).
>
> It will therefore only be in language that the limit can be drawn, and what lies on the other side of the limit will simply be nonsense [*einfach Unsinn*]. (TLP 3)

The clipped confidence of Wittgenstein's prose compensates for a momentary flinch in his reasoning, his apparent meticulousness functioning to a certain extent as a sleight of hand. He begins by claiming that the aim of his book is to draw a limit to thought but then immediately retracts that statement, specifying that to draw a limit to "the expression of thoughts" constitutes the text's aim. The relationship between the limits to thought and the limits to the expression of thoughts, however, is precisely what is at issue in the *Tractatus*, and this passage leaves uncertain whether language displaces thought as the proper object of study — as that to which the *Tractatus* draws the limit — or instead functions as Wittgenstein's method of delimiting thought. To further complicate matters, the same logic that thwarts his initial attempt at stating the aim of the text — the fact that to draw the limit to thought would require that he think the unthinkable — also troubles his revised statement of that aim, for to draw the limits to the expression of thoughts, in language, would seem to entail speaking the unspeakable, that which is "simply nonsense."

Recognizing the necessity of engaging in nonsense in order to reveal the limits of sense — whether psychological or linguistic — helps to explain Wittgenstein's characterization of his own propositions as "nonsensical," but it also lands his readers in an interpretive dilemma, for they must decide how, or whether, to make sense of his nonsense. That decision rests in turn on how a given reader understands the aim of the book and the method it employs to achieve that aim—on whether Wittgenstein's nonsense marks a failure of the book's philosophical project, or instead constitutes a key to the success of the text's immanent critique of that project. Wittgenstein does not specify what relationship between language and thought would allow his readers to understand him in spite of, or perhaps because of, his nonsensical propositions. This undetermined relationship, moreover, risks the dangers of "unessential psychological investigations," since in the absence of a clearly delimited relationship between language and thought, Wittgenstein's multiple references to his own and his readers' "thoughts and feelings" threaten to exceed their intended function.[18]

The Senses of Nonsense, the Feelings of Philosophy

If what lies beyond the limits of language is "simply nonsense," nonsense is, nonetheless, no simple matter, and on its vagaries turn the alternate readings of the *Tractatus* as a modernist text.[19] One possible interpretation, which presents itself perhaps most readily and certainly boasts the most distinguished lineage, can be traced back to Russell's Introduction as well as to the logical positivists of the Vienna Circle, for whom the *Tractatus* served as something of a sacred text. This possibility, call it the *modernity*-modernist reading, holds that the *Tractatus* attempts to rid ordinary language of nonsense and, as Russell states, to investigate "the conditions which would have to be fulfilled by a logically perfect language" (TLP ix). With this end in mind, the story goes, Wittgenstein sets out to distinguish what we can speak about and what we must pass over in silence, what can be said and what can only be shown. He draws these distinctions in what has come to be known as the text's "picture theory of language," which holds that, because the same "logical form" underlies language and reality, propositions are able to "represent the whole of reality" (TLP 4.12). Propositions cannot, however, represent their own logical form, they can only "show" it: "What *can* be shown, *cannot* be said. Now, too, we understand our feeling [*unser Gefühl*] that once we have a sign-language [*Zeichensprache*] in which everything is all right, we already have a correct logical point of view" (TLP 4.1212–4.1213). To determine what can be said and what can only be shown is to

Wittgenstein's *Tractatus*

imply further that the limits of language and the limits of thought are co-extensive, that nonsensical propositions betray nonsensical thoughts. "Our feeling," therefore, arises as an aftereffect, not as an essential component of the logical investigation but as a symptom that corroborates psychologically what necessarily precedes it logically: first we must achieve the correct logical point of view, and only then will we feel that everything is right with our language. Unlike the modern worldview, Wittgenstein's study of language avoids confusing empirical accidents (such as our feeling about a given problem) with logical necessities by "showing" the limits that separate them.

This effort to establish the conditions for a logically perfect language, and, even further, "to formulate a method of communication unmediated by any particularity whatever," makes the *Tractatus*, Michael North claims, "in some ways the finest and most extreme expression of . . . the ambition to lift thought free of all specificity, all contingency."[20] And yet, as North convincingly shows, the translation history of the *Tractatus* testifies to the failure, indeed the impossibility, of achieving such a goal. The vicissitudes of natural languages belie the dream of a perfect logical one. North notes that even the term *Grenze*, "in some sense perhaps the most important single word in the book," can be translated either as "limit" or as "boundary," thus presenting the translator with a choice between the logical and the empirical, forcing a decision precisely where the criteria for deciding are at stake: "The very word that Wittgenstein chose to represent the unity and impermeability of language thus turns out to have within it possibilities that would not emerge explicitly in his work until many years later. 'Limit' is unitary and metaphysical; 'boundary' is multiple and empirical."[21] The possibilities inherent within language disrupt the attempt to delimit language from within. The external history of the *Tractatus* thus thwarts its internal logic, demonstrating that to determine the limits of logic is not entirely a logical matter.[22]

In locating the text's failure in its external history, however, North limits the reach of his own insights, foreclosing the possibility that the *Tractatus* deliberately unsettles its own project. He suggests that "the inversion of modernity's 'dream of reason' was always inherent within it," but there is much evidence to suggest that this "inversion" is not only endemic to the project of philosophical modernity but internal to the *Tractatus* itself.[23] In the first place, Wittgenstein makes a number of remarks that flatly contradict a view of the *Tractatus* as an attempt to "expose and clarify the logical incoherence of natural languages."[24] He claims, for example, that "all propositions of our everyday language, just as they stand, are in perfect logical order" (TLP 5.5563). Second, and more significantly, to maintain Russell's understanding of the aim of the *Tractatus* requires that one entirely ignore Wittgenstein's own characterization of his propositions as nonsense and that one largely dismiss the "mystical" sections of the work—those which, Russell confessed, left him with "a certain sense of intellectual discomfort" (TLP xxi). That is not to say that North is wrong to claim that "in some respects" the *Tractatus* is the "finest and most extreme expression" of the project of philosophical modernity; it is to say, however, that in other respects the *Tractatus* is one of the most cogent critiques of that project. Logic and nonsense coexist, often appearing in successive remarks, or even within the same one:

> The correct method in philosophy would really be the following: to say nothing except what can be said, i.e., propositions of natural science—i.e. something that has nothing to do with philosophy—and then, whenever someone else wanted to say something metaphysical, to demonstrate to him that he had failed to give a meaning to certain signs in his propositions. Although it would not be satisfying to the other person—he would not have the feeling [*das Gefühl*] that we were teaching him philosophy—*this* method would be the only strictly correct one. (TLP 6.53)

The "correct method in philosophy" suits the objective of developing a logically perfect language, one that conforms to the limits of what can be said. However, such a method does not arouse the feeling that the hypothetical interlocutor typically associates with philosophy. The absence of this feeling seems to run counter to Wittgenstein's earlier explanation of "our feeling" (the one that arises when we develop a proper sign-language and then realize we have already achieved a "correct logical point of view"). But this apparent contradiction—the correct method appears to lack the feeling that the correct point of view inspires—in fact represents two sides of the same coin. The "problems of philosophy," Wittgenstein writes in the Preface, arise when we misunderstand "the logic of our language" (*TLP* 3). As a result, if we practice a method that conforms to the correct logical point of view, we will not feel like we are addressing philosophical problems, or at least what we typically understand to be philosophical problems. The absence of the feeling that we are doing philosophy thus serves as a negative counterpart to our feeling that we have attained the correct point of view: both confirm that we have correctly construed the relationship between logic and language. We might therefore answer affirmatively the Wittgensteinian question that serves as the second epigraph to this essay: the absence of a feeling is indeed itself a feeling.

To reconcile this apparent contradiction concerning Wittgenstein's definition of the correct philosophical method, however, is to invite yet another pertaining to his implementation of that method. Wittgenstein immediately follows his definition of the correct method with his claim that his own propositions are nonsense. This juxtaposition suggests that Wittgenstein's method in the *Tractatus* is not the strictly correct one and that the text's language is not a logically perfect one. It thus suggests further that the feeling that is absent from the correct method might arise as one reads the *Tractatus*. Indeed, the text offers a number of potential candidates for the feeling that one typically associates with the practice of philosophy but that fails to arise when practicing the strictly correct method. For example, on the next-to-last page of the book, in the midst of the "mystical" propositions, Wittgenstein remarks: "To view the world sub specie aeterni [*sic*] is to view it as a whole—a limited whole. Feeling the world as a limited whole—it is this that is mystical [*Das Gefühl der Welt als begrenztes Ganzes ist das mystische*.]" (*TLP* 6.45). Unlike "our feeling" that results from the "correct logical point of view," the experience of "feeling the world as a limited whole" suggests a transcendental point of view. In an earlier version of the remark that appears in Wittgenstein's notebooks, he discusses such a point of view in explicitly aesthetic, and ethical, terms:

> The work of art is the object seen *sub specie aeternitatis*; and the good life is the world seen *sub specie aeternitatis*. This is the connexion between art and ethics. The usual way of looking at things sees objects as it were from the midst of them, the view *sub specie aeternitatis* from outside. In

such a way that they have the whole world as a background. Is this it perhaps? . . . (The thought forces itself upon one): The thing seen *sub specie aeternitatis* is the thing seen together with the whole logical space.[25]

One sees in this passage Wittgenstein grappling with the limits of his own ideas about the limits of language and thought, attempting to capture in language a perspective that potentially transcends it, one that would allow him to see things "from outside." He abandons many of these remarks in the *Tractatus*, for the most part dropping the idea of viewing the world from the outside and instead, as we have seen, defining that which lies beyond the limits of language as "simply nonsense." But if Wittgenstein appears to abandon transcendence for immanence, he nonetheless finds the "force" of the former hard to resist, and he does not entirely relinquish the possibility of a view from above, preserving in the *Tractatus* the remark regarding the view *sub specie aeternitatis* and indicating that to feel the world as a limited whole is perhaps to have one foot on either side of the limit.

This transcendental residue figures into a second reading of the *Tractatus* as a modernist text: call this the *modernism*-modernist reading. What the *modernity*-modernist reading inscribes as a logical failure becomes on the *modernism*-modernist reading legible as an aesthetic success.[26] If we cannot entirely transcend the limits of the logic of language, this reading suggests, we might nevertheless "feel" beyond them.[27] A familiar cousin of this idea is the Kantian sublime, wherein apprehension, which is theoretically unlimited, exceeds comprehension, which is strictly limited.[28] Perloff touches on the possibility of feeling what one cannot say by emphasizing the poetic qualities of the text's concluding remarks and the feelings that accompany them.[29] Commenting on Wittgenstein's wartime experiences and his proposition concerning the relation between life and death ("Death is not an event in life: we do not live to experience death" [TLP 6.4311]), Perloff writes: "[W]e *feel* that we have witnessed the process whereby this 'mystical' insight has been earned. The diarist [Wittgenstein] has witnessed countless deaths, but they are not, he *feels* obliged to insist, 'events' of his own life. The point cannot be argued; it can merely be *felt*. And in this sense the *Tractatus* must be understood as a poetic construct."[30]

The literary protocols of reading that Perloff brings to bear on the *Tractatus* offer a way to understand Wittgenstein's apparently nonsensical, or "mystical," propositions—those that appear to exceed the limits of language—not as a failure of the text's philosophical project but as a key to recognizing its literary objectives. Perloff emphasizes "feeling" in two respects: Wittgenstein "feels" a certain way about his wartime experience and this feeling "cannot be argued" in language but only "felt" through language. Perloff's language parallels the passive voice construction that Wittgenstein employs in stating the distinction between saying and showing, and she adapts that logical point to reflect an empirical fact. Whereas Wittgenstein claims that what *can* be shown *cannot* be said, on this reading what *cannot* be argued *can* (merely) be felt. Both Wittgenstein and his readers share in this feeling: Wittgenstein's act of witnessing death produces a feeling in him, and our own act of witnessing Wittgenstein struggle to express this insight allows us to "feel," in some sense, the process whereby he arrives at it. Thus while Wittgenstein's "gnomic utterances" may appear nonsensical, they nevertheless allow his readers to feel the import of his thoughts, and it is "in this sense" that "the *Tractatus* must be understood as a poetic construct."

While this last imperative reflects the force of the text's literary aspects, logical necessity delimits even what Perloff points to as Wittgenstein's poetic, experiential epiphany—or, perhaps better, logical necessity dictates that the content of the epiphany is not limited to any particular experience whatsoever. Wittgenstein presents his remark about death not as an insight gained through experience but instead as the definitional limit of experience. The claim that death is not an event in life holds true independent of any particular experience of death; in fact it defines death as the impossibility of experience. Death marks the limit of the empirical, the limit of eventfulness. "Our life," Wittgenstein goes on to remark in this same passage, "has no end in just the way in which our visual field has no limits." One can witness the death of others, but one cannot experience one's own death, the limit of one's own life. In this respect, the literary sections of the *Tractatus*, those that for Perloff "break abruptly" with the remarks that precede them, seem to replicate the logical points of the text's more strictly philosophical sections.[31] Perhaps, then, it is not the logician who makes a poetic point but the poet who makes a logical one: the bell, by *necessity*, must always toll for *thee*.

Thus while at times the text's philosophical aspects give way to empirical contingencies, at others its literary aspects take the form of logical necessities. Wittgenstein's attempts to delimit necessity and contingency result in a knot of significations that alternately appear under the aspects of logical positivism and empirical psychology, of the text's more patently "philosophical" propositions and its more ineffably "literary" remarks. Untangling that knot demands a judgment regarding the relationship between truth and method in the *Tractatus*. Does the text aim to formulate a logical language or to unsettle the possibility of one? Do the text's "feelings" remain subordinate to logical necessities or instead touch on empirical contingencies and mystical insights? Wittgenstein does not supply a set of clear and distinct criteria by which one would choose definitively between these two options. However, Cora Diamond suggests that if we take seriously Wittgenstein's claim that we must recognize his propositions as nonsense in order to understand him — if we adopt what she calls "an austere view of nonsense" — then we can also understand the method of the *Tractatus* in such a way as to recognize that it is a false choice "to read Wittgenstein either as a mystic or as a logical positivist."[32] Along with James Conant, Diamond convincingly argues that the *Tractatus* shows how nonsense neither transgresses the logical limits of reality nor illuminates what lies beyond those limits.[33] Nonsense is, rather, "simply nonsense," a sentence with no determinate structure or a word with no determinate meaning, and Wittgenstein's claim that his own propositions are nonsensical is also to be read in the same "austere" spirit. The aim of the nonsensical propositions in the *Tractatus* is to "elucidate" nothing more than their own nonsensical status, thus aligning the *Tractatus* with Wittgenstein's later philosophy in its aim of teaching the reader "to pass from a piece of disguised nonsense to something that is patent nonsense."[34] This therapeutic aim delivers, moreover, an ethical payoff, for the *Tractatus* teaches us, Diamond claims, to engage in "an imaginative activity of understanding" nonsense by imagining ourselves occupying the illusory perspective from which a person who utters nonsense fancies himself to be speaking sensibly — by allowing ourselves, in other words, "to be taken in by the appearance of sense that some nonsense presents to us."[35]

One could do worse than to describe this last idea, which has a familiar ring, as a type of "negative capability": the capacity to disregard one's own knowledge of nonsense in order to engage ethically with another who lacks that knowledge. One wonders, however, how the *Tractatus* manages to assure us that we know which of its propositions are nonsensical. Are those that present the criteria for distinguishing between sense and nonsense, for example, themselves nonsensical? In order to avoid contradiction and circularity, to avoid unseating logical positivism with what one might call "logical negativism," the "austerity" interpretation of the *Tractatus* must locate those propositions of the text that are not "simply nonsense" and, furthermore, those that teach us to recognize the ones that are. Hence the importance Conant and Diamond attach to "the frame of the book — its Preface and closing sentences," where "Wittgenstein combines remarks about the aim of the book and the kind of reading it requires."[36] But if the frame of the book teaches its readers to recognize the propositions of the text proper as nonsense, what about those propositions in the body of the text that agree with or reiterate points made in the frame? Do they too enjoy a privileged, more trustworthy status? Conant stipulates that a given proposition's status as a "framing" remark is a function not only of its location in the text but also of "how it occurs," and that determination is in turn a function of what "aspect" a given proposition presents to a given reader.[37] This criterion shifts to a different interpretive level the same types of decisions that face the *modernity*-modernist and *modernism*-modernist readings of the *Tractatus*. However, although the question migrates to another hermeneutic field, from the body of the text to its frame, it retains largely the same shape — and the same difficulty — since deciding what "aspect" a given proposition presents in a text that is Janus-faced, strictly philosophical and simultaneously literary, is never a straightforward exercise. To begin with the assumption that Wittgenstein's propositions represent not sense but simply nonsense is still to leave undetermined the criteria for distinguishing between the two. We hang upside-down on the horns of the same dilemma.

Feelers and Figures

The attempt to determine the text's frame might lead us, if initially for no more than the accidental reasons of metaphorical resonance, to the text's much maligned picture theory of language. And if the decision between reading the *Tractatus* as a document of philosophical modernity or one of aesthetic modernism rests in part on a decision between two conflicting feelings, we might ask, in keeping with this metaphorical logic rather than a strictly philosophical one, how the picture theory frames that decision. As it turns out, "feeling" plays a determining role even in this most quintessentially logical doctrine, this time not as a state of mind but as an act of touching.[38] We might recall here that the dominant trope of the picture theory is *isomorphism*, a symmetrical relation between the elements that make up one structure, in this case the words in a proposition, and those that make up another, in this case the objects in a state of affairs. This formal relation establishes the conditions of possibility that allow language to refer to reality:

> **2.151** Pictorial form is the possibility that things are related to one another in the same way as the elements of the picture.

> **2.1511** *That* is how a picture is attached to reality; it reaches right out to it.

> **2.1512** It is laid against reality like a measure.

> **2.15121** Only the end-points of the graduating lines actually *touch* the object that is to be measured.

> **2.1513** So a picture, conceived in this way, also includes the pictorial relationship, which makes it into a picture.

> **2.1514** The pictorial relationship consists of the correlations of the picture's elements with things.

> **2.1515** These correlations are, as it were, the feelers [*die Fühler*] of the picture's elements with which the picture touches reality.

The measuring-stick metaphor is fitting, for pictorial form allows pictures and reality, two otherwise incommensurable structures, to become commensurable. But if pictorial form establishes the conditions of possibility for a referential relation, this leaves untouched the question of how such a relation becomes actual, how the two structures become not only isomorphic but contiguous. Wittgenstein introduces the figure of "feelers" to bridge that gap. The feelers are, first of all, the necessary "correlations" between the elements in a picture and the elements in a state of affairs; they are not themselves "pictures of reality" but a figure of the formal correspondence underlying the two structures that enter into a pictorial relationship. The feelers are thus "senseless" insofar as they logically precede distinctions between sense and nonsense, in much the same way that Derrida's *différance* is the condition that allows for conceptual thinking but is itself not a concept.[39] At the same time, however, the feelers are also part of, or proper to, the picture itself. They function not only as the logical conditions of possibility for representation but also as the empirical means by which the picture represents reality. Wittgenstein describes the feelers as that with which the picture touches reality, and a more literal translation might emphasize this aspect by rendering *die Fühler* as "antennae." The feelers thus mark the interface between subject and object, simultaneously a logical limit and an empirical boundary, both separating language from reality and binding language to reality.

Wittgenstein subordinates neither the logical nor the empirical function of the feelers because his argument requires both, and his depiction of the pictorial relation as simultaneously active and passive reflects this double duty: the picture first reaches out and touches the world and is then laid against it. Furthermore, note how, in the second proposition cited above, the italicized *that* ("*That* is how a picture is attached to reality; it reaches right out to it") graphically reaches out in an act of demonstration or ostention, a figure of pointing that itself doubles as both a precondition of reference and an act of referring. Although Wittgenstein would come to repudiate the picture theory of language—a "*picture* held us captive," he would later reflect in the *Investigations*—the feelers touch on an ambiguity that extends beyond the local context in which they appear.[40] We can read the doubled aspect that the feelers present as itself a figure for the doubled aspects of the text as a whole. Time and again the *Tractatus* presents two aspects of a phenomenon that are not placed in a relation of subordination but instead set side by side: necessary and contingent, logical and empirical, philosophical and, at the same time, literary.

With this in mind, consider yet another "frame" of the book, this one decidedly contingent. On June 22, 1912, not long before the inception of the *Tractatus*, Wittgenstein wrote to Russell: "Whenever I have time I now read James's 'Varieties of religious exp[erience].' The book does me a *lot* of good."[41] Seven years later, Russell met with Wittgenstein, after an extended absence, on neutral ground in The Hague. On December 20, 1919, he wrote to Lady Ottoline Morrell about his impressions: "I had felt in his book a flavour of mysticism, but was astonished when I found that he has become a complete mystic . . . It all started from William James's *Varieties of Religious Experience* . . . He has penetrated deep into mystical ways of thought and feeling, but I think (though he wouldn't agree) that what he likes best in mysticism is its power to make him stop thinking."[42]

Perhaps Wittgenstein would have agreed with Russell's characterization of his attraction to mystical "thought and feeling," with but one qualification: that it was not mysticism's power to make him stop thinking, but its power to alert him when to stop thinking *philosophically*, that was valuable. In *Varieties of Religious Experience*, James writes: "Feeling is private and dumb, and unable to give an account of itself. It allows that its results are mysteries and enigmas, declines to justify them rationally, and on occasion is willing that they should even pass for paradoxical and absurd. Philosophy takes just the opposite attitude. Her aspiration is to reclaim from mystery and paradox whatever territory she touches."[43] One can detect an echo of this remark in the *Tractatus*: "We feel [*fühlen*] that even when all possible scientific questions have been answered, the problems of life remain untouched [*nicht berührt sind*]. Of course then there are no questions left, and this itself is the answer" (*TLP* 6.52). For Wittgenstein as for James, philosophy desires to subject feeling to logical analysis, whereas feeling indicates where logical analysis ends, where its reach does not extend. This remark suggests why the strictly correct method in philosophy, which limits itself to the propositions of natural science, fails to produce the feeling that one is doing philosophy: such a method leaves us with the feeling that the problems of life remain untouched. Yet although Wittgenstein follows this remark with a definition of the mystical as "that which cannot be put into words" (*TLP* 6.522), he does not present our feeling that the problems of life remain untouched as a special sort of mystical insight into the nature of those problems, as an intimation of what lies beyond the limits of language. Rather, he simply places "scientific questions" and "the problems of life" — the logical and the mystical — alongside one another. The relationship between the two remains unframed.

For Habermas, this refusal to determine the relationship between the answers to scientific questions and the problems of life amounts to an abdication of responsibility, and he thus dismisses the *Tractatus* as a mystical retreat, discarding Wittgenstein's ladder as yet one more failed attempt to escape the philosophical problems of modernity.[44] I want to suggest, however, that it is precisely this undetermined relationship that provides a key to understanding Wittgenstein's conception of the ethical. This is not to say that Wittgenstein means "ethical problems" when he speaks of the "problems of life." Unlike Habermas, who imagines a modernity in which epistemology, ethics, and aesthetics each develop according to the inner logic of their respective spheres, Wittgenstein maintains that there is no ethical sphere, no distinct set of ethical problems: "[I]t is impossible for there to be propositions of ethics. Propositions can express nothing that is higher. It is clear that ethics cannot be put into words. Ethics is transcendental. (Ethics and aesthetics are one and the same.)" (*TLP* 6.42, 6.421).[45] These remarks put a different face on what by this point in the text has become a familiar interpretive stalemate: from a logical point of view, ethical propositions are no propositions at all but simply nonsense; from a transcendental point of view, they are that which cannot be put into words but merely felt through words. Like the text's philosophical and literary aspects, or the relationship between scientific questions and the problems of life, Wittgenstein provides no grammar by which one would conjugate the relationship between these two features of ethical discourse, or of what at least appears to be ethical discourse.

Wittgenstein nevertheless maintains, in another letter to Ludwig von Ficker, that the point of the *Tractatus* is "ethical" — not despite its lack of a circumscribed ethical sphere, but precisely because of it. Wittgenstein explains that even though Ficker might find the content of the book strange, he should not be misled by this initial impression:

> In reality, it isn't strange to you, for the point of the book is ethical. I once wanted to give a few words in the foreword which now actually are not in it, which, however, I'll write to you now because they might be a key for you: I wanted to write that my work consists of two parts: of the one which is here, and of everything which I have *not* written. And precisely this second part is the important one. For the Ethical is delimited from within, as it were, by my book; and I'm convinced that, strictly speaking, it can ONLY be delimited in this way. In brief, I think: All of that

which *many* are *babbling* [*schwefeln*] today, I have defined in my book by remaining silent [*schweige*] about it.[46]

One can imagine the dismay with which Wittgenstein's prospective publisher greeted this letter. As Wittgenstein describes it, the *Tractatus* is an incomplete text in more than one sense. Not only does the most important part of the book remain unwritten but this very piece of information, which is the key to understanding the text, is also left out. Note, however, that the two "parts" of the text, one written and the other unwritten, are not the literary and philosophical aspects: those aspects together form the part that is written. What remains "unwritten" is the ethical aspect, and, what's more, the ethical *must*, by necessity, remain unwritten.

The *Tractatus*'s final proposition manifests this compulsion: "What we cannot speak about we must pass over in silence." Both by virtue of its position in the *Tractatus* and in light of the nature of its content, this concluding remark seems to join the text's written and unwritten parts. As such, it seems to complete readings of the text as a narrative of either philosophical modernity or aesthetic modernism: in terms of the first, it marks the limit of what language can say and what it can only show; in terms of the second, it intimates the boundary separating what can be argued in language from what can merely be felt through language. Yet Wittgenstein's imperative neither reconciles these competing perspectives nor allows one to subsume the other; like the *Tractatus* as a whole, it holds the two in suspension, leaving their relationship unsettled. "What we cannot speak about we must pass over in silence": I want to suggest that we read this closing assertion neither as a logical necessity nor as an empirical generalization, but as an ethical injunction that enacts what it enjoins precisely by maintaining the suspension between the two competing options.

What we might call a *bad*-modernist reading of the *Tractatus*, then, locates the emergence of the ethical precisely in the text's refusal to close off, reconcile, or circumscribe the competing perspectives that it exemplifies—those represented by the *modernity*-modernist and the *modernism*-modernist readings. However, in remaining open to what Wittgenstein claims is the ethical point of the *Tractatus*, a *bad*-modernist reading does not thereby redeem itself from its own badness; it does not, that is to say, show us how to read well or teach us how to be good. If we conscientiously refuse to choose between the text's strictly philosophical and simultaneously literary elements—if we attribute to the *Tractatus* neither a logical point of view nor a mystical one—we are not rewarded for our steadfastness with a distinct "ethical point of view."

And this stricture, this "austere" view of ethics, so to speak, extends even to our negative capability of imaginatively engaging what we take to be another's nonsense. Diamond allows that the text supplies no criteria by which one would determine whether one's attempt to occupy imaginatively another's nonsensical point of view is "well or badly done." Indeed, because for Wittgenstein the ethical is "a non-category," it follows that there is no categorical imperative, no universal rule—not even an unwritten one—that would determine in general what counts as nonsense and thus determine in advance of our engagement with another whether that person is in fact speaking nonsensically.[47] The text provides no measuring stick or feelers— neither a symptomatic feeling nor a mystical one. It provokes instead only the feeling that we will yet again be forced to choose between competing perspectives and yet again be unable to decide. The risk that we might decide badly is the ethical challenge that the *Tractatus* places upon its readers.

I suggested at the outset that, although Wittgenstein acknowledges a debt to Frege and Russell, his indifference to the philosophical tradition, his desire not "to judge" the coincidence or lack thereof between his thoughts and "those of other philosophers," questioned the very possibility of making any judgment about the "modernism" of the *Tractatus*. But what appears at first glance as indifference to the past might in the end be a disposition toward the future, as Wittgenstein seems to suggest in a letter to Russell concerning the latter's Introduction to the *Tractatus*: "I am not quite in agreement with a lot of it: both where you criticize me, and where you are merely trying to expound my views. But it doesn't matter. The future will judge between us. Or it won't—and if silent, that will be a judgment too."[48] For Wittgenstein, ethics is a matter not of agreement, reconciliation, or completion—a matter not of closure but of an opening, or indebtedness, to the possibility of a future judgment that cannot be known in advance and that may never be spoken.[49]

Notes

1. Unless otherwise noted, all citations of the *Tractatus Logico-Philosophicus* refer to D. F. Pears and B. F. McGuinness's translation (London: Routledge, 1961), with reference to the page number when citing the Preface (as well as Russell's "Introduction") and to the section number in all other instances. German citations refer to *Werkausgabe Band 1 (Tractatus logico-philosophicus, Tagebücher 1914–1916, Philosophische Untersuchungen)* (Frankfurt a.M: Suhrkamp, 1984).

2. *Wittgenstein: Sources and Perspectives*, ed. C. G. Luckhardt (Ithaca, N.Y.: Cornell University Press, 1979), 94.

3. See Habermas, *The Philosophical Discourse of Modernity*, trans. Frederick G. Lawrence (Cambridge, Mass.: MIT Press, 1987), 185.

4. Michael Fischer, "Wittgenstein as a Modernist Philosopher," *Philosophy and Literature* 17 (1993): 279. For a seminal discussion of the *Tractatus* in a modernist context, see Allan Janik and Stephen Toulmin, *Wittgenstein's Vienna* (New York: Simon and Schuster, 1973).

5. Michael North, *Reading 1922: A Return to the Scene of the Modern* (New York: Oxford University Press, 1999), 33.

6. Marjorie Perloff, *Wittgenstein's Ladder: Poetic Language and the Strangeness of the Ordinary* (Chicago: University of Chicago Press, 1996), 44–45.

7. Habermas, "Modernity—An Incomplete Project," in *Postmodernism: A Reader*, ed. Thomas Docherty (New York: Columbia University Press, 1993), 103. Further references in this paragraph cited parenthetically.

8. Habermas, *Philosophical Discourse of Modernity*, 185.

9. Wittgenstein, *Notebooks 1914–1916*, 2d ed., ed. G. H. von Wright and G. E. M. Anscombe, trans. Anscombe (Chicago: University of Chicago Press, 1979), 72.

10. Pears and McGuinness translate *Weltanschauung* as "conception of the world."

11. See, for example, Wittgenstein's "Lecture on Ethics," where he remarks that "the superficial curiosity about the latest discoveries of science" constitutes "one of the lowest desires of modern people." *Philosophical Occasions, 1912–1951*, ed. James C. Klagge and Alfred Nordmann (Indianapolis, Ind.: Hackett, 1993), 37.

12. Wittgenstein's argument runs on two parallel tracks that never quite intersect. In a first line of reasoning he stipulates that the only necessity, or "compulsion," is logical necessity. Because the laws of nature, he implies, are empirical generalizations arrived at through inductive reasoning, they have "no logical justification but only a psychological one," and thus to treat them as "inviolable" in the sense of being "necessary" is to commit a category error, to confuse a logical justification with a psychological, or empirical, one. A second line of reasoning, or at least a second implication of the remarks, is that logical truths bear no explanatory value. Thus while the law of contradiction holds that "either *p* or not *p*," to remark that "it is either raining or not raining" is to *explain* absolutely nothing about the weather, despite the logical necessity of the proposition (and leaving aside whatever semantic ambiguities that a mist or a drizzle might introduce). But to say, on the one hand, that the laws of nature are not logical necessities, and, on the other, that necessary truths bear no explanatory value, is not to explain why the laws of nature are not explanations of natural phenomena. Furthermore, Wittgenstein does not offer an argument in support of his claim that the only necessity is logical necessity and thereby seems to rely on a de facto definitional necessity. As I hope to show, this type of shifting between different registers troubles attempts to read the *Tractatus* as an exemplification of either philosophical modernity or aesthetic modernism.

13. Wittgenstein, *Notebooks*, 72.

14. Wittgenstein, *Philosophical Investigations*, rev. 3rd ed., trans. G. E. M. Anscombe (Malden, Mass.: Blackwell, 2001), §1.

15. In this regard the *Tractatus* clearly bears the marks of Frege's influential critique, which charged psychologism with "confusing the act of judgement with its object, and so projecting the psychological character of the former on to the latter." Michael Dummett, *Frege and Other Philosophers* (Oxford: Oxford University Press, 1991), 224.

16. Wittgenstein, *Philosophical Remarks*, ed. Rush Rhees, trans. Raymond Hargreaves and Roger White (Chicago: University of Chicago Press, 1975), 7.

17. Wittgenstein, *Philosophical Remarks*, §6.

18. Frank Cioffi notes of Wittgenstein's "Remarks on Frazer's *Golden Bough*": "The striking thing . . . is not just how often, in commenting on what is ostensibly a hermeneutic enterprise, Wittgenstein turns away from interpreting the phenomena to relating them 'to our own feelings and thoughts' but that these much outnumber his straightforwardly interpretive efforts." *Wittgenstein on Freud and Frazier* (Cambridge: Cambridge University Press, 1998), 5. Indeed, Wittgenstein makes something of a psychological speculation in the text's very first sentence: "Perhaps this book will be understood only by someone who has himself already had the thoughts that are expressed in it — or at least similar thoughts" (*TLP* 3). This remark presents a prima facie case against reading the work as a critique of all forms of "psychologism."

19. My understanding of the importance of nonsense to Wittgenstein's philosophical method owes a debt to the work of James Conant and Cora Diamond. See Conant, "The Method of the *Tractatus*," *From Frege to Wittgenstein*, ed. Erich H. Reck (Oxford: Oxford University Press, 2002); and Diamond, "Ethics, Imagination, and the Method of Wittgenstein's *Tractatus*," in *The New Wittgenstein*, ed. Alice Crary and Rupert Read (London: Routledge, 2000). For P. M. S. Hacker's objections to Conant's and Diamond's interpretations, see "Philosophy" in *Wittgenstein: A Critical Reader*, 322–47; as well as "Was He Trying to Whistle It?" and "When the Whistling Had to Stop," both in Hacker, *Wittgenstein: Connections and Controversies* (Oxford: Clarendon, 2001), 98–140, 141–169.

20. North, *Reading 1922*, 33, 39.

21. Ibid., 36–37.

22. Winfried Menninghaus notes how the nominally logical distinction between sense and nonsense is itself "subject to historical change." See *In Praise of Nonsense: Kant and Bluebeard*, trans. Henry Pickford (Stanford, Calif.: Stanford University Press, 1999), 5.

23. North, *Reading 1922*, 39.

24. Ibid., 35.

Michael LeMahieu

25. Wittgenstein, *Notebooks*, 83.

26. Allan Janik also advances a version of what I am calling the *modernism*-modernist reading of the *Tractatus* in *Wittgenstein's Vienna Revisited* (New Brunswick, N.J.: Transaction, 2001).

27. Conant describes this effort as an attempt to "touch in thought" that which one cannot "embrace in thought." "The Search for Logically Alien Thought: Descartes, Kant, Frege and the *Tractatus*," *Philosophical Topics* 20 (1991): 121.

28. "Comprehension has a limit or, rather, is limitation itself, for it consists in a putting into form, and form is a limitation." Jean-François Lyotard, *Lessons on the Analytic of the Sublime*, trans. Elizabeth Rottenberg (Stanford, Calif.: Stanford University Press, 1994), 100–101.

29. Thus the very remarks that produced in Russell a feeling of "intellectual discomfort" are the same ones that capture Perloff's interest: "My own interest is less in what the *Tractatus* 'says' about propositionality, tautology, etc., than in what it *is*, especially in its later sections, which break abruptly with the 'clarity' of its opening and turn to matters of ethics and religion in a series of gnomic utterances." *Wittgenstein's Ladder*, 19.

30. Ibid., 45, emphasis added.

31. Ibid., 19.

32. Diamond, "Ethics, Imagination, and the Method of Wittgenstein's *Tractatus*," 153, 164.

33. Conant refers to these two options as the "positivist" and "ineffability" interpretations of nonsense, and they correspond, *mutatis mutandis*, to what I am calling the *modernity*-modernist and *modernism*-modernist readings of the *Tractatus*, respectively. See Conant, "The Method of the *Tractatus*," 375.

34. *Philosophical Investigations*, §464.

35. Diamond, "Ethics, Imagination, and the Method of Wittgenstein's *Tractatus*," 165.

36. Ibid., 164, 149.

37. Conant, "The Method of the *Tractatus*," 458.

38. Rei Terada discusses the psychological and physiological ambiguities of the term "feeling" in *Feeling in Theory: Emotion after the "Death of the Subject"* (Cambridge, Mass.: Harvard University Press, 2001); see also Eve Kosofsky Sedgwick, *Touching Feeling: Affect, Pedagogy, Performativity* (Durham, N.C.: Duke University Press, 2003).

39. In this respect, the feelers occupy a place in the text's tropological system analogous to that of tautology and contradiction in its logical system—neither sense nor nonsense, but rather senseless: "Tautologies and contradictions lack sense [*sind sinnlos*] . . . Tautologies and contradictions are not, however, nonsensical. They are part of the symbolism, much as '0' is part of the symbolism of mathematics . . . Tautologies and contradictions are not pictures of reality" (*TLP* 4.461, 4.4611, 4.462).

40. Wittgenstein, *Philosophical Investigations*, §115.

41. *Ludwig Wittgenstein: Cambridge Letters*, ed. Brian McGuinness and G. H. von Wright (Oxford: Blackwell, 1995), 14.

42. Ibid., 140.

43. William James, *The Varieties of Religious Experience: A Study in Human Nature*, ed. Martin E. Murray (1902; New York: Penguin, 1982), 432.

44. "According to one thesis, science, when properly understood, has become irrevocably meaningless for the orientation of the life-world . . . (One could name here the early Wittgenstein . . .)" Habermas, "Modernity—An Incomplete Project," 108.

45. Diamond argues that, "from the point of view of the *Tractatus*, there is no class of sentences distinguishable by their subject matter as 'ethical sentences.' " "Ethics, Imagination, and the Method of Wittgenstein's *Tractatus*," 160.

46. Wittgenstein, *Sources and Perspectives*, 94–95.

47. Diamond, "Ethics, Imagination, and the Method of Wittgenstein's *Tractatus*," 165, 164.

48. Wittgenstein, *Notebooks*, 132.

49. My thanks to Elizabeth Rivlin, Eric Rothstein, and John Tiedemann—and to the editors of this volume—for incisively commenting on earlier versions of the essay. I also owe a more general debt to Jacques Lezra, who first suggested that I write about the *Tractatus*, and whose essay "The Indecisive Muse" (presented to the English Institute and forthcoming from Routledge in a volume tentatively entitled *Divided Loyalties*) sharpened my understanding of how the impossible task of deciding between Wittgenstein's literary and philosophical aspects ultimately arrives at an ethical point.

Laura Frost

The Romance of Cliché: E. M. Hull,

D. H. Lawrence, and Interwar Erotic Fiction

On October 15, 1927, the debut issue of *My Story Weekly* appeared in London with a cover image calculated to draw an audience: a sleek flapper, glamorous and dreamy, against a background oasis complete with camel, palm tree, and a male figure in a turban and robes. Inside, in a tone that simulates an intimate chat at the local ABC teashop, with frequent addresses to the reader, Irene Speller's "How I Was Loved by a Sheik!" recounts the author's trip to Damascus with a British dance troupe. There, "in the East," Speller confides, she "met with adventure and romance, which make all the sheik stories ever written pale into insignificance."[1] She and her dancer friend Winnie compare their first glimpse of the Saharan sky to images they have seen on "glowing posters . . . outside the picture palace at Shepherd's Bush. [H]aven't you seen them, too," Speller asks her reader, "outside the picture palace in your neighborhood?" (2). But the East is "not much like Shepherd's Bush," Speller and Winnie conclude, especially when a dashing sheik appears one night in the theater in which they are performing and fixes his "amazing dark eyes" (3) on Speller ("dark, flashing eyes that you never see in the men here in England"). The sheik makes his move and invites her to his elegant desert tent. Amid clichés such as "Love knows no boundaries" and "There was something in the air that night," he woos Speller while other characters repeatedly warn her that he "has got different ideas to the sort of men we know." As Speller obsesses about how the sheik might kidnap her and make her his "desert queen," it becomes clear that alterity and danger are a central part of the story's thrill. And yet as the tale's clichéd language and multiple references to "sheik stories" indicate, the appeal of Speller's adventure is not its novelty but its reiteration of an excitingly predictable formula with which Speller assumes her readers are familiar. The narrative concludes with Speller tearfully leaving the sheik, and the final sentence of the story — "We were East and West, and, of course, it is true now that 'never the twain shall meet' " — contains no less than two clichés, one so hackneyed that the writer herself sets it off in quotes.[2]

My Story Weekly proceeded to become one of the most popular British women's magazines, and its editors' choice of Speller's story for its inaugural issue is indicative of interwar reading tastes. "How I Was Loved by a Sheik!" is a less violent and sexually explicit imitation of one of the most successful fictions in early-twentieth-century British publishing history, E. M. (Edith Maude) Hull's 1919 novel *The Sheik*. In this Orientalist fantasy, Diana Mayo, an arrogant English aristocrat who rejects marriage and other trappings of womanliness, dares to take a trip into the Algerian Sahara with only Arab guides. She is captured by a handsome sheik and taken to his luxurious caravan in the desert, where he forces himself — along with lavish jewelry and dresses — upon her. After much bosom heaving and bodice ripping, Diana becomes conscious of her love for the "lawless savage" and she decides to stay with him in their love oasis.[3] British readers of 1919 thrilled to this sadomasochistic fantasy, sending the novel through 108 reprintings in the UK by 1923.[4] Two years later, audiences came to the cinema by the millions to watch Rudolph Valentino, in the title role that made his reputation, kidnap and ravish his way through George Melford's adaptation of *The Sheik*.

Hull followed *The Sheik* with *The Shadow of the East*, *The Desert Healer*, and *The Sons of the Sheik*, and these narratives joined a plethora of fictions with similarly suggestive titles by other authors: *Desert Love*, *The Hawk of Egypt*, *The Lure of the Desert*, *Burning Sands*, *Harem Love*, and so on. *The Sheik* inspired so many imitators that we can accurately speak of an interwar "desert romance genre." The elements were intensely formulaic: a beautiful woman, usually British, leaves the home country for the "Arab East" (including a diversity of locales such as Algeria, Egypt, and Morocco), which was routinely signified by the same images of endless deserts and skies, jasmine-scented nights, ill-tempered camels, and lustful, gorgeous sheiks.[5] Above all, the heroine is "swept away" and made more exquisitely feminine (that is, pleasurably passive) by her encounter with a relentlessly masculine sheik. The dominant imagery in desert romance is the cliché of "burning desire" or "consuming passion": there is no body part of the sheik that does not "sear" the heroine, and no emotion that is not experienced as a "conflagration." While the stories were of varying degrees of sexual frankness and violence, Hull's novel was the supreme model for "sheik stories" in the interwar period.[6]

In *The Long Week End*, Robert Graves and Alan Hodge note that "Tarzan of the Apes was the most popular fictional character among the low-brow [British] public of the Twenties; though the passionate Sheikh of Araby, as portrayed by E. M. Hull and her many imitators, ran him pretty close." The terms "Sheikh" and "Sheikhy" entered the popular lexicon as synonyms "for the passionately conquering male."[7] Sheet music and gramophone records and a number of "sheik films" capitalized on the hunger for desert romance between the wars.[8] And then in the 1930s, with a few exceptions, the desert romance waned.[9] This was a relatively short shelf life, given the fervor with which British readers consumed "sheik stories."[10] Interestingly, this genre—a celebration of male power and female submission—reached the pinnacle of its popularity in Britain at a time of vigorous debate about new possibilities for gender roles in the wake of World War I. Moreover, the desert romance's triumph coincides with the height of British literary modernism. In the interwar period, modernists strove to define themselves against the earnest, predictably Victorian novel and "materialist" Edwardian fiction, as well as contemporary popular culture, epitomized by the predictable formula and banal prose of genre fiction. If there is a retrospective irony in the fact that the desert romance, one of the most clichéd and deliberately derivative of popular fiction genres, peaked at the same moment that modernist fiction was pursuing originality and "making it new," that irony was just as legible to the modernists themselves. *The Sheik* has a surprisingly prominent place in some of the most significant formulations of British modernism by key critics, for whom Hull was not just a bad writer and *The Sheik* not merely a bad novel but a chief representative of cultural degeneracy.

This essay will examine the modernist critique of aesthetic and political "badness" through Hull and one of her most important critics: D. H. Lawrence. Lawrence, perhaps more self-consciously than any other modern novelist, set out to transform the representation of sexuality as a means of liberating consciousness in general. Although Lawrence now tends to be classified as a transitional modernist figure, insofar as his work does not show the technical experimentation of Woolf or Joyce, for example, early critics such as Q. D. Leavis and F. R. Leavis (and modernist arbiters of the next generation, such as Frank Kermode) present him as an exemplary modernist.[11] Lawrence thought of his own writing as quite radical; his admiration for the avant-gardism of the Futurists colors his apocalyptic descriptions of his work as cultural "surgery" or a "bomb." But it is Lawrence's writing on sexuality that marks him most strongly as a modernist. In his fiction and essays alike, Lawrence proclaimed his intention to revitalize sexuality by writing about it without repression, abstraction, romanticism, or cliché.

Lawrence's sexual politics are notoriously perplexing in his interwar fiction, in which he shifts from being a supporter of women's autonomy and sexual freedom to being a defensive promoter of phallic power.[12] The Lawrence of "Tickets Please," terrified of women's castrating power, and the Lawrence of *Lady Chatterley's Lover*, for whom "the bridge to the future is the phallus," are difficult to reconcile with the Lawrence of *Women in Love* and other earlier works in which he explored the possibility of men and women as equal partners.[13] Even as he pushed the boundaries of sexual and erotic representation, Lawrence produced increasingly stereotypical, polarized images of masculinity and femininity. And it was at this moment that Lawrence's writing was influenced by the "bad" writer E. M. Hull.

Lawrence and Hull figure in very different narratives of literary history, but each contributed to the modern exploration of sexuality and eroticism. Hull is by no means "modernist," but her fiction has a significant, if auxiliary, role in early-twentieth-century British literature. A growing body of work has explored how modernism is inflected by repudiated popular genre fictions, particularly those coded as "feminine."[14] I am interested in another dimension of the gendered mass culture phenomenon, and that is the modernist critique of cliché in relation to erotic representation. While "bad" fiction is increasingly making its way into modernist studies as we find that the modernists themselves were interested in genre fiction such as adventure, thrillers, and romance—the kind of material George Orwell called "good bad books"[15]—the discussion, from the Cambridge critics to the Frankfurt School to the present, continues to be cast primarily in terms of aesthetic innovation versus cliché, or as revolutionary versus reactionary politics. Critics generally trace the modern figuring of sexuality to Flaubert, Zola, the Goncourts, and other sophisticated literary sources; however, many British genre novels of the same period also exerted an important influence. The case of Lawrence and Hull suggests that "clichéd" popular fictions underpin modernism's supposedly "innovative" representations of sexuality and eroticism in spite of the modernist repudiation of this "badness." Ultimately, the modernist turn to "bad" fiction raises a more fundamental question of whether erotic fantasy, by its very nature, may elude the much-prized modernist value of innovation.

"Are you not woman enough to know?"

Few locales were more infused with British women's erotic fantasy in the interwar period than Biskra, a city in northeastern Algeria. In setting her novel of sexual awakening in Biskra, Hull not only inaugurated an Orientalist psycho-geography for women but also initiated a kind of female sexual tourism in that area. In the early twentieth century, solo British female travelers were increasingly common; but, writes Osman Bencherif, it was "E. M. Hull who, with *The Sheik*, first put the desert on the map as an exotic place of sexual indulgence" (180). In 1924 the *Daily Express* journalist H. V. Morton wrote a multi-installment column from Biskra, "In the Garden of Allah." Morton describes a city full of British and Americans seeking erotic adventure: women like Irene Speller, "English girls, advertising the fact that they are wearing non-stop silk stockings . . . riding past on camels," in search of passionate sheiks. Morton himself admits, "I want sheiks. I want the real Edith M. Hull stuff. I want to see how perfectly ordinary people from London, Paris, and New York behave under the influence of the Sahara."[16] Zelda Fitzgerald wrote of Biskra that since the publication of *The Sheik*, "the town has been filled with frustrated women."[17]

As Hull's novel opens, Diana Mayo seems an unlikely model of sexual adventurism. She appears to have no libido at all, but by the end of the story this ice-cold androgyne is begging for the love of a "fierce desert man." The commonplace reading of *The Sheik* as a taming of the New Woman is not strictly accurate.[18] Diana has none of the political concerns of the typical New Woman (although she does have fashionably bobbed hair). Her dec-

The Romance of Cliché

laration that "marriage for a woman means the end of independence" is quickly undercut by her modification, "that is, marriage with a man who is a man, in spite of all that the most modern woman may say" (12). Diana is an orphan who was raised by her brother, Aubrey. "You have brought me up to ignore the restrictions attached to my sex" (24), she reminds him when he tries to curb her independence. This privilege is more a matter of spoiled will than political consciousness, and Hull's depiction of this boy-girl is clearly intended to strike her romance readers as unnatural.

Hull performs an unusual balancing act as she encourages the reader to identify narcissistically with Diana while colluding against her. As with all romances, physiognomy is destiny; Diana is beautiful but also haughty and must give up her willfulness so that the romance plot can unfold. When Diana tells Aubrey "I will never obey any will but my own," his response — "Then I hope to Heaven that one day you will fall into the hands of a man who will make you obey" (24) — is a desire that Hull develops in the reader, too, and it proves to be prognostic. The story of Diana's abduction, captivity, and rape (of which more later) are told in a breathless manner culminating in victorious debasement: "The girl who had started out so triumphantly from Biskra had become a woman through bitter knowledge and humiliating experience" (102).

Against all warnings, Diana rides out into the desert with an entourage of "natives." On the second day, the party is ambushed; a turbaned figure on horseback chases Diana across the "burning sands" and lifts her off her horse onto his with one sweep of his powerful arm. He takes her into a tent of magnificent luxury and throws her on a well-appointed divan (sartorial and interior design details feature prominently in *The Sheik*). Flinging aside his cloak, the sheik stands before her, "tall and broad-shouldered," with "the handsomest and the cruelest face that she had ever seen." Nature triumphs over culture as Diana finds herself "dragging the lapels of her riding jacket together over her breast with clutching hands, obeying an impulse that she hardly understood." In an instant, the sheik undoes Aubrey's years of cultivating boyishness in Diana, and she reverts to a performance of melodramatic womanhood.

"Who are you?" she gasped hoarsely.
"I am the Sheik Ahmed Ben Hassan. . . ."

"Why have you brought me here?" . . .

He repeated her words with a slow smile. "Why have I brought you here? *Bon Dieu!* Are you not woman enough to know?" (48)

But Hull's reader is woman enough to know, and this superior knowledge aligns the "womanly" reader with Ahmed and his desires.

Critics routinely describe the first encounters between Diana and Ahmed as extended rape scenarios, which they are, technically, but the significance of which is crucially modified by Hull's language. Throughout Diana's struggles with Ahmed, Hull dwells on "the consuming fire" of his "ardent gaze," and his "pulsating body." Hull's repetition of and endless variation on "burning desire" has a cumulative effect, suggesting desire and somatic excitement where there is also violence and moral outrage: "The flaming light of desire burning in his eyes turned her sick and faint. Her body throbbed with the consciousness of a knowledge that appalled her. She understood his purpose with a horror that made each separate nerve in her system shrink against the understanding that had come to her under the consuming fire of his ardent gaze" (49).

Hull generates an erotic dynamic from the oscillation between knowledge and innocence, physical sensation and ethical indignation. All the pulsating, flaming, and throbbing signal the eroticism of these scenes. Hull encourages the reader to identify with Diana while hoping, like the sheik himself, for her fall into passion. In Hull's forerunners among romance, sensational, Gothic, and seduction novels, a direct identification with the heroine is always central to the formula. No matter what the heroine's shortcomings may be, the reader is rarely encouraged to desire, with the male "villain," her demise. When Diana is "shaken to the very foundation of her being with the upheaval of her convictions and the ruthless violence done to her cold, sexless temperament" (77), Hull's construction suggests that Diana's sexlessness is as repugnant as Ahmed's cruelty. These unorthodox arrangements of sympathy, identification, and sensation are key to an accurate reading of *The Sheik*.

Hull handles racial stereotype in much the same way, with a double movement of attraction and repulsion, predictability and exception. Desert romance inverts the gender positions in Orientalism by imagining an eroticized masculine "Oriental" subject and casting the fantasy from a woman's perspective, but the terms of that eroticization are just as stereotypical.[19] Hull pedantically insists that "the position of a woman in the desert was a very precarious one" because of Arab men's "pitiless . . . disregard of the woman's subjugation" (78). But this is all in bad faith, as Diana comes to love a version of that subjugation. The moment Diana realizes her feelings for Ahmed also involves such contradictions and polarizations:

> Her heart was given for all time to the fierce desert man who was so different from all other men whom she had met, a lawless savage who had taken her to satisfy a passing fancy and who had treated her with merciless cruelty. He was a brute, but she loved him, loved him for his very brutality and superb animal strength. And he was an Arab! A man of different race and colour, a native; Aubrey would indiscriminately class him as a "damned nigger." She did not care. . . . She was deliriously, insanely happy. (112–13)

That Hull emphasizes stereotypes at this turning point suggests that the frisson of alterity and polarity is a central part of the erotics of *The Sheik*, and it remains so long after Diana "discovers" her erotic feelings for Ahmed (as when she "pant[s] for" his embraces [123]). Diana continues to imagine herself and Ahmed as, respectively, a "primeval woman" (152) and a "lawless savage" even after evidence to the contrary.

At the end of the novel, Hull springs a surprise on the reader. Ahmed is actually the son of an English earl and a Spanish mother. Hence, it would appear that the sexual compromises of the previous two hundred pages and the "horror" of loving an Arab are recuperated with an aristocratic marriage. This is surely the most clichéd part of Hull's novel: the ubiquitous marriage denouement that the modernists jettisoned from their own novels. And yet, while the subject of marriage bookends the narrative (Diana rejects marriage at the beginning of the story but marries at the end), in between, there is no attention to marriage whatsoever. As Billie Melman observes, "both the marriage and the discovery, by Diana, of Ahmed's 'real' identity are gratuitous. At no point in the whole story is matrimony presented as a necessary alternative to an unlawful but happy concubinage" (102–3). Despite the conventional frame, *The Sheik* presents an erotic fantasy almost completely unmediated by proprietary concerns, which, I would argue, accounts not only for the tremendous popularity of Hull's novel but also for the unusual attention that an unlikely modernist audience gave to *The Sheik*.

"... the typist's day-dream"

The London *Times Literary Supplement* reviewed *The Sheik* in 1919 and focused exclusively on the novel's plot, without making any judgment about the quality of the writing. It was the last time that Hull would be reviewed so neutrally. "It is a bold novelist who takes his [*sic*] heroine into the Garden of Allah by the gates of Biskra, as heroes are so hard to find there who comply alike with the requirements of the proper local culture and the conventions of romance as written for Western people."[20] Despite misattributing male authorship, the *Times* reviewer shows a canny understanding of the dilemma of genre and geography in which Hull finds him/herself. But the *Times* conclusion is amiss: "If there be a moral here in this simple tale it is one of warning to young European ladies not to ride alone into the Sahara." The translation of Hull's fantasy novel into a cautionary tale is the first of many misreadings of *The Sheik*.

In 1919 Hull's novel looked like a "simple tale," yet critics were soon writing about *The Sheik* as a symptom of cultural decline. Q. D. Leavis's *Fiction and the Reading Public* (1932) is a key summary of this critical development. Leavis is most concerned with the fact that "what is considered by the critical minority to be the significant works in fiction," the novels of D. H. Lawrence, Virginia Woolf, James Joyce, T. F. Powys, and E. M. Forster, are not read by the public or stocked by libraries or booksellers. Reading contemporary best-sellers against the glory days of the novel in the eighteenth century, Leavis's main critique of contemporary fiction—"as distinct from literature"—is that it is "mere tissues of clichés."[21] Extending the modernist claim of aesthetic originality, Leavis adds a psychological and moral interpretation of the dangers of "bad" fiction. "[N]ovel-reading now is largely a drug habit" (31), Leavis asserts, a "masturbatory" (136) form of "self-indulgence" (55), and "a habit of reading poor novels not only destroys the ability to distinguish between literature and trash, it creates a positive taste for a certain kind of writing, if only because it does not demand the effort of a fresh response." Not only, then, is the quality of the writing at fault but so is the response that it summons up in the reader. Leavis contends that popular fiction cultivates the reader's passivity through "the consistent use of clichés (stock phrases to evoke stock responses)" (194). The "stock response" is inauthentic or ersatz, as opposed to the "fresh response," which is critical and "spontaneous."

> [N]early all popular novelists are now trying to dramatize problems of feeling and sentiment far too complex for their handling, and in an idiom which inevitably vulgarizes whatever it has to convey. They are thus not so much what is often described as 'falsifying life' as interfering with the reader's spontaneities. (195)

The connection between bad fiction, cliché, and stock response culminates, for Leavis, in a habit more dangerous than addiction: "fantasying." Leavis's example is a classic one: Gerty MacDowell in *Ulysses*, whose consciousness has been colonized by bad fiction. "For Gerty MacDowell every situation has a prescribed attitude provided by memories of slightly similar situations in cheap fiction; she thinks in terms of clichés drawn from the same source, and is completely out of touch with reality. Such a life is not only crude, impoverished, and narrow, it is dangerous" (195). Such a life is also fiction, but never mind. It is the "fantasying" reader, even more than the drugged or indolent reader, who alarms Leavis. Gerty is, of course, a reader of sensational, sentimental, and romantic fiction. In a rare moment of genre distinction, Leavis argues that reading "novels like *The Way of an Eagle, The Sheik,* [and] *The Blue Lagoon*" (the contemporary equivalents, to Leavis, of *The Lamplighter* and Princess novelettes) constitutes "a more detrimental diet than the detective story in so far as a habit of fantasying will lead to maladjustment in actual life" (55). Presumably, one could put the deductive method of detection to use in real life, while the "fantasying" of romance novels lacks such application. While Leavis never substantiates this claim of *Madame Bovary*–like corruption, romance is the genre on which her argument about the connection between cliché and fantasy leans most heavily, and *The Sheik* is one of the central pillars. Attempting to anatomize the popular novel, Leavis notes that "ten of the fourteen novelists advertised by the 3d. circulating libraries [in a catalog] specialize in fantasy-spinning" (55). The titles are, predictably, romances, but what is startling (although Leavis does not acknowledge it) is that most of these titles are desert romances: *The Desert Dreamers, The Lure of the Desert, Sands of Gold, The City of Palms, The Mirage of the Dawn,* and *East o' the Sun* (55–56). In the questionnaire about popular fiction that Leavis distributed to sixty authors, *The Sheik* is one of four titles specified as examples of "great bestseller[s]" (48), and at least one respondent similarly singles out *The Sheik* as his primary example of "rotten primitive stuff" (50). In demonstrating how low the popular novel has fallen, Leavis suggests that we "compare *Pamela* with *The Sheik*, which in the year of its publication was to be seen in the hands of every typist and may be taken as embodying the typist's day-dream, and it is obvious that *Pamela* is only incidentally serving the purposes for which *The Sheik* exists and even then serving it very indifferently" (116). Rather than providing a "scaffolding for castle-building" (117), the eighteenth-century novel promoted the destruction of illusions and fantasy. Leavis's apparent throwaway line about "the typist's day-dream" is telling of how tightly connected female subjectivity, popular culture, the working or lower middle class, and fantasy are in the modernist critical paradigm. In "The Little Shopgirls Go to the Movies," for example, Siegfried Kracauer argues that "sensational film hits and life usually correspond to each other because the Little Miss Typists model themselves after the examples they see on the screen."[22] Again, the iconographic typist (for Eliot in *The Waste Land*, among other modernist fictions) stands in for a whole demographic of women consumers whose fantasies are apparently simple to comprehend, and who live out their lives in mindless imitation. Fantasy — as both an activity and a literary genre — is passive, mindless, simplistic, and based on clichés. It is divorced from the processes of imagination, distinction, and activity, all of which Leavis (and Kracauer) associate with modernist fiction.

If *The Sheik*, for Leavis, epitomizes the dangerous way in which popular fiction cultivates fantasy in the contemporary reader, the antidote is modernist fiction, with its intelligently critical "shocks." For both Q. D. and F. R. Leavis, one of the modernists most capable of delivering these shocks was D. H. Lawrence. Many of Leavis's central arguments about popular fiction are anticipated by Lawrence's own essays, in which Hull makes several appearances. Lawrence presents the typical modernist case against Hull's "badness" in both the aesthetic and the political sense. However, he then goes on to incorporate *The Sheik* into his own work in a way that calls into question the modernist critique of "badness."

In "Surgery for the Novel—Or a Bomb" (1923) Lawrence begins by making the same generic distinction Leavis does between "serious" and popular fiction: "On the one hand [is the] pale-faced, high-browed, earnest novel, which you have to take seriously; on the other, that smirking, rather plausible hussy, the popular novel."[23] Unlike Leavis, Lawrence jeers at the high modernists—Joyce, Proust, Richardson, and Stein—whose self-absorption and abstraction sabotage spontaneity. In a famous letter on Joyce's "journalistic dirty-mindedness" Lawrence carps about *Ulysses*'s "too terribly would-be and done-on-purpose, utterly without spontaneity or real life" (*Selected* 148–48). Within this reading of high modernism, Lawrence creates a demand for his own kind of fiction, a "convulsion or cataclysm" that would wrench "this serious novel out of its self-consciousness" (*Selected* 115).

The popular novel, Lawrence writes, is obvious and formulaic: "Always the same sort of baking-powder gas to make you rise" (116). In this analysis, Hull's novel is the paradigmatic popular novel: "The mass of the populace 'find themselves' in the popular novels. But nowadays it's a funny sort of self they find. A sheik with a whip up his sleeve, and a heroine with weals on her back, but adored in the end, adored, the whip out of sight, but the weals still faintly visible. . . . Sheik heroines, duly whipped, wildly adored" (116). While Ahmed whips an insubordinate servant in one brief scene, the whip does not play the memorable role that Lawrence suggests; certainly, Ahmed never whips Diana. But there are scenes of sadomasochistic eroticism in Hull's novel that seem right out of Lawrence's own pages (even though Lawrence warns readers to resist "the throb of *The Sheik*" [114]). For example, in a highly charged scene, Diana sees Ahmed brutally break a colt, an encounter that is reminiscent of Gudrun and Ursula watching Gerald Crich terrorize a mare in *Women in Love*. Hull is perhaps the only romance writer to pay as much attention to the rhetoric of "will" as Lawrence does, making it a central trope of Ahmed's dynamic with Diana. Moreover, Ahmed is a man who commands other men, a posture that Lawrence found fascinating.

Whether or not Lawrence consciously recognized these affinities, he returned to *The Sheik* in "Pornography and Obscenity" (1929), an essay prompted by the censorship of *Lady Chatterley's Lover*. Lawrence maintains that genuine pornography can be recognized "by the insult it offers, invariably, to sex, and to the human spirit. Pornography is the attempt to insult sex, to do dirt on it." Pornography, for Lawrence, represents a concrete threat to society:

> The pornography of to-day, whether it be the pornography of the rubber-goods shop or the pornography of the popular novel, film, and play, is an invariable stimulant to the vice of self-abuse, onanism, masturbation, call it what you will. . . . And the mass of our popular literature, the bulk of our popular amusements just exists to provoke masturbation. (*Selected* 41)

Unlike Leavis, Lawrence does not limit this theory of pernicious masturbation to popular literature alone; "most of our modern literature," he asserts, shows symptoms of "self-abuse" (43). Building on this premise, Lawrence goes on to draw some unexpected distinctions among a group of diverse texts. Weighing Boccaccio, Rabelais, Wagner, Richardson, Brontë, Fielding, and Keats against one another, Lawrence now includes Hull in this company: "I'm sure poor Charlotte Brontë, or the authoress of *The Sheik*, did not have any deliberate intention to stimulate sex feelings in the reader." (This is an odd interpretation, as one only has to read a couple pages of *The Sheik* to realize that it is meant precisely to "stimulate sex feelings.") Lawrence continues, "Yet I find *Jane Eyre* verging towards pornography and Boccaccio seems to me always fresh and wholesome" (37). What grounds this distinction? The texts Lawrence rejects are those that, in his view, treat sex as furtive and dirty instead of healthy and clean. Although Lawrence suggests that *The Sheik* falls into the category of pornography, Hull moves several notches up the literary genre ladder, and now she is credited with more honorable intentions than she was in 1923.

Even as he employs Hull's novel to establish what is to be avoided in fiction, Lawrence's own fiction in the period between "Surgery for the Novel" and "Pornography and Obscenity" takes a decidedly Hullian turn. As several critics have noted, Lawrence's story "The Woman Who Rode Away" (1924) and, even more explicitly, his novel *The Plumed Serpent* (1926) reference and recast Hull's novel.[24] In both, an aloof modern heroine (American in one case, and British in the other) goes to Mexico and falls in thrall to swarthy "Indian" men whose ideology is founded on Aztec cosmology, human sacrifice, and male dominance. But while critics concur that Lawrence was "adapting the clichés of the desert romance" (Horsley, *Fictions of Power*) in these works, the reason Lawrence does so is not self-evident.

"The Woman Who Rode Away" and *The Plumed Serpent* are variations on the common interwar theme of leaving a troubled Britain for another, less apparently complicated, country. Lawrence had an unusually literal understanding of this theme, as he enacted the flight from Britain himself, to Australia, Italy, New Mexico, and other locales that seemed to offer alternatives to the moribund UK. Lawrence's bizarre plan to found a utopian community, "Rananim," indicates the degree to which he was actively trying to "ride away" from interwar Britain. Unlike Hull, who once praised "the really fine work that the French Government has done" in Algeria,[25] Lawrence was staunchly anti-imperial, and his fictions support the autonomy of native cultures. Lawrence's setting of the desert romance in Mexico reflects where he was living when he wrote the stories. Mexico, like Algeria, offered racial, religious, and linguistic otherness, a foreign landscape, a "primitive" culture that was free of the gender upheavals of Britain. Finally, neither Algeria nor Mexico has a history of British imperialism (but rather French and Spanish), so the exoticism is less fettered by political complications.

"The Woman Who Rode Away" presents many of the themes that are explored in *The Plumed Serpent*, but in a different tone. The unnamed American female protagonist lives in Mexico with her children and her husband, who "admired his wife to extinction. . . . Like any sheikh, he kept her guarded." The woman hears about a local tribe of Indians who are the "descendants of Montezuma and the old Aztec or Totonac kings," and the next time her husband is traveling, she rides out into the hills alone, where a group of "dark-faced," "strongly-built" Indian men surround her. In a less dramatic version of Hull's kidnapping on horseback, one of the men seizes the reins of the woman's horse and they lead her to their village, where they drug her and keep her captive.[26] But this is no sexual utopia; there is "nothing sensual or sexual" (560) in the way the men regard the woman. Rather, they give her unbearably earnest lectures about how the white man has stolen the Aztec sun and moon, and only the sacrifice of a white woman will return the cosmos to its proper order. The woman, in her pulque haze, accepts it all: "The sharpness and the quivering nervous consciousness of the highly-bred white woman was to be destroyed" so that "the great primeval symbols were to tower once more" (570). In the final scene of the story, the woman is taken into an ice cave, fumigated, stripped naked on a table, and the story ends with the men gathered around her, watching the sun's rays creeping into the cave and waiting for a priest to plunge a knife into her. Lawrence takes up Hull's erotic fantasy of escape and pleasurable submission and transposes it into a desexualized and de-eroticized register in order to imagine how enervated culture, represented by the submissive white woman, might be dominated by a "great primeval" culture of dark, powerful men.

Lawrence gives more attention to the erotic content of Hull's novel in *The Plumed Serpent*, the third of his so-called leadership novels, where anti-democratic politics are combined with male domination. The first two leadership novels (*Aaron's Rod* and *Kangaroo*) feature a British male protagonist who is disillusioned with postwar democracy and searches for a political "master" abroad but can never bring himself to fully submit.[27] In *The Plumed Serpent*, the submission of Kate Leslie, a middle-aged woman, is achieved through a heavy narrative reliance on *The Sheik*. In Mexico City, Kate hears about and is fascinated by a growing underground movement calling for the return of the gods of antiquity—the Aztecs' plumed serpent Quetzalcoatl, the god of culture, and Tlaloc, the god of fertility. When she meets the powerfully charismatic general Cipriano, who, with Don Ramon, is leading the Quetzalcoatl movement, Kate has a strongly imaginative response: "There was something undeveloped and intense in him, the intensity and the crudity of the semi-savage. . . . Something smooth, undeveloped, yet vital in this man suggested the heavy-ebbing blood of reptiles in his veins" (74). This is the first of many reptilian metaphors that prove aphrodisiac to Kate. When she contemplates returning to America, the thought of Cipriano's reptilian body slithering around hers makes her hesitate: "She felt like a bird round whose body a snake has coiled itself. Mexico was the snake" (79). The discourse of colonialism and imperial conquest is reversed in this masochistic, reptilian embrace. Here the "conquering" race finds itself squeezed by the potent "semi-savages" of Mexico—and is aroused. Throughout the novel, Lawrence's idioms of eroticism—the virile and animalistic Quetzalcoatl men, the conflict between Kate's "modern"

The Romance of Cliché

ideas and the allure of gender regression — are borrowed from Hull. Just as Hull's Diana imagines the sheik's arms around her as "the coils of a great serpent closing round its victim" (96), Kate's response to reptilian domination is submission. Even in the transposed setting of Mexico, Hull's desert romance tropes creep in. Kate thinks of the Quetzalcoatl women as "harem type[s]" with "harem tricks."

As Hull's Diana is able to dominate British and American men but meets her match in Ahmed, so the Quetzalcoatl men present Kate with a kind of masculinity she has never seen before. Western influences have not slackened Cipriano's primitive virility: his Oxford education "lay like a film of white oil on the black lake of his barbarian consciousness" (89). Similarly, Hull's Ahmed manages to keep his nails pared and his robes spotless, but these Western conventions do not ruin his primitive appeal. Lawrence reproduces Hull's fantasy of polarity, but he then adds to it an idiosyncratic political agenda. Anti-democratic and anti-Marxist, the Quetzalcoatl movement wants to reinstate the Aztec religion and racial and gender hierarchy. Ramón declares himself "the First Man of Quetzalcoatl," and Cipriano is named the "First Man of Huizilopochtli" (261), the god of war and sacrifice. When Cipriano asks Kate to marry him and become "First Woman of Itzpapoltl," she initially resists, wondering "how could she marry Cipriano, and give her body to this death?" (259). But

> she felt herself submitting, succumbing. He was once more the old dominant male [and] she was swooned prone beneath, perfect in her proneness. It was the ancient phallic mystery. . . . Ah! and what a mystery of prone submission, on her part, this huge erection would imply! . . . Ah! what a marriage! How terrible! and how complete! . . . She could conceive now her marriage with Cipriano; the supreme passivity, like the earth below the twilight, consummate in living lifelessness, the sheer solid mystery of passivity. (324–25)

As in Hull's novel, surrender comes with knowledge and acceptance; however, there is an important difference between Kate's "prone submission" and Diana's. In the beginning of The Plumed Serpent, Kate's libidinal drive is a crucial part of her attraction to the Quetzalcoatl men, and this is where the desert romance formula is most powerful for Lawrence. However, by the end of the novel, with Kate's marriage to Cipriano, this changes. One of many conditions Cipriano imposes upon her is that they must maintain emotional and sexual distance, and this includes control of her orgasm:

> He made her aware of her own desire for frictional, irritant sensation . . . and the spasms of frictional voluptuousness.
>
> Cipriano . . . refus[ed] to share any of this with her. . . . When, in their love, it came back on her, the seething electric female ecstasy, which knows such spasms of delirium, he recoiled from her. . . . And succeeding the first moment of disappointment, when this sort of "satisfaction" was denied her, came the knowledge that she did not really want it, that it was really nauseous to her. (439)

Critics have generally translated this inchoate passage as Cipriano demanding that Kate give up clitoral "spasms of frictional voluptuousness" for more "potent" (and, presumably, less labor-intensive for Cipriano) vaginal orgasms. A central difference between Hull and Lawrence is illustrated by a comparison of the "knowledge" at which Kate arrives (that certain forms of sexual "satisfaction" are "really nauseous to her") and Diana Mayo's erotic enlightenment. As euphemistic as Hull's narrative is, there is no question that Diana's captivity is an erotic experience, whereas, as Marianna Torgovnick argues of *The Plumed Serpent*, "Kate's attraction to Mexican men is clearly sexual, but — she insists and Lawrence insists — sex is not the point, is not more than a metaphor, a means to an end, an expression of larger, cosmic unities."[28] Kate's conclusion only emphasizes "sex suppression": "Without Cipriano to touch me and limit me and submerge my will, I shall become a horrible, elderly female. I ought to *want* to be limited" (457). Despite what Lawrence suggests here, he uses Hull's narrative of female eroticism toward anti-erotic ends, to achieve a "limiting" of women's sexuality and a concomitant embrace of Queztalcoatl authoritarianism.

The Lustful Sheik

Lawrence subordinates Hull's version of eroticism to two other interlinked purposes: artistic (the innovative modernist text) and political (the new phallic order). Most critical debate about Hull's novel similarly imposes political or modernist-aesthetic readings, with the same vocabulary of regression and innovation. One of the most common arguments is that while Hull's politics are retrogressive and her language is banal, *The Sheik* points out the need for a new vocabulary to account for female sexuality: an argument that comes directly out of the modernist idea that new linguistic and discursive models are needed to represent the complexities of modernity. Other arguments are based on innovation within genre. Patricia Raub writes that "while Hull's desert backdrop and her emphasis upon sex were scarcely innovative by 1919, the way in which she handled the nineteenth-century seduction novel format was new" (124). At the other end of the regressive/progressive scale, *The Sheik* looks soundly "bad" in Lee Horsley's analysis, which casts Hull's fantasy of male domination in terms of fascism—a point announced by Horsley's pairing of an epigraph from *The Sheik* with *Mein Kampf.* One is hard pressed to argue that Hull's politics and writing are anything but "bad," but her novel obviously had another kind of appeal that eludes these readings. The attraction of *The Sheik* seems to baffle Leavis and Lawrence: how could anyone enjoy anything so bad? Still, it is Lawrence himself who seemed to have the best sense of what *The Sheik* really is: pornography.

Isolated, remote, striving to minimize historical referents and problems except those that are part of the erotic frisson, the setting of desert romance resembles nothing so much as what Steven Marcus has called "pornotopia."[29] Billie Melman argues that "the desert-passion industry" (104) is "one of the earliest examples of mass, commercialised erotic literature" (104). The complex double identification that Hull cultivates (the reader's sympathy for Diana's plight and alignment with Ahmed's erotic desires) is uncharacteristic of romance. But in pornography—most notoriously in texts such as Sade's *Justine*—the reader is commonly primed to will the heroine's chastisement or comeuppance. Although there are strong echoes of *Clarissa* and *Pamela*, for example, in *The Sheik*, Hull's language and her handling of somatic response are more resolutely pornographic. Although Hull never mentions body parts or acts that would constitute obscenity, the novel's repetition, in terms of language and content, resembles nothing so much as pornographic replication. Just as pornography endlessly recycles a limited vocabulary without, apparently, any inhibition of its pleasurable affect, so Hull (and her readers) never seems to tire of clichés of burning passion. The episodic pacing of *The Sheik* is also reminiscent of pornography; the way Diana comes to each encounter with Ahmed as if for the first time, with her feelings and his body reiterated in only subtle variation over the last time, resembles the phenomenon of "renewable virginity" in pornography, where each episode presupposes its own novelty and excitement. The relationship between the desert romance author and her readers is as intimate as the pornographer's, reflecting an almost naïve faith that the same scenario, told again and again, from a slightly different angle, or with a slightly different set of props, is sure to incite arousal.

In fact, *The Sheik* is less closely related to *Pamela* or *Jane Eyre* than it is to the anonymous mid-nineteenth-century pornographic classic *The Lustful Turk*.[30] Emily Barlow, the supposed narrator of this epistolary novel, is a British ingénue traveling in "the East." She is swept off her horse and captured by Ali, the Dey of Algiers. ("Dey" was the title for governor used before the French conquest in 1830.) The Dey carries Emily to his "sumptuous chambers," complete with beautiful clothes, attentive maids, and contemporary novels. This gorgeous but barbarous swain immediately assaults Emily's virginity. Although she puts up a fight, the protest quickly gives way to, as Emily reports, "a sensation it is quite impossible to describe . . . [a] sudden, new and wild sensation blended with . . . shame and rage."[31] Emily's archetypically pornographic awakening—the rape that turns to arousal—is strikingly like Diana Mayo's, although it takes about a tenth of the time to achieve. Within just a few pages, Emily is utterly in thrall to the Dey and his wicked ways, and in no time she proves to be a gifted libertine. It is only with great reluctance that at the end of the novel she is shipped home to England, her erotic education complete. "I will never marry," Emily writes, "until I am assured that the chosen [man] possesses sufficient charm and weight not only to erase the Dey's impression from my heart, but also from a more sensitive part." The flimsy way in which marriage is invoked at the end of *The Lustful Turk*—more as a setup for a coy joke than anything else—is typical of pornography, in the world of which marriage is not just insignificant but a turn-off. Just so, the marriage at the end of *The Sheik* is gratuitous, and Hull's main concession to traditional novel conventions is perfectly in keeping with its pornographic progenitor.

What would Lawrence have found useful in a style of writing he purported to detest? First, the desert romances were supposedly an insight into what for Lawrence was a lifelong mystery: female consciousness and sexuality. Second, the desert romance managed, in its clichéd manner, to achieve a readerly effect of immediacy and response that Lawrence valued highly. As Allison Pease has shown, many modern writers, including Lawrence, "strove to incorporate mass-cultural pornographic representations of the body, sex, and sexuality into their works even as they affirmed the aesthetic value of their appropriations."[32] Pease contends that the only representations of sexualized bodies available to the modernists were in conventional pornography, but Lawrence knew—and he says this in "Pornography and Obscenity"—that popular fiction was already bringing pornographic representation into its discourse, if not precisely in the explicit fashion of classic pornography, then in a language that we might call "porno-romance," the idiom of the desert romance. There is a suggestive connection between pornography's arousing function and Lawrence's desire to wrest the reader out of passivity and into spontaneity, reviving the libidinalized body from the stranglehold of consciousness. Nowhere are clichés so effective, and readerly affect so unmediated and immediate, as in pornography. What is pornography but a "tissue of clichés (stock phrases to evoke stock responses)"? But in the realm of pornography, the stock response is the ideal response.

Lawrence's appropriation of *The Sheik* turns out to be symptomatic of the modernist reading of erotic fantasy. Hull strives to isolate the fantasy of *The Sheik* from the "here and now" (as the race-change and hasty marriage indicate), while Lawrence seeks to deploy fantasy toward an enacted, realized (and anti-erotic) end. Similarly, modernist reading of erotic fantasy typically puts it toward a particular political use. In a symptomatic interwar example of casting erotic fantasy in terms of politics, the British MP Ellen Wilkinson once remarked of Sir Oswald Mosley, head of the British Union of Fascists, that his allure was not that of "the nice kind hero who rescues the girl at the point of torture, but the one who hisses, 'At last . . . we meet.'" He was, she claimed, "The Sheik."[33] As rhetorically amusing as this politicization of Hull's romantic-sadistic desert lover is, it sidesteps the real argument of Hull's novel: that fantasies of stereotypical gender roles and relationships of oppression continued to have a hold on the imagination at the same time that enlightened modernity was fighting political oppression and liberating women. That "nice kind hero," it seems, was simply not as erotically exciting to Hull and her readers as "The Sheik."

Erotic fantasy is notoriously difficult to read in terms of progressive or regressive politics, not because it precludes or is exempt from politics but because the goal of erotic fantasy—pleasure—does not easily lend itself to clear political readings.[34] The compulsion to translate erotic fantasy into a political form is analogous to how modernism and its critics tend to read "regressive" or banal fantasy. For example, Lee Horsley juxtaposes *The Sheik* and *The Plumed Serpent* with "progressive and feminist" works by Virginia Woolf, Rebecca West, and Katherine Burdekin, which Horsley credits with "changing those aspects of the female response to male power which are sometimes characterized as passive and masochistic. They contest the assumption . . . that passivity and decadence are normal in women" (116). Just as Leavis argues that "stock responses" could be corrected by the "spontaneous" and "fresh responses" of modernism, all too often readings of fantasy are based on a hope that we can overcome cliché and fantasy as we would unenlightened political positions. This corrective or rehabilitative approach—and the hope that politically threatening fantasies can be consciously changed, overcome, or replaced with "better" ones—is predicated on an understanding of fantasy as a kind of "false consciousness."[35] But fantasy and its most unmediated literary forms, including pornography, articulate structures of desire that, while stimulated by and responding to politics, have their own logic that is, at times, all too genuine.

If women in great numbers responded to the desert romance, they did so, it seems, out of an attraction to a kind of novelty (alterity or escape) combined with an anti-novelty. The former includes an exotic locale, a certain explicitness about women's desire, and the appearance of a kind of man one ordinarily didn't meet, apparently, if one was a typist; the latter includes formulaic repetitions, clichés of genre, stereotypes, and conventional plots. What *The Sheik* tells us is that along with the desire for equality, innovation, and individual power, erotic fantasy can be equally constructed around stereotype, cliché, and predictability: "badness" in its most unfashionable sense. Even as erotic representation is often construed as the realm of transgression and novelty, erotic fantasy may also actively resist innovation, which makes it almost antithetical to prevailing modernist tenets.

Modernism has many models for reading erotic fantasy, but the case of Lawrence and Hull indicates that we should look not just at the most transgressive or non-normative representations but also at the most conventional. For a body of art that claims to be deeply invested in exploring interiority, the "dark places of psychology,"[36] modernism turns out to have a quite limited idea of which places are worth exploring. As critics including Suzanne Clark, Jane Tompkins, and Rita Felski have argued of "feminine" forms of writing such as sentimentalism and melodrama, modernist artists and critics are quick to exclude forms of writing that do not fit into their aesthetic or political paradigms.[37] The point is not that Hull should be included in the canon of modernism or that her work should be championed as feminist or original, but that "bad" fictions such as *The Sheik* underpin many of the most ostensibly "innovative" modernist sexual representations. Indeed, several central features of *The Plumed Serpent* — female submission, male primitivism, and orgasmic discipline — return, re-eroticized, in *Lady Chatterley's Lover*, Lawrence's most explicit and "innovative" treatment of sexuality. The fact that Lawrence derived many of these tropes from Hull's novel suggests his recognition that erotic fantasy and its literary representation may necessarily converge with cliché in ways that are at odds with traditional definitions of modernism. Accordingly, a literary history that accurately describes the modernist interest in libidinal life must be capacious enough to include not only the shock of the new but also the pleasures of cliché.

Notes

I presented an earlier version of this paper at a December 2000 MLA panel on "The Other Britain I: Late Victorian and Early Modernist Orientalism"; my thanks to John Paul Riquelme for inviting me to participate. Thanks also to Ruth Bernard Yeazell for her suggestion that I look at *The Lustful Turk*.

1. Irene Speller, "How I Was Loved by a Sheik!," *My Story Weekly*, October 15, 22, 29, November 5, 1927: 3.

2. Ibid., November 5, 1927.

3. *The Sheik* (London: Virago Books, 1996), 112.

4. David Trotter, *The English Novel in History: 1895–1920* (London: Routledge, 1993), 185. Billie Melman estimates that "the first filmed version of *The Sheik* (1921) was seen by 125 million viewers, the majority of them — to judge from the contemporary press reports — women" (*Women and the Popular Imagination in the Twenties: Flappers and Nymphs* [London: Palgrave MacMillan, 1988], 90).

5. Melman argues that "the desert romance is one of the most consciously topographical and ethnological genres in popular fiction" (*Women and the Popular Imagination*, 95) and describes the different styles of the main geographical areas of desert romance.

6. For contemporary responses to desert romance and *The Sheik*, see Evelyn Bach's "Sheik Fantasies: Orientalism and Feminine Desire in the Desert Romance," *Hecate: An Interdisciplinary Journal of Women's Liberation* 23, no. 1 (1997): 9–40; Julia Bettinotti and Marie-Françoise Truel's "Lust and Dust: Desert Fabula in Romances and Media," *Paradoxa* 3, nos. 1–2 (1997): 184–94; and Karen Chow's "Popular Sexual Knowledges and Women's Agency in 1920s England: Marie Stopes's *Married Love* and E. M. Hull's *The Sheik*," *Feminist Review* no. 63 (Autumn 1999): 64–87. See also Tania Modleski's *Loving with a Vengeance: Mass-Produced Fantasies for Women* (Hamden, Conn.: Archon Books, 1982) for more general observations about fantasy and the romance genre.

7. *The Long Week End: A Social History of Great Britain, 1918–1939* (New York: Macmillan, 1941), 41.

8. See Gaylyn Studlar's *This Mad Masquerade: Stardom and Masculinity in the Jazz Age* (New York: Columbia University Press, 1996); Studlar's " 'Out-Salomeing Salome': Dance, the New Woman, and Fan Magazine Orientalism," in *Visions of the East: Orientalism in Film*, ed. Matthew Bernstein and Gaylyn Studlar (New Brunswick, N. J.: Rutgers University Press, 1998); and Miriam Hansen's "Pleasure, Ambivalence, Identification: Valentino and Female Spectatorship," *Cinema Journal* 25, no. 4 (1986) for excellent readings of Hollywood desert romance films and particularly *The Sheik*.

9. Although critics agree that the desert romance was an interwar genre (Melman, *Women and the Popular Imagination*; Osman Bencherif, *The Image of Algeria in Anglo-American Writings, 1785–1962* [Lanham, Md.: University Press of America, 1997], and Patricia Raub, "Issues of Passion and Power in *The Sheik*," *Women's Studies* 21 [1992]), its forerunners include novels by Ouida, Marie Corelli, Kathlyn Rhodes, and Robert Hichens. Especially notable is Hichens's 1904 novel, *The Garden of Allah*, which is often associated with *The Sheik* but is much more complex. It includes a strong theological narrative, and has none of *The Sheik*'s sadomasochistic eroticism.

10. While *The Sheik* and its film adaptation were immensely popular in America as well as Britain, according to Raub, "With the exception of *The Sheik* it appears these British-written [desert romances] were much more popular with British women readers than with American readers. None of these romances appeared on the American Booklist's monthly lists of best-selling fiction during this period, much less upon the yearly best-seller lists" (ibid., 128).

11. F. R. Leavis, *D. H. Lawrence: Novelist* (New York: Knopf, 1956), Q. D. Leavis, *Fiction and the Reading Public* (London: Penguin, 1979), and Frank Kermode, *D. H. Lawrence* (New York: Viking, 1973).

12. See Hilary Simpson's discussion of Lawrence's "abrupt espousal of male supremacy which coincides with the end of the war" in *D. H. Lawrence and Feminism* (DeKalb: Northern Illinois University Press, 1982), 66.

13. See "A Propos of *Lady Chatterley's Lover*," in *Lady Chatterley's Lover*, ed. Michael Squires (London: Penguin, 1993), 327.

14. See, for example, Maria Di Battista and Lucy McDiarmid, eds., *High and Low Moderns: Literature and Culture, 1889–1939* (New York: Oxford University Press, 1996); Michael North, *Reading 1922: A Return to the Scene of the Modern* (New York: Oxford University Press, 1999); James Naremore and Patrick Brantlinger, *Modernity and Mass Culture* (Bloomington: Indiana University Press, 1991); and Rita Felski, *The Gender of Modernity* (Cambridge, Mass.: Harvard University Press, 1995).

15. Orwell, "Good Bad Books," *The Collected Essays, Journalism and Letters of George Orwell*, ed. Sonia Orwell and Ian Angus, vol. 4, *In Front of Your Nose: 1945–1950* (London: Penguin, 1968), 37–41.

16. "In the Garden of Allah," *Daily Express*, January 23, 1924: 5.

17. *The Crack-Up*, ed. Edmund Wilson (New York: New Directions, 1945), 51–52. Qtd. in Bencherif, *Image of Algeria*, 203.

18. See Lee Horsley, *Fictions of Power in English Literature: 1900–1950* (London: Longman, 1995). Billie Melman and Gaylyn Studlar, for example, read Diana as a New Woman.

19. See Reina Lewis, *Gendering Orientalism: Race, Femininity and Representation* (London: Routledge, 1996); Gina Marchetti, *Romance and the "Yellow Peril"* (Berkeley: University of California Press, 1993); and Meyda Yegenoglu, *Colonial Fantasies: Towards a Feminist Reading of Orientalism* (Cambridge: Cambridge University Press, 1998), on gender and Orientalism.

20. *Times Literary Supplement*, "*The Sheik*" (review), November 6, 1919: 633.

21. Q. D. Leavis, *Fiction and the Reading Public* (London: Penguin, 1979), xxxiv, 250.

22. "The Little Shopgirls Go to the Movies," in *The Mass Ornament: Weimar Essays*, ed. and trans. Thomas Y. Levin (Cambridge, Mass.: Harvard University Press, 1995), 291–304.

23. D. H. Lawrence, *Selected Literary Criticism*, ed. Anthony Beal (London: Heinemann, 1973).

24. See, for example, Simpson, *D.H. Lawrence and Feminism*; Melman, *Women and the Popular Imagination*; Trotter, *English Novel*; and Horsley, *Fictions of Power*.

25. Hull, "Why I Wrote 'The Sheik,'" *Movie Weekly*, November 19, 1921: 3.

26. D. H. Lawrence, "The Woman Who Rode Away," *The Complete Short Stories* (New York: Penguin Books, 1981), 3: 546–81; 550.

27. D. H. Lawrence, *Aaron's Rod*, ed. Mara Kalnins (Cambridge: Cambridge University Press, 1988); *Kangaroo* (New York: Penguin Books, 1980); and *The Plumed Serpent*, ed. L. D. Clark and Virginia Crosswhite Hyde (London: Penguin, 1995).

28. *Gone Primitive: Savage Intellectuals, Modern Lives* (Chicago: University of Chicago Press, 1990), 164.

29. Steven Marcus, *The Other Victorians* (New York: Basic Books, 1966).

30. See Ruth Bernard Yeazell's reading of *The Lustful Turk* in *Harems of the Mind: Passages of Western Art and Literature* (New Haven: Yale University Press, 2000).

31. Anon., *The Lustful Turk* (Ware, Hertfordshire: Wordsworth Editions, 1995), 16.

32. *Modernism, Mass Culture, and the Aesthetics of Obscenity* (Cambridge: Cambridge University Press, 2000).

33. Cited in Horsley, *Fictions of Power*, 112.

34. Some of the best attempts to come to terms with sadomasochism in women's erotic fantasies include Marianne Noble's *The Masochistic Pleasures of Sentimental Literature*

(Princeton, N.J.: Princeton University Press, 2000) and Ann Snitow's "Mass Market Romance: Pornography for Women is Different," in *Powers of Desire: The Politics of Sexuality*, ed. Ann Snitow, Christine Stansell, and Sharon Thompson (New York: Monthly Review Press, 1983), 258–75.

35. Marianne Noble contends that "to deny the abiding power of fantasies is to reify rather than dissipate their power. If a woman really does not want to have masochistic fantasies, is repression really the best way of achieving a personal transformative liberation? Particularly if she is secretly deriving power and pleasure from fantasies of submission?" (*Masochistic Pleasures*, 205 n. 22).

36. Virginia Woolf, "Modern Fiction" (1925), *Collected Essays*, 4 vols. (New York: Harcourt, Brace, 1967), 2: 108.

37. Suzanne Clark, *Sentimental Modernism: Women Writers and the Revolution of the Word* (Bloomington: Indiana University Press, 1991); Jane Tompkins, *Sensational Designs: The Cultural Work of American Fiction, 1790–1860* (New York: Oxford, 1985); Rita Felski, *The Gender of Modernity* (Cambridge, Mass.: Harvard University Press, 1995).

The Romance of Cliché

Rebecca L. Walkowitz

Virginia Woolf's Evasion: Critical Cosmopolitanism and British Modernism

Oh! thought Clarissa, in the middle
of my party, here's death, she thought.
Virginia Woolf, *Mrs. Dalloway*

In his recent work on international feelings, Bruce Robbins looks to contemporary novels about fascism, imperialism, and world war to investigate "the proper tone" of cosmopolitanism. The novel, Robbins proposes, is "a place where such matters of tone are most searchingly experimented and reflected on."[1] Robbins's gambit is telling in three important ways. First, it suggests that any philosophy or ethics of cosmopolitanism must have a "tone," a way of thinking about people whose lives are geographically or culturally unrelated to one's own and a way of acknowledging, though not only acknowledging, the ethical or affective compromises that may go with that thinking. Second, it suggests that there are many possible "tones" (sympathetic, indifferent, arrogant, tolerant, outraged), which need to be examined and tested. And third, it directs the project of tone to the project of the novel and thus suggests that the tradition of narrative in the twentieth century has helped to develop existing strategies of cosmopolitanism. The echoes of this tradition have become increasingly audible in old and new essays about international conflict and wartime patriotism; and while some of the authors of these essays are trained as literary critics, as Robbins is, others are importing the techniques and metaphors of narrative — and of modernist narrative, in particular — into disciplines such as philosophy and performance studies. Judith Butler, for example, has argued that U. S. patriotism, as it was formulated after the World Trade Center attacks, demands a "first-person point of view" that precludes "accounts that might involve the decentering of the narrative 'I' within the international political domain."[2] To conceive a just role for U. S. foreign policy, one that acknowledges the global underpinnings of local conditions, Butler asserts, "we will need to emerge from the narrative perspective of U. S. unilateralism and, as it were, its defensive structures, to consider the ways in which our lives are profoundly implicated in the lives of others" (181). Butler proposes that a more responsible view of global history requires less coherent, less exclusive perspectives.

Fred Moten has argued similarly that the rhetoric of terrorism promoted by the U.S. government has generated a new political "homogenization," which is based on the "equality" of suffering and fear, and not on the equality of persons.[3] This is manifest, Moten proposes, "not only as the liquidation of dissent or of whatever marks the possibility of another way of being political, but even as the suppression of alternative tones or modes of phrasing as well" (189). Moten takes the title of his essay, "The New International of Decent Feelings," from Louis Althusser, whose early treatise "The International of Decent Feelings," first published in 1946, argues that the proper tone of internationalism after the catastrophe of the Second World War is not a "moralizing socialism" of equality in suffering but an analytic, antagonistic socialism of judgment and differentiation.[4] Wanting to preserve the class struggle against postwar existentialism, Althusser argues that the rhetoric of universal suffering by all tends to obscure the significance and reality of social and economic suffering by some. And these generalizations about class struggle allow him to see other generalizations about international violence and world politics. He shares with Butler and Moten a critique of self-absorbed "decency." Butler and Moten contest the assumptions of universal or "planetary" cosmopolitanism: that all people in the world have the same relationship to international events; that all people living in a single nation should have the same views about these events; that any one view is unambivalent and unchanging; that decent feelings are more important than dissenting thought.[5]

Decentering the first-person point of view, rejecting tones of comfort or confidence, risking indecency: arguably, these are the principal hallmarks of modernist fiction. Indeed, the tension between decent feelings and dissenting thought is crucial to Virginia Woolf's writing and to the project of many early-twentieth-century artists who sought to imagine models of social critique that would resist social codification. Recent theorists of humanism, such as Edward Said and Jacques Lezra, see in Woolf's fiction a model of what Lezra has called, after Said, "critical heroism": the attempt to "[operate] in the world with sympathy toward the richness of the past, [while] preserving a posture of resistance and critique towards that richness and towards the institutions in which its study is enabled and its value measured and propounded, and maintaining that sympathy, and that critical and resisting stance, without end."[6] Said proposes that "the practice of humanistic service" in which Woolf and other modernists engaged "always entails a heroic unwillingness to rest in the consolidation of previously existing attitudes."[7] Yet, as Lezra and Said acknowledge, it is not easy to be both critical and heroic. How does one resist social postures of euphemism and blinding generalization—postures, Woolf felt, that led to acts of imperialism and militarism, such as the First World War—without resorting to literalism or to narrow description? How does one resist inattentiveness if one's attention can never rest, if one must always look away in order to keep looking? As these questions suggest, as the phrase "critical heroism" implies, one must risk being bad—uncertain, distracted, and unsuccessful—in order to keep being good.

Focusing on the past and on the margins of social activity, on useless pleasures but also on invisible labors, Woolf directs her readers to notice those aspects of British society that have gone almost unseen: the mundane activities of upper-class women, but also the activities and existence of servants, immigrants, homosexuals, divorced women, educated working women, the insane, and the dissident or angry.[8] Offering only glimpses of servants, immigrants, and others on the margins of upper-class life, Woolf emphasizes the social conditions of blindness rather more than she rectifies invisibility. Indeed, Woolf will purposefully exclude significant episodes—a suicide, an engagement, or the break-up of a relationship but also the destruction of bodies during wartime and the procedures of colonial efficiency—in order to emphasize episodes of unsocialized pleasure, as well as echoes, tangential effects, and memories. In the past, critics have argued that Woolf's fiction is quietist and insufficiently patriotic because it speaks of fascism and war but fails to address those topics directly or appropriately: she mentions a newspaper but does not tell us what the headlines say; she describes someone thinking of war but does not describe a battle. For these reasons, M. C. Bradbrook called "the style of Mrs. Woolf" self-indulgent and "evasive," arguing that her books give primary attention to minor events, such as a party, and only indirect attention to major events, such as war and death.[9] Writing in the inaugural issue of *Scrutiny* in 1932, Bradbrook condemned Woolf's novels for failing to express unambiguous political values and then attributed this opacity to a "trick of style": namely, Woolf's tendency to disrupt or qualify narrated thoughts with dependent clauses and frequent asides. Woolf is evasive, Bradbrook explains, in refusing to devote her novels, or even her sentences, to any single topic, and in refusing to limit her topics to those that seem pertinent or suitable to war.

In the 1930s, the critique of Woolf came from both sides of the political aisle: the socialist writer R. D. Charques submitted that Woolf finds "refuge or immunity from the worst in contemplation of—what shall we say?—a mark on the wall," while the right-wing Wyndham Lewis argued that Woolf represents "mere personality" instead of "ideas."[10] In a scornful review from 1938, Q. D. Leavis asserted that Woolf's writing lacks the characteristics of true argument and thus achieves only "argument" (the word appears in quotation marks in Leavis's text [205]). These writers contended that Woolf seems too various in her sympathies, too distracted in her commitments, and too cosmopolitan in her analogies between the psychology of marriages and the philosophy of treaties, between the world of parties at home and the wars of fascism abroad. The early critics of Woolf's style believed that art should be unwaveringly attentive, that any failure of attention led not only to bad writing but, worse, to "nasty," "preposterous," and "dangerous" writing. In Leavis's view, Woolf's work is dangerous because it refuses to generalize (about Germany) and because it generalizes too much (about misogyny and sexism).[11] Decrying what she sees as Woolf's evasion of important matters (for example, her apparent failure to emphasize the risk of German militarism), Leavis is also critical of what she sees as Woolf's fixation on matters overly narrow, literal, or petty (for example, her observation that Hitler's efforts to limit women's roles in public life resonate with the sentiments of many English politicians).

The point here is that those who identify evasiveness in others assume some agreement within a community or among readers about the topics that deserve attention and the kinds of attentiveness that are attentive enough. For Woolf, there is no such agreement. She examines in her fiction the literary classifications — evasion, argument, euphemism, literalism, generalization, and others — that many of her critics take for granted, and she asks readers to see that interpretive judgments operate historically: that they help to shape the boundaries and meanings of British society; that they are, in turn, shaped by social contestations. Woolf's writing represents conflicts about international action and national culture as conflicts about attention. This is true not only of those works that seem to focus on domestic minutiae but also of those that seem to focus on peripheral spaces (*To the Lighthouse*, *The Voyage Out*), education policies (*A Room of One's Own*), and the relationship between fascism and gender (*Three Guineas*). Her point is not simply to create a new ideal of attentiveness, more expansive and extensive, but to display the customs and conventions, social and psychological, that control what can be seen and what can be said.

Woolf does not replace the euphemisms of British patriotism with explicitness, transparency, or heroic action, and in this sense her modernism is purposefully bad. I share Melba Cuddy-Keane's belief that "Woolf's commitment to independent, critical thinking . . . was the foundation for the model of social equality that she upheld," but I argue also that Woolf often expressed this commitment by developing narrative strategies that are *evasive* rather than *descriptive* or *utopian*.[12] Woolf may have participated in civic projects and written directly against war and gender inequality, but her writing remains challenging and often disturbing because she proposes that international sympathy and national dissent are nourished in part by those evasions of syntax and plot that qualify, unsettle, and redirect enduring habits of attentiveness.

Woolf's novels and essays return, over and over again, to the problem of comparison and to conflicts about tone. How should artists present sociability or pleasure in the context of international catastrophe? How does one display systemic conditions without seeming to ignore the particularity of events or diminish their singular importance? How can one offer fresh associations among different experiences without seeming to treat the experiences as the same? For Woolf and her contemporaries, as Michèle Barrett has argued in an essay on modernism and memory, these questions were prompted not only by the task of looking backward but also by the social and geographic conditions of the war: the spatial proximity of the trenches in France and gentleman's clubs in London, such that an officer might spend his morning in one place and his evening in the other; the horror of devastating losses at the front reported in newspapers side by side with racing results and other commonplace records of everyday life.[13] Is it more appropriate for artists to rectify the confusion of tones by representing only the direct, violent experience of war in the trenches? Or should artists represent a more expansive, more entangled conception of war, one that includes the spaces of newspaper, gentleman's club, trench, and racetrack?

Woolf begins to engage these questions in her very first published story, "The Mark on the Wall." Given her subject matter — the value of questioning in a time of unsatisfactory answers — it is perhaps not surprising that this story has been central to Woolf's reputation as an evasive writer. "The Mark" occasioned this review from E. M. Forster: "Mrs Woolf's art is of a very unusual type, and one realizes that quite good critics, especially of the academic kind, may think it insignificant. It has no moral, no philosophy, nor has it what is usually understood by Form. It aims deliberately at aimlessness."[14] While Forster may have recognized the purposeful "aimlessness" of Woolf's literary project, other critics have transformed "The Mark on the Wall" into a metaphor of futility and lassitude: they invoke the story to assert the naïve myopia of Woolf's entire oeuvre. This is the implication of R. D. Charques's comment, when he claims that Woolf finds "refuge or immunity from the worst in contemplation of — what shall we say? — a mark on the wall," as if the story's title represents all that Woolf contemplates and as if it merely replaces the contemplation of other, more serious concerns. Charques proposes that looking at a mark on the wall allows one to avoid social and political conditions that are otherwise legible and definitive. In his quip, he pretends to speculate ("what shall we say?") about Woolf's interests in much the same way that Woolf is said to speculate about the mark: he imagines that Woolf's writing, once it ignores "the worst," might focus on anything at all, that its wandering has no aim whatsoever.

Charques implies that those who write speculatively in a time of catastrophe help to perpetuate catastrophe by refusing to address it directly. Theodor W. Adorno would later argue that this criticism, which targets a literary style, promotes a rigid politics of affiliation and exclusion. Adorno

Virginia Woolf's Evasion

provides an important context for Woolf's work because both writers share the conviction that social norms are embedded in traditions of literary style and that literary style is embedded in the politics of national culture. Adorno makes these connections explicit. Like Woolf, Adorno asserts throughout his career that the homogenization of writing—at the level of narrative structure, diction, and syntax—helps to produce the homogenization of culture, which Adorno associates with fascism. Adorno addresses the dangers besetting projects such as Woolf's in an essay on literary form, in which he claims that the demand for political writing that is always literal and direct is a demand for legible and consistent social classifications:

> The person who interprets instead of accepting what is given and classifying it is marked with the yellow star of one who squanders his intelligence in impotent speculation, reading things in where there is nothing to interpret. A man with his feet on the ground or a man with his head in the clouds—those are the only alternatives. But letting oneself be terrorized by the prohibition against saying more than was meant right then and there means complying with the false conceptions that people and things harbor concerning themselves.[15]

Adorno proposes that those who suspend the work of classification become themselves classified; they are marked as traitors, outcasts, and degenerates. The "yellow star" is compensatory: it creates ocular proof where self-evidence is no longer visible. Refusing to classify a mark on the wall, Woolf's narrator shows how intellectual speculation, because it thwarts compliance, resists the passivity of wartime.

"The Mark on the Wall" was published in July 1917, bound with Leonard Woolf's "Three Jews" in a pamphlet entitled *Two Stories*.[16] Circulated privately among friends and literary colleagues, *Two Stories* inaugurated the Woolfs' new Hogarth Press, which was later to publish all of Virginia Woolf's remaining novels, T. S. Eliot's *The Waste Land*, the collected writings of Sigmund Freud, English translations of Dostoevsky and Gorky, and many other important works of British modernism.[17] Most readers know "The Mark on the Wall" from its third publication in *Monday or Tuesday* (1921), the only volume of short stories published during Woolf's lifetime, and from its later republication in posthumous volumes assembled by Leonard Woolf after the Second World War.[18] The 1917 publication is significant, however, because Leonard's "Three Jews" orients readers of Virginia's story to the production of national collectivity.[19] Both stories remind readers that there are diverse ways of being British, even or especially during wartime, and both stories imply that one must resist the pressure to assimilate. The 1917 publication presents Virginia Woolf, unmistakably, as the wife of a person both British and Jewish, a person of both national and international affiliations; and it presents Woolf's literary project within a social context of anti-Semitism and strong international feeling about the relative patriotism of British Jews.[20]

Leonard's story relates a conversation between two Jewish men who wonder together whether they can be part of the "orderly English way," or whether they can have or should have only their own, separate order.[21] The story focuses on the difference between wishing that England "belongs to us" and wishing that we "belonged to *it*" (emphasis in original). These are two models of assimilation: in the first model, English Jews change what counts as "English," while in the second model, English Jews accommodate religious and social norms whose characteristics are static and definable (8). One of the two characters tells of an acquaintance, the story's third Jew, who decides that his son no longer belongs to his family because he has married a Christian servant. The son is disinherited not because he has married a Christian, however, but because he has married a servant, which is to say that the father makes himself more English by emphasizing class rather than religion as a standard of exclusion. The story thus asserts that exclusion can be a characteristic of Jewish as well as English belonging, though it ends, inconclusively, with one character observing to the other that "times change" (18). This phrase could mean that the standards of national belonging merely shift from one category to another over time, as in the anecdote, but it may also mean — and the story's irony points to this unachieved but preferable outcome — that, over time, belonging could come to have fewer, or less rigid, standards: England could belong to "us" because the meaning of England changes, from a homogeneous community defined by manners or race to a heterogeneous community defined by location or citizenship.

While Leonard's story reminds wartime readers that national collectivity tends to impose cultural norms, Virginia's focuses on social rules of attentiveness, feeling, and thought to address, more specifically, cultural norms about war. The 1917 publication of "The Mark on the Wall" is significant not only because Virginia's story echoes Leonard's topic—England's diversity—but also because it examines an ongoing historical event: it depends on the progress of war for the drama of its ending and for its effect of distracted thought and entangled spaces. "The Mark" is narrated in the first person by a woman remembering a day in the recent past ("it was the middle of January in the present year" [83]) when she saw a mark on the wall above the fireplace. Sitting in her living room, she imagines what the mark might be, though she does not get up to see what it is for certain; neither the narrator's name nor the location of the house is ever given; the entire episode, we learn explicitly at the end, takes place during a war, whose damnation ("Curse this war; God damn this war!") by an unnamed person addressing the narrator is the most dramatic activity and only conversation that the story relates.[22] Contentiously and self-consciously, "The Mark" is a story about the refusal to act without thinking. It is about the refusal to *substitute* patriotic comfort or static outrage for critical anger and curiosity, and the refusal to *separate* the political "facts" of a European war (casualties and official reports) from the disarray of a living room in England. These are related gestures: redirecting outrage and yet refusing comfort, the story suggests, allows the narrator to consider how the social history of attentiveness creates the conditions for wartime complacency.

"The Mark on the Wall" may serve as a metaphor for evasion (evading the "fact" of the mark on the wall; evading the "fact" of the war), but it is also a story that considers directly what evasion evades. First of all, "The Mark" is in a sense narrated backward: although one might paraphrase the story as a tale about a woman who is trying not to think about the war, the context of wartime is announced only at the end of the story, when a comment about the war disrupts the narrator's thinking about the mark. The disruption of the narrator's thoughts about the mark makes the reader notice, really for the first time, that the story is trying to represent the experience of wartime thinking. Of course, anyone reading the story in 1917, as British casualties continued to mount, would have known this from the beginning. Indeed, there are clues at the beginning, even if one needs the ending to make them fully legible: in the first paragraph, seeing the mark interrupts the narrator's "fancy of the crimson flag flapping from the castle tower," which she imagines when she looks at the burning coals in the fire before her (83). The narrator is relieved to have this vision disrupted: this is the story's first image of militarism, and it gestures toward the fighting not many miles away. One imagines that the narrator is relieved because thoughts of war are distressing in themselves, but she attributes her relief to a more specific distaste: the narrator calls her vision of war "an old fancy, an automatic fancy"; it is a vision shaped by worn images of heroism and chivalry rather than by personal experiences or singular thought (83).[23]

Evading automatic fancies, Woolf's narrator is trying to evade "generalisation," which she associates with the social rituals and fashions of the past. The narrator criticizes the generalizations of British culture and then attempts to avoid generalizing rhetoric: as she speculates about the future of the novel, how it will tend to omit the description of reality in favor of reality reflected in the minds of individuals, she breaks off, dismissing "these generalisations" as "very worthless" and then noting "the military sound of the word" (85–86). Woolf critiques "standard" interpretations and pious rules by first dismissing generalization and then engaging in it. She shows, by speaking abstractly and theoretically about genre, that all rhetorical terms have social contexts:

> The military sound of the word is enough. It recalls leading articles, cabinet ministers—a whole class of things indeed which as a child one thought the thing itself, the standard thing, the real thing, from which one could not depart save at the risk of nameless damnation. Generalisations bring back somehow Sunday in London, Sunday afternoon walks, Sunday luncheons, and also ways of speaking of the dead, clothes, and habits—like the habit of sitting all together in one room until a certain hour, although nobody liked it. There was a rule for everything. (86)

The military sound of the word is enough to remind the narrator that speculative thought can diversify a single perspective and also that a single perspective makes it difficult to think speculatively at all. Moreover, by noticing the *sound* of "generalisation," the narrator refuses to take the word literally; she refuses the efficiency of meaning in favor of sensation, poetry, and art. This strategy, insisting on sound rather than meaning, turning poetry against efficiency, will be important to Woolf's later work—not because she values the play of the signifier, although she does, but because she uses the provocation and vitality of figurative language to invigorate and replace dead or deadened thought.

Woolf demonstrates in "The Mark," as she will elsewhere, that to critique euphemism, which translates intense experiences into language that is habitual and therefore invisible, one must also critique literalism, which proposes that there is only one, objective experience to present. She demonstrates also, however, that the critique of euphemism and literalism will have to involve gestures that are in some ways both euphemistic and literal, because writing a novel or making an argument or maintaining a friendship requires moments of purposeful blindness as well as moments of direct attention. To put it another way, Woolf cannot reject generalization outright because she actually values some of the things that generalization facilitates: new analogies, strategic overlooking, parties, and even, as I'll suggest, national monuments. Nevertheless, we might distinguish Woolf's use of euphemism and literalism from the uses she criticizes by her effort to treat these styles politically, to show that civic language (the rhetoric of leading articles, ways of speaking of the dead) and literary classifications (generalization, evasion) help to shape the social meanings of war, colonialism, and education.

By the time of the story, as the narrator tells it, the "standard things" of childhood have been replaced by Whitaker's Table of Precedency and its list of the peerage, whose official order complements the informal rituals of upper-class norms. If as a child the narrator mistook a "class of things" for the repertoire of all things and thus was unable to see that there was anything that she had neglected to notice, as an adult the narrator observes that Whitaker's tends to minimize thought by providing the "comfort" of precedency:

> The Archbishop of Canterbury is followed by the Lord High Chancellor; the Lord High Chancellor is followed by the Archbishop of York. Everybody follows somebody, such is the philosophy of Whitaker; the great thing is to know who follows whom. Whitaker knows, and let that, so Nature counsels, comfort you, instead of enraging you; and if you can't be comforted, if you must shatter this hour of peace, think of the mark on the wall. (88)

The surprising logic of this passage is that thinking of the mark on the wall provides not a refuge from discomfort but an alternative, implicitly superior way of shattering peace. The narrator has "contempt for men . . . [who] take action as a way of ending any thought that threatens to excite or pain," but she puts an end to those "disagreeable thoughts" by thinking of the mark on the wall (88): that is, for the narrator, the discomfort of thinking about the mark works to combat the discomfort of thinking about the blind comforts of others. It is action without thought that the narrator finds complacent. It is habitual patriotism that the narrator finds contemptible. Yet the story does not suggest that one should rest in this contempt: while acknowledging rage as the appropriate response to obsequious order and anesthetizing action, the narrator prefers the wandering unpeacefulness of agitated thinking (the form and content of the story) to the static unpeacefulness of sheer frustration (the desire to classify the mark).

The story ends with a disruption: the narrator's thoughts are broken when the voice of practicality arrives, like some person from Porlock, to announce, "I'm going to buy a newspaper" (89). The unnamed person introduces the story's conclusion, providing the cause of the mark, the political context of the narrator's thoughts, and the facts of a newspaper. Official reports thus replace speculation about the production of official knowledge:

> Someone is standing over me and saying–
> "I'm going out to buy a newspaper."
> "Yes?"
> "Though it's no good buying newspapers. . . . Nothing ever happens. Curse this war; God damn this war! All the same, I don't see why we should have a snail on our wall."
> Ah, the mark on the wall! It was a snail. (89)

Woolf contrasts the contention that "nothing ever happens" with the happenings of the story: she resists the passive experience of war by making thought happen and by arguing that what "happens" in the world involves not only the events that newspapers report but also the daily sociability that shapes, interprets, opposes, and ignores those events. With "The Mark on the Wall," Woolf introduces a central trope of her career, speculating about what "happens" while war is happening, or while war, in its violence and its precedency, keeps one from noticing that anything else does happen.

"The Mark on the Wall" does not observe a sense of order: its narrative progresses by way of association rather than by way of cause or efficiency; it tends to stop, change direction, turn in on itself. While Leonard

Woolf contests the orthodoxy of national culture, Virginia Woolf contests the habits of wartime attention. Speculating instead of accepting what is given, Woolf marks out the lines of entanglement between the public, official, and faraway spaces where men fight and the small, private, enclosed spaces where women think. Woolf's narrator uses private speculation and poetic language to introduce the topics and tones of cosmopolitanism.

In "The Mark on the Wall," Woolf is critical of traditional narrative aims, those of realism and of linear narrative progress, because she finds them all too comfortable, like euphemism, in a time of radical discomfort and international crisis. And yet a wide range of literary and cultural observers today —filmmakers such as Marleen Gorris as well as critics such as Alex Zwerdling—have suggested that Woolf's hostility to social euphemism means that her approach to war, to patriotism, and to individual desire must repudiate indirection and artifice as symptoms of ethical complacency and political negligence.[24] In her 1997 film adaptation, *Virginia Woolf's Mrs. Dalloway*, Gorris adds transparency and explicitness to Woolf's project by rearranging the plot of her novel. While the book begins with Mrs. Dalloway's trip through London to buy flowers for a party in the evening, Gorris's film begins with Septimus Warren Smith's experience of trench warfare: the camera focuses on his terrified face, as mortars and gunfire explode chaotically around him. Woolf's novel begins in London, in 1923. Gorris's film begins in Italy, in 1918. The time and place of the film's beginning are announced by a caption superimposed on a single shot of Septimus: we watch Septimus, who watches (the camera does not show what he sees) the death of his friend, Evans, who is killed by a mortar or a mine. The film seems to remedy what it establishes as a problem both of equation—death and a party—and of evasion—having a party instead of thinking wholly of death. The film tries to make good on Woolf's politics by clarifying the novel's concerns. Gorris's image of good modernism is a modernism matched to narrative clarity, direct representation, and achieved ethical priorities.

Of course, the first line of Woolf's novel is not a beginning but a middle: "Mrs. Dalloway said she would buy the flowers herself."[25] The first scene of the film has been added by Gorris—it exists nowhere in the novel—and it preempts the trip to the flower shop, which now follows in the echo of the war. It is worth noting these differences, not so much to complain that Gorris has deviated from a sacred original as to emphasize that the new

Rebecca L. Walkowitz

scene seems to correct Woolf's omission. The invention of the scene in the trenches and its placement at the beginning of Gorris's film introduces the war as a preeminent topic, because it comes first and because it is the only historical episode presented as an objective past rather than as a remembered one. Gorris's film reverses the structure of "A Mark on the Wall": it starts with war, not with distraction; it gives precedence to casualties, trenches, and men at the front, not to women in living rooms or in flower shops or at parties. By beginning her film with a war in Italy instead of a shopping trip in London, by beginning her film with a war that we see directly rather than through the memory or consciousness of one of the characters, Gorris gives Woolf's narrative a sharper, more definite face. Gorris contrasts a style of euphemism — common among most of the upper-class characters in the story, including Clarissa Dalloway — with a style of transparency, which is visible in the film's commitment to show what is made to seem like everything, even those scenes that Woolf chose never to describe.[26] Gorris's adaptation of Woolf seems to argue that social indifference and national triumphalism, which Woolf criticizes in her novel, are best defeated by a narrative style that is linear and unequivocal.

For Woolf, however, it is unequivocal style that generates upper-class euphemism. The face that Gorris gives to her film — a focused, objective image of war — is similar to the face that Clarissa Dalloway gives to herself, as Woolf describes it:

How many million times she had seen her face, and always with that same imperceptible contraction! She pursed her lips when she looked in the glass. It was to give her face point. That was her self — pointed; dartlike; definite. That was her self when some effort, some call on her to be her self, drew the parts together, she alone knew how different, how incompatible and composed so for the world only into one centre, one diamond, one woman who sat in her drawing-room and made a meeting-point, a radiancy no doubt in some dull lives, a refuge for the lonely to come to, perhaps; she had helped young people, who were grateful to her; had tried to be the same always, never showing a sign of all of the other sides of her — faults, jealousies, vanities, suspicions, like this of Lady Bruton not asking her to lunch; which, she thought (combing her hair finally), is utterly base! Now, where was her dress? (37)

Between the distraction of looking into her mirror and the distraction of looking for her dress falls an account of a single-mindedness that Clarissa's mind labors to assemble. The face is the result of compositional effort, the "contraction" of many parts and varieties of the self into one "pointed; dart-like; definite" image. Woolf presents this image as the face of social decorum: Clarissa displays only one self and also makes sure to conceal that there are any other selves to display. Woolf registers this sense of concealment in the doubling of selves: "that was her *self* when . . . some call on her to be her *self* drew the parts together." Clarissa's socialized face promises socialized thoughts and conceals the emotional intensity that Clarissa remembers from her youth. Later in the novel, Woolf will suggest that English patriotism, also, has a pointed, dartlike face, which in turn conceals the multiple attachments and unruly desires of cosmopolitan Britain. At the same time, Woolf will acknowledge that contraction makes possible those communities that serve as alternatives or supplements to patriotism: in the novel, communities of friendship; in Woolf's milieu, the subcultural communities of pacifist artists and the transnational communities of women. Indeed, Clarissa's euphemism of self, as grim as it may be, allows her to assemble the party that concludes the novel—a party that occasions the comparison of selves and the acknowledgment of unresolved differences.

To meet the demands of marriage and upper-class propriety, Clarissa generates a consistent, public self that does not reflect her many, momentary, private desires. Her contracted face is marmoreal—not only definite but also unchanging, like the marble faces of the uniformed boys whom Peter Walsh, just returned from India, admires in the London street:

> Boys in uniform, carrying guns, marched with their eyes ahead of them, marched, their arms stiff, and on their faces an expression like the letters of a legend written round the base of a statue praising duty, gratitude, fidelity, love of England. (51)

Less purposeful than Clarissa, Peter allows his thoughts of a rebellious past to be "drummed" into step by the "regular thudding" of young men marching past him. Peter's thoughts are regularized in theme and in style: they become like the concrete letters written "round the base of a statue" both because Peter has some sympathy for the specific praise of duty and because his sympathy is almost as automatic as the legend's cliché. Peter's agitated,

Rebecca L. Walkowitz

recursive thoughts of the past as it lives in the present are replaced momentarily by the deadened march of syntax, by the march of feet, and by the forward momentum of certainty and progress. Like Clarissa's social world, which requires contraction, the march of British triumphalism requires "renunciation," as Peter reports:

> . . . on they marched, past him, past every one, in their steady way, as if one will worked legs and arms uniformly, and life, with its varieties, its irreticences, had been laid under a pavement of monuments and wreaths and drugged into a stiff yet staring corpse by discipline. (51)

It is through renunciation of varieties and irreticences, Peter explains, that the marching boys come to resemble the military heroes whose statues they pass; having "trampled under" the temptations of life, the boys likewise achieve a "marble stare."

In this important passage, only a few pages after Clarissa's encounter with the mirror, Woolf indicates that public triumphalism requires an undistracted attentiveness: a face that is stiff and recognizable, that shows no "varieties" or "irreticences." Moreover, Woolf presents triumphalism as a style of history. Whereas the boys march steadily forward, never looking back, Clarissa and Peter remember moments from the past that change and develop, and that disorder the narrative progress of living. Clarissa's relationship with Sally Seton, for example, occasions "the most exquisite moment of her whole life" (35). Unlike the boys "drugged into a stiff yet staring corpse," Sally is remembered by Clarissa as a person of "abandonment, as if she could say anything, do anything; a quality much commoner in foreigners than in Englishwomen" (33). Woolf knows that a style of behavior that abandons social conventions will tend to seem foreign, and she also knows that the decorum of gender—how women and men are expected to behave—is crucial to the definition of national culture. Sally is one of the many English characters in *Mrs. Dalloway* who are said to seem or act like foreigners: there is Miss Kilman, who loves Clarissa's daughter and whose friends and family are German; Peter Walsh, who has been living in India and who has fallen in love with a married woman; Septimus, whose thoughts are in Italy and not with his Italian emigrée wife. Abandonment, like agitation, leads to improvisation and flexibility, but also to surprise and often pain. The heroic past, captured in marble, is familiar and etched in stone; the momentary past, on the contrary, is "a present, wrapped up," which one uncovers slowly over time (35–36).

Resisting imperceptible contractions and the march of progress, Woolf extends the grammar of parataxis—in her novel, not only the lists of phrases and images that appear within a single sentence but also the many scenes that follow each other without immediate rationale—to the insubordinate arrangement of political imperatives and everyday pleasures. Adorno describes parataxis as "artificial disturbances that evade the logical hierarchy of a subordinating syntax."[27] In *Mrs. Dalloway*, parataxis serves to evade "a sense of proportion," which functions in the novel as a rule not only of thought and society but also of speech (96). Proportion is the social theory promoted by Sir William Bradshaw, the specialist physician who treats Septimus for shell shock on his return from the European war. The symptoms of Septimus's condition, as Sir William identifies them, are disorders of thought and language: Septimus overinterprets and over-elaborates; he distrusts the normative meanings of words and shows an unwillingness to follow conventional patterns of expression. Septimus's symptoms, like Woolf's strategies of evasion, tend to resist the "logical hierarchy" needed for patriotism and normative masculinity. One should see, also, that Woolf's critique of "logical hierarchy" extends to the foundations of British society, represented by imperial conquest and compulsory marriage: as agitation interferes with patriotism, so "susceptibility" makes Peter Walsh a mediocre colonial administrator, and so remembering threatens to derail Clarissa's studied social poise (151).

During times of international crisis, Woolf proposes, boundaries of thought are patrolled even more rigorously than boundaries of land. Sir William exists to correct women like Miss Kilman, whom he never meets in the novel but whose forceful heterodoxy would conflict with his own, more socially acceptable brand of pushiness. Kilman tutors the Dalloways' daughter in history because she lost her position in a girls' school at the beginning of the war; fired because her family was of German origin and she had German friends, her career ruined as a result of patriotism, she feels "bitter and burning" (124) much of the time. Though she tries to feel "calm," (124), having learned to think of God, she is "stricken once, twice, thrice by suffering" (133). Miss Kilman's bitterness seems too much for Woolf, who values pleasure as well as anger and has little sympathy, at least here, for the critique of economic privilege. Yet though her resentment is ugly (as is Miss Kilman herself, in Woolf's description), Woolf uses her story to show that the control of independent women (Miss Kilman) and shell-shocked men (Septimus) in England helps to prepare the control of independent cultures abroad.

Sir William's desire to discourage thinking is legible in his diagnosis of Septimus, whose illness he pronounces after "two or three" minutes of questioning (95). As Sir William interrogates Septimus, Woolf's narrative shifts from the doctor's point of view to the point of view of "the patient":

> "You served with great distinction in the War?"
>
> The patient repeated the word "war" interrogatively.
>
> He was attaching meanings to words of a symbolical kind. A serious symptom, to be noted on the card.
>
> "The War?" the patient asked. The European War — that little shindy of schoolboys with gunpowder? Had he served with distinction? He really forgot. In the War itself he had failed. (96)

Septimus's wife, Lucrezia Warren Smith, answers Sir William's question on Septimus's behalf, as if the doctor had asked for a fact that Septimus could not remember. She assures Sir William that, "Yes, he served with the greatest distinction" and "was promoted" as a result (96). But Septimus has forgotten what "distinction" means; he no longer values the rhetoric of valor and military heroism. He says "he had failed" not because he did not fight but because "he did not feel" (91). "War," "failure," and "distinction" are words whose meanings are no longer certain. By repeating the words, Septimus insists that he does not assume, as Sir William does, that he and the doctor are talking about the same idea of war, or that there is only one idea of war to talk about. The multiplication of perspectives, the fact of perspective at all, Sir William identifies as a sign of illness: "He was attaching meanings to words of a symbolical kind." In the shift of perspective from Sir William to Septimus, from "the patient" and "the War" to "the European War" and "that little shindy of schoolboys with gunpowder," Septimus recites the several names for which Sir William has only one name and, moreover, invents a new name along the way. Septimus insists that his war is not Sir William's war and also refuses to call his event a war at all; for Septimus, "war" celebrates and finalizes without modifying or analyzing.

While Septimus suggests that words might have multiple, contested meanings, Sir William invokes euphemism, making words mean as little as possible. Euphemism is the opposite of symbolization because it does not "attach" one meaning to another but replaces one meaning with a muted, more comfortable interpretation. The point of euphemism is to make what it has replaced and the act of replacement invisible. Sir William explains to Rezia, who wants to know if Septimus is "mad," that "he never spoke of 'madness'; he called it not having a sense of proportion" (96). Septimus shows, through deflation, the fatuous spectacle that "war" covers up (a "little shindy of schoolboys with gunpowder"), while Sir William gives "madness" a cover, a new name, so he does not have to speak of it at all. Giving uncomfortable experiences new names and embracing these names in lieu of discomfort, euphemism demonstrates a sense of proportion. Of course, it is perfectly true that Septimus's response is also in some ways evasive: he does not speak of bodily destruction, the death of friends, or the intensity of remorse. Yet unlike Sir William's euphemism, Septimus's deflation creates greater discomfort: speaking of the war sarcastically, he declines explicitness, to be sure, but he also declines mythification. That Septimus does not share Sir William's sense (meaning) of war is taken as a sign that he lacks sense (sanity) altogether. Woolf explains that Sir William's method works by excluding any element that would challenge his views: "Worshipping proportion, Sir William not only prospered himself but made England prosper, secluded its lunatics, forbade childbirth, penalised despair, made it impossible for the unfit to propagate their views until they, too, shared his sense of proportion" (99). Proportion requires seclusion and prohibition: it makes things fit by calling them "unfit" until they do.

Fighting proportion as a system of representation, Woolf is fighting to reverse the contraction of individuality and antagonism within civic debates about national and international thinking. To do this, Woolf promotes several strategies of thought that correspond to strategies of writing: poetic language, nicknaming, excitement, stammering, revision, and parataxis. These strategies are most visible in *Mrs. Dalloway*, where Woolf develops an analogy between symptoms of shell-shock and tactics of social critique, but they are noticeable throughout her work: Rachel Bowlby describes the feminist logic of "Woolf's equivocations" in *A Room of One's Own* and other essays (70), and Michèle Barrett proposes that Woolf's use of parentheses and square brackets "form part of a general writing strategy that represents the really important things for Woolf—the war, death, grief, the meaning of life, as well as love—only obliquely."[28] Barrett argues persuasively that the "strange withdrawal of obvious affect in the writing of Woolf" (195–96), part of what I have been calling "evasion," reflects Woolf's commitment to the multiple, transient self, as opposed to the contracted, marmoreal self required by proportion, conversion, and triumphalism.

Woolf contests the war by rejecting its models of attention; she approaches the war parenthetically, never erasing its violence, but not allowing violence to absorb, in the total attention violence demands, the partial attention that resists it. *Mrs. Dalloway*, in particular, reproduces a conflict about attention at several levels of attention (syntax, theme, plot). The novel shuttles between remembering and forgetting, between the rejection of complacency and the suspicion of prescribed action, whether this action involves forgetting or remembering to the exclusion of everything else. With the arrival of Sir William at her home, Clarissa hears that Septimus has killed himself: "Oh! thought Clarissa, in the middle of my party, here's death, she thought" (183). If one thinks that the gravity of death means considering death first and by itself, and not in the middle of a party, and not in the middle of a sentence about a party, then Clarissa's thought may seem insensitive and unsympathetic. But there may be something valuable in a reiterated "thought" that equates the significance of a party with the significance of death—that places these topics, syntactically and ethically, on the same plane. Clarissa recognizes in Septimus "an attempt to communicate" (184). She admires his death because he has done something unreasonable. He has rejected the "corruption" of life: "A thing there was that mattered; a thing, wreathed about with chatter, defaced, obscured in her own life, let drop every day in corruption, lies, chatter. This he had preserved" (184). As for herself, Clarissa reports: "She had schemed; she had pilfered. She was never wholly admirable" (185). Clarissa's party may facilitate chatter and perpetuate exclusion (Miss Kilman was not invited), but it creates opportunities also—for measuring the past, recognizing friends, and saying "things you couldn't say anyhow else, things that needed an effort" (171). Presenting death in the middle of a party, Woolf refuses to accept the structure of choice—war or peace; party or death; reasonableness or insanity— that Clarissa's milieu takes for granted. The refusal of choice and linearity is a signal characteristic of Woolf's modernism, and it is one of the reasons why aesthetic success in her terms often seems like political failure.

Arguably, *Mrs. Dalloway* achieves its climax not at the party, where Septimus's suicide is announced and considered, but at the start of the novel's penultimate section, in which Peter Walsh declares that a passing ambulance is "one of the triumphs of civilisation" (151). Woolf places this phrase among Peter's thoughts only sentences after Septimus has killed himself and Dr. Holmes has disclaimed all responsibility. While Peter's comment does refer to the ambulance, it seems also, by proximity, to describe the scene of suicide that appeared in the novel (though not to Peter) immediately before. Woolf uses Peter's interior monologue to register both the cruelty and the kindness of civilization's triumph and to suggest that technologies of kindness, which arrive in the novel as a doctor or as an ambulance, may generate cruelty in their wake. Throughout *Mrs. Dalloway*, Woolf makes the monuments of English civilization into symbols in Sir William's very sense: progress, an ambulance, war, even a wedding ring, all of which seem at first to have definitive meanings, no longer convey an unequivocal achievement.

In the novel's sudden shift from death to "triumph," we see right away that even in an ambulance there is nothing "wholly admirable." Peter sees the ambulance as a triumph because it functions as an agent of rescue and as an example of imperial "efficiency" and "communal spirit" (151)—it symbolizes both English society at its most humane and the beneficence of this superior nation's rule elsewhere (as in India, from whose colonial service Peter has just returned). While the first may seem to us far more appealing than the second, Woolf would have us notice, by the nearness of the ambulance to the suicide and by Peter's clanging words (he repeats the word "civilisation" several times), that the very doctors who tend to the injured may be those who have driven Septimus to his death. Peter's appreciation of efficiency is made possible by three kinds of blindness: he does not know about the suicide of Septimus, or even that the medical treatment that Septimus has received has worsened rather than corrected his injury; he does not recognize that the "communal spirit" at home, which he unreservedly admires, has been financed by the exploitation of communities abroad; and he cannot see that the social values he admires (progress, efficiency, usefulness) are continuous with those that led Clarissa to marry Richard, making

Peter "more unhappy than I've ever been since" (42). In this scene, Woolf proposes forcefully what she has suggested elsewhere: that English manners have a "cosmopolitan geography";[29] efficiency and "communal spirit" are made possible—and compromised—by colonialism on the one hand and by European war on the other.

Peter's thoughts of efficiency may distract readers from the contemplation of Septimus's mangled body and his wife's misery, and from wondering whether it is, indeed, Septimus whom the ambulance carries. Yet turning away from death, the novel brings to light the uncivil, unwavering attention of triumphalist thought, represented in the novel by the affective priorities of upper-class marriage, colonialism, and patriotism. By creating this diversion, Woolf's style of composition rejects what Adorno has called "the dream of an existence without shame."[30] For Adorno—who is perhaps best known for insisting that poetry after Auschwitz is impossible, and who is perhaps least known for retracting or at least revising this declaration[31]—writers seeking to resist social conformity must develop strategies of critique that exceed homogeneous or merely pious styles of expression. They must accept, if not embrace, the profanity of conflicting sensibilities—beautiful metaphors and ugly events, acts of kindness and scenes of cruelty, suicide in the afternoon and a party in the evening—and they must accept the ethical discomfort that this profanity may evoke. Adorno argues that the writer must acknowledge "the complicity that enfolds all those who, in the face of unspeakable collective events, speak of individual matters at all."[32] While "collaboration" should be resisted, Adorno asserts, "there is no way out of entanglement" (26–27). In *Mrs. Dalloway*, Woolf's shame is marked by her willingness to contemplate both the opportunities and the dangers of evasion.

By cultivating moments of diversion and rejecting wartime priorities of attention, Woolf makes her readers more aware of social networks and helps them to distinguish between single perspectives and universal ones. For example, Peter transforms a specific triumph into triumphalism by assuming that the limited success of the ambulance in recovering injured bodies can be simply extended to the entire success of London; that London's success can be extended to the success of the British Empire; that the success of the British Empire is equivalent to the success of civilization. Whereas the generalizing perspective assumes that triumph extends to every action and every actor, the agitated perspective acknowledges that one person's triumph is often the cause of someone else's loss. This is the point that Walter Benjamin offers in his claim that "there is no document of civilization which is not at the same time a document of barbarism." Benjamin observes that "cultural treasures," now collected in museums, are the spoils of forgotten wars; that those discoveries which mark the advance of science and technology, however much they owe to individual inspiration, have been produced in part by anonymous laborers who received no benefit and no credit for their efforts.[33] Benjamin's observation emphasizes causality and history, but it also speaks of the present and the future—the "triumphal procession," as he puts it, "that steps over those who are lying prostrate" (256). For Benjamin, forgetting and ignoring are not the unintended or necessary consequences of civilization's triumph but rather the inaugural moments in which destructive self-righteousness is achieved. Writing in a time of too many processions, Benjamin proposes, as Woolf does, that looking backward and looking below are principal tactics of anti-triumphalism.

And thus for Woolf even monuments are usable and potentially critical, when their marmoreal substance is tempered by the incitement to speculation. In *The Years* (1938), one of Woolf's characters refers to the statue of Edith Cavell, a British nurse who was executed by the Germans in 1915 and whose monument was erected near Trafalgar Square in 1920.[34] Initially, the statue was inscribed with the usual patriotic phrases: "fortitude," "devotion," "for King and country." Four years later, however, the Labour government added a statement that Cavell made before her death: "Patriotism is not enough, I must have no hatred or bitterness for anyone."[35] In Woolf's novel, Eleanor calls these words "[t]he only fine thing that was said in the war" (319). Neither embracing patriotism nor rejecting it outright, Cavell's tentative universalism forces readers to speculate about the statue's message and about its function as a national monument. Woolf seems to appreciate the statue for its articulate evasiveness: the way it acknowledges (and even records) a history of conflict about the appropriate meanings and necessary objects of British devotion.

Woolf suggests that political engagement in an international context requires the willingness to march but also to think; the willingness to have a mind but also to change it; and the willingness to embrace uncommitted styles of attention. Ultimately, Woolf's evasiveness is bad because it can't be good: its analytic strategies depend on the persistence of effort rather than the production of efficiency. Rejecting the consistency and intensity of affect that she associates with imperial progress and civic hypocrisy, Woolf's evasion borrows from two traditions of cosmopolitanism: a decadent, urbane tradition of dissenting individualism and a philosophical tradition of transnational collectivity based on similarities greater or less than the nation. Seeing these traditions together in Woolf's work has two principal consequences for the field of modernist studies: first, it suggests that Anglo-American modernism includes anti-heroic impulses that help to shape alternative modes of political consciousness; second, it suggests that European critiques of modernity such as Woolf's share analytic insights with non-European critiques such as those that emphasize the experiences of colonialism. Among these insights is the belief that resisting the politics of imperialism, as well as the politics of marriage and epic masculinity, may involve refining or even at times rejecting some kinds of attentiveness. Reading Woolf's fiction in the context of theories of cosmopolitanism and social dissent allows us to see and to question what is valued as literary innovation, political critique, and international sympathy in the early twentieth century.

Notes

My thanks to those who responded to earlier versions of this essay presented at the Institute for Research in the Humanities at the University of Wisconsin-Madison (2003), the "Bad Modernisms" conference at Harvard University (2002), the Narrative conference at Rice University (2001), and the Modernist Studies Association conference at Rice University (2001). I am grateful for the generous comments of several interlocutors: Philip Fisher, Susan Stanford Friedman, Marjorie Garber, Barbara Johnson, Caroline Levine, and Sianne Ngai. Special thanks to Michèle Barrett and Douglas Mao for their warm provocations.

1. Bruce Robbins, "The Village of the Liberal Managerial Class," in *Cosmopolitan Geographies: New Locations in Literature and Culture*, ed. Vinay Dharwadker (New York: Routledge, 2001), 16.

2. Judith Butler, "Explanation and Exoneration, or What We Can Hear," *Social Text* 72 (Fall 2002): 180.

3. Fred Moten, "The New International of Decent Feelings," *Social Text* 72 (Fall 2002): 189.

4. Louis Althusser, "The International of Decent Feelings," in *The Spectre of Hegel: Early Writings*, trans. G. M. Goshgarian (London: Verso, 1997), 30.

5. For examples of cosmopolitanism as "planetary humanism," see Paul Gilroy, *Against Race: Imagining Political Culture beyond the Color Line* (Cambridge, Mass.: Harvard University Press, 2000), 356; Ross Posnock, *Color and Culture: Black Writers and the Making of the Modern Intellectual* (Cambridge, Mass.: Harvard University Press, 1998), 21; and Martha Nussbaum, "Patriotism and Cosmopolitanism?," in *Respondents, For Love of Country: Debating the Limits of Patriotism*, ed. Joshua Cohen (Boston: Beacon Press, 1996).

6. Jacques Lezra, "Unrelated Passions," *differences: A journal of Feminist Cultural Studies* 14, no.1 (2003): 83–84.

7. Edward Said, "Heroism and Humanism," *Al-Ahram Weekly On-line*, Issue No. 463 (January 6–12, 2000).

8. I am grateful to Amanda Claybaugh for leading me to think about the semi-visibility of servants in *Mrs. Dalloway*.

9. M. C. Bradbrook, "Notes on the Style of Mrs. Woolf," *Scrutiny* 1, no. 1 (1932): 33–38; Q. D. Leavis, "Caterpillars of the Commonwealth Unite!," *Scrutiny* 7, no. 1 (1938): 203–14.

10. R. D. Charques, "The Bourgeois Novel," *Contemporary Literature and Social Revolution* (1933), 108–14. Reprinted in *Virginia Woolf: The Critical Heritage*, ed. Robin Majumdar and Allen McLaurin (London: Routledge, 1997), 344. Wyndham Lewis, *Men without Art* [1934] (Santa Rosa, Calif.: Black Sparrow Press, 1987), 11.

11. While Leavis's review is focused on *Three Guineas* (1938), in which Woolf explicitly and contentiously aligns British tyranny at home with fascist tyranny abroad, Leavis's disdain is continuous with the criticism that others directed at Woolf's earlier works of fiction and criticism (204).

12. Melba Cuddy-Keane, *Virginia Woolf, the Intellectual, and the Public Sphere* (Cambridge: Cambridge University Press, 2003), 9.

13. Michèle Barrett presents these examples, taken from Paul Fussell's *The Great War and Modern Memory*, in the context of an argument about contemporary critical debates in "The Great War and Post-Modern Memory," *New Formations* 41 (August 2000): 139.

14. E. M. Forster, "Visions" in *Daily News* (31 July 1919), 2. Reprinted in *Virginia Woolf: The Critical Heritage*, 69.

15. Theodor W. Adorno, "The Essay as Form," *Notes to Literature: Volume One*, ed. Rolf Tiedemann, trans. Shierry Weber Nicholsen (New York: Columbia University Press, 1991), 4.

16. Leonard Woolf and Virginia Woolf, *Two Stories* (London: Hogarth Press, 1917).

17. Leonard Woolf discusses the history of the Hogarth Press in *Beginning Again: An Autobiography of the Years 1911 to 1918* (London: Hogarth Press, 1972), 241–42.

18. The Hogarth Press published a slightly revised version of "The Mark on the Wall" in 1919, under its own cover; the story was further revised for *Monday or Tuesday* in 1921.

19. Leonard's story precedes Virginia's in this publication.

20. See David Cesarani, "An Embattled Minority: The Jews in Britain during the First World War," *The Politics of Marginality: Race, the Radical Right, and Minorities in Twentieth Century Britain*, ed. Tony Kushner and Kenneth Lunn (London: Frank Cass, 1990), 61–81.

21. Leonard Woolf, "Three Jews," in *Two Stories*, 6–8.

22. Virginia Woolf, "The Mark on the Wall," *The Complete Shorter Fiction of Virginia Woolf*, 2d ed., ed. Susan Dick (New York: Harcourt, 1989), 89.

23. Also writing in 1917, Victor Shklovsky warns that habitual thought "devours works, clothes, furniture, one's wife, and the fear of war." Like Woolf, Shklovsky brings together the perception of everyday, domestic objects and the perception of war, arguing that stereotypes and metonymic thinking impede the experience both of furniture and of fear. Victor Shklovsky, "Art as Technique" [1917], *Russian Formalist Criticism: Four Essays* (Lincoln: University of Nebraska Press, 1965), 12.

24. *Virginia Woolf's Mrs Dalloway* (dir. Marleen Gorris), 1997; Alex Zwerdling, *Virginia Woolf and the Real World* (Berkeley: University of California Press, 1986).

25. Virginia Woolf, *Mrs Dalloway* [1925] (New York: Harcourt, 1981), 3.

26. The film shows another scene from the past that the novel, strikingly, omits: the scene of Clarissa's engagement to Richard, which in the film involves a kiss between Richard and Clarissa.

27. Theodor W. Adorno, "Parataxis: On Hölderlin's Late Poetry," *Notes to Literature: Volume Two*, ed. Rolf Tiedemann, trans. Shierry Weber Nicholsen (New York: Columbia University Press, 1992), 131.

28. Michèle Barrett, "Virginia Woolf Meets Michel Foucault," *Imagination in Theory: Essays on Writing and Culture* (Cambridge: Polity Press, 1999), 195.

29. Robbins, "The Village," 30.

30. Theodor W. Adorno, *Minima Moralia: Reflections from a Damaged Life*, trans. E. F. N. Jephcott (London: Verso, 1978), 86.

31. Adorno makes the first comment many times in his work and takes it back on at least two occasions: once in *Negative Dialectics* and once in his late essay "Is Art Lighthearted?" Theodor W. Adorno, *Negative Dialectics*, trans. E. B. Ashton (New York: Continuum, 1983), 362, and "Is Art Lighthearted?," *Notes to Literature: Volume Two*, 251. For an excellent account of the development of Adorno's thinking on this topic, see Lyn Hejinian, "Barbarism," *The Language of Inquiry* (Berkeley: University of California Press, 2000), 325.

32. Adorno, *Minima Moralia*, 18.

33. Walter Benjamin, *Illuminations*, trans. Harry Zohn (New York: Schocken, 1968), 256.

34. Virginia Woolf, *The Years*, ed. Hermione Lee (Oxford: Oxford University Press, 1992), 319. My thanks to Michèle Barrett for alerting me to Woolf's reference to the Cavell monument.

35. See editor's note in *The Years*, 477–78, and Rowland Ryder, *Edith Cavell* (London: Hamish Hamilton, 1975), 237.

Sianne Ngai

Black Venus, *Blonde Venus*

That German cow has copied me all my life.
The only thing left for her to copy will be my funeral.
Josephine Baker[1]

No one could take umbrage at paying tribute to another.
Josef von Sternberg[2]

The speakers in my epigraphs, aesthetic innovators in entertainment industries whose careers effloresced in the late 1920s on opposite sides of the Atlantic, are referring to the same person — Marlene Dietrich — in a similarly bitter fashion. Dancer, cabaret artist, and "International Star of the Screen" Josephine Baker accuses Dietrich of an imitation that cannot be counted the sincerest form of flattery, as the aphorism has it, but only read as appropriation, even theft. (The two performers did, incidentally, end up having similarly elaborate, state-sponsored funerals.)[3] Hollywood director Josef von Sternberg's remark, by contrast, might almost sound like a defense of his female star's perceived copying, or aping, of Baker. Yet in this comment from his memoir about the German actress he brought to Hollywood, and with whom he made seven films for Paramount Studios over a period of five years, Sternberg is in fact referring, just as acrimoniously, to Dietrich's aggressive *use* of praise, which discomfits him as much as her mimicry bothers Baker. Though the director initially interprets Dietrich's "excessive" public tributes to his artistic merits sympathetically (as an unconscious defense against the overwhelming experience of her adulation by others), he eventually suspects that she is marshalling her praise as a substitute for its rhetorical antithesis: criticism.

During her first film with me in Berlin [*The Blue Angel*, 1930], when she was unimportant and no one outside her immediate circle took notice of her, it was easy to complain that nothing on earth was worth such torture. But those who had listened so eagerly before might not be so sympathetic to her woes following the unique success her woes took on.

She now retailed her "torments" not as a complaint, but managed to turn this by shrewd indirection into an outstanding virtue. She flipped the other side of the coin, and with commendable instinct turned into a martyr who praised the divine grace which favored her with lacerations. She told everyone . . . that [during the filming of *Morocco*, 1930] I let her walk out into a blazing desert, barefooted . . . and that when she had fainted with exhaustion . . . I corrected her English when she had recovered enough to ask if I required another close up. This was not said to inform anyone that she had been mistreated. On the contrary, it was twisted into a form of praise for me. "Isn't he wonderful? He even corrects my English when I don't come out of a fainting spell properly." (*FCL*, 253–54, my italics)

The director's suspicion that the seemingly morally unassailable and even virtuous rhetoric of praise ("No one could take umbrage at paying tribute to another") has been adopted by Dietrich to disguise a more acid language of blame eventually culminates in his comparison of her praise to a violent discharge ("A geyser of praise began to shoot, hot and steaming, on the hour and every hour, and there was nothing I could do to avoid being scalded"), and its effects to that of a weapon, "spark[ing] a detonation that backfired on me" (254, 257). Yet even as Sternberg interprets Dietrich's praise as calculatedly and even injuriously aggressive, we can sense his grudging admiration of her "shrewd indirection," her ability to "[flip] the other side of the coin," to twist complaint or criticism into its difficult-to-criticize opposite. In other words, what Sternberg seems to admire most, even in the context of his own criticism of Dietrich, is the female performer's skill at *inversion*: "As the voice of the charming woman discovered by me became stronger in extolling her director, the slander in opposition to her 'praise' became thunderous. The scale always remained in balance" (257).

The awareness evidently shared by director and star of the fine line between praise and criticism (and Sternberg's belief in Dietrich's ability to manipulate it) brings us back full circle to Baker's accusation, which, paralleling Sternberg's interpretation of Dietrich's praise as slander, insists on reading imitation not as homage but as mere aping or theft. If the sign of Dietrich thus links Josef and Josephine together, connecting Austrian American auteur to African American cabaret performer, it can also be said to connect these aesthetic concerns: imitation and the problem of gauging its affect, "ethos," or encoded intent; praise and its surprisingly close relationship to criticism and other agonistic modes of discourse; and last, questions raised by the representational strategy of inversion. All of these questions are clearly central to the intertextual bouncing of what Linda Hutcheon calls modernist parody, an imitation characterized by inversion that often involves, as John Fowles has said, "*both* an homage *and* a kind of thumbed nose" to "an obvious previous iconography."[4] While this essay will continue to revolve around the figures of Baker, Dietrich, and Sternberg — as constellated, in particular, by *Blonde Venus* (1932), fifth of the seven Sternberg-Dietrich films in their Paramount Corporation cycle — it will do so primarily to explore affectively ambiguous acts of imitation and inversion as they inform a representational genre favored by first-wave modernists such as Stein, Joyce, and Schiele: the portrait of the artist or auteur.

Though *Blonde Venus* is frequently read as a portrait-of-the-artist film, it is one that immediately raises questions about who that artist might be. While all products of the American film industry, and those of the vertically integrated studio system of the thirties in particular, complicate the notion of individual authorship, Paramount's final version of *Blonde Venus* — which was based on a story co-written by its star and director, and in script form proliferated, between March and September 1932, into no fewer than six versions shaped by contributors with conflicting professional and aesthetic agendas — might be said to do so in an especially pronounced way.[5] In addition to Sternberg and Dietrich and screenwriters Jules Furthman and S. K. Lauren, executives representing different sectors of the integrated but internally unstable Paramount Publix Corporation, such as producer B. P. Schulberg and exhibition head Sam Katz, played significant roles in finalizing the script for the movie that was eventually released. So did MPPDA official Jason Joy and censors at Hollywood's self-regulating Studio Relations Committee, with whom Schulberg and Katz were reluctantly compelled to enter into further authorial "collaborations." Yet while there are clearly multiple authors behind this cinematic portrait of the artist, Dietrich and Sternberg remain the strongest competitors for the role in the world of *Blonde Venus*'s story, which traces the transformation of German immigrant and housewife Helen Faraday into cosmopolitan cabaret diva Helen Jones. While critics have noted that the Depression-era picture draws partly on Sternberg's childhood experiences as the son of Austrian immigrants for its story, it does so in order to chart not the rise of a Hollywood auteur but the emergence of a transatlantic female star who more obviously doubles as a figure for Dietrich. More specifically, in narrating the rise to stardom of a German immigrant ambiguously involved with a rich playboy (Cary Grant), who is consequently estranged from her husband (Herbert Marshall) and eventually forced into kidnapping her own child Johnny (Dickie Moore), the melodramatic plot mirrored the much publicized circumstances in which Dietrich crossed the Atlantic to work with Sternberg at Paramount, eventually bringing her daughter Maria, but leaving behind husband Rudolf Sieber.[6] Critics have also read *Blonde Venus* as a commentary on the power of cinematic illusionism that "establishes a parallel between Sternberg's performance and his character's, between his spectacle and Helen's."[7] Helen's efforts to exert control over her image, in other words, make her character as viable a double for the film's male director as for its female star. Approached as an allegory about the struggle for directorial control *over* female spectacle, Sternberg's film might be said to wrest Dietrich's representation of "herself" from herself, in order to generate a portrait of its director qua auteur. Though Helen's eventual success in directing and controlling the meaning of her diegetic performances (marked by her appearing dressed in male finery in the film's final musical number) reinforces this parallel between her character and Sternberg, his presence is as strongly suggested by the "strangely perverse and aggressive" figure of Johnny,[8] who not only provides the point of view of the film's culminating shot but is twice shown, near the film's beginning and at its conclusion, "directing" his mother and father in a theatrical reenactment of their courtship.[9]

And yet there is a third internationally known artist working in the interstitial zone between the avant-garde and the world of popular amusements, and one with no hand, direct or indirect, in the authorship of *Blonde Venus*, whom the film might be said to portray in a much more distorted, oblique, and one could thus even say paradigmatically modernist fashion. For in its account of a white European chorus girl who emigrates to the United States, attains fame and notoriety as a revue star by performing a primitivist jungle act, and is endowed with the name "Blonde Venus," *Blonde Venus* can be viewed as retelling, in what historical audiences would have perceived as an almost perfectly symmetrical "reversal," the story of Dietrich's much more famous contemporary Josephine Baker — a black American chorus girl who emigrates to Europe, attains fame and notoriety as a revue star by perfecting a primitivist *danse sauvage*, and eventually acquires the name "Black Venus."[10] In striking contrast to the correspondences inviting us to read the film as a self-reflexive allegory of the making of a transatlantic star (a portrait of Dietrich), or of the struggle for directorial control *over* female spectacle (a portrait of Sternberg), what we have here is less a parallel foregrounding likeness than a reversal foregrounding contrast and opposition.

How do we read this "inverted" portrait of an artist? Should it be taken as a respectful homage, a more aggressive act of parody, or simply an imitation that borders on theft?

Born in 1906 in poverty-stricken East St. Louis, Baker had been transformed into a "Black Venus" nearly a decade prior to the year-long production of *Blonde Venus*, and five years prior to Dietrich's first meeting and collaboration with Sternberg on *The Blue Angel* (1930) in Berlin. After traveling the American South on the black vaudeville circuit with blues singer Clara Smith and the Dixie Steppers, Baker had chorus-line roles in a second run of Noble Sissle and Eubie Blake's 1922 crossover hit *Shuffle Along* (which in its first run, on Broadway, starred Florence Mills and Paul Robeson) and their following 1924 musical *Chocolate Dandies*. She then took a job as a dancer at the Plantation Club, located above the Winter Garden Theater burlesqued by Hart Crane in *The Bridge* (1923–30). It was there that jazz composer Spencer Williams and socialite-producer Caroline Dudley approached Baker with an offer of a lead role in *La Revue Nègre*, an all-black show Reagan had pitched and managed to book for a season at Théâtre des Champs-Elysées, site of the 1913 premiere of Stravinsky's infamous *Le Sacre du Printemps*.

Given the immediate success of *La Revue Nègre*, by the end of 1925 Baker was well established as a star of the Parisian music hall circuit that had become an object of renewed interest to E. E. Cummings, Jean Cocteau, and other modernists "looking to popular culture to reinvigorate high art" after World War I, and admiring the revue shows for their eclectic pluralism and what Cummings called their "plotless drama."[11] Though Baker was best known for primitivist acts such as her *danse sauvage* with Martinique performer Joe Alex in *La Revue Nègre*, and her "banana dance" at the Folies-Bergère, the pluralist aesthetic of the music hall allowed her to become associated equally with American jazz and the Charleston, and thus to embody both "jungle and skyscraper elements," as Berlin writer Harry Kessler noted in his diary.[12] Emulating singer Florence Jones of the popular Chez Florence, by 1926 Baker was herself owner and hostess of Chez Joséphine, a Montmartre cabaret frequented by artists and intellectuals including Ernest Hemingway and Langston Hughes. She was also an astonishingly synergistic presence across French popular culture, spanning print media, the music recording industry, and film.[13] French critic André Levinson anticipates this in an early review of Baker's dancing, in which he suggestively describes her as a figure for intermediality itself—mixing American music and minstrel comedy, African sculpture, and French poetry in her performances:

> There seemed to emanate from her violently shuddering body, her bold dislocations, her spring movements, a gushing stream of rhythm. . . . It was as though the jazz, catching on the wing the vibrations of the body, was interpreting word by word its fantastic monologue. The music is born from the dance, and what a dance! The gyrations of this cynical yet merry mountebank, the good-natured grin on her large mouth, suddenly give way to visions from which good humor is entirely absent. In the short *pas de deux* of the savages, which came as the finale of *La Revue Nègre*, there was a wild splendor and magnificent animality. Certain of Miss Baker's poses, back arched, haunches protruding, arms entwined and uplifted in a phallic symbol, had the compelling potency of the finest examples of Negro sculpture. The plastic sense of a race of sculptors came to life and the frenzy of African Eros swept over the audience. It was no longer a grotesque dancing girl who stood before them, but the black Venus that haunted Baudelaire.[14]

Crossing cultural domains as well as media, portraits of Baker in a full range of styles — realist, post-impressionist, primitivist, cubist, fauvist, art deco — appeared in the form of biographies (the 1927 *Les Mémoires de Joséphine Baker*, written by Marcel Sauvage with illustrations by Paul Colin, whose *Le Tumulte Noir*, a portfolio of lithographs featuring Baker in *La Revue Nègre*, was published to wide acclaim earlier the same year), films, photographs, paintings, essays, sculpture, poetry, advertising (for products ranging from cigarettes to hair oil), and even recipes for food.[15] By the end of the decade Baker not only dominated the French media but had become a major presence in the African American and white American press, with her lifestyle and career tracked by publications ranging from the *Chicago Defender* to *Vogue* and *Vanity Fair*. And expanding her fame well beyond Paris and the United States, between 1928 and 1930 Baker embarked on a major tour across Europe and South America, performing in Vienna and Berlin (where an antagonistic reception put an early end to a theater booking originally planned for six months, as well as plans to launch a German Chez Joséphine), as well as Dresden, Brussels, Budapest, Prague, Zagreb, Agram, Basel, Amsterdam, Stockholm, Oslo, Copenhagen, Buenos Aires, Cordoba, Mendoza, Santiago, São Paulo, and Rio. Given Baker's iconicity and international celebrity, it would have been impossible for Sternberg and Dietrich not to have been aware of the Black Venus prior to their collaboration on the story that would eventually be filmed and titled *Blonde Venus* — or for that matter, given the intense reactions to Baker's Berlin performances in 1928, prior to their first meeting and collaboration on *The Blue Angel* in 1930.

Noting that there are historical grounds for reading *Blonde Venus* as an inverted portrait of the Black Venus still begs, however, the questions about imitation and homage raised by the confrontation between Baker, Dietrich, and Sternberg we viewed at the beginning of this essay. Moreover, from the perspective of an aesthetic modernism institutionalized as a reflexive turn to each medium's essential properties, there is a sense in which this reading of the film — based so far only on an observation about its plot structure — is a decidedly bad one. If the good modernism of an artwork continues to be indexed by an attention to medium specificity,[16] and in the case of Hollywood film in particular, by the capacity of *style* to disrupt and dominate *narrative* (a disruption which critics since Laura

Mulvey have routinely relied on to redeem industrial pictures ideologically and/or elevate them aesthetically), this truism becomes all the more pronounced in a Sternberg-Dietrich film, given what critics from 1932 forward have either praised or criticized as the director's conspicuous foregrounding of visual elements at the *expense* of story, form at the *expense* of content. As one 1936 critic, Andreas Mackenzie, put it simply in a profile called "Leonardo of the Lenses": "The story does not move his picture, it is his picture which moves the story."[17] Sternberg himself is repeatedly quoted as saying "the narrative means nothing," and that his films should be projected upside down so "that the actors and story become no longer noticeable, so that the values produced by the camera alone could not escape study."[18] When Mulvey, Carole Zucker, Bill Nichols, and other critics have considered films in Sternberg-Dietrich's Paramount cycle *as* modernism, they have focused on the contrast between the abstraction and complexity of the films' movement-images and their hackneyed and implausible storylines, on their use of visual style to resist or rebel against the narrative conventions of industrial genre pictures.[19]

But if visual style is as overt and manifest in Sternberg's films as it would appear, affirming what Nichols claims as his "disinterest in narrative per se" (*II* 115), it could be argued that *Blonde Venus*'s most latent layer, or its "unconscious," is actually its *story*. Moreover, if we approach modernism as a movement characterized by racial roleplaying and an obsession "with personae, metamorphoses, doubles, and mythic parallels," as Michael North argues in *The Dialect of Modernism*, it could be argued that the "bad" modernism of *Blonde Venus* resides in the fact that its particular preoccupation with racial doubles and personae — in this case, the Black Venus — is expressed primarily in terms of plot structure *rather* than style.[20] As such, the image of the black star called forth by *Blonde Venus* could be described as an anamorphic portrait: a distorted image that assumes its proper proportions only when viewed from an unconventional perspective.[21] Pushing this pictorial metaphor further, as seems appropriate in the case of a director famous for his "form of cinema in *suspension*" — that is, "long and elaborate shots . . . developed internally, by camera movement and dramatic lighting" rather than "the 'cutting' process of montage"[22] — the film's portrait of Josephine Baker could be said to rely on two of the most common forms of anamorphosis in the medium of painting: "oblique," in which "the unconventionality arises from the fact that the image must be viewed from a position that is very far from the usual in-front and straight-ahead position from which we normally expect images to be looked at" (as when we read a visually stunning Sternberg film for its "tenuous" story); and "catoptric," in which "the image must be seen reflected in a distorting mirror" (as when the film signals us to subject that story to a structural reversal, to read it in *inverted* form).[23] In the second case, the "image," or more accurately, the *story*, of a black cabaret performer (*Blonde Venus*'s "symbolic truth") emerges through the distortion of a distortion—a redoubling in which, as Slavoj Žižek might put it, distortion itself is distorted back into proportion.[24]

In a manner that inverts Sternberg's own prototypically modernist polemic that his films should be projected upside down to prevent story and characters from interfering with visual imagery, *Blonde Venus* thus gives the viewer cues to read its plot—that of a white European who crosses the Atlantic and launches a career as a cabaret performer in America by means of a primitivist stage act—"upside down." One of the strongest signals we are given to invert this basic story, generating the ghostly "anti-story" of a *black* American who crosses the Atlantic and launches a career in *Europe* as a cabaret performer by means of a primitivist stage act—the anti-story that *is*, I am arguing, the film's anamorphic portrait of Josephine Baker, the most famous transatlantic cabaret performer of not only her own time but arguably all time—is the primitivist stage act in the diegesis itself. "Hot Voodoo" is in fact a dizzying mise-en-abyme, in which an actress "discovered" in Germany and brought to America (Dietrich) plays a German actress in America (Helen) performing a theatrical act under a stage name (Blonde Venus), in which she undergoes metamorphosis, after entering on stage in a literally "apish" fashion (wearing a gorilla costume), into a persona with a blonde afro who sings a song about how a particular genre of song or music ("that African tempo") produces a metamorphosis in her persona or character—converting her from demure white woman to "African queen," from a person with a "conscience" to one who "want[s] to be bad!" (Figures 1–3).

"Hot Voodoo" is thus a strikingly overdetermined allegory of transformation. More specifically, it is an allegory of how a white woman's transformation into a performing artist/star, or, say, *Helen's* transformation into

Helen's multi-stage transformation into
"Marlene Dietrich" in a New York cabaret.

Marlene Dietrich (who is more truly, as Lea Jacobs argues, the Blonde
Venus), becomes predicated on a performance of racial, national, and cultural "reversals."[25] As an account, then, of the making of Blonde Venus (and
thus also an account, if we lean hard on the shared title, of the making of the
very film we are watching), *Blonde Venus*'s primitivist stage act suggests that
the film is in its largest and most abstract sense a film *about* reversal. There
is thus a sense in which the film invites us to perceive its story of a white
European's transformation into an American star as *already inverted*, such
that a story of a black American's transformation into a European star — as
epitomized in this iconic image of Baker from the 1934 French film *Zou Zou*

Josephine Baker playing the role
of a Parisian cabaret star in *Zou Zou*
(dir. Marc Allegret, 1934).

(Figure 4) — comes to haunt the former as its racial and national antithesis and double. And indeed, in a manner that anticipates Josephine Baker's
accusation of Dietrich's haunting of *her* as her double: "That German cow
has copied me all my life."

The highly stylized transformation of a white woman into a performing
artist/star allegorized in "Hot Voodoo," is also, however, predicated on a
more literal act of "aping." Here we should pause to ask: why does Helen's
metamorphosis into Dietrich require the preliminary step, prior to her im-
personation of the "African Queen," of aping a gorilla? We might immediately chalk this up to the film's reliance on a crudely racist metonymy: the
image of the ape is designed to function "atavistically," as a necessary pre-
quel to the intermediary image of African royalty that more directly facilitates the transition from Helen to Dietrich. However, if we read the ape, in
its apishness, as a figure not for the black primitive but for the very imitativeness of which Baker accused Dietrich, it could be argued that in aping
apishness, the Blonde Venus gestures at her indebtedness to some unspeci-
fied original *being* imitated or "aped." We thus have a redoubling in which
"apish imitation" itself is apishly imitated into difference, generating the
ironic distance on which parody depends — a redoubling that parallels the
convention of distorting a distorted image back to its correct proportions
in anamorphic portraiture. It is crucial to note here, however, that the target of the irony generated by the Blonde Venus's aping of apishness is less
some original "text" being copied (let us remember that this original is not
specified) than the general disposition or attitude of imitativeness itself.
Contrary to the way in which this scene is typically read, what the white
woman's aping seems to ridicule or criticize is not "blackness" (to say that

it does would in fact be to consent to and replicate the racist equation of human to ape) but a kind of *white* mimicry.

There are other, complementary ways of reading this scene. It could be argued, for instance, if we follow Michael Rogin's lead in *Blackface, White Noise*, that Helen's performance of blackness offers a way for the Paramount film to assimilate and Americanize the German immigrant played by Dietrich (and by extension, Dietrich herself).[26] The white subject plays "black"—or, more accurately, plays "African"—to secure an American identity: paradoxically, Helen/Dietrich's "Africanness" signifies Americanness. North's influential argument in *The Dialect of Modernism* offers another interpretation: that the European expatriate's highly stylized race-change becomes a way for her (and by extension, the film) to secure its *modernist* credentials. But if it is stressed that becoming "African" also paradoxically enables Helen to become Marlene Dietrich (reversing the conventional trajectory from reality to fiction in which actors are perceived to "become" their characters), becoming an "African queen" seems not only the way for a white immigrant to become a good modernist or a good American but a way for her to become a *star*. "Africanness" equals stardom—at least, if not especially, in the cabaret. This no less unproblematic equation is, of course, something to which Baker's own success as a primitivist performer attested.

My argument is thus that *Blonde Venus* generates its own anti-story, gives us multiple signals to subject its own plot structure to a reversal, by making the very process of reversal central to its story about the production of a "Blonde Venus" qua transatlantic female star. One could argue that the film in fact projects its story upside down to ensure that for all its insistent presence, the visually transfixing image of Dietrich—the image of an unmistakably white and European star—does not entirely obfuscate the portrait of her African American contemporary that the film simultaneously produces yet cannot quite bring itself to produce in a positive or undistorted fashion. The preoccupations with reversal established in "Hot Voodoo," the first musical performance of the film, come to a head in the last musical performance of the film—a scene set, significantly, in a Parisian cabaret, a cultural space marking Helen/Dietrich's final success, after she escapes poverty in the American South, as star of her own eponymous revue. For inversions in natural and social or conventional order—and a publicly announced ease or comfort with them—are explicitly thematized in the song sung by the new star of the *Super Revue Avec Helen Jones*: "I Couldn't Be Annoyed." Paralleling not just the manner in which the story of the Blonde Venus generates its own anti-story but also Dietrich's ability to invert praise into criticism, the song's lyrics (written by Dick Whiting) exaggerate the facility of "flipp[ing] the other side of the coin":

If everyone stood on their heads
And on their heads were shoes
I'd still eat crackers in my bed
What have I got to lose?

If you ate soup with a fork
Or if babies brought the stork
Do you think I'd care
I'd still declare
I couldn't be annoyed.[27]

If the film's story is that of a white European who becomes a "Blonde Venus" in America (the story of Helen/Dietrich), and its "anti-story" that of a black American who becomes a "Black Venus" in Europe (the story of Josephine Baker), then the scene of the Blonde Venus's *return* to the site of the Black Venus's origins—by 1932, nothing would signify "Josephine Baker" to film audiences more than a Parisian music hall—might be thought of as the crossroads of a narrative chiasmus, the moment in which the film's story and anti-story converge. And it is here, I would argue, that the film's "anamorphic" portrait of Baker comes most to the fore, in the form of a visual distortion. Recalling that catoptric anamorphoses in painting are traditionally made intelligible by conical or cylindrical mirrors, we might note that the Paris cabaret scene opens with a strikingly rounded, even fishbowl-like image of the stage where Helen/Dietrich stands. The visual field is given a distorted look that we might at first associate with wide-angle cinematography (Figure 5), until the camera draws back and reveals that the convex or warped effect stems from the grotesque design of the expressionist stage scenery (that is, stems from something in the world of the film's story) and is actually not a product of the photographic process or the camera's lens (Figure 6). A theatrical illusion in the diegesis, rather than a technical or cinematic trick, thus plays the role of the "distorting

5

6

Distortion in the depiction of Helen/ Dietrich on a Parisian stage.

mirror" that makes catoptric anamorphoses intelligible. And this suggests a tipping of the hat to the aesthetic power of revue theater in the one scene where the stories of Baker and Dietrich might be imagined to "meet" one another. What is fascinating about this scene is that the collision of inverted plots or narrative trajectories, of story and anti-story, produces a warping in the film's visual look or style. And it is in and as this narrative disturbance of style, I am arguing, that Baker's negative presence, as anti-story, most makes itself known.

The black international cabaret star's uncanny appearance — as a distorted distortion — in the scene featuring the white expatriate's triumphant success as star of a Parisian revue itself inverts an early scene in which the legacy of black stage performance comes to haunt the story of *Blonde Venus*. Both moments, like the "Hot Voodoo" performance, involve acts of renaming or transforming Dietrich's persona. When she pursues work on the American stage to earn money to pay for her husband's cure for radium poisoning, talent agent Ben Smith agrees to represent Helen Faraday ("Nah, we gotta get something different, something unusual!") on the condition that she be renamed Helen Jones. In the switch from Faraday to Jones,

Helen acquires a more "black" surname not only shared by Baker's fellow African American expatriate and famous cabaret owner Florence Jones but made most famous, *as* an African American surname, by the protagonist of Eugene O'Neill's "crossover" success *The Emperor Jones* (1920). Depicting the "atavistic" regression — or gradual primitivization — of colonial ruler and ex-Pullman porter Brutus Jones into an African savage, O'Neill's expressionist drama is often credited for creating the first important part for a black actor in America: Charles Gilpin, to be followed by Paul Robeson when the play was turned into a film.[28] Given that Helen's transformation into Jones is immediately followed by her own primitivist spectacle, in which she enters the stage aping an ape, the story of the primitivization of one Jones in *The Emperor Jones* (which was followed by O'Neill's play about a *white* primitive, *The Hairy Ape*, in 1922) could be said to provide a template for the primitivization of the other.

After Helen has been turned into Jones, Smith takes her to visit the theater owner who will eventually hire her on the condition that her name be changed again, to Blonde Venus. Becoming Blonde Venus requires passing through Jones, though Helen will eventually readopt the erased surname upon her triumph in Paris, as star of the *Super Revue Avec Helen Jones*. The scene marking the transition from Jones to Blonde Venus opens by showing the white theater producer, O'Connor, standing in front of an open rectangular window whose drawn curtains suggest the curtains of a stage. We see and hear an African American woman and man, framed by those drawn curtains and dressed in strangely anachronistic-looking clothing, talking audibly on a stoop raised just slightly, like a platform, above the window's bottom sill (Figure 7). O'Connor's negotiation with Smith over hiring Helen as the Blonde Venus begins only after he shuts the window (Figure 8), drowning out the dialogue of the African American actors on the "stage." He also turns his back to the actors — though because the window he has pulled down is transparent, their now silent performance continues to provide a theatrical backdrop for his negotiations (Figure 9).

Anticipating his erasure of the surname Jones, what the white producer allegorically shuts out — though not entirely successfully — in this second reinvention of Dietrich's character is a kind of black theater. And it is this black performance that becomes the "backgrounded text" (literally, as well as metaphorically) of *Blonde Venus*'s account of how a Blonde Venus is

The New York producer shuts out African American "theater" as Helen Jones is renamed "Blonde Venus."

made. The theater producer's exaggerated performance of excluding black performance also visually enacts a real elision made during the script's revisions by studio censors. As Lea Jacobs notes, the film's MPPDA case file contains a memo indicating that legal department official Harold Hurley was worried by the fact that in the first version (March 1932) of the script, Helen works in a *Harlem* nightclub, performing for *black* audiences (WS 89). The memo reads, "Mr. Hurley seems to share our [the Studio Relations Committee's] feeling that this would be questionable, especially in Southern States where such equality is frowned upon" (quoted in WS 89). As Jacobs notes, "There are several references to blacks, as well as a reference to Harlem, which are eliminated in the second and third versions of the script." In the March draft, for instance, the scene where O'Connor re-fashions Jones as Blonde Venus opens with this description of his theater's location: "A side street in the neighborhood of Lenox Ave and 135th St; show the exterior of the MAGNOLIA CLUB. Colored children are playing in the street; colored men and women are passing by." And in the original script, O'Connor is described as talking to "two colored girls" when Helen arrives with Smith; his office is also "covered with theatrical photographs, most of them young girls of all colors and in various stages of undress" (quoted in ws 177–78, n. 16). There is thus a sense in which this Hollywood film about a white chorus girl turned international revue star could be described as haunted not just by a single black female performer but by many. Yet apart from the "actors" excluded by O'Connor, in the released version of *Blonde Venus* the only diegetic remnant of the originally intended African-American specificity of the theatrical culture (from which both the fictional Blonde Venus *and* the Black Venus derive their beginnings) seems to be the black orchestra leader and bartender in the nightclub where Helen/Dietrich performs "Hot Voodoo" — figures who play, in a solitary and reduced form, the roles of black performer and black audience occluded from the final script.

Here we return to the issue raised by the Black Venus's spectral presence throughout *Blonde Venus*: the question of whether portraiture by means of inversion should be taken as a tribute or parody, as respectful or aggressive. The first possibility seems the most remote, given that inversion is not a formal strategy we conventionally associate with praise. It is certainly, however, one we conventionally associate with parody — Linda Hutcheon in fact suggests that "inversion is a characteristic of *all* parody" (TP 6). And from Pound's inversion of Dante's *Commedia* in *Hugh Selwyn Mauberley*, to Max Ernst's "Oedipal inversion" of Michelangelo's *Pieta* (in which the living mother and dead son in Michelangelo's original are replaced by a wooden father holding a living son), parody is — as Hutcheon notes, citing these examples — "the genre that has been described as both a symptom and a critical tool of the modernist episteme" (6, 2). As these and other examples of the "bitextual synthesis" so central to modernism demonstrate (and here we can add the appropriations of the *Odyssey* by Joyce, of opera by Brecht, of Elizabethan tragedy by Djuna Barnes, and of Ingres and Manet by Picasso), modernist parody involves a repetition that emphasizes difference rather than similarity (*TP* 33). For Hutcheon, it is this emphasis on difference that ultimately distinguishes parody from allusion, citation, pastiche, and other kinds of intertextuality: "While the act and form of parody are those of incorporation, its function is one of separation and contrast. Unlike imitation, quotation, or even allusion, parody requires that critical ironic distance" (34).

But while the necessity of separation and contrast would seem to reinforce the oft-perceived incompatibility of parody and praise, the modernist works above illustrate the central thesis of Hutcheon's study: that while parody is "a form of imitation . . . characterized by ironic inversion," the inversion is "not always at the expense of the parodied text" (6). The expansion of parody beyond the function of derision or ridicule, Hutcheon suggests, is in fact distinctive, if not exclusive, to modernism:

> [T]he critical distancing between the parody itself and its *backgrounded text* does not always lead to irony at the expense of the parodied work . . .
> [M]any parodies . . . do not ridicule the backgrounded texts but use them as standards by which to place the contemporary under scrutiny. The modernist verse of Eliot and Pound is probably the most obvious example of this kind of attitude, one that suggests almost a respectful or deferential ethos. (57)

The spatial or perspectival metaphor—background versus foreground—that informs Hutcheon's expanded concept of parody takes on particularly resonant meanings in *Blonde Venus*. If the film's backgrounded text is the story of chorus-girl-turned-international-cabaret-star Josephine Baker—or more precisely, if what *Blonde Venus* imitates and inverts is the story of Josephine Baker's transformation into the Black Venus—this backgrounded text has a "background" of its own: the artistic context or tradition from which Baker emerged and to which she owed her own eventual elevation into transatlantic stardom. But there are in fact two traditions or backgrounds behind the story of Black Venus: African American theater and the French music hall. Both traditions, significantly, are represented in the scenes involving the transformation of Helen/Dietrich's identity discussed above. This is emphasized by the fact that the visual backgrounds of these scenes are, in either a strongly literal or a metaphoric way, *theatrical backdrops*. Behind the white theater producer who will eventually remake Jones into the Blonde Venus is a "stage" with African American actors; behind Helen Jones in the Paris cabaret, as she launches into her song about inversions, is expressionist stage scenery recalling the exaggeratedly stylized and even cartoonish set designs for *La Revue Nègre* by Miguel Covarrubias, the caricaturist who famously depicted Carl Van Vechten in blackface. Both backdrops are used to suggest some kind of contestation between the mediums and traditions of cabaret theater and film.

This becomes particularly evident when the junglesque background of "Hot Voodoo," Helen/Dietrich's first diegetic performance of racial and cultural "reversals," begins to aggressively press into the film's foreground. As Nichols notes, though the "tropical décor motif begins as a theatrical backdrop for Helen's first stage number . . . as her career rises and then plummets during her flight from [her husband] Ned, the tropical motif begins to envelop her, on stage and off. What began as a stage role — a 'play' with lush imagery — becomes an existential trap whose imagery pervades her entire life" (*II* 125). Reinforcing the "intimacy between character and environment" produced by Sternberg's general preference for shallow compositions and unusually congested and cluttered frames,[29] the theatrical backdrop's struggle to take over the film's foreground not only parallels the *trompe l'oeil* in the Paris cabaret (where the expressionist stage scenery momentarily fools us into thinking that the distorted image we see is a cinema-specific effect) but suggests the same "privileging of the relationship of character to background or décor over the relationship between characters" produced by "the film's use of sequences dominated by one shot between characters who do not look directly at each other" (*II* 112). "As a corollary," Nichols notes, "changes in [background and décor] take on considerable significance." It is worth noting here that the mirrored background in the dressing room of the star of the Parisian *Super Revue Avec Helen Jones* is covered with highly stylized drawings of dancers — apparently drawn by Sternberg himself — strikingly reminiscent of Paul Colin's poster designs for *La Revue Nègre* and his lithographs of Baker in *Le Tumulte Noir*.

Hence while *Blonde Venus*, in addition to generating its own anti-story about the making of the Black Venus, paradoxically renders this "back-grounded text" intelligible by means of strenuous negations, reversals, and distortions, and while it simultaneously excises and preserves the African American specificity of Baker's own theatrical background by turning it, literally, into a theatrical backdrop, all these "backgrounds" and "backdrops" might be said to resist, in a strikingly antagonistic fashion, their formally subordinate position in Sternberg's film. Like Dietrich's clever flip-flopping of praise into criticism, the film absorbs and pays its respects to a competing medium; in a similar vein, it seems to simultaneously elevate and subordinate the story of Baker by generating it through negation and inversion. Like the highly stylized Busby Berkeley backstage musicals made for Warner's in the 1930s, the film demonstrates its superiority as a medium by its thematic/diegetic *incorporation* of theater, and yet this very act of dominating-by-incorporating appears to backfire as its backgrounded tradition pushes into the fore. In particular, the gradual seeping of the backdrop of the film's primitivist stage act into its nontheatrical reality, which becomes most pronounced when Helen abandons theater altogether and goes deeper and deeper into the American South, is paralleled by the fact that her racially ambiguous image as the white-afroed Blonde Venus or African Queen—a stage image that is not chosen or authored by Helen, as the scene in O'Connor's office makes clear, but rather "the design of others for the pleasure of others"—eventually becomes what Nichols also calls "a mask she cannot remove," pursuing her, in the form of a photograph on an FBI "Wanted" poster, as she heads South with her kidnapped son (*II* 125). As Nichols notes, "She is hunted *by* her stage appearance" (125, my italics).

Thus although African masking became a sign of *liberating* expatriation for modernists like Stein and Picasso, as North has persuasively argued, instrumentalized by the international avant-garde to intensify their rebellion against the mores and conventions of European and Anglo-American culture and "complete their defection from bourgeois society" (*DM* 67), there is a sense in which *Blonde Venus*, and its disobedient backgrounded texts in particular, suggests that "the role of the racial alien" may not be as flexible as it would seem—even for a professional or expert shape-shifter like Helen/Dietrich. In fact, the film suggests that far from completing any process of expatriation in a liberating sense, the African mask donned by Helen/Dietrich actually threatens an oppressive *repatriation*, in the sense of recapture by her husband and the law. The surprising inflexibility, even for a white performer, of the racial roleplaying central to the modernism of Pound, Stein, and Picasso is already anticipated by Sam Coslow's "Hot Voodoo" lyrics. While roughly half the lines sung by Helen/Dietrich equate her blonde-afroed persona's "Africanization" with some form of liberating release, either from social conventions or sexual or moral constraints ("Hot voodoo, makes me brave"), the other half equate racial masking with being intoxicated (not necessarily in a pleasurable way), under a spell, and generally subject to some form of external control ("That African tempo / has made me a slave"). At times, these depictions of freedom and slavery are made to alternate in a single verse or refrain.[30]

Is there, then, in the Black Venus's own relentless pursuit of Helen/ Dietrich throughout the film — in the aggressive efforts by a "backgrounded text" to overtake its parody — a retort to this instrumental use of "the role of racial alien" by whites? A critique of the avant-garde's effort to secure its revolt against European and American cultural traditions by claiming to be, as Pound put it, "the heirs of the witch doctor and voodoo"?[31] In any case, it should be noted that the reversals in *Blonde Venus* that simultaneously produce and suppress the story of the Black Venus are not exclusively racial. The relationship between the film's story and anti-story, the parody and its backgrounded text, is as strongly marked by a reversal of patterns of movement between nations, continents, and cultures. Inverting the trajectory of Baker's career, from her initial tour of the South with the Dixie Steppers on the all-black TOBA circuit, to all-black musicals on Broadway, to *La Revue Nègre* — the trajectory of a chorus girl who moves from the American South to New York to Europe — *Blonde Venus* tracks the movements of a chorus girl who moves from Europe to New York to the American South. As much preoccupied with the patterns of migration and immigration that "defined the new social base of Modernism" as with race, *Blonde Venus* might be said to flip the other side of the coin in more ways than one.[32]

Hence while the stylistic richness of *Blonde Venus* and all the optically stunning Sternberg-Dietrich films at Paramount do give some basis to the director's good modernist pronouncement that it would make no substantial difference to the viewer's aesthetic experience if his films were projected upside down (inviting, in turn, a good modernist interpretation of the film as a reflexive meditation on the internal properties of the cinematic medium), the aggressive resurfacing of *Blonde Venus*'s various theatrical "backgrounds" ultimately attests to the aesthetic power of the cabaret stage — the origin, foundation, and predominant site of production for Baker's own innovative and aesthetically powerful modernism, for all her later appearances in film and other media. If praise can take the form of a *respectful* "imitation characterized by ironic inversion," as in the affectively expanded concept of parody Hutcheon credits twentieth-century art forms with creating, we might say that *Blonde Venus*, the story of the making of an international cabaret star, is both an homage to and a parody of the life, career, and star-text of Josephine Baker—and that this "both/and" is aesthetically and ideologically nontrivial.

It is tempting to solidify my own bad or predominantly story-based reading of *Blonde Venus* by pointing out numerous correspondences between Baker and Dietrich—parallels drawn not just from extracinematic content but also from the ignoble content derived from mass genres like biographies, fan discourse, and gossip. I'll indulge myself in this vein in a footnote.[33] It is important to note, however, that both media icons became floating signifiers for just about any kind of racial, ethnic, or national otherness. Through a chain of visual and narrative metonymies (and in spite of her fair coloring and unmistakably German accent), Dietrich is presented as vaguely or figuratively "Arab" and "Chinese" in *Morocco* (1930) and *Shanghai Express* (1932); she becomes explicitly Russian in *The Scarlet Empress* (1934) and Spanish in *The Devil Is a Woman* (1935). Scholars have similarly remarked on Baker's "generalized ethnic exoticism," which allowed Kessler, in 1926, to imagine collaborating with Richard Strauss on a "half jazz, half Oriental" ballet version of *The Song of Solomon*, in which Baker, playing the role of the Shulamite, "would be dressed (or not dressed) on the lines of Oriental Antiquity" (*BL* 280). Though Baker's status as "generic" exotic also allowed her, in spite of her Americanness, to be named Queen of the Exposition Coloniale Internationale in 1930, as Elizabeth Coffman notes, her generalized ethnicity comes most to the fore in *Princess Tam-Tam* (directed by Edmond Greville, 1935), a film in which Baker plays Alwina, a Tunisian woman posing as an Indian princess to Parisian high society, and in which "all types of non-white ethnicity are collapsed into a generalized 'African' or 'Arab' or 'Oriental.' "[34] At the film's climax, which takes place in a Parisian revue theater, a jealous rival tricks a drunk Alwina into jumping out of the audience to join the dancers performing on stage. But this act of malice, designed to expose the princess's real identity as savage, backfires when Alwina's wild dancing is greeted by the Parisian audience with thunderous applause. In a striking parallel to Helen's "reverse" transformation into Marlene Dietrich during the performance of "Hot Voodoo," the dance number that draws Alwina in as an involuntarily "animated" participant (primitivizing the princess or "Africanizing" the regal "Indian" and simultaneously revealing her true identity *as a dancer* to the Parisian audience) is a strange mélange of "Mexican" and "African" themes (Figures 10–15). It is as if Alwina's final and eagerly awaited transformation into *Josephine Baker*, much to the satisfaction of both the French audience represented within the film and the French audience for whom it was intended, were a direct response to, or in some sense explicitly set off or "caused" by, this ironically distinctive representation of "ethnicity in general."

In spite of the ethnic and national fluidity associated as much with their personal lives as with their screen and stage images, Baker and Dietrich came to exemplify forms of failed repatriation.[35] Baker's highly anticipated and much publicized return to the United States to perform in the 1935 *Ziegfield Follies* was disastrously received by the mainstream American press and considered by herself to have been a terrible career mistake. Following her early departure from and much publicized refusal to return to Germany during the Second World War, which included turning down an invitation from Hitler to assume an executive position in the nationalized film industry, Dietrich experienced a similar reception from the German public on her return to Berlin for a 1960 concert tour: "They didn't want me. They were angry with me. . . . They claimed, 'She left us. She didn't want us.'"[36] And since the image of Dietrich as having "rejected" Germany persisted among Germans long after the war, as Gertrud Koch has noted, the elaborate funeral ceremony planned in Berlin, where Dietrich requested to be buried, had to be called off because state officials were unsure how her "return" would be welcomed.[37] These moments of thwarted transnationalism eerily parallel the miscarriage of the attempt by Sternberg, once known widely as a Hollywood moviemaker, to refashion himself as an international director by making films he perceived as homages to the countries featured in them. Though in his autobiography he notes that he designed *The Devil Is a Woman*, originally titled *Capriccio Espagnol* and adapted from a Pierre Louÿs novel by John Dos Passos, as "an affectionate salute to Spain and its traditions" (*FCL* 266–67), his cinematic "salute to the Spanish people" was banned by the pre-Franco Spanish government. Not only was *Shanghai Express* banned in China, but Sternberg was told he would be arrested

if he entered the country on further occasions. The outcome of Sternberg's efforts to praise the people and traditions of other nations thus might be described in the same words he uses to describe Dietrich's aggressive praise of himself: "[it] sparked a detonation that backfired on me."

As *Experimental Cinema* critic B. G. Braver-Mann acidly noted in 1934, "Sternberg is no different than his directorial contemporaries in Holly-wood whom he regards patronizingly." Like the author of "Leonardo of the Lenses," Braver-Mann describes Sternberg as a "pictorialist" rather than montagist or filmmaker proper—for Braver-Mann, however, the term is pejorative. He gives the screw a further twist by adding, "Beside . . . the

Alwina's transformation into "Josephine Baker" on a Parisian stage in *Princess Tam-Tam* (dir. Edmond Greville, 1935).

images of Dovzhenko, Dreyer, or Eisenstein, [his] little pictorial talent is analogous to an insipid magazine illustration."[38] As a twentieth-century artist whose innovations in her primary medium, dance, were framed by an entertainment industry that always kept her modernist credentials slightly suspect, Baker was placed in a position strikingly similar to *Blonde Venus*'s director. Both Baker and Sternberg, significantly, were primarily concerned with *abstracting movement*. As Braver-Mann noted, "[Sternberg] *moves* rather than *cuts*, which is typical of all directors who build their films either in the non-cinematic pictorial or the semi-theatre traditions of the motion picture" (*S* 31–32).[39] Paralleling Sternberg's claim that "the motion picture's most important asset is that the images are in motion . . . a film is built out of a *succession* of mobile images, each replacing the last" (313, 315), in a February 1926 entry from his diaries, Kessler notes that "Miss Baker danced with brilliant . . . purity of style . . . performing an intricate series of movements without ever losing the basic pattern . . . for hours on end, without tiring and continually inventing new figures" (279). Drawing on this entry, Hans Gumbrecht describes Baker's dancing as "a pure surface phenomenon consisting of endless varieties of forms"—a reading that doubles as a description of Sternberg's oft-noted obsession with sliding and layered surfaces, abstract patterns of movement, and dynamic plays of light and darkness.[40] The implication here is that Baker's dancing, like Sternberg's movies, could be inverted without much aesthetic loss to a good modernist viewer; as Janet Lyon notes, "Josephine Baker's dance qua dance followed the anti-representational contours of [most of her contemporaries's] avant-garde projects" (*JBH* 40). Pushing the argument further, Lyon provocatively argues that as "pure surface phenomenon," Baker's experimental dancing "resisted the interpretative act" to such an extent that it subverted attempts to anchor the "primitiveness" of her dancing in race or racialist paradigms: "For . . . if her rhythmic 'wildness' did not 'mean' anything other than an inexhaustible improvisational ability . . . then her figure could not coherently anchor the binarism of wildness and civilization on which colonial ideology depended" (41).

Yet in contrast to Gumbrecht's and Lyon's interpretation of Baker's dancing as desemanticized, asignifying, purely formal play, critics like Wendy Martin have read her dancing as already parodying the modernist obsession with the primitive body as well as conventions of American blackface minstrelsy. Martin argues, for instance, that Baker's deliberate manipulation of primitivist conventions "to gain a measurable amount of control over her audience" in *La Revue Nègre* was prefigured by her earlier performance in Sissle and Blake's *Shuffle Along*, where "she rolled her eyes, contorted her face, and swiveled her body in a deliberate parody of the blackface vaudeville routines and the conventions of the Negro minstrel show" (313, 311).[41] The Black Venus's entire career, Martin suggests, could in fact be read as a "trajectory from parodic savagery to parodic royalty" (314). Though Martin identifies parody with ridicule and does not extend its ethos to include the respect or admiration associated with praise, her reading provocatively suggests that *Blonde Venus* might be read as a parody of the story of a brilliant parodist. But if *Blonde Venus* is also, in some sense, an homage to the Black Venus, why does it go to such lengths to ensure that the latter's portrait appears only upside down, as anti-story or as an oblique distortion? If the inverted imitation of the story of Baker is genuinely respectful, why the need for such unusually strenuous, even overstrained acts of negation and reversal?

There is a generous as well as skeptical way of answering this question — though in both cases we can presume that the film's formal difficulties in praising Baker ensue from discrepancies in power and cultural capital related to race. One has to be suspicious that this Hollywood film, on which the struggling Paramount Corporation relied heavily to thwart its impending bankruptcy, simply cannot bring itself to pay tribute to a black expatriate, not to mention a female entertainer in a competing medium and national tradition, in the racist climate of the 1930s. But we might also suspect that the very overwroughtness of the film's inversions, the excessively labored quality of its negations and reversals, enable it to problematize its *right* to praise Baker — in the same way that *The Band Wagon*, according to Stanley Cavell, raises the question of Fred Astaire's right to praise African American dance.[42] For the act of paying tribute to another text or tradition, by imitating or even parodying it, immediately becomes problematic when the praised object is, for one reason or another, a socially or historically subordinated text or tradition. Hence in the case of a white art form that praises (by directly or overtly imitating) a black art form or tradition, any respect and admiration, however intended or encoded *as* intent, will inevitably risk nonrecognition, being readable only as ridicule or naked appropriation. The parody/praise also risks appearing patronizing or presumptuous, as if it assumes its evaluation or comment on the "backgrounded text," however positive, to be an unquestionable prerogative. Paying tribute, in this case, veers dangerously close to an assertion of cultural entitlement, if not mastery or domination. Hence we might speculate that *Blonde Venus*'s inversions become necessary to avoid the problem of what Cavell calls vain or blasphemous praise, where what is to be considered is whether the subject is entitled to praise the object, or whether the very act of giving praise is "earned or acceptable." Cavell distinguishes this problem from "false" praise or idolatry, where the question is whether the object *deserves* to be praised, or whether the praise given is "sufficient or accurate" (66). It is not surprising that Sternberg, a personage we certainly can't accuse of excessive humility, implies that Dietrich is guilty of the blasphemous rather than idolatrous variety.

> In Argentina, in Las Vegas, in Wiesbaden, in Paris, wherever it may be, she *waves the banner of her indebtedness*, includes me in her act, and since few are familiar with even the most rudimentary functioning of a film director, *has almost succeeded in making me a subsidiary requisite.* Her constant praise is rated as one of her admirable virtues — by others, not me. (*FCL* 224–25)

It could be argued that *Blonde Venus* cannot "wave the banner of its indebtedness" to the story of the Black Venus as overtly as Dietrich supposedly does to Sternberg, and must for this reason rely on its exaggerated and at times overstrained reversals, because to do so might too nakedly disclose the uneasy proximity between praise and domination. To humbly or virtuously wave a banner of indebtedness to the life and career of Josephine Baker, in other words, by portraying her explicitly and without distortion, would be to risk reducing the film's story of the cabaret star to a "subsidiary requisite" — another form of mastery by incorporation.

It could also be argued that the negativity of Baker's portrait in *Blonde Venus* strategically protects her from being reduced to a modernist theme or motif. The film's insistence on presenting Baker as *anti*-story rather than story, its refraining from paying tribute to her in a positive or direct fashion, might be understood as a critical response to the extent to which Baker became "obvious previous iconography" for the parodic works of other modernists — to the extent to which her image or portrait became a way of signaling the modernism of others. Baker posed for Pablo Picasso, though no images of her by him survive; her portrait also appeared in wire sculptures by Alexander Calder, in essays by Kurt Weill and Nancy Cunard, and in Gertrude Stein's 1928 *Useful Knowledge*, "A story of the Three of you Josephine Baker Maud de Forest and Ida Lewelyn and Mr. and Mrs. Paul Robeson and as they never met and as they never met."[43] Baker was also the occasion/inspiration of a house design by Adolf Loos ("the outwall is covered with crosslined black and white marble slabs"),[44] set designs by Covarrubias, costume and ballet designs by Le Corbusier, and in a particularly sweet, if not particularly lofty tribute, a pudding recipe invented by Alice B. Toklas called "Custard Joséphine Baker" (in which the primary ingredient was bananas).[45] Though the portraiture of modernists by fellow modernists in their coterie was, of course, a familiar practice — the best-known example being Picasso's portrait of Stein and Stein's portrait of Picasso — *Blonde Venus*'s story of a female cabaret star's struggle for control over her image, a struggle that could only be intensified in the case of the *black* performer, suggests a more cautious attitude about such overt acts of portraiture as homage.

This reading of *Blonde Venus* as an inverted homage to the Black Venus, which is based on a complexity in its story rather than visual style, is partly intended to foreground an intimate and even dialectical relationship between modernism as critical reading practice and modernism as aesthetic or cultural object. If aesthetic modernism has become institutionalized as the disruption of routinized expectations on the part of producers and audiences, and modernist criticism as a rebellion against reading artworks from "the usual in-front and straight-ahead position," it is paradoxically when one chooses a decidedly unmodernist way of approaching *Blonde Venus* — an approach that, say, turns on the film's plot rather than its visual elements, on extra-medial discourse rather than its medium specificity — that unnoticed dimensions of the aesthetic object suddenly rise to the foreground, much like an anamorphic design, or the various theatrical backdrops competing for attention in the film itself. In other words, since modernism has become a canonized style of interpreting aesthetic objects as well as of making them, a bad version of such interpretation might disclose new or previously unsuspected examples of such making — examples that might, in turn, provide ways of addressing the critique of aesthetic modernism's institutional rigidification. (Such critiques would include Raymond Williams's insistence, as summarized by Tony Pinkney, that "Modernism as a historical and cultural phenomenon cannot possibly be grasped by brands of [theory and criticism] which, in a self-serving circularity, are actually born out of its own procedures and strategies."[46])

The bad modernism of such a reading inheres also in the fact that it may seem to appraise or even "praise" its object too much. In other words, it is easy to object that understanding *Blonde Venus* as an inverted homage to, rather than mere appropriation of, the Black Venus is too generous, or

insufficiently aggressive, to be good *criticism*. Yet as the confrontation between Baker, Dietrich, and Sternberg staged at the opening of this essay
reminds us, criticism and praise are not as incompatible as one might think.
There is a sense, then, in which it would be appropriate for me to close by
echoing the closing line of "Hot Voodoo" sung by Helen/Dietrich: "I want
to be bad!" However, I will instead give the last word—or parting shot—to
her unceremoniously ousted rival Taxi, the greatest skeptic in and we could
even say *of* the film. We might even imagine Taxi's comment as spoken on
Josephine Baker's behalf. "So you're the Blonde Venus. Don't tell me you
thought of that label all by yourself!"

Notes

This essay is dedicated to Stanley Cavell, whose work on problematic praise has been its
primary inspiration. I am grateful to my research assistant, Caley Horan, and the Feminist Studies Program at Stanford University for providing the summer research grant
(2001) that enabled us to work together. Thanks also to Mark McGurl, Arthur Knight,
Rebecca Walkowitz, and Doug Mao for their critical comments and insights.
1. Jean-Claude Baker and Chris Chase, *Josephine: The Hungry Heart* (New York: Random
House, 1993), 456. Hereafter designated as *HH*.
2. Josef von Sternberg, *Fun in a Chinese Laundry* (New York: Macmillan, 1965), 254.
Hereafter referred to as FCL.
3. The moniker "International Star of the Screen" appears in an ad for Baker's first full-
length sound film, *La Sirène des Tropiques* (dir. Mario Nalpas, 1927), carried in the St.
Louis newspaper *The Argus*. Cited in *HH*, 164.
4. Linda Hutcheon, *A Theory of Parody: The Teachings of Twentieth Century Art Forms*
(Urbana: University of Illinois Press, 2000), 33. Hereafter designated as TP. John Fowles,
The Ebony Tower (Boston: Little, Brown, 1974), 18; cited in TP, 33.
5. For more detailed accounts of *Blonde Venus*'s production history—and its significant
effects on the eventual fate of Paramount Publix Corporation—see Peter Baxter, *Just
Watch! Sternberg, Paramount and America* (London: BFI, 1993), 39–69; and Lea Jacobs,
"Something Other Than a Sob Story," *The Wages of Sin: Censorship and the Fallen Woman
Film, 1928–1942* (Berkeley: University of California Press, 1995), 85–105. Jacobs makes the
fascinating argument that contrary to what one might expect, efforts by studio and industry censors to "soften" aspects of the film's fallen woman narrative did not conflict
with, but actually supported and enhanced, Sternberg's elliptical directorial style.
6. Reinforcing a reading of the film as an allegory of the production of female stardom
(a portrait of Dietrich), or even as a parable of the American studio system's capacity
to assimilate female foreignness and turn European immigrants into stars (a portrait of

Paramount Publix Corporation as auteur), numerous other parallels between Dietrich and Helen abound, at times strategically amplified (if not overtly manufactured) by the studio. Paralleling Helen's usurpation of Nick Townsend's former actress-paramour Taxi (Rita La Roy), a lawsuit against Dietrich for the alienation of Sternberg's affection filed by actress Riza Royce, his divorced American wife, increased tabloid speculations of a romantic involvement between director and star. In May 1932, moreover, when the script for *Blonde Venus* was undergoing its first major revisions, an anonymous extortion note threatening to kidnap Dietrich's daughter—leading to what *the Los Angeles Times* called an "intense search for the author"—would have eerily prefigured the film's kidnapping subplot for viewers when it opened in September. And perhaps suspiciously so, as Peter Baxter suggests: "It is just possible that the whole affair was a publicity stunt," invented to bolster Dietrich's image as a devoted mother in preparation for her role in the forthcoming woman's picture (*Just Watch*, 134). It was likely that Paramount saw this domestic image as sorely needing fortification of some sort, given that Dietrich had exclusively played tarts, prostitutes, and transients in her four previous films with Sternberg: Lola Lola in *The Blue Angel*, Amy Jolly in *Morocco*, X-27 in *Dishonored*, and Shanghai Lily in the box-office success *Shanghai Express*.

7. Bill Nichols, *Ideology and the Image: Social Representation in the Cinema and Other Media* (Bloomington: Indiana University Press, 1981), 125. Hereafter designated as *II*.

8. E. Ann Kaplan, "Fetishism and the Repression of Motherhood in Von Sternberg's *Blonde* Venus (1932)," in *Women and Film: Both Sides of the Camera*, ed. E. Ann Kaplan (New York: Methuen, 1983), 49–60, 56. As Kaplan notes, Johnny is consistently associated with aggressive forms of illusion and artifice, such as grotesque male masks and phallic toys like guns, trumpets, and crocodiles.

9. Since these parallels between Sternberg and Johnny can also be reinforced biographically, as Sternberg was the child of European immigrants raised by his mother, it may be worth noting that during the first major revisions of *Blonde Venus* in the spring of 1932 (and around the same time as the anonymous kidnapping threat that placed Dietrich in the spotlight), the director commissioned a portrait of himself from Mexican muralist David Alfaro Siqueiros, adding it to a collection of international art that already included works by experts of modernist portraiture such as Schiele, Picasso, and Modigliani. Siqueiros was also known as a favorite painter of Sergei Eisenstein, who was on tour in the Americas when the portrait of Sternberg was comissioned. On Siqueiros's influence on Sternberg, and the history of their relationship, see Baxter, *JW*, 178–91.

10. That fame and notoriety were reinforced in 1932 when Baker sang "Si J'Etais Blanche" in a blonde wig at the Casino de Paris. *HH*, 177.

11. Phyllis Rose, *Jazz Cleopatra: Josephine Baker in Her Time* (New York: Doubleday, 1989), 92; E. E. Cummings, "Vive La Folie! An Analysis of the *Revue* in General and the Parisian Revue in Particular," *Vanity Fair*, September 1926, 55. Cited in Rose, 94.

12. Harry Kessler, *Berlin in Lights: The Diaries of Count Harry Kessler: 1918–1937* (New York: Grove Press, 1999), 282. As Kessler notes in this same entry (February 17, 1926),

"The same [mixture of jungle and skyscraper elements in the negro revues] holds good for the tone and rhythm of their music, jazz. Ultramodern and ultraprimitive. The extremes they bridge render their style compulsive, just as it does with the Russians."

13. On Baker as "modernist hostess" and the Parisian nightclub as salon, see Janet Lyon, "Josephine Baker's Hothouse," in *Modernism, Inc: Body, Memory, Capital,* ed. Jani Scandura and Michael Thurston (New York: New York University Press, 2001), 29–47. Hereafter designated as JBH.

14. Cited in Henry Louis Gates Jr. and Karen C. C. Dalton, introduction to *Josphine Baker and La Revue Nègre: Paul Colin's Lithographs of* Le Tumulte Noir *in Paris, 1927* (New York: Henry Abrams, 1998), 7.

15. After appearing in two silent shorts based on the *Folies-Bergère* revue (1926, 1927), Baker starred in *La Sirène des Tropiques* (dir. Mario Nalpas, 1927), on which Luis Buñuel worked as an assistant director; its American premiere, in September 1929 at the Lafayette Theater in Harlem, was attended by New York City mayor James Walker.

16. For a critique of the traditional way of understanding "medium specificity," and Clement Greenberg's articulation of it with modernism, see Rosalind Krauss, *"A Voyage on the North Sea": Art in the Age of the Post-Medium Condition* (London: Thames and Hudson, 1999).

17. Aeneas Mackenzie, "Leonardo of the Lenses," *Life and Letters Today* 14, no. 2 (1936): 170–75; rpt. in Peter Baxter, ed., *Sternberg* (London: BFI, 1980), 43.

18. "Were I to instruct others how to use the camera, the first step would be . . . to project a film upside down . . . [so] that the actors and story become no longer noticeable, so that the values produced by the camera alone could not escape study (FCL, 325). This oft-quoted pronouncement (appearing most famously in Laura Mulvey's "Visual Pleasure and Narrative Cinema") is located just above a paragraph in which Sternberg states that "the [camera's] greatest asset, superb and unique, is motion" (325).

19. Though critics like Jacobs and Nichols have also argued that visual style and narrative strategy are consciously *integrated* in the Sternberg-Dietrich films, Gaylyn Studlar notes that even arguments on behalf of cohesion assume that style dominates and takes precedence over the latter. See Studlar, *In the Realm of Pleasure: Von Sternberg, Dietrich, and the Masochistic Aesthetic* (Urbana: University of Illinois Press, 1988), 110.

20. Michael North, *The Dialect of Modernism: Race, Language, and Twentieth-Century Literature* (Oxford: Oxford University Press, 1994), 67. Hereafter referred to as DM.

21. For more on the concept of black stardom and its relation to the American "race" films of the 1920s and 30s, see Arthur Knight, "Star Dances: African-American Constructions of Stardom, 1925–1960," in *Classic Hollywood, Classic Whiteness*, ed. Daniel Bernardi (Minneapolis: Univ. of Minnesota Press, 2001), 386–414, and also Knight's *Disintegrating the Musical: Black Performance and American Musical Film* (Durham and London: Duke University Press, 2002), especially " 'Aping' Hollywood: Deformation and Mastery in *The Duke is Tops* and *Swing!*," 169–194.

22. Aeneas MacKenzie, "Leonardo of the Lenses," 43.

23. Philip Kent, "What is Anamorphosis?" (website), http://www.anamorphosis.com/.

24. This sentence borrows the syntax of Slavoj Žižek's comment on the Platonic fear of "imitation of imitation." See *For They Know Not What They Do: Enjoyment as a Political Factor* (London: Verso, 1991), 15.

25. Lea Jacobs, *The Wages of Sin*, 102.

26. Michael Rogin, *Blackface, White Noise: Jewish Immigrants in the Hollywood Melting Pot* (Berkeley; University of California Press, 1996).

27. "I Couldn't Be Annoyed"; music by Leo Robin, lyrics by Dick Whiting.

28. Normand Berlin, *Eugene O'Neill* (New York: Grove Press, 1982), 61.

29. Carole Zucker, *The Idea of the Image: Josef von Sternberg's Dietrich Films* (London: Associated University Presses, 1988), 20.

30. I am grateful to Adeline Azrack, a student in my "Gender and American Cinema" course at Stanford (Fall 2000), for this observation.

31. Ezra Pound, "The New Sculpture," *Egoist*, February 16, 1914: 67–68. Cited in *DM* 67.

32. Tony Pinkney, "Editor's Introduction: Modernism and Cultural Theory," in Raymond Williams, *The Politics of Modernism: Against the New Conformists*, ed. Tony Pinkney (London: Verso, 1989), 15. Hereafter referred to as *PM*.

33. Josephine Baker became a friend of Berlin theater director Max Reinhardt in the late 1920s; in the early 1920s, Marlene Dietrich was enrolled as a student in his famous dramatic school. Both were intimates with Paris cabaret performer Maurice Chevalier (Dietrich was his lover, Baker was his co-star). And biographers Jean-Claude Baker and Chris Chase inform us that upon Baker's return to Paris from Algiers in 1944, "Her apartment on Avenue Bugeaud had been allocated to Jean Gabin, who was sharing it with his current lover, Marlene Dietrich. Josephine felt possessive not only about the apartment, but about Gabin, who played her brother in *Zou Zou* [Marc Allegret, 1934]. 'When I think that German cow is sleeping in my blue satin sheets!' she raved" (*HH* 263). Nasty (and apocryphal) comments about "German cow" notwithstanding, there are accounts of Baker and Dietrich socializing pleasantly together in Paris in 1937—the year of Baker's performance in *En Super Folies*. Strongly committed to anti-Nazism, both women worked for the French Resistance and entertained Allied troops during World War II, for which they both received medals from the French Legion of Honor.

34. Elizabeth Coffman, "Uncanny Performances in Colonial Narratives: Josephine Baker in *Princess Tam Tam*," *Paradoxa* 3, nos. 3–4 (1997): 379–94, 379.

35. It may also be worth noting here that while Baker was mother to her "Rainbow Tribe," which began, as she requested in a memo to friend Miki Sawada, with the adoption of "a Japanese, a black from South Africa, an Indian from Peru, a Nordic child, and an Israelite" (*HH* 326), Dietrich, as noted in her daughter Maria's biography, was the obsessed "mother" of two black and Chinese dolls, given to her by Sternberg and featured prominently (for no obvious, narratively motivated reason) in the mise en scène of both *Morocco* and *The Blue Angel*. See Maria Riva, *Marlene Dietrich* (New York: Alfred A. Knopf, 1993), 70–73.

36. Dietrich, interview with Maximilian Schell in *Marlene* (dir. Schell, 1984).

37. Gertrud Koch, "Exorcised: Marlene Dietrich and German Nationalism," in *Women* *and Film: A Sight and Sound Reader*, ed. Pam Cook and Philip Dodd (London: Scarlet Press, n.d.), 10–15.

38. B. G. Braver-Mann, "Josef Von Sternberg," *Experimental Cinema* 1, no. 5 (1934): 17–21; rpt. in Baxter, ed., *Sternberg*, 28–34.

39. As we have seen, Mackenzie makes a similar observation about Sternberg's reliance on movement *within* the shot, with this camera mobility "substituted for the 'cutting' process of montage." "Leonardo of the Lenses," 43.

40. Hans Ulrich Gumbrecht, *In 1926: Living at the Edge of Time* (Cambridge, Mass.: Harvard University Press, 1997), 67; cited in Janet Lyon, JBH, 40–41.

41. Wendy Martin, "'Remembering the Jungle': Josephine Baker and Modernist Parody," in *Prehistories of the Future: The Primitivist Project and the Culture of Modernism*, ed. Elazeur Barler and Ronald Bush (Stanford, Calif.: Stanford University Press, 1995), 310–25. Martin's comment points to, without directly addressing, the artistic difficulty of exaggerating a form or genre that is inherently dependent on exaggerations. This raises another question: to the predominantly white audiences of this Broadway musical, would Baker's performance have been recognizable as a parody with a critical ethos?

42. Stanley Cavell, "Fred Astaire Asserts the Right to Praise" in *Philosophy the Day After Tomorrow* (Cambridge: Harvard University Press, 2005), 61–82.

43. Gertrude Stein, *Useful Knowledge* (New York: Payson and Clarke, 1928), 60. Cited in Bryan Hammond and Patrick O'Connor, *Josephine Baker* (London: Jonathan Cape, 1988), 52.

44. Paul Groenendijk, *Adolf Loos huis voor Jospehine Baker*, cited in Hammond and O'Connor, *Josephine Baker*, 53. Though the Josephine Baker House in Paris was never built, Loos would eventually come to quote its design in his World Savings and Loan Association building in Santa Ana, California.

45. Alice B. Toklas, *The Alice B. Toklas Cookbook* (New York: Anchor Books, 1960), 127. Cited in Hammond and O'Conner, *Josephine Baker*, 52.

46. Tony Pinkney, "Introduction," from Raymond Williams, *The Politics of Modernism*, 3.

Monica L. Miller

The Black Dandy as Bad Modernist

Listening and Looking for Black Modernism

In his first disquisition on African American modernism, *Modernism and the Harlem Renaissance* (1989), Houston Baker sets out to save black America's first modernist movement, the Harlem Renaissance, from consideration as a modernist failure. In order to do so, he identifies Afro-American modernism as a movement separate from modernism, a move that he later revises and with which I will disagree. For Baker, in 1989, modernism is associated with the following "successful" "objects or processes": the "collaged allusiveness of T. S. Eliot's *The Waste Land* and Joyce's *Ulysses*, the cubist reveries of Picasso, the imagism of Pound, the subversive politics of the surrealists."[1] Because modernism is so much the product of a "bourgeois, characteristically twentieth-century, white Western mentality," it is a record of the breakdown of the cultural confidence of "an assumed supremacy of boorishly racist, indisputably sexist, and unbelievably wealthy Anglo-Saxon males," rather than a "threat" to "the towers of civilization."[2] This modernism is not only elitist and inviolable but, as such, irrelevant to the cultural condition of those, such as African Americans, for whom there is not the luxury or "need to pose, in ironical Auden-esque ways, questions such as 'Are we happy? Are we content? Are we free?'"[3] In *Modernism and the Harlem Renaissance*, Baker insists that in order to recognize the way in which the Harlem Renaissance's artists and intellectuals may have had success in "defining themselves in 'modern' terms," we must "listen" for the modern in the Harlem Renaissance, the emergence and critical use of "*modern Afro-American sound*, as a function of a *specifically* Afro-American discursive practice."[4] For Baker, this sound of Afro-American modernism emerges as black artists learn the "mastery of form" and "the deformation of mastery," the former beginning with black-authored confrontations with the representational strategies of blackface minstrelsy, the latter with a turn to indigenous art forms, particularly the blues, as a basis for an "authentic" black modern identity.

In his most recent discourse on modernism, *Turning South Again: Re-Thinking Modernism/Re-Reading Booker T.* (2001), Baker changes his mind about that which would be the "marker" of black modernism and, as a result, the very definition of modernism itself. He will no longer listen for a separate black modernism or that which sounds or seems authentically or *"specifically"* black,[5] but will rather look for modernism in examples of "the achievement of a life-enhancing and empowering public sphere mobility and economic mobility of the black majority."[6] This change in his definition of modernism, from the sociocultural to the more political, and the change in his methodology in seeking it, from listening to looking, bring him, surprisingly, to the figure of the black dandy. In particular, he finds this revised black modernism in the dandyism and performativity of Booker T. Washington. Baker reads Washington's dandyism — his performativity and ambivalence — as dangerous and even "treacherous."[7] For him dandyism can be only this because Washington "performs" in his white father's "weeds," "the black dandy (kid-gloved ghost of the 'educated black man' in the white imaginary) . . . all dressed up without any fully modern, urban place to go."[8] Baker calls this Washington's "mulatto modernism" "a bourgeois, middle-class individualism, vestimentary and hygienic impeccability, oratorical and double-conscious race pride and protonationalism."[9] According to Baker, this dandyism prevents modernist possibilities for the black majority as well as any productive connection between modernism in black and white.

Though Baker would dismiss the black dandy and his mulatto nature as an example of the failure of African America to reach the "modern," I will argue that looking to an alternative history of black dandies and dandyism does disclose a certain black modern identity and a potential for mobility in a world grappling with an "acknowledgement of radical uncertainty"[10] in a newly established urban locale — Harlem, the "Negro capital of the world." A few years after Washington's death, we can see Harlemites practicing a

The Black Dandy as Bad Modernist

different, more subversive dandyism that helps us to revise this perception of both black or mulatto modernism and modernism generally as exclusive phenomena. This alternative history establishes the black dandy as a figure with both European and African/American origins, who expresses with his performative body and dress the fact that modern identity, in both black and white, is necessarily syncretic, or mulatto, but in a liberating, rather than constraining, way. For both Baker and myself, the black dandy figure is a sign of "bad" modernism, but how we read that dandy and his mulatto nature in the early twentieth century matters much for our respective analyses of his effectiveness as a modernist sign. For Baker, dandyism is betrayal and "mulatto modernism" is "bad" in the sense that it has no group objective. For me, the dandyism that erupted in early-twentieth-century Harlem is not a group performance of whiteness or staged for the benefit of the individual only but rather a visible sign of the modern black imaginary, a kind of "freedom dream."[11] This other dandy's particular history, his syncretic and palimpsestic nature, enables the figure to display a knowingness about representation; this knowingness makes the "look" of black modernism much more complicated than an explanation of white imitation suggests.

Because their provenance and escapades in fiction both permit and disturb the fit between European and African American modernism, the black dandies that I find in Harlem will allow me to argue for a certain presence of a black modern consciousness. The suitability and dissonance of the black dandy figure as a modernist or black modernist marker — ironically through his anti-essentialist character — generate a productive struggle between the movements, rather than a separation between them or the denial of the very existence of Harlem's modernist moment. Such a tension identifies black modernism, with the black dandy as its sign, as that which challenges the conventional wisdom about modernism's success and the subsequent failure of the Harlem Renaissance, just as it enables their mutual redefinition. The "mixed" origins of the movement and its dandy connect African American modernism and modernism indelibly. By concentrating on the dandy figure as appropriated and articulated by African Americans who sought to define their own modernity, I aim to demonstrate the importance of the black dandy's failure to embody authenticity of race and culture and thus create fixity of these ideas. Although deeply regrettable and trouble-some to Harlem Renaissance architects as well as to more contemporary critics, this failure to espouse or promulgate a blackness that could be pack-aged as "the" or "a" New Negro aesthetic is precisely that which identifies the movement as a success.[12]

Dandy History—in White and Black

As a social practice that mounts a critique against the hierarchies that order society, dandyism appears to be a phenomenon naturally suited to blacks experiencing an attempted erasure or reordering of their identities in the slave trade and its aftermath.[13] For example, in order to survive the inhu-manity of slavery, those Africans arriving in England, America, or the West Indies had to fashion new identities, make the most out of the little that they were given—and significantly, their new lives nearly always began with the issuance of a new set of clothes. To back up a little: even from dandy-ism's beginnings in late 1700s Europe, a dandy's "look," the clothing on his performative body, has always signified more than excessive attention to personal style. As Ellen Moers implicitly argues in the standard volume on European dandyism, *The Dandy: Brummell to Beerbohm*, whether heir to the austere dandy père Beau Brummell or acolyte of the more decadent Beerbohm, the dandy uses his characteristic style and charisma to distin-guish himself when privileges of birth, wealth, and social standing might be absent. Dandies are people who have made themselves "an independent somebody," those who have a "self-fashioned nobility."[14] Moers and other historians of dandies identify the dandy's genius as precisely this ability to find power and influence in an attitude generated from the pointed deploy-ment of the everyday object of clothing, to communicate self-possession and self-creation. Therefore, dandyism is nothing less than symbolic of the transition between hierarchies of "wealth and birth" and the oppor-tunities afforded by "style and pose."[15] As a potentially socially and cul-turally critical and subversive practice, dandyism requires a sense of self-possession and self-consciousness about style as a combination of dress and attitude that signifies "dignity, elegance, refinement, self-control, pride and lucidity."[16] It is this extra-sartorial perspicuity concerning social position and its manipulation, above all, that enables the dandy to capitalize on moments of transition, to access the "power to fascinate, to puzzle, to travel, to persist and figure in an ambiguous social situation in a revolutionary climate."[17]

With this Brummellian beginning, dandies and dandyism took many forms (as actual people, as fictional characters and caricatures, as ascetics and flamboyants), crossed geographic boundaries (between England and France and back again; across the Atlantic), and became symbolic of border crossings in terms of class lines, gender roles, sexualities, and (later) racial identities. In addition to a talent for incisive social and cultural analysis that manifests itself in sartorial and attitudinal style, the figure is a consummate semiotician in that he exposes the "arbitrariness of all systems of codification," converts absence into presence, nothing into something.[18] Along with a characteristic exhibition of "innovation and eccentricity, paradox and hyperbole," the dandy "transform[s] every pertinent element of [his] body, dress or ornamentation, manners, speech into a system of poetic signs laden with secret, nondiscursive meanings."[19] In so doing, the dandy resists delimitation by "time, place, or coterie," because he is "the riddle, the ever-expanding set of questions which forms about the changing answer of human identity itself."[20]

In *Gender on the Divide: The Dandy in Modernist Literature*, Jessica Feldman does delimit, for a moment, the dandy's multiplicity as she elaborates on the figure as a "sign" for modernism, particularly in relation to performances of gender.[21] In fact, we can look to the modernist dandy's intersection with gender to tell us something about modernism's and the dandy's intersection with race. Feldman's insights on the dandy as a figure that reveals the cultural transition that modernism embodies adds an important footnote to Andreas Huyssen's famous observation that modernism has "woman" or the feminized as its "other."[22] The dandy is, for Feldman, primarily a figure that could embody the displacement of binaries that this "otherness" implies:

> He is the figure who practices, and even impersonates, the fascinating acts of self-creation and presentation. He is the figure of paradox created by many societies in order to express whatever it is that the culture feels it must, but cannot, synthesize. This dandy is neither spirit nor flesh, nature nor artifice, ethical nor aesthetic, active nor passive, male nor

female. He is the figure who casts into doubt, even while he underscores, the very binary oppositions by which his culture lives.[23]

If the dandy's attention to style and cultivation of artificiality of the self is traditionally labeled a feminine trait in a patriarchal world, then the figure's status as analogous to women and the feminine, rather than opposite to them, breaks down the gender divide, presenting a perhaps liberating challenge to patriarchy for women and men. Dandy style in the modernist period highlights the presence of a cultural condition in which the binaries that unnecessarily limit identity can be and are being challenged. Modernism is then a state in which "a true change of style implies the ability of [the dandy's] genius to see, and by seeing to create, however dimly and intuitively, at the farthest reaches of culture and, blindly, one startling step beyond."[24] Beyond male and female, beyond black and white, beyond success or failure?

If "woman" is modernism's "other," and the dandy modernism's subversive sign of a mediation between identity's potential binaries, then can we not see blackness and the black dandy as modernism's other "other"? If the "radical uncertainty" of the times is now associated with "the fear of the masses . . . always also a fear of woman, a fear of nature out of control, a fear of the unconscious, of sexuality, of the loss of identity and stable ego boundaries in the mass," then can we not look to the black dandy figure to simultaneously mitigate and exaggerate this fear through an absolutely dogged sense of self-invention?[25] As a creature of the streets, the paradigmatic actual and philosophical flaneur, the dandy in black and white can help us look at the mass, the crowd, not as a space of fear but as a revelation, an experimental space, a place to challenge conventions of identity—can help us to look, as Feldman suggests, "one startling step beyond." Therefore, dandyism does not matter only to those keeping up with haute couture; instead, such fastidiousness or ostentation in dress, arch social and personal style, biting wit and gesture describe radical changes in social life, new expressions of class, gender, and sexual and racial identities, for black *and* white, especially in the period we call "modernist." It is this style of critique, the astute cultural observation that it requires, in addition to its textual or literary quality, that defines the dandy's fitness as a discursive sign for black and white modernisms and as an articulation of the relationship between these modernisms. This is especially so if we remember that according to Baudelaire, the dandy *"cherche ce quelque chose qu'ons nous permettra d'appeler la modernité,"* "seeks that indefinable something we may be allowed to call modernity."[26]

If we want to find a black modernism that is not a separate modernist tradition but rather a movement in dialogue with the Baudelairian dandy's "indefinable something" expressive of modern life, then Harlem in the 1920s is an excellent place to look. The mecca for early-twentieth-century blacks, Harlem was a place that James Weldon Johnson describes in his 1930 history as the locus of a new style of blackness, a place capable of "strik[ing] the uninformed observer as a phenomenon, a miracle straight out of the skies."[27] In *Black Manhattan* Johnson insists on communicating and assessing the impact of this "miracle" and its relation to a modern identity for blacks, when, for example, he opens his discourse on Harlem culture with the following:

> If you ride northward the length of Manhattan Island, going through Central Park and coming out on Seventh Avenue or Lenox Avenue at One Hundred and Tenth Street, you cannot escape being struck by the sudden change in the character of the people you see. In the middle and lower parts of the city you have, perhaps, noted Negro faces here and there; but when you emerge from the Park, you see them everywhere, and as you go up either of these two great arteries leading out from the city to the north, you see more and more Negroes, walking in the streets, looking from the windows, trading in the shops, eating in the restaurants, going in and coming out of the theatres, until, nearing One Hundred and Thirty-Fifth Street, ninety percent of the people you see, including the traffic officers, are Negroes. And it is not until you cross the Harlem River that the population whitens again, which it does as suddenly as it began to darken at One Hundred and Tenth Street. You have been having an outside glimpse of Harlem, the Negro metropolis.[28]

This remarkable portrait of African Americans and other members of the black diaspora, "everywhere" in Harlem streets, shops, and restaurants, speaks to both the material and philosophical origins of the Harlem Renaissance. In numbers and on the streets there is both safety and strategy — Harlem became a black community interested in rethinking its "look" in

1

Armistice Day, Harlem, 1919, Lenox Avenue and West 134th Street. Reproduced courtesy of Photographs and Prints Division, Schomburg Center for Research in Black Culture, the New York Public Library, Astor, Lenox and Tilden Foundations.

the aftermath of the northward migration of blacks from other New York City neighborhoods and an unprecedented influx of migrants from the South and the Caribbean during the Great Migration. Black real estate savvy enabled this newly constituted group to settle into a middle-class neighborhood that had been overbuilt, a neighborhood originally intended for whites. Indeed Harlem was unique among black urban spaces in being full of decent housing situated on broad avenues. As an actual and metaphorical space, Harlem was a ready canvas for black *self*-display, a location from which to make "nothing into something" (Figure 1).

The striking visual impact that black New Yorkers had on each other and the world helped them to understand that they had a particular opportunity to revise their self-image and their image in other people's eyes, in both small ways and ways with much more significance. In fact, in the era-

The Black Dandy as Bad Modernist

defining 1925 volume *The New Negro*, Alain Locke explains that in Harlem "each group has come [from the rural North and South, Africa, the West Indies] with their own separate motives and for its own special ends, but their greatest experience has been the finding of one another."[29] Indeed, this finding of one another, the recognition of their mutual talents, and their deliberate use of those talents to re-imagine African American people and their culture was the hallmark of the movement. As Locke says, as early as 1925, "in Harlem, Negro life is seizing upon its first chances of group expression and self-determination."[30] James Weldon Johnson echoes this sentiment when he says that Harlem was, from the beginning, "more than a community; it is a large scale laboratory experiment in the race problem."[31] A signal concern in this experiment would be to find a method of combating debilitating stereotypes, especially those stereotypes originating from the blackface minstrel stage. As people who were subject to horrific racial violence regularly, whose civil rights had been denied or questioned for much of their history in America, whose culture and character had been ridiculed and demeaned in print, on stage, in film, African Americans had, until the Great Migration, toiled for rights and against stereotypes, but not with the numbers or diversity of strategies that Harlem made available. Fittingly — or not — a paradoxical catalyst and product of this experiment with stereotypes and modernism would be a particular denizen of this new black metropolis, the black dandy, a figure with that "indefinable something" important for a description of black modernism.

As the black community studied, adjusted, and upgraded its "look" in 1920s Harlem, dandies erupted everywhere. They could be seen in the guise of well-dressed doctors and lawyers inhabiting brownstones on Striver's Row; in flamboyantly dressed street peddlers of women and "hooch"; in dancers, musicians, and patrons at speakeasies; and in artists ensconced in salons. Of course, the majority of Harlem's residents were not aware of themselves as dandies, but many could be seen that way — depending on who was looking. Although the dandies on the streets of Harlem seemed to be particular to that urban space, they were, in fact, the result of earlier competing, but interrelated traditions concerning black identity formation and the visual in the Atlantic diaspora. Black dandies, like their European counterparts, were made, not born. And, in America, reading the black dandy on the street or in a text requires one to take account of the fact that throughout American history dandies have been black *and* in black-face. Therefore, in order to process the figure's self-fashioning impulse as an exemplification of modernity during the Harlem Renaissance, we have to analyze the figure's play with race, class, and dress, in black and blackface. If we do so, we see that the black look seen on Harlem streets is not that which can possibly constitute a *separate* modernist tradition, a *specifically* black voice, because the look is a result of a kind of call and response between black and white efforts at black representation. Instead, this look is a sign that blackness has always been and will always be collaged.

Because of the new attitude they communicated with their style, the figures now confidently strolling in Harlem were of increasing actual and symbolic concern to the leaders and members of the art-for-progress crowd. This concern on the part of Harlem notables like Locke, Johnson, and W. E. B. Du Bois (all dandies themselves or authors of dandy books) had to do with how to control or target the figure's performativity. On the one hand, they desired to use the figure to exhibit black sophistication and "knowingness" concerning the history of black representation; on the other, they wanted to limit that knowledge to the project of "uplift," or the practice of a politics of respectability that worked against stereotypes. While dandyism in white and black does have as its hallmark a self-consciousness about identity construction—about the way in which society, culture, and politics influence a sense of self and community—as a practice, it takes advantage of and manipulates the space between image and identity. By definition, dandyism refuses to stand for any one thing. To use the dandy then as an emblem of black urbanity, sophistication, and modernity was, in some ways, a brilliant and doomed act, an act foretold by the dandy's complicated pre-history and performance in and during the Harlem Renaissance.

During the nineteenth century, black dandyism constituted not only cultural commentary, like its European counterpart, but also a cultural fear.[32] Best known from the minstrel stage, the blackface dandy was one half of the "dandy and darky" team that precisely exemplified white fears of black social and cultural mobility in a world in which most blacks were making the transition from slavery to freedom. On the blackface stage, the dandy was haphazardly dressed, accidentally educated, and always desirous

The Black Dandy as Bad Modernist

of getting ahead — in a blue plaid suit, cane, and top hat, delivering a lecture on the importance of "libin' well," the figure mocked all African American pretensions to a life outside the actual and psychic restrictions of slavery. Not merely a figment of the white imagination, these stage dandies were also a response to the gradual emancipation and the growth of small, politically active and culturally sophisticated black communities in Northern cities.[33] In addition, the dandies in blackface mocked an earlier indigenous black tradition of race and class play, best exemplified by the colonial American festivals of Negro Election Day and Pinkster.[34] From as early as the 1750s, in late spring and early summer in colonial New England and early America, African American slaves and free people celebrated their New World identities in festivals that, like rituals of reversal and the Bakhtinian carnivalesque, mockingly and lovingly displayed their self-consciousness about the constructedness of their identities.[35] Sartorial display exhibited this knowledge; in the case of both Pinkster and Negro Election Day, black slaves and free people held festivals in which they elected and/or celebrated their own leaders by pompously parading through town dressed up in, most often, a combination of their own and their masters' best clothing.[36] According to contemporary observers, the slaves and free blacks participating in the festivals wore "uniforms — [that were] anything but uniform," outfits that communicated a tone of mock-seriousness and parody, rather than mere imitation (Figure 2).[37]

Early American blacks looked forward to these days when the black community could give speeches, vote, party, and parade down colonial streets at the literal expense of their masters. Additionally, these festivals displayed the power of memory, a memory specifically associated with image and clothing.[38] From the point of contact with Europeans, the West African elite had eagerly incorporated into their wardrobes European cloth and clothing they received in trade for people and goods; items of European origin quickly became part of the process of visually displaying authority and power within African communities.[39] Transported to the other side of the Atlantic, West Africans remembered and re-invigorated the importance that European fancy dress had had in communicating and destabilizing nobility, authority, and respect, especially for fellow Africans, as "Kings" and "Governors" were often African-born members of the com-

2

Zip Coon, 1834: blackface minstrel sheet music cover. Reproduced courtesy of Photographs and Prints Division, Schomburg Center for Research in Black Culture, the New York Public Library, Astor, Lenox and Tilden Foundations.

munity. Thus the Negro "Governors," like the Pinkster "Kings," sometimes had actual as well as symbolic power that was not limited to the day's celebrations. In its African origins and American manifestation, their dandyism also displayed a long-standing cultural disposition to exploring hybridity and syncretism.[40]

Because of the richness of this indigenous play with race and class, especially the way in which it acknowledged black identity as hybrid and black discursive style as syncretic, these festivals lasted only so long. When the slave trade and then slavery were abolished in the North, around 1830, the performativity that characterized the festival began to play very differently.[41] The class and racial cross-dressing came to have increased symbolic value as the status mockingly achieved in the festivals actually became theoretically, if not materially, attainable for blacks no longer enslaved. Such a threat or opportunity meant the end of the festivals, but not the end of black dandies and dandyism. Co-existent with the end of the festivals was the beginning of blackface minstrelsy, a counter-burlesque of the kind of racial play and class crossing that was performed in the festivals. On the black-face stage, the dandy expressed white anxiety about black self-stylization as well as a desire for social regard or cultural recognition. At once a symbol of a self-conscious subversion of authority by means of self-fashioning *and* an attempted denigratory parody of free black pride and enterprise, the black dandy—pre-Harlem—was poised to encapsulate the complexities of African America's quest for cultural recognition in the modernist period. Coming through the cracks of Western civilization would then be a black discursive style that took advantage of the cultural commentary of European dandyism but with a distinctive black difference.

Strangely, then, as the Harlem Renaissance emerged, its architects attempted to use a figure born out of cultural syncretism and symbolic and actual class and race cross-dressing to do the impossible: not only to embody but also to translate artistically a "blackness" or black modernism that everyone could or should recognize. Though appreciated as a symbol of cultural arrival, the figure of the black dandy would fail in this task, especially when deployed in literature concerning the demands a cultural renaissance makes on resolutely modern people. Renaissance architects initially seemed to think that using the black dandy as a sign of black modernity would be "good" in that the figure re-presented by Harlemites would be one free of the minstrel mask, a figure self-fashioning, rather than one fashioned by others. Having transcended the limitations of blackface, the figure would then be capable of exemplifying the striving that was initially mocked by the caricature: desire for education, social mobility, a cosmopolitanism not prohibited by black and white manipulation of the color line. What they did not realize, perhaps, was that this effort to modify the dandy for modernity would also, in some way, uncover the dandy in black, an earlier version of black self-fashioning that would be difficult to channel into a definitive statement on blackness. So while *good* at pointing out the commonalities between modernism in black and modernism in white, the black dandy was *bad* for black modernism as delimited by its architects in that it prevented the movement from defining blackness in a way that satisfied either its shepherds or future critics. This lack of definition counterintuitively saved Renaissance aesthetics from being too narrowly defined.

Black Dandies and New Negroes

If the business of Harlem as laboratory would be black America's new attitude about itself, the turn of Renaissance architects to art and culture as the vehicle was a bet that "artistic and literary achievement could do more for the black cause at this particular historical moment than any economic or political gains."[42] In artistic manifestos written by Locke and Du Bois, for example, each cultural gatekeeper attempted to shape a modernist movement according to his own vision. Although they had very different methodologies, and were successful at communicating these methodologies within the confines of essays and collections like "The Criteria of Negro Art" and *The New Negro*, they were unable to carry their visions beyond these texts. Unsurprisingly, given black dandyism's history and effect, they were particularly thwarted when they attempted to use the dandy as a vehicle for expressing black modernism in their own fiction, or, in the case of Locke, when the figure was used in fiction by "the younger generation," to whom he dedicates *The New Negro*. In both cases, the attempt to build a movement defined by what is and is not art or propaganda (Du Bois) or a proper identification and use of the ancestral arts (Locke) disappointed, but in a way that revealed the difficulty, even the impossibility, of describing the New Negro and his or her art in a conclusive way.

Although seemingly unlikely to entertain the dandy figure as part of a definition of blackness for modernity, W. E. B. Du Bois was deeply invested in the strategic redeployment of incongruous (to him) ideas or concepts for black advantage.[43] To that end, in 1926's "Criteria of Negro Art," Du Bois attempted to identify black art as propaganda, but in so doing, he redefined propaganda away from overtly didactic, ideological art toward that which insists on "the right of black folk to love and enjoy."[44] Although he declares in the "Criteria" that "all Art is propaganda and ever must be, despite the wailing of the purists," Du Bois understands black art as propaganda insofar as art matters to black folk not as an escapist dream but as a weapon.[45] Indeed, Du Bois's next sentence, "But I do care when propaganda is confined to one side while the other is stripped and silent," provides a clue to his thinking about appropriate weapons. In his formulation, centuries of racist propaganda have naturalized black depravity, creating conditions in which African Americans have been "stripped and silent," naked or without cover

3

Portrait of W. E. B. Du Bois at nineteen. Reproduced courtesy of Special Collections and Archives, W. E. B. Du Bois Library, University of Massachusetts, Amherst.

of their own making. Here, we might read an intimation of a connection between the necessary counter-propaganda and clothing. Strangely, but fascinatingly, Du Bois provides this cover in his 1928 novel *Dark Princess* — primarily by inventing a protagonist who sounds, looks, and acts much like a dandy. Art, politics, and dandyism are major concerns in the novel; in fact, Du Bois combines them in the hope of fomenting nothing less than a revolution (Figure 3).

In the novel, the dandy figure, Matthew Towns, is a beautifully turned-out, well-mannered Talented Tenth type, described by Du Bois as a handsome creature, especially when "wearing the new suit made for the opening school term . . . his newest dark crimson tie that burned with the red in his smooth brown face . . . carr[ying] cane and gloves."[46] Self-exiled in Europe, in flight from discrimination at medical school, he falls in with a group of radicals, the Council of the Darker Peoples of the World. Though dedicated to its plan to effect a worldwide revolution against white hegemony and color lines (partly because he is in love with its leader, the South Asian Indian Princess of the title), Matthew refuses to toe the party line when some of his fellow revolutionaries question black fitness for the cause. Forced to prove that African Americans and their culture are sufficiently "civilized" or "modern" for inclusion in the revolution, Matthew finds himself at a black tie affair singing a Negro spiritual in defense of African American civilization:

> The blood rushed to Matthew's face. He threw back his head and closed his eyes, and with the movement he heard again the Great Song. He saw his father in the old log church by the river, leading the moaning singers in the Great Song of Emancipation. Clearly, plainly he heard that mighty voice and saw the rhythmic swing and beat of the thick brown arm. Matthew swung his arm and beat the table; the silver tinkled. Silence dropped on all, and suddenly Matthew found himself singing. His voice full, untrained but mellow, quivered down the first plaintive bar. . . .
>
> "That," said Matthew, "came out of the black rabble of America." And he trilled his "r." They all smiled as the tension broke.
>
> "You assume then," said the Princess at last, "that the mass of the workers of the world can rule as well as be ruled?"
>
> "Yes, — or rather can work as well as be worked, can live as well as be kept alive. America is teaching the world one thing of real value, and that is, the ability and capacity for culture is not the hereditary monopoly of the few, but the widespread possibility for the majority of mankind if they only have a decent chance in life."[47]

Here, Matthew effectively re-presents the race and ushers it into the modern world by removing the corrupting effects of blackface from the performance and himself as performer; as such, this moment in the text seems to demonstrate the "mastery of form and the deformation of mastery." Therefore, Matthew's song could be read as an example of the emergence of Baker's initially desired "successful" and "specific" black voice, the dismissal of stereotype and a return to "pure" Negro art. But that a dandy sings this song or performs this sign of modernity is extremely important for Du Bois's project and for the claim of black modernism as an autochthonous or "mulatto" phenomenon. Because the song emanates from a performing body, a body doubly performative and "impure" or "mulatto" because dandified, it cannot be heard as merely or only the arrival of a "*specifically* Afro-American" modern voice. Instead of a fulfillment or an excavation of an originary, discernible blackness, this moment is rather a provocation to redefine black identity in the face of color and class lines. That this is not an arrival as much as an opportunity is also suggested by the fact that this scene occurs very early on in the novel. From this moment, *Dark Princess*'s re-formed dandy and his art are propelled forward—not toward an elaboration of a "*specifically* Afro-American discursive practice," or to an individualistic betrayal of black progress, but rather to a claim for cosmopolitanism as black modernist goal and process. This cosmopolitanism denies limitations and especially those constituted on or by the color line—what Matthew wants *for all* is counterintuitively modest and extreme, "a decent chance at life." Therefore, the combination of the "sound" of modernism with its "look" signals that a black modernist discursive strategy will be that which insists on "the right to love and enjoy" beyond the color line, but only after the debilitating effects of the color line (as represented by blackface) have been understood and displaced.

After this scene, in which Matthew converts a specifically African American moment of aesthetic struggle into a more universal triumph (but one that does not forget the specificities of history), *Dark Princess*'s dandy becomes a kind of visionary. However, he proves unable to work for the immediate "success" of racially bound causes: his work for the Council stalls, he abandons a later turn to politics on Chicago's South Side, and in the end, the revolution of Darker Peoples seems possible but not particularly imminent. In the latter half of *Dark Princess*, the dandy chooses to abandon his job in order to spend his time looking at modern art in museums, contemplating how its abstractions inspire self-discovery and personal and group freedom, and exercising the right for black people to "love and enjoy." Though this dilettantism might seem like a failure, in truth it is an accomplishment of sorts as it manifests Matthew's conception of a lived experience in a world in which the color line no longer rules. Not a traditional revolutionary, this dandy makes a Byron-esque gesture in that he works for and exemplifies a broader sense of what it means to be a world citizen, a citizen not limited by, but attentive to, his or her particular history. Du Bois's use of the dandy in *Dark Princess* illustrates the phenomenon of African American identity responding to and emerging from the minstrel mask; and as the novel concludes, we see what happens "one startling step beyond" that trumping of the color line. In the end, *Dark Princess* and its dandy do indeed exceed the lines of color and class, leaving an inconclusive but instructive, multicultural collage behind. The novel closes as the dandy marries the Dark Princess, after producing an heir, who, in the course of the marriage ceremony, is recognized by representatives of all the world's darker people as "King of the Snows of Gaurisankar!," "Protector of Ganga the Holy!," "Incarnate Son of the Buddha!," "Grand Mughal of Utter India!," and "Messenger and Messiah to all the Darker Worlds!"[48]

What frustrates and fascinates about Du Bois's use of the dandy in the novel is the way in which the figure uncannily responds to its own history *and* imbrication in modernist discourse, all the while fashioning a future that in true dandy style extends well beyond white imitation. No less important, however, is that in going "one startling step beyond," the dandy also brings us back to and beyond Baker's effort to *listen* for the emergence of an "Afro-American sound" and to see the dandy trapped in his white father's "weeds." In its hope of covering African American cultural "nakedness," Du Bois's use of the dandy as modernist sign was both shrewd and naïve—shrewd because the dandy had always played on the lines of color and culture, assembled fragments of identity into a workable collage; naïve because, as kind of palimpsestic creature, the figure best represents the act of representation, rather than a particular represented identity. In addition, the dandy figure's tendency to exceed boundaries, used by Du Bois in the novel to redefine debilitating notions of identity and cultural nationalism, affected not only the plot of *Dark Princess* but its reception. Despite the novel's revolutionary reconception of African American identity, *Dark Princess*'s melodrama (the plot features, among other trying moments, the rescue of the Princess from a train about to be blown up in a terrorist plot) and sensationalism (we should not forget that it is a novel authored by an NAACP official and dramatizes interracial sex and intercultural romance) challenged many readers of Du Bois's text and rendered it a critical conundrum in the Harlem Renaissance. White reviewers took the genre mix—a combination of sociology, didacticism, love story, and adventure—as evidence of Du Bois's confused artistic goals.[49] Black reviewers merely lamented their fates, as did Langston Hughes, who wrote in a letter to Alain Locke: "Tonight I have to do *Dark Princess* for [New York Herald

Tribune] Books. God help me."[50] Some even privately regarded *Dark Princess* as "a dirty old man's fantasy that should have never been published."[51] The book did poorly, failing to sell out its initial printing of approximately 5,000 copies, prompting Du Bois to ask his editor for " 'frank advice' as to whether or not there existed 'a market for my fiction.' "[52] Although the revolution of Darker Peoples fails to ignite within the book and precious few even read of this radical possibility, the novel clearly demonstrates its author's desire to imagine a "mulatto modernism" potentially beneficial to all.

Although Du Bois's attempt to define modern black identity through the refinement of propaganda seems a tactic very different from that of his colleague Alain Locke, their efforts had similarly destabilizing and productive results. In his capacity as "midwife" of the Harlem Renaissance, Locke, like Du Bois, wrote much about aesthetics that acknowledged and promoted African American artistic achievement, while at the same time providing instructions on how to do more. *The New Negro*, edited by Locke and containing no less than five Locke pieces, certainly best exemplifies his tactics for guiding the movement toward fruition. Serving as the actual and perhaps proverbial last Locke word in *The New Negro*, "The Legacy of the Ancestral Arts" is an essay in which he gives a lesson in art history, appreciates current artistic efforts, and then very clearly establishes a program for aspiring and established artists to follow in the hope of inspiring (or dictating) future artistic production.

As the title implies, "Legacy" lobbies for African American use of and inspiration from African art, the Negro's "ancestral art." Acknowledging that "the American Negro, even when he confronts the various forms of African art expression, with a sense of its ethnic claims upon him, meets them in as alienated and misunderstanding an attitude as the average European Westerner," Locke also understands that it is precisely these Europeans who made the effort to bridge this gap and took advantage of African art's lessons in stylization in creating modern art.[53] His purpose in the essay is then to answer the question asked in other quarters, "What is Africa to me?," by stating very clearly that, if Europeans are inspired by African art, "surely this [the use of an African legacy] is not too much to expect of . . . the culturally awakened Negro artist of the present generation?"[54] While he says explicitly that he does not wish to "dictate a style" to the young Negro artist

4

Portrait of Alain Locke by
James Latimer Allen, 1943.
Reproduced courtesy of Pho-
tographs and Prints Division,
Schomburg Center for Research
in Black Culture, the New York
Public Library, Astor, Lenox
and Tilden Foundations.

in developing a "racial art," he nonetheless hopes that "there is the possibility that the sensitive artistic mind of the American Negro, stimulated
by a cultural pride and interest, will receive from African art a profound
and galvanizing influence. The legacy is there, at least, with prospects of
a rich yield."[55] In admonishing young artists to tap the "yet unexhausted
reservoir" of highly stylized African art, Locke seemingly contradicts or
certainly complicates his program. On the one hand, Negro artists have no
particular feeling for their "ancestral legacy"; on the other hand, expressing black modernism seems to depend on their finding and claiming such
a "racial feeling," because if they do not, someone else will. Modern "racial
art" for Locke is then a combination of history and fantasy, but one that
needs to suppress its artificiality (Figure 4).

Locke himself did not write of the dandy; nevertheless, he comes up for
criticism from a fictional counterpart who dares to teach him a dandy lesson that, as a frequent visitor to France and a gay black man in the early
1920s, perhaps he should have already known. Certainly to Locke's chagrin,
one of the highly stylized creatures also monitoring the Harlem Renaissance
did not let the potential contradictions of his aesthetic program go by. In

The Black Dandy as Bad Modernist

1932 Wallace Thurman parodied Locke and his aesthetic theory (especially its self-consciousness) brilliantly in *Infants of the Spring*, his satire on the Harlem phenomenon. A "bad" book in that it is a wholly irreverent roman à clef, *Infants* held little back in its knocks at the Harlem principals, even those like Langston Hughes, Zora Neale Hurston, and Richard Bruce Nugent who were intimates of Thurman. Those who had attempted to be at all proscriptive in their work for black cultural arrival came under particular attack — Du Bois and Locke especially.

The most memorable chapter of the book, chapter 21, features a gathering initiated by the Locke figure, called Dr. Parkes, at the Harlem rooming house where the younger artists had established a kind of salon; Sweetie May Carr, the Hurston character, facetiously nicknames the house Niggerati Manor, as Hurston did a similar rooming house in real life. At the beginning of the chapter, Parkes writes to the Thurman character, Raymond, instructing him to gather the group to "bring into active being a concerted movement that would establish the younger Negro talent once and for all as a vital artistic force" — Parkes would, of course, preside.[56] True to character, Parkes tells the group that the realization of this talent will depend on "going back to your racial roots, and cultivating a healthy paganism based on African traditions."[57] Doing so will allow this younger group to forge the "future of the race," to establish "for the Negro everywhere . . . complete freedom and equality."[58]

The content and specific nature of this advice please some, like DeWitt Clinton, the Eric Walrond character, and appall others, particularly the dandy among them, Paul Arbian, a poet and painter modeled after Richard Bruce Nugent. A self-declared "genius" and devoted to Wilde, Huysmans, and Baudelaire, Paul is highly unconventional even as a dandy, affecting a "habit not to wear a necktie because he knew his neck was too well modeled to be hidden from public gaze," and "no sox either, nor underwear, and those few clothes he did deign to affect were musty and disheveled."[59] Self-styled as a bohemian and consummate naysayer, Paul responds wittily to Parkes's call for art for "Africa's sake." Reluctant to limit his ancestral legacy to the African, he refuses the burden of authenticity that the times and Dr. Parkes would place on them. Facetiously asking if his "German, English and Indian" forefathers also would be included in the ancestral heritage he would bring to his work, he declares that he "ain't got no African spirit" and spends the rest of the meeting listening amusedly as the group fights over the possibility of establishing any concert in their efforts, whether based around African tradition, or not.[60] Shocked by the group's unwillingness to sacrifice the multiplicity of individual expression to a fantasy of group liberation, Dr. Parkes "visibly recoiled from Carl's [Aaron Douglas's] incoherent expository barrage, and wilted in his chair, willing but unable to effect a courteous exit."[61] While Paul's attitude and the melee it inspires might have struck Locke and other Renaissance architects as rebellious and counterproductive, it is consistent with his general policy of indeterminacy. Against Dr. Parkes/Locke, Paul and others of "the younger generation" insist on a definition of modernity that will take advantage of the fact that, as Raymond later declares, "Negroes are the only people in America not standardized."[62]

While the dandy in Thurman's book makes a claim for Harlem's modernist aesthetics as that which should not or cannot be standardized, this lesson is one that applies to modernism in general. In these books the dandies perform a "bad" black modernism that places modernism in conversation with the Harlem Renaissance while at the same time proposing a black modernist discursive practice that finds its specificity in heterogeneity, not authenticity or imitation. What the black dandy as "bad" modernist in these texts reveals—the productive necessity of play and indeterminacy—forces us to see modernism as modernisms, and modernisms in *and as* both black and white, mulatto. What is "good" about this dandy's "badness" is that the figure's redefinition of blackness and modernism does not allow for either concept to be entirely recognizable—for to present blackness as something discernible would be to play too close to the lines of stereotype; to present modernism as that which is the concern of those on "high," as audible as a distinctive "sound," or as a derivative "look," would limit its power as a tool of group- and self-fashioning. Instead, when looking through the lens of the black dandy in the modernist period, what we see are performances of modernity in "uniforms—anything but uniform," the communication of a sense of self and culture, in black and white, that is experimental out of fear, necessity, strategy, and joy. When we search for signs of modernist arrival and participation, what emerges is a sense of what modernism means for blackness and what blackness means for modernism: a notion that modern identity is—if at all definitive—essentially "mixed."

As such, the black dandy affirms the importance of the "mix" to the cultural survival and evolution of all, while arguing for a conception of blackness and modernity as perceptible processes, rather than voices or looks that we have heard and seen before.

Notes

1. Houston Baker, *Modernism and the Harlem Renaissance* (Chicago: University of Chicago Press, 1989), xvi, xiii. For details on the ways in which critics have judged the success and failure of the Harlem Renaissance, see especially chapter 2 of *Modernism and the Harlem Renaissance* and David Levering Lewis's preface to the 1997 edition of *When Harlem Was in Vogue* (New York: Penguin, 1997).

2. Baker, *Modernism*, 8, 7, 4.

3. Ibid., 7.

4. Ibid., 9 (Baker's emphasis), xiv (emphasis added).

5. Ibid., 106.

6. Baker, *Turning South Again: Re-Thinking Modernism/Re-Reading Booker T* (Durham, N.C.: Duke University Press, 2001), 33.

7. Ibid., 70.

8. Ibid., 75.

9. Ibid., 33.

10. Baker, *Modernism*, 3.

11. I borrow this phrase from Robin Kelley's *Freedom Dreams: The Black Radical Imagination* (Boston: Beacon Press, 2000).

12. Both Baker's rethinking of *Modernism and the Harlem Renaissance* and my own bring us to the black dandy, but our very different conclusions on how to read the figure reveal the different purposes of our projects. For Baker, as for Washington in *Up from Slavery*, dandyism is frivolous; see *Up From Slavery*, chapter 8, p. 57, when Washington rails against the "educated Negro, with high hat, imitation gold eye-glasses, a showy walking stick, kid gloves, fancy boots and what not," a distraction from what Baker calls the "achievement of a black citizenship that entails documented mobility (driver's license, passport, green card, social security card) and access to a decent job at a decent rate of pay" (*Turning* 33). For me, black dandyism is practice that reveals the black imaginary, is a location of one kind of expressive or creative response to oppression in the field of representation.

13. Although historical and cultural studies of European dandyism describe the practice as a strategy that seems appropriate, even necessary, for blacks in their uncertain social, political, and cultural positions in and after the slave trade, black dandies have been largely ignored in those contexts. Exceptions include Richard J. Powell, "Sartor Africanus," in *Dandies: Fashion and Finesse in Art and Culture*, ed. Susan Fillin-Yeh (New

York: New York University Press, 2001), 217–42, an article that treats the black dandy in American visual culture; and Elisa Glick, "Harlem's Queer Dandy: African-American Modernism and the Artifice of Blackness," *MFS: Modern Fiction Studies* 49, no. 3 (Fall 2003): 414–42, which also reads the black dandy-aesthete in the Harlem Renaissance as a "queer" critique of the era's attempted formulation of an "authentic" African American identity. See also my dissertation, "Figuring the Black Dandy: Negro Art, Black Bodies, and African-Diasporic Ambitions" (Ph.D. diss., Harvard University, 2000), for a cultural history of the black dandy in a transhistorical, diasporic context.

14. Ellen Moers, *The Dandy: Brummell to Beerbohm* (New York: Viking Press, 1960), 26; Rhonda Garelick, *Rising Star: Dandyism, Gender, and Performance in the Fin de Siècle* (Princeton, N.J.: Princeton University Press, 1998), 21.

15. Moers, *The Dandy*, 12.

16. Ibid., 30.

17. Ibid., 11.

18. Domna Stanton, *The Aristocrat as Art: A Study of the* honnête homme *and the Dandy in Seventeenth and Nineteenth Century France* (New York: Columbia University Press, 1980), 174.

19. Ibid., 173.

20. Jessica Feldman, *Gender on the Divide: The Dandy in Modernist Literature* (Ithaca, N.Y.: Cornell University Press, 1993), 1. For a collection of essays on the variety of dandies and dandyisms in nineteenth- and twentieth-century culture, see also *Dandies: Fashion and Finesse in Art and Culture*, ed. Susan Fillin-Yeh.

21. In *Turning South Again*, Baker also mentions the way in which Booker T's dandyism feminizes him; for Baker this feminization is, like the dandyism, dangerous, rather than a potential experiment with masculine styles. In *Turning South Again*, both "mulatto" and "feminization" are "bad" words. For more on how the dandy's play with gender might be liberating, see my article on Du Bois, "W. E. B. Du Bois and the Dandy as Diasporic Race Man," *Callaloo* 26, no. 3(2003): 738–65.

22. Andreas Huyssen, "Mass Culture as Woman: Modernism's Other," *After the Great Divide: Modernism, Mass Culture, Postmodernism* (Bloomington: Indiana University Press, 1986), 44–62.

23. Feldman, *Gender on the Divide*, 4.

24. Ibid., 9.

25. Huyssen, "Mass Culture as Woman," 52.

26. Charles Baudelaire, "The Painter of Modern Life," *Selected Writings on Art and Literature*, trans. and ed. P. E. Charvet (New York: Penguin, 1992), 402.

27. James Weldon Johnson, *Black Manhattan* (New York, De Capo Press, 1991), 4.

28. Ibid., 144.

29. Alain Locke, "The New Negro," *The New Negro*, ed. Alain Locke (New York: Atheneum, 1992), 6.

30. Ibid.

31. Johnson, *Black Manhattan*, 281.

32. For more about the black dandy and the fear (and sexual threat) that he signified, especially in the nineteenth century, see Eric Lott's seminal volume, *Love and Theft: Blackface Minstrelsy and the American Working Class* (New York: Oxford University Press, 1993); Gary Nash's *Forging Freedom: The Formation of Philadelphia's Black Community, 1720–1840* (Cambridge, Mass.: Harvard University Press, 1988); Barbara Lewis's "Daddy Blue: The Evolution of the Dark Daddy," in *Inside the Minstrel Mask: Readings in Nineteenth-Century Blackface Minstrelsy*, ed. Annemarie Bean, James V. Hatch, and Brooks McNamara (Hanover, N.H.: University Press of New England, 1996): 257–74; and William Mahar's *Behind the Burnt Cork Mask: Early Blackface Minstrelsy and Antebellum Popular Culture* (Urbana: University of Illinois Press, 1999).

33. See especially Nash, *Forging Freedom*.

34. Best sources for more details on Election Day in New England are William D. Piersen, *Black Yankees: The Development of Afro-American Subculture in Eighteenth-Century New England* (Amherst: University of Massachusetts Press, 1988); Oliver H. Platt, "Negro Governors," *Papers of the New England Historical Society* 6 (1900): 315–35; Shane White, *Somewhat More Independent: The End of Slavery in New York City, 1770–1810* (Athens: University of Georgia Press, 1991); and Shane White and Graham White, *Stylin': African American Expressive Culture from its Beginnings to the Zoot Suit* (Ithaca, N.Y.: Cornell University Press, 1998). For Pinkster, see Geneviève Fabre, "Pinkster Carnival: 1776–1811: An African-American Celebration," in *Feasts and Celebrations in Northern American Ethnic Communities*, ed. Ramón Gutiérrez and Geneviève Fabre (Albuquerque: University of New Mexico Press, 1995), 13–29; Melvin Wade, " 'Shining in Borrowed Plummage': Affirmation of Community in the Black Coronation Festivals of New England (c. 1750–c. 1850)," *Western Folklore* 40, no. 3 (1981): 211–31; and A. J. Williams-Meyers, "Pinkster Carnival: Africanisms in the Hudson Valley," *Afro-Americans in New York Life and History* 9, no. 1 (1985): 7–18. While I rely on these historians for excellent archival research and cogent arguments concerning the cultural context in which these festivals took place (especially Shane White and Graham White), none of them has yet explored how this process of play with clothing, in the days before blackface minstrelsy, might have influenced the representation of dandies and the black middle class after emancipation.

35. According to Victor Turner in *The Ritual Process: Structure and Anti-Structure* (New York: Aldine, 1969), "rituals of reversal" feature a temporary exchange of power in which "inferiors affect[ed] the rank and style of superiors, sometimes . . . arraying themselves in a hierarchy mimicking that of their so-called betters" (168–69). This is clearly similar to the Bakhtinian carinivalesque, which, as an expression of folk understanding of and subversion of hierarchy, "celebrated temporary liberation from the prevailing truth and from the established order; it marked the suspension of all hierarchical rank, privileges, norms, and prohibitions. Carnival was a feast of time, the feast of becoming, change and renewal. It was hostile to all that was immortalized and completed," Mikhail Bakhtin, *Rabelais and his World*, trans. Helene Iswolsky (Bloomington: Indiana University Press, 1984), 10.

36. Jane Shelton, "The New England Negro: A Remnant," *Harper's Magazine* 88, no. 526 (1894): 535.

37. Ibid., 537.

38. In the introduction to *Feasts and Celebrations*, Geneviève Fabre claims that festivals in general "offer a way of performing experience and of identifying 'sites of memory' for the communities that perform them" (6).

39. Helen Bradley Foster, *"New Raiments of Self": African American Clothing in the Antebellum South* (New York: Berg, 1997), 29, 64. Foster provides an amazing list of European or European-traded cloth types available in Benin from the early 1500s to the early 1770s, suggesting that some form of African play with cloth and clothing could date from the sixteenth century (61).

40. In the South and Caribbean, similar festivals were those celebrating John Canoe or Jonkonnu; the later manifestation of the sartorial subversion in these festivals in the South is the cakewalk. See Elizabeth Fenn, " 'A Perfect Equality Seemed to Reign': Slave Society and Jonkonnu," *North Carolina Historical Review* 65 (April 1988): 127–53, and Brooke Baldwin, "The Cakewalk: A Study in Stereotype and Reality," *Journal of Social History* 15 (Winter 1981): 205–18.

41. See Piersen, *Black Yankees*, 159, for more on lower-class white resentment; for more on the festivals' later perceived threat to law and order, see Williams-Meyers and Joseph P. Reidy, " 'Negro Election Day' and Black Community Life in New England, 1750–1860," *Marxist Perspectives* 1, no. 3 (1978): 102–17.

42. Ann Douglas, *Terrible Honesty: Mongrel Manhattan in the 1920s* (New York: Farrar, Straus and Giroux, 1995), 323, 213.

43. This argument about Du Bois and dandyism appears in a slightly different form in my "W. E. B. Du Bois and the Dandy as Diasporic Race Man."

44. W. E. B. Du Bois, "The Criteria of Negro Art," *Writings* (New York: Literary Classics of the United States [Library of America], 1986), 1000.

45. Ibid., 1000. See also Keith Byerman's *Seizing the Word: History, Art, and the Self in the Work of W. E. B. Du Bois* (Athens: University of Georgia Press, 1994), especially chapter 5, "The Propaganda of Art: Ideology and Literary Practice." Byerman very helpfully provides an extended reading of the "Criteria" which emphasizes the way in which Du Bois sought to redefine (or seize) certain concepts like "propaganda" and "beauty" for his own use.

46. W. E. B. Du Bois, *Dark Princess: A Romance* (Jackson: University of Mississippi Press, 1995).

47. Ibid., 25–26.

48. Ibid., 310–11.

49. For a summary of the novel's reception by both black and white reviewers, see Herbert Aptheker, introduction to *Dark Princess: A Romance*, by W. E. B. Du Bois (Millwood, N.Y.: Kraus-Thomason Organization, 1974), 5–29.

50. Claudia Tate, introduction to *Dark Princess: A Romance*, by W. E. B. Du Bois (Jackson: University of Mississippi Press, 1995), xxiv.

51. Ibid.

52. Aptheker, introduction, 20.

53. Alain Locke, "The Legacy of the Ancestral Arts," *The New Negro* (New York Atheneum, 1992), 254, 255.

54. Ibid., 267.

55. Ibid., 266, 256.

56. Wallace Thurman, *Infants of the Spring* (Boston: Northeastern University Press, 1992), 228.

57. Ibid., 235.

58. Ibid., 234.

59. Ibid., 24, 21.

60. Ibid., 236, 237.

61. Ibid., 245.

62. Ibid., 241.

Douglas Mao

A Shaman in Common: Lewis, Auden,

and the Queerness of Liberalism

I s there any point in continuing to assess the politics of modernism? Even were we to discount recent scholarship's case that early-twentieth-century culture is best approached in terms of a variety of *modernisms* and restrict our attention to the narrowest plausible canon of innovative works, we would still encounter a range of political positions among those works' makers. What label — to take for example the still smaller subfield of British-Irish and American modernist literature — accommodates Pound, Woolf, Eliot, Dos Passos, Toomer, Stein, Rukeyser, Yeats, Joyce, Williams, and Hemingway? When we consider in addition that many modernist artists changed their political positions over time or professed affiliations that seem objectively antithetical to their own beliefs, it becomes clear (should any doubts have lingered) that there was no single modernist political line. Yet still one wonders. If the divisions are so intractable, why do the works of these writers continue to seem meaningfully constellated, to speak to each other in ways that cannot, except under the most willfully repressive and selective kind of reading, be deemed apolitical? How could their differences have been articulated at all if they did not share some framework of agreement, if they did not operate within a larger discourse whose contours we might be able to specify? Might it not be worthwhile to look again for underlying continuities of belief out of which a variety of partisan affiliations could have germinated?

In this essay, I want to suggest that one important (but hitherto underappreciated) continuity of this kind is staged by an intriguing (but hitherto unnoticed) intertextual convergence between two writers whom historical memory has assigned to opposing political camps. The first is Wyndham Lewis, whom many students of literature still know chiefly from the title of Fredric Jameson's 1979 monograph, *Fables of Aggression: Wyndham Lewis, the Modernist as Fascist*, and whom W. H. Auden called "[t]hat lonely old volcano of the Right" in 1936.[1] The second is Auden himself, widely invoked of late as a kind of general spokesman for people of conscience wondering how to live in an unjust and dangerous world, but for many decades identified as the point man for a cohort of leftist writers who came into prominence in the 1930s. Students of Lewis know that his support of fascism was predicated on a curious mixture of admiration and contempt; that this support overlapped with an endorsement — tepid to the point of irony, but not quite ironic — of communism for some countries; and that his beliefs changed frequently over the several decades of his writing career. Students of Auden know that he very briefly entertained the idea of joining the communist party, but never did, and shortly thereafter developed a resistance to strict partisan affiliations that would not prevent him from writing in socially engaged ways. Even so, there had been no attention to possible convergences between the politics of these writers until a recent essay in which Stan Smith examines the "largely unacknowledged debt to Wyndham Lewis in the work of the early Auden and his contemporaries." Smith not only shows that Auden's circle and Lewis had some surprisingly cordial things to say about each other but also illustrates, via careful attention to political groupings and regroupings in interwar England, how "the two systems of thought, feeling and action which hindsight dichotomises into Left and Right were not so obviously incompatible in the individual mindsets of many in the early 1930s."[2]

In what follows, I will be arguing that the political continuity between Lewis and Auden operates also at what we might call a more theoretical level, and specifically that the two writers share a commitment to certain core tenets of liberalism. This commitment goes well beyond mere introjection of a broadly post-Enlightenment worldview, even as it remains obscured by these writers' tendency — shared by liberals in many times and places — to disavow the liberal label. I will also suggest that this commitment is inseparable from a vision of the liberal intelligence as a kind of virtuous badness subject to certain exclusions: very precariously available to adult heterosexual Western men, it appears to Lewis and Auden virtually unavailable to members of "primitive" societies (and to Lewis out of the reach, also, of most modern children, homosexuals, and women). I will go on to claim that although this complex of views obviously does not generalize to all modernist writers, it does bear crucially on a wide range of high modernist performances. And I will conclude by arguing that in being so touched, these performances have something to say—even when they least seem to—about the revelations of comparative ethnography, the vicissitudes of liberal democracy, and the teleology of the human individual.

In his 1926 polemic *The Art of Being Ruled*, Wyndham Lewis argues that the condition of *l'entre deux guerres* is at once symptomatized and partly induced by three closely interrelated movements: feminism, the cult of youth, and homosexuality. About each, he unburdens himself of a multitude of opinions likely to strike readers today as variously fascinating, odious, prescient, and mad, but it is homosexuality that elicits his most extensive and surprising engagement. In Lewis's view, homosexuality per se is neither to be celebrated nor condemned: the "sternest moralists," he insists, "could not devise a better system for dealing with" it "than treating it on equal terms with other forms of sex emotion. . . . At its most natural (in the case of the congenital invert) it is always a passion, colouring everything about the life of the individual marked down as its prey; but, this intensity apart, it has a right to rank without comment alongside other forms of sex liveliness."[3] Professing even a certain fondness for those "true-blue" male inverts "who, whatever the orthodoxy of the moment, would . . . be there busy with all the rather complicated arrangements incident to their favorite pursuit" (238), he decries those—by far the greater fraction, in his estimate— who take up homosexuality out of conformity *to* an orthodoxy, or rather to fashion.[4] For there is, he asserts, a fashion for inversion sweeping through the cosmopolitan West and answering dangerously to certain psychic and political needs.

But what needs? The psychic need that Lewis discerns is essentially transhistorical, and arises from the hitherto little noticed fragility of the construct called "masculinity." Two decades before Simone de Beauvoir's declaration that "[o]ne is not born, but rather becomes, a woman,"[5] and seven before the performativity of gender became an academic commonplace, Lewis was observing that

> [m]en were only made into "men" with great difficulty even in primitive society: the male is not naturally "a man" any more than the woman. He has to be propped up into that position with some ingenuity, and is always likely to collapse. . . . A man . . . is made, not born: and he is made . . . with very great difficulty. From the time he yells and kicks in the cradle, to the time he receives his last kick at school, he is recalcitrant. And it is not until he is about thirty years old that the present European becomes resigned to an erect position. (279–80)

Given how discouragingly taxing it is to maintain the status of "man," Lewis avers, we will hardly be surprised to find many male persons attempting to evade its burdens. This would be true under all kinds of social conditions, but Lewis suspects that the problem became especially intense in Europe in the wake of 1914, which led many men to say "to themselves subconsciously that at last . . . the game was not worth the candle . . . that the institution of manhood had in some way overreached itself or got into the caricatural stage" (279). No wonder, given the Great War's lesson in how masculinity is rewarded, that the 1920s should witness a wave of "demasculinization developing like a prairie fire in . . . the great european centres" (294); no wonder that many males should rush to embrace a movement promising a release from the duties associated with manhood.

This alone would be consequential enough, but in Lewis's view the flight from masculine duty is a flight from duty generally, since all "normal human effort or competitive ambition has for its end to place you in a position of power or prestige," on attaining which you enter into "a position of *responsibility*" inseparable from "the male category of initiative" (270). Voguish homosexuality is thus less about any liberation of sexual desire than about a certain resistance to growing up. "[M]ale sex-inversion," according to Lewis, "can be regarded . . . as the prognostication of a deep revolution in the european character" under which freedom is identified with irresponsibility, authority is abjured, and validation attaches not to the overburdened man but to the carefree child, the never-quite-mature invert, and the passive woman (270).[6] "The education and press encouragement for the mood favourable to the development of such fashions is very striking," Lewis remarks,

> indeed there is little trouble in showing even the obtusest person how . . . extremely disagreeable it is to be in a position of authority, how very foolish it is to desire authority, how authority, responsibility, is in every form to be shunned: how it is *much pleasanter in everything to be the under dog*. Even the *male* — that queer expression of the masculine pride of the race: is it worth being *him*? It is not difficult to show that *he* . . . is no great shakes . . . and any woman, let alone a child, is better off than he is. (271)

Lewis's reference to "education and press encouragement" brings us to the political requirement answered by the elevation of woman, child, and homosexual, a requirement not of these vogues' authority-eschewing followers but, on the contrary, of those who wish to wield authority at all costs. And this requirement is simply that most people remain incapable of thinking for themselves. If one wants to manipulate a docile populace, Lewis observes, one's best bet will be not to silence dissent overtly and violently but rather to make the very capacity to dissent seem unattractively burdensome. In other words, the psychic requirement of the herd answers all too beautifully the political requirement of the power-hungry:

> Traditionally women and children are the most helpless and ill-equipped categories of mankind. Up to the present, equality of opportunity has not been achieved, and they are still the most credulous and influenceable of us. It is natural, therefore, that a great political power, interested only in domination and in nothing else, would seize on them as its most readily manipulated tools. By flattery and coercion it would discipline their ignorance and weakness into an organized instrument of social and political domination. . . . [T]he mass of the ill equipped, easily influenced, and credulous can be used to destroy the minority that knows a little more than it is proper that it should know, that is not so easy to fool, therefore, and is not so helpless. The "war" of the low-brow against the highbrow is a conflict fomented on the same principle. (206–07)

And this war of the lowbrow against the highbrow turns out to be Lewis's governing interest in *The Art of Being Ruled*, which is professedly the work of an intellectual anxious about the political ends to which anti-intellectualism is mobilized.[7]

Yet here we might pause, noting how strange it is that Lewis puts inverts and highbrows, both traditionally suspect from the point of normative masculinity, into opposing camps. How does he enforce this polarization? The answer lies, once again, in his identification of the male with responsibly critical thinking. In place of the coldly reflective intellect that could give rise to dissent, the powers that be offer the masses the sensuous, the irrational, and the unconscious; and the proselytizing invert abets this work by promoting a "natural feminine hostility to the intellect," a *"philosophy of sensation"* at war with thought (275, 244). Like its confreres (or consoeurs) feminism and the cult of the child, the homosexual vogue pits the body against the mind, which is why "Proust himself"—as Lewis asserts with characteristic outrageousness—"is an arch sex-mixer, a great democrat, a great enemy of the intellect. For he desires in the deepest way to see everything converted into terms of sex" (275).

Into this heady atmosphere, Lewis introduces what must surely count as one of the most extraordinary and exasperating of confrontations between high modernism and anthropology: his comparison of the European invert to the transgendered shaman of the Chukchee people of Siberia. Here is Lewis quoting at length from his principal source of information, *The Chukchee* (1909), a massive record of fieldwork undertaken between 1890 and 1901 by the ethnographer Waldemar Bogoras:

> A young man who is undergoing [shamanistic transformation] leaves off all pursuits and customs of his sex, and takes up those of a woman. He throws away the rifle and the lance. . . . Even his pronunciation changes from the male to the female mode. . . . He loses masculine strength . . . and acquires instead the helplessness of a woman . . . loses his brute courage and fighting spirit, and becomes shy of strangers, even fond of small talk and of nursing small children. . . .
>
> . . . . He seeks to win the good graces of men, and succeeds easily with the aid of "spirits." Thus he has all the young men he would wish for striving to obtain his favour. From them he chooses his lover, and after

a time takes a husband. The marriage is performed with the usual rites, and I must say that it forms a quite solid union which often lasts till the death of one of the parties. The couple live in much the same way as do other people. . . . They cohabit in a perverse way, *modo Socratis*, in which the transformed wife always plays the passive rôle. . . .

The state of a transformed man is so peculiar that it attracts much gossip and jests on the part of the neighbours. Such jests are of course interchanged in whispers, because the people are extremely afraid of the transformed, much more so than of ordinary *shamans*. (ABR 298–99)[8]

As we have seen, Lewis opposes the singling out of homosexuality for special moral condemnation in *The Art of Being Ruled*, and indeed in a prefatory chapter devoted to the "Universal Character of Inversion" he draws on Edward Westermarck's *Origin and Development of Moral Ideas* (1906–08) to show that homosexuality cannot be a mere by-product of European modernity.[9] Given that Lewis seemed to regard his own treatment of shamanism as central to his analysis of the European predicament, and that at least one reader of a manuscript version thought this treatment legible as propaganda *on behalf of* inversion,[10] we might expect Lewis to enlist Bogoras in the service of intercultural contrast. We might expect him, that is, to use the ethnographer's description of a socially integrated or organic kind of homosexuality as a foil to both European modishness and European homophobia.

In fact, however, Lewis dwells on points of *resemblance* between the Chukchee shaman and the noncongenital European invert, recurring particularly to the claim that in both cultures the appeal of shamanism lies in its promise of emancipation from difficult masculinity. Declaring that in "primitive life" puberty "is almost invariably accompanied by rites of rebirth and initiation, by means of which the postulant, if a male, is introduced to the male mysteries of his tribe . . . and in some cases . . . severs his connection with the women and children," Lewis remarks that it is only

natural that at this juncture, faced with the often very unnerving and disagreeable tests which accompany initiation, a certain percentage of boys should shrink from crossing this bridge to *responsibility* and *manhood*. The "spoilt child" would no doubt much rather stop with its mother.

Also the initiatory ceremonies are . . . surrounded by a great deal of mystery, and made very terrifying, for the benefit of the women and children. (301–02)

In order to advance this claim, Lewis has to suppress some key features of Bogoras's account, features later emphasized by writers on shamanism from Mircea Eliade to Michael Taussig.[11] Among these are that the shamanic vocation is *itself* associated with frightening rituals of death and rebirth, that those who receive the shamanic call often resist the vocation because it seems so fearful, and that the shaman is nearly always a figure who has suffered from and triumphed over a severe illness. Anthropological accounts concur, in other words, that the election of shamanism has little to do with any refusal either of development or of painful initiation. By pretending that it is premised on such timidity, however, Lewis is able to confirm a transculturally persistent connection among homosexuality, feminization, and immaturity, which then supports his linkage of voguish inversion with feminism and the cult of the child.

A related point that Lewis claims (in this case with more justice) to draw from ethnography is that the shaman parlays a certain kind of abnormality into a peculiar kind of authority. In the aforementioned prefatory chapter, Lewis draws on Westermarck for confirmation that homosexuality, male-to-female transformation, and epilepsy (to which we will return further on) have long been associated with magic and "divinity," their practitioners regarded as "a class apart . . . strange creatures not like other men" (289). Citing Westermarck's view that shamanism is often associated with awe of the mysterious powers of woman (not corroborated in the Chukchee case by Bogoras[12]), Lewis concludes,

> [I]t is natural that men should come to think that one of the first steps towards a career as a magician was to change their sex. . . . It is the example of a far-sighted calculation or strategy: one of the maddest flights of primitive human cunning attempting to harness supernatural energy by a *feigning*, for the easily deceived powers of the natural world, of femininity. (291–92)

In this rendering, the boy who chooses shamanism fools not only the powers of nature but also those of society, defying the standards of a group that—warily—recuperates this very defiance. The shaman becomes a licensed rebel, a countenanced transgressor, a normalized abnormal.[13]

Thus acquiring social position through the ability to inspire wonder in others, the shaman would seem to find a natural counterpart in the figure of the artist, as Lewis acknowledges elsewhere. In *Time and Western Man*, which was published in 1927 and apparently evolved from the same lost ur-manuscript as *The Art of Being Ruled*, he writes that we are entitled to describe "creative art" as "a spell, a talisman, an incantation . . . *magic*" or as "the civilized *substitute* for magic" and that in writing *King Lear* Shakespeare "was evidently in some sort of trance"[14]—a point the more freighted because in *The Lion and the Fox*, yet another outgrowth of the same ur-text, Lewis ventures that Shakespeare was almost certainly gay.[15] Yet in *The Art of Being Ruled*, Lewis aligns the duplicitous shaman not with the true artist but with the false.

Specifically, he associates the shaman with the monied faux-bohemian (often a feminist, child-cultist, or invert as well) whom he would pillory in the gigantic *Apes of God* (1930) and at dozens of other junctures in his writing, including a section on the "bohemian millionaire" in *The Art of Being Ruled* itself. For the always struggling and insubordinate Lewis, nothing was as infuriating as the spectacle of privileged "amateur" artists—Sitwells and Morrells, Woolfs and Bells—disporting themselves with the good will of a public that could refuse these loveable eccentrics nothing, provided it was not asked to pay for their prolonged juvenescense. Like the wily shaman, in Lewis's view, these shrewd operators cut a deal with society in which deference and glamour are obtained by a relinquishing of the burden of authority as we usually conceive it. The true artist and the meaningful intellectual, meanwhile, suffer painful marginalization precisely because they attempt to remain responsible: refusing to disencumber itself of critical thinking, the authentic highbrow "minority" becomes a threat because it "knows a little more than it is proper that it should know." In other words, Lewis locates the genuine highbrow's claim to authority in a capacity to think *against* authority.

Such a formulation may sound paradoxical, but it should also sound familiar, for the artist or intellectual so conceived looks very much like the classical liberal subject, or the ideal citizen as framed by democratic liberalism. In virtually all its forms, in fact, liberalism incorporates a belief in the importance of dissent, along with a view that social change over time is both inevitable and desirable. Liberalism admits and even requires, that is to say, a certain resistance to the status quo, a recuperable badness, that serves society's best interests in the long run.[16] That Lewis profoundly valued this kind of badness is clear from *The Art of Being Ruled* and *Time and Western Man*: both books commence with an insistence that modernity brings with it an irresistible, unending "revolution," but what Lewis means by this is continuous technical and ideological evolution, not violent political upheaval (indeed he declares himself opposed both to the soi-disant Revolutionary and the soi-disant Reactionary [24]). His ideal was, as Paul Edwards precisely condenses it, "the kind of society where true revolution (the will to spiritual change and progress) is not impeded by the conservative majority . . . nor . . . by those men of the world who flourish as parasites on the genuinely creative."[17]

In much of Lewis's writing, however, this thin core of aspiration comes thickly sheathed in skepticism and disappointment, and no book is more skeptical or disappointed than *The Art of Being Ruled*. Here, Lewis insists that liberalism makes a disastrous mistake in supposing it possible that all members of a society can be responsibly critical citizens, since the "true heart's desire" of the majority is a "disciplined, well-policed, herd-life," existence as "a blind, dependent, obedient cell of a crowd organism" in which thinking and governing are left to someone else (35–36). If all or even most people could be intelligent evaluators of their polities, liberal democracy would obviously be the best system imaginable. But in fact, Lewis asserts, *"men, as a whole, will never be ready"* for the civilization prepared for them by scientific progress (423, Lewis's emphasis). And liberalism, with its emphasis on "kindliness" as a political principle, "idly taunt[s] the Yahoo with what he can never hope to possess" (50).

There is "nothing wrong with democracy," then, "except the people who compose it" (374). Yet instead of meeting this state of affairs openly, modern liberal states use the press and the educational system to instill in the masses the false idea that they want to be responsible political agents and are everywhere achieving individuality. "A person is trained up stringently to certain opinions," Lewis writes in anticipation of Adorno, Althusser, and Foucault, then he is given a vote, called a "free" and fully enfranchised person; then he votes . . . strictly in accordance with his training. His support for everything that he has been taught to support can be practically guaranteed. Hence, of course, the vote of the free citizen is a farce: education and suggestion, the imposition of the will of the ruler through the press and other publicity channels, cancelling it. So "democratic" government is far more effective than subjugation by physical conquest. (111)

Supplementing these other strategies of manipulation, moreover, are vogues and trends, the harbingers of a "a political state in which no legislation, police, or any physical compulsion would be required: in which everything would be effected by public opinion, snobbery, and the magic of *fashion*" (419).

In place of liberal democracy (and "english liberalism" in particular), *The Art of Being Ruled* recommends communism for the East and fascism for the Anglo-Saxon West (27, 369). And it does so on the grounds of comparative transparency and efficiency. Ruling by naked force, the "present rulers of Russia or Italy" recognize that the average human being "finds his greatest happiness in a state of dependence and subservience" (91), and Mussolini, in particular, opens for Italy a future in which politics and economics as such will disappear because those troubling the central government will simply be assassinated. This "[c]omplete political standardization," Lewis declares,

> will rescue masses of energy otherwise wasted in politics for more productive ends. All the humbug of a democratic suffrage, all the imbecility that is so wastefully manufactured, will henceforth be spared this happy people. There will not be an extremely efficient ruling caste, pretending to possess a "liberal" section, or soft place in its heart for the struggling people. . . . There will be instead an organization that proclaims its intention to rule without interminable palaver. (370)

What brought Lewis to this astonishing a repudiation was, of course, a double disappointment—that human beings seemed unwilling to resist burgeoning technologies of mass manipulation and (inseparably) that liberal democracy had failed to prevent the Great War or the stagnation that followed. This feeling led many intellectuals to conclude that liberalism had to go (ironically, one might say, since the conviction that its moment had passed is itself whiggish in form), but it was especially dangerous to an imagination like Lewis's, which not only delighted in its ability to formulate unpopular positions but also believed itself morally bound to disseminate them.

Lewis would continue to praise fascism's comparative transparency well into the 1930s, but after *The Art of Being Ruled* his rhetoric grows a shade more prone to irony at the expense of fascists as well as liberals.[18] Even in 1926 he had promoted fascism from the vantage of cold observer rather than warm adherent, and in *Time and Western Man* he remarks how fascism has things in common with other tendencies he scorns: *passéism* (to which would-be revivers of the Naughty Nineties are also addicted, as are feminists wanting to return "to the supposed conditions of the primitive Matriarchate" [35]), demagoguéry (Mussolini has "an actor-mind . . . with all the instincts bred behind the footlights" [342]), and the promotion of doing over thinking (the fascists "have the word *action* on their lips from morning till night" [201]). More instructive still are the terms in which Lewis *explicitly* backs away from *The Art of Being Ruled* in the book of the following year. "I have now somewhat modified my views," he writes in *Time and Western Man*,

> I now believe . . . that people should be compelled to be freer and more "individualistic" than they naturally desire to be, rather than that their native unfreedom and instinct towards slavery should be encouraged and organized. I believe they could with advantage be compelled to remain absolutely alone for several hours every day; and a week's solitary confinement, under pleasant conditions (say in mountain scenery), every two months, would be an excellent provision. (118)

Lewis's tongue is in his cheek, here, but not altogether. If the human material could be reshaped, induced by whatever means necessary to think, democracy might yet have a chance.[19]

To return, now, to the figure of the shaman. If, as we have seen, Lewis aligns the shaman with the responsibility-shunning crew of false artist, child-cultist, feminist, and invert, we might expect him to align the *true* artist or intellectual with the non-shamanic adult male tribe member, responsibly exercising critical judgment and dissenting conscientiously when necessary. The problem here is that as Lewis and many early-twentieth-century Europeans understood matters, this kind of person was not to be found in "primitive" cultures. On the contrary, the absence of such a dissenting consciousness was taken to be, virtually, what made primitives primitive. One of the lessons supposedly extracted from anthropology (though in fact challenged by leading anthropologists) was that "advanced" Western societies show a high degree of differentiation and individualism, whereas "savage" ones are marked by a unity of imagination so thorough as to make critical distance on social transactions nearly impossible.

If this assumption is more or less tacit in *The Art of Being Ruled*, it could be overt and indeed preoccupying in other writings by other writers, including the early W. H. Auden. In a strange, speculative essay appearing in a leftist encyclopedia for children, for example, Auden observes confidently that people in less advanced societies do not need language as much as we do because they are less highly individuated.[20] "Among savage tribes," he notes,

> news travels much quicker than a messenger could carry it, by a sympathy which we, ignorant of its nature and incapable of practising it, call telepathy. Dr. [W. H. R.] Rivers tells a story of some natives in Melanesia getting into a rowing-boat. There was no discussion as to who should stroke or steer. All found their places, as we should say, by instinct. (EA 303)[21]

Language, he tells his young readers, originated precisely as a substitute for a feeling of unity lost in more advanced cultures, from a "need to bridge over the gulf" between self and neighbor (EA 303). And while this essay does exude a faint yearning for the undivided life, a preeminent theme of Auden's writing in this period is the undesirability of regression for individuals as for societies.

Nor is this true of the early Auden only. As I have argued elsewhere, the necessity of increasing individuation remained one of Auden's central convictions over the long arc of his career.[22] Particularly impressive, in this regard, is how neatly the secular version of this view that he held in the thirties harmonizes with the style of Christianity he would adopt after his return to Anglicanism in 1939. For the earlier Auden, self-consciousness was the burdensome, complicated, painful asset that (paradoxically) installed human beings at the summit of biological evolution, just as the differentiation that makes dissent possible rendered modern Western societies incomparably the most advanced. Of the many poems Auden wrote in celebration of this troubled complexity, the earliest is probably "Our hunting fathers" of 1934, in the first stanza of which he imagines "our" ancestors seeing

> in the lion's intolerant look,
> Behind the quarry's dying glare,
> Love raging for the personal glory
>   That reason's gift would add,
> The liberal appetite and the power,
>   The rightness of a god.

In the second stanza, however, he corrects this expectation: contra our ancestors, he insists, we see that love is not associated with simple mastery but "by nature suited to / The intricate ways of guilt" and desire (EA 151). With an economy unsurpassed in any of his later poems on this theme, Auden here manages a double movement, first from the proto-humanity of animals to the imaginative projection performed by "our" primitive forebears, then from those ancestors to the still more richly complicated beings "we" are. The post-1939 Auden would then complement this evolutionary view— in which uncertainty, vexation, and changefulness are the very indices of evolutionary superiority—with a persistent gratitude for the fortunate fall. "There must be sorrow if there can be love," he writes in 1942's "Canzone," while the chorus in 1944's *For the Time Being* declares, "*The distresses of choice are our chance to be blessed.*"[23]

Within this paradigm, the highbrow turns out to occupy a position of unrivaled importance as both end and means. As end, because he stands as the most evolved being within the most evolved species, and thus obtains the highest metaphysical value; as means, because his exercise of the critical faculty is essential to society's continuing evolution.[24] In a 1933 review Auden defines the highbrow as

[s]omeone who is not passive to his experience but who tries to organise, explain and alter it, someone in fact, who tries to influence his history: a man struggling for life in the water is for the time being a highbrow.

The decisive factor is a conflict between the person and his environment; most of the people who are usually called highbrows had either an unhappy childhood and adolescence or suffer from physical defects. (*EA* 317 / *P1* 37–38)

In a 1939 Hogarth Press pamphlet on education, Auden and his co-author T. C. Worsley would insist that there "must always be a conflict between the loyalty necessary for society to be, and the intelligence necessary for society to become" (*P1* 415). And Auden's writing of the preceding years suggests that only a childhood marked by an obscure sense of divergence from imposed norms—what we might today describe as a queer childhood—can produce this felicitously disloyal intelligence. In 1936's "Letter to Lord Byron" (the same poem in which he christens Lewis "that lonely old volcano of the Right"), for instance, he comes out against "the modern trick" of "straightening out the kinks in the young mind"; exhorts, "Let each child have that's in our care / As much neurosis as the child can bear"; and, with an echo of Woolf's allegory of the sisters Proportion and Conversion in *Mrs. Dalloway*, denounces that "[g]oddess of bossy underlings, Normality" for the "murders . . . committed in [her] name" (*EA* 193). Where Lewis drew an analogy between children and the infantalization-embracing masses, then, Auden was interested in what kinds of children would grow up to be critical intellectuals.

Auden would vociferate against efforts to raise healthy, unconflicted children repeatedly from the mid-1930s on, always associating such sanitary projects with "liberalism" in spite of the fact that his own position constituted a sort of liberalism-by-default in its acceptance of Western democratic structures and its rejection of fascism, communism, and most conservatism. In the early 1930s, however, this stance had not yet solidified, nor had his poetry taken the turn toward more traditional forms that would later predominate. In this period, the very beginning of his career as a published author, he famously wrestled with the attractions not only of more disjunctive poetic modes but also of more radical political movements, producing what for some remains his most vital and significant work. Among the products of this rich and strange period, arguably the richest and strangest is *The Orators: An English Study*—which, as it happens, includes an encounter with the Chukchee shaman.

On its publication in 1932, this complicated work seems to have been received as a sort of *Waste Land* for the new decade: few reviewers professed to
understand it, but it cemented Auden's literary celebrity nonetheless. And
while this opacity prevents any summary of the text from doing it justice,
some survey will have to be attempted here. Book I, "The Initiates," opens
with "Address for a Prize-Day," a parody of an English public school oration
in which the young audience is instructed to locate abnormals in its midst
and which ends with the frightening imperatives, "Quick, guard that door.
Stop that man. Good. Now boys hustle them, ready, steady—go" (EA 64).[25]
The rest of Book I is written from the viewpoint of the adolescent followers
of a charismatic young quasi-fascist leader whose attempt to topple mainstream English society eventually fails. The size and nature of this group
remain unclear: it may be a revolutionary insurgency that draws its forms
from English public school bonding, but it may be a band of English public schoolboys imagining themselves as a revolutionary insurgency. (It even
seems possible that the whole is the projective fantasy of a single adolescent.) Book II, the "Journal of an Airman," is written from the point of view
of the leader himself, and includes poetic catalogues in celebration of avia-
tion, meditations on the nature of the "enemy," and fragmentary notations
of hopes, doubts, and interactions with friend and foe. This book draws to
a close with the Airman concluding that "the power of the enemy is a function of our resistance" and that "self-destruction" is therefore the only path
to victory; its final lines suggest that the Airman commits literal or figurative suicide by crashing his literal or figurative plane (EA 93–94). Book III
consists of six odes echoing the themes of the first two books and built
mainly around the experience of English private-school education. (Auden
was teaching at the Larchfield Academy, a small school near Glasgow, at the
time of their writing.)

As Peter Firchow, and after him other scholars such as Edward Mendelson, John Fuller, and Richard Bozorth, have noted,[26] *The Orators* owes a
great deal to two ethnographic essays published by Auden's friend John
Layard in the *Journal of the Royal Anthropological Institute of Great Britain and Ireland* in 1930.[27] The first is titled "Malekula: Flying Tricksters,
Ghosts, Gods, and Epileptics" and draws on fieldwork Layard had done
in the New Hebrides (now Vanuatu) in 1914–15; in it, Layard describes the

Bwili, or flying tricksters of Malekula. These are men who, according to native informants, "all fly, in the form of fowls" and can assume as well other forms, in which "they indulge their spite by killing their enemies, though at other times their activities take the form of playing practical jokes on their friends." The Bwili "cannot be said to constitute a society," according to Layard, since they provide "little mutual assistance" and "are as liable to direct their attentions against one another as against the rest of mankind," but his informants do describe an initiation ritual in which the candidate, who is always "the sister's son of the initiator," has his arms, legs, and head cut off. If he "can laugh throughout the operation . . . he will survive and himself become a Bwili," but if "he cannot laugh, he dies."[28]

In the speculative discussion that he appends to his recording of Bwili lore, Layard connects the dismemberment, resurrection, and flying motifs of the Bwili initiation with tropes from the mythology of Osiris, and hazards that the practical joking and "impish behaviour" of the Bwili, in combination with the resurrection figure, imply an origin in "ritual epilepsy." The epileptic, according to Layard, "retains an infantile mentality, with the result that he is apt to be child-like in his tastes, irresponsible, roguish, and playful, while the misunderstanding he invariably meets with tends at times to render him spiteful and malicious" (519–20). Some epileptics, however, can produce the living death of epileptic seizures at will, and in cases like the Malekulan, "where the subject would find himself neither pitied nor despised, but actually venerated on account of his attacks, the inducement of religious ecstasy . . . would probably be sufficient to produce the desired state of mind" (522). Noting further that one "of the hitherto inexplicable activities of the Malekulan ghost is that of anally penetrating the candidates during their 30 days' seclusion in the main initiation rite" (523), he suggests that homosexuality is woven into the system because both epilepsy and homosexuality originate in regressive behavior. Both involve an avoidance of difficult situations by reversion to childlike states and suppression of "the adult side of" psychic conflicts, and indeed "epileptics are also apt to become homosexual" (523–24). He rounds out the essay by pointing to an ancient Egyptian papyrus "dealing with the anal penetration of Horus by Set" and asking whether, in addition to being "irresponsible and homosexual," Set was "also epileptic" (524).

The resonances with Lewis are striking, of course. Here, as in the sha-

A Shaman in Common

man section of *The Art of Being Ruled*, homosexuality appears as a failure of maturation (acknowledgment of their own homosexuality preventing neither Layard nor Auden from theorizing an etiology in regression) and the primitive magician uses the awe associated with sickness, strangeness, and death to transform marginalization into authority. But the convergence with Lewis becomes even more dramatic in the second of Layard's 1930 essays, "Shamanism: An Analysis Based on Comparison with the Flying Tricksters of Malekula." For in that piece Layard turns, for confirmation of his theories, to comparable data on the Siberian shaman. Layard's principal source for information on Siberian shamanism is M. A. Czaplicka's 1914 volume, *Aboriginal Siberia*, but it turns out that Czaplicka (whose project was to synthesize reports from a variety of investigators) gets much of her data from Waldemar Bogoras, the same source principally used by Lewis.

In this second essay, Layard observes that entry into the shamanic vocation coincides with recovery from an intense period of nervous illness, so that the shaman may be described as "one of those persons, not absent among ourselves, who know how to turn their 'affliction' into an asset."[29] He goes on to refer to shamanic affinities for birds and flight; to the "erratic, malicious, and childish" character of the spirits with whom shamans confer; and to a belief held by some peoples (not including the Chukchee) that the spirit possessing the shaman may be an ancestor (536, 539, 531). Next, he turns to the "ritual homosexuality" associated with shamanism, dwelling particularly on the transformed man of the Chukchee and reproducing passages from Czaplicka that prove near quotations of some of the very sentences from Bogoras that we have seen Lewis working into *The Art of Being Ruled*. Concerning the transformed shaman's domestic life, for example, Czaplicka writes, and Layard quotes:

> The marriage is performed with the usual rites, and the union is as durable as any other. The "man" goes hunting and fishing, the "woman" does domestic work. Bogoras thinks they cohabit *modo Socratis*. . . . [P]ublic opinion is always against them, but as the transformed shamans are very dangerous, they are not opposed and no outward objections are raised. (542–43)[30]

Layard goes on to remark that both the shamans and the Bwili "are individualists," their practice marked by "an entire lack of organization such as is found elsewhere between the different practitioners of a homogeneous cult" (548–49). This absence of organization, he concludes, may be attributed to these magicians' reliance on the spectacular production of "epileptoid symptoms," an affair of "individual inspiration" whose "ritually disintegrating effect" seems confirmed by a parallel Western case: "Catholicism, firmly based on ritual," maintains its unity, whereas Protestant sects, with their stress on individual relationship to the deity, continue to multiply (549–50).

As Firchow and other scholars after him have noted, Auden works many of Layard's motifs into his "English Study." Flying is discussed obsessively in *The Orators* (the Airman's journal even includes poetic allusions to one who "keep[s] on trying to be a bird" and to "a flying trickster" in the woods [EA 76, 77]), and references to practical joking, neurosis, ancestors, and resurrection abound:[31] the "[t]hree signs of an airman" are "practical jokes — nervousness before taking off — rapid healing after injury" and the "[t]hree counter attacks" to be used against the enemy are "complete mastery of the air — ancestor worship — practical jokes" (EA 81–82). Most significant for our purposes, however, is Auden's ingenious use of the transposition to England to establish another kind of link between homosexuality and the uncle-nephew initiation pattern. In one of the Bwili legends Layard recounts, a boy who has become a Bwili tries to conceal from his mother that he has undergone transformation, the story ending as follows:

> And when they got home the son was there. And now his mother was angry with him, and said, "What were you doing all the seven days that you were with your uncle?" "Nothing special," he said. "Oh," she replied, "Do you think I'm a fool? You have deceived me three times now. First you pretended you were a pig, then a fowl, and now you've been pretending to be a *wawa* tree and making me miss it all the time. Don't deceive me any more. Tell me about it." And he said, "Yes, it was me."[32]

In Auden's version, the Airman records his mother's inexplicable hostility to his Uncle Henry, then recalls, "It wasn't till I was sixteen and a half that he invited me to his flat. We had champagne for dinner. When I left I knew who and what he was — my real ancestor" (EA 85). The Airman, fashioning himself an heir-man, leaves no doubt that he wishes always to honor the memory of this uncle, who seems to have committed suicide too. (Here ritual death and resurrection are linked yet again to ancestral transmission.) But it is not clear whether uncle and nephew have sexual contact or simply acknowledge some kind of common disposition.[33]

Nor is it clear, for that matter, that the common disposition even has to do with sexuality—an important ambiguity, because it complements Auden's refusal to reveal whether the bond between the Airman and his followers is homosexual or strictly homosocial. Abnormality in love is the quality that the Prize Day orator in the first part of Book I seeks to eradicate: he condemns those guilty of "excessive love towards themselves or their neighbours, those guilty of defective love towards God, and those guilty of perverted love," and while he encourages his auditors to help the first two classes of faulty lover, he suggests that the third is not only the "worst" but also beyond help, destined absolutely for the ranks of "proscribed persons" (EA 62–64). Yet the relationship between the Airman's group and the Prize Day orator is ambiguous. Do the boys follow the behests of that speaker, or do they hope to destroy him and those who resemble him? Do they recognize themselves as guilty of perverted love and practice gay sex, or do they number homosexuals among the enemy? Or both at once? In the first edition of the book, the Airman's love object, identified only as "E," is female; in the second edition, male,[34] but even in the latter case it is not clear whether language like "O understand, darling" (EA 94) is that of homosexual attachment or of romantic male friendship—neither of which, of course, is incompatible with homophobic aggression.[35]

As if these ambiguities were not sufficient, *The Orators* requires us to consider another possibility: that the real matter of interest is less the homosexual versus the homosocial than something that we might, with contemporary terminology but also with some precision, denominate "the queer." The Prize Day orator notably says nothing at all about sex when cataloguing the symptoms of aberrant love: "[e]xcessive lovers of self" are not expressly accused of masturbation, but rather of being, among other curious things, "[h]abituees of the mirror, famous readers" who "fall in love with historical characters," like to "develop photographs," and "even in childhood played in their corner." Excessive lovers of neighbours are "heavy smokers" who (counterintuitively) resist "pass[ing] the ball" in team sports; defective lovers "sit by fires they can't make up their minds to light" and are "[a]naemic, muscularly undeveloped and rather mean"; perverted lovers are prone to influenza, afraid of cows, and exhibit a "gait wooden like a galvanised doll." The orator then discerns that some of the boys he is addressing "have no daydreams . . . wince at no curse," and "are never ill" — but all of these prove *undesirable* traits, inasmuch as he next asks the boys to promise him that they'll "never be like that" (EA 62–64). What makes the Prize Day orator's catalogue so unsettling is thus not only its arbitrariness but also its breadth. It seems to demonize every possible adherence to norms as well as every possible deviation from them, leaving one hard pressed to see who can remain free of suspicion or censure. By the time it concludes, virtually everyone has been rendered queer and dangerous.

A similar complexity informs the ensuing sections of *The Orators*, wherein the relationship between the Airman's band and queerness firmly resists specification. The members of the group seem highly conscious, indeed protective, of their neuroses and are given to rhetoric and rituals (including the aforementioned practical joking) that seem as idiosyncratic as they are inventive. If the band anticipates suppressing queerly individual behavior on accession to power, therefore, it would — like British public schools and fascist parties — have at the very least to make exceptions for its own tendencies, customs, and priorities.

Queerness also emanates from the group members' covert spurning of the bourgeois milieu they continue to inhabit: in the second section of the first book, one of them writes, "Smile inwardly on their day handing round tea," as if what anneals their bond is a superiority-conferring knowledge of their impending revolution (EA 64). Such secret knowledge is a privilege of the espionage ring, of course, but it is also central to the epistemology of the closet. The epigraph to the Airman's discussion of the enemy, moreover, is a familiar caricature of the respectable Englishman of the older generation, full of talk of responsibility but guilty of the most catastrophic irresponsibility in sending younger men to die in the Great War ("His collar was spotless; he talked very well, / He spoke of our homes and duty and we fell" [EA 81]). Further, many of the enemy's characteristics seem typical of the mainstream English liberal: "Three enemy questions — Am I boring you? — Could you tell me the time? — Are you sure you're fit enough?" (EA 81). Yet in other cases the enemy seems abundantly queer; the three kinds of enemy walk, for example, are "the grandiose stunt — the melancholic stagger — the paranoic [*sic*] sidle" (EA 81–82).

Whether on the side of the Prize Day speaker or opposed to him, then, the Airman's group replicates that orator's move of rendering everyone potentially queer. Nor is this effect confined to individuals, for every kind of social vision also seems at risk of demonization in this text. The Airman names as the enemy's first wave of attack "Flux-mongers (shock-troops for destruction)," as if he has read Lewis's diatribes against the legacy of Bergson in *The Art of Being Ruled* and *Time and Western Man*, but he designates as the second wave, "Order-doctrinaires (establishment of martial law)" (EA 84). Opposed both to flux and to imposed order, the Airman professes to believe that a "system organises itself, if interaction is undisturbed" (EA 73), but this anti-entropic libertarianism is undercut by his own attempt at revolutionary intervention, as he perhaps comes to realize at the very end of his journal. These contradictions reach their boiling point in the slightly amusing but mostly disturbing fourth ode of Book III, in which Auden's speaker disparages the proletariat, the upper classes, the younger generation, a series of world leaders (including MacDonald, Hoover, Mussolini, and Hitler), a series of writers ("Where is Lewis? Under the sofa. / Where is Eliot? Dreaming of nuns"), and "the Simonites, the Moselyites, and the I.L.P" (EA 101–05). No one past the age of infancy can be trusted with the future, then; the one who will rescue England, who will "save John Bull / From losing his wool" (and who, incidentally, appears "[q]ueer to" all of these other "birds: yes, very queer") is John, the newborn son of Lewis's friends Rex and Frances Warner (EA 103, 105). Only the young Auden, perhaps, would put the occasion of a birth to such use, but his temerity is felicitous: few texts convey more keenly the vital ideological exhaustion, the energetic cynicism, of the interwar years.

The moral of *The Orators* thus seems to be that if fascism and other movements emphasizing collective action demand some relinquishing of the queer individualism that Auden so greatly prized, liberalism does so no less relentlessly. The queer society of the Airman's followers cannot succeed in renovating England, but the surrender of eccentricity, romance, plans, secrets, and practical jokes that would come with reabsorption by the genial liberal mainstream looks equally unacceptable. Moreover, the liberal form of the demand may be more insidious and damaging because it is so much less transparent. The discovery that "the power of the enemy is a function of our resistance" is especially apposite if the enemy is a liberal, since it is precisely resistance that liberalism pretends, up to a point, to encourage. Here Auden crucially meets Lewis, and yet one might say that Auden is even more profoundly hostile to liberalism in *The Orators* than Lewis is in *The Art of Being Ruled*. For whereas Lewis would not mind liberal democracy if only everybody could be intelligent, Auden suggests that tolerance itself may be pernicious, antipathetic both in its rhetoric and in its practice to individuation. This is perhaps why, even though contemporary readers may have trouble finding much of a recommendation for fascism in *The Orators*, Auden wrote in 1966 that the book seems the work of "someone else, someone talented but near the border of sanity, who might well, in a year or two, become a Nazi."[36]

For conservatives, one might say, good is good in the sense that good behavior toward the status quo (or toward a prior condition taken to be normative) is generally esteemed. For radicals, on the other hand, good can be said to be bad, since what is required for the realization of a better world is behavior that the regime in power will count threatening and evil. What both Lewis and Auden preferred, once again, was the good badness of the critical intelligence, the principled dissent that had long been part of liberalism's self-definition. Why, then, did they so vociferously reject the term "liberal"? As we have seen, the answer lies in a shared sense not only that liberal democracy had failed to live up to its vast aspirations but also that liberalism pretended to encourage free thought while in fact aiming (principally by means of the educational system and the press) to eradicate it. For both, in other words, liberalism named a bad goodness *masquerading as* good badness, an inhibition of dissent disguised as the sponsoring of freedom.

Yet if this perceived fraudulence compromised liberal democracy well into the thirties for Lewis, Auden's outlook changed rapidly after *The Orators*. To be sure, he would continue to disavow liberalism and to mistrust forms of tolerance that he perceived as systematically mandated. But he also began to think that the prevailing order might be accepted so long as it provided room for the dissenters who would help it to evolve—began to have hope, that is, that modern democracies would yet provide their queers, their highbrows, their neurotic children, and their other dissidents something like a shamanic role. The reasons why Auden's views should change so much more quickly than Lewis's are multiple. One was that in the early

A Shaman in Common

1930s Auden was still a young man exploring rather than defending possible political orientations; another, surely, was that he would have experienced his swift entry into literary lionhood as confirmation that highbrows and others of critically queer disposition might be allowed to wield their integrity against the forces of deceit. (Such a possibility would have been much harder for Lewis to entertain in this period: while the young rebel found himself suddenly a sage, the "lonely old volcano" believed himself at odds with most literati, struggled with physical illness, and turned out book after book in a grinding effort to make ends meet.)

Another key reason, however, lies in these writers' respective understandings — both mediated through the figure of the shaman — of the queer subject in European society. For Lewis (and for Auden's friend Layard), shamanized individuals, whether savage or modern, "turn their 'affliction' into an asset," use their relegation to the social periphery to carve a niche in the social center. In the modern European case, as in the Chukchee, the privilege of shamanhood is a kind of authority without responsibility, possible because other members of society, whether out of condescension or awe, grant special license to the figure whose development seems arrested. How Auden departs from this view is legible in two features of Layard's anthropology that he *omits* from his modern "English Study."

One is that of the shaman-trickster's deviously successful integration. Far from using his sense of his own difference to acquire standing within the prevailing order, the Airman refuses flatly to compromise or surrender: on recognizing that the enemy's power is a function of his resistance, he commits suicide, or withdraws in some other fashion that presumably prevents the enemy from profiting by his struggle. The other feature Auden omits, which is closely entangled with the first but harder to see, is the premise that the magician embraces childishness out of a wish to evade responsibility. Whatever else the Airman and his fellow practical jokers may be, they are evidently earnest and idealistic, interested not in merely pretending to serve society's interests but in *actually* serving those interests (albeit as they — alarmingly — construe them). In other words, *The Orators* allows for, if it does not quite present, an aligning of the responsible citizen with the queer personality, and in this at least opens the door to a certain rapprochement between society and critical intelligences as Auden conceived them (a rapprochement in which the latter would assume responsibility for the former's perpetual reinvention). For Lewis, by contrast, the possibility of reconciliation between critical intellectuals and liberal democracy was further weakened by a fantasy that an ensconced cult of inversion was already undercutting the serious efforts of true artists and intellectuals.[37] In Lewis's vision—which no doubt seemed confirmed by the very eminence of the sexually ambiguous Auden generation—shamanic queerness was already in power, and out not to amend the present condition of Europe but to intensify its most baleful characteristics.

One final point. Although certain kinds of modern individuals could be likened to the shaman at crucial textual junctures, as we have seen, this metaphoric relation could never quite modulate into an identity. If for Lewis and Auden the shaman and the Western highbrow resembled each other in being more individuated than other members of their respective societies, it remained the case that on another axis—that of absolute rather than relative individuation—Western intellectuals would inevitably resemble other Westerners more nearly than they would any Malekulan or Chukchee. In the view of neither writer could the non-Western shaman actually attain the Western intellectual's level of individuality, for the simple reason that no "primitive" could—at least not without ceasing to be primitive. Nor was this assumption limited to Lewis and Auden. Certainly, the putative discovery that the modern soul and the "savage" one had much in common animated a great deal of modernist art and writing; this is indeed the very essence of primitivism as we have lately come to understand it. But there remained in the background of high modernism—its highly various eruptions of primitivist fantasy, cross-cultural sensitivity, and xenophobic intolerance notwithstanding—a potent sense of residual difference between the modern "we" and the primitive "they," a difference whose most essential parameter was degree of individuation.

This point carries significance even for texts that seem far from the orbit of the primitive, because no human quality was more consistently precious to modernists than individuation manifested as critical intelligence. If one feature links Lewis's persecuted artist and Auden's self-conscious highbrow with Clarissa Dalloway and Leopold Bloom and Quentin Compson and the poetic voices of Eliot, Stein, Stevens, and company, it is the possession of independence of mind. Even D. H. Lawrence, remembered by some as a strident unifier, in fact abominates merging in his central pronouncements, precisely on the ground that total melding would render impossible the relating between separate individuals that counts as the very highest good. This extraordinary privileging of the individualized critical intelligence clearly distinguishes modernist priorities from those of the mainstream nineteenth century, not because the latter failed to value individualism, intellection, or difference, but because it was much more comfortable with normativity — much less suspicious of what we might call the un-queer angle of view. In this elevation of the dissenting imagination we encounter something more like an inheritance from Romanticism (by way, in the Anglo-American case at least, of Wildean aestheticism's privileging of "Individualism" and "Personality"). And we encounter too a kind of general version of something we observed in the Auden of the mid-1930s and after. For in modernism's attachment to critical consciousness generally, as in Auden's more specific praise of the highbrow, esteem for a certain kind of political disposition passes into something more than political: a sense that surrender of the dissenting faculty would (for Westerners, at least) constitute a regression tantamount to self-erasure. The good badness of modernism is finally very difficult to separate from the good badness of liberalism because both are variants of an individuation presumed to arrive at the culmination of some evolution, an evolution it would be unthinkable to try to reverse except in the direst extremity.

The Art of Being Ruled and The Orators venture that just such an extremity may have materialized with the stagnation of l'entre deux guerres. Neither book validates regression in any global sense — to do so would, after all, go against their authors' leading convictions — but both entertain the idea that a sort of temporary, peculiarly circumscribed regression (associated with fascism) could assist the cause of progress in the long run. By the end of the 1930s, of course, extremity had taken the very different form of possible conquest by the Axis powers, and regression had lost the last of its always limited charm. In The Hitler Cult of 1939, part of his atonement for 1931's disastrously misguided Hitler, Lewis finds in the "intemperate crudity" of fascism not a step backward by means of which society might paradoxically move ahead, but backwardness pure and simple; in a Nation article of February 11, 1941, Auden would describe "[m]odern society" as "a differentiated society in disorder," whose problems the fascists propose to remedy by means of "a return to primitive uniformity . . . a theirs-not-to-reason-why obedience."[38]

The alternative that Auden presents in this period is also instructive. Instead of promoting cultivation of the dissenting, neurotic consciousness as he had through the 1930s, he argues in the *Nation* essay that the "cohesion of a differentiated and open society can only be secured through a common agreement upon a small number of carefully defined general presuppositions"—though (and this is important) such agreement must be coupled with a recognition "that these presuppositions are not knowledge" and that "as a society changes, its constellation of presuppositions . . . changes too" (*P2* 102). In a piece appearing the following month in the *Yale Daily News*, he adds that "every psychological resource, every trick of advertisement and propaganda" should be used to indoctrinate children in certain basic moral principles (reverence, obligation, justice, sociality) and notably faults "Liberalism" for concluding, from the "psychological damage often done to the young by faulty techniques in teaching . . . virtues" that it is wrong to try to teach virtue at all (*P2* 122). In the terrifying shadow of fascist regression, in other words, Auden proposes just the kind of indoctrination he had once found utterly untenable, but only in tandem with a grown-up recognition that no principle is immune to challenge, no authority above critique. In this remedy for the disorder of modern societies, the moral trajectory of each individual would recapitulate the progress of humankind as Auden understood it—from an undifferentiated good behavior to a badness honed with infinite solicitude.

Notes

1. W. H. Auden, *The English Auden: Poems, Essays, and Dramatic Writings 1927–1939* (London: Faber, 1977), 198. Hereafter designated as *EA*.
2. Stan Smith, "Re-Righting Lefty: Wyndham and Wystan in the Thirties," *Wyndham Lewis Annual* 9–10 (2002–03): 36. Smith—whose eloquent article I encountered after the present essay was mostly complete—dwells heavily on *The Orators*, as I do here, but focuses on quite different strands within that text.
3. Wyndham Lewis, *The Art of Being Ruled* (New York: Haskell House, 1972), 310. Reprint of the 1926 edition. Hereafter designated as *ABR*.
4. Lewis has little to say about lesbians in *The Art of Being Ruled*, though they figure prominently in novels like *The Apes of God* and *The Revenge for Love*.

5. Simone de Beauvoir, *The Second Sex* (New York: Vintage, 1974), 301.

6. Lewis's position on women and feminism in *The Art of Being Ruled*, which seems the result of an attempt to reconcile reflexive misogyny with the more disinterested recognition that women are not innately inferior, requires a little clarification. Lewis insists that by the interwar years, feminism's original (and praiseworthy) struggle for equality of opportunity had been hijacked by those who, for reasons discussed below, were interested in rendering all authority suspect. Feminism as conjured by Lewis has to do not with the empowering, educating, and rallying of female persons but with a fetishizing of powerlessness, ignorance, and political passivity for all persons. Instead of protesting the transmutation of women into dolls, this spectral feminism advocates the dollification of all people by insisting that "woman" (a socially constructed phenomenon) is better than (the equally constructed) "man." "It is not more natural for one sex than for the other to be heroic or to be responsible," Lewis writes at one point; the "position of the male today, and the symbolism of the word MAN, are purely artificial: no more for one sex than for the other are the heroic ardours, 'intellectuality,' *responsibility*, and so forth, that we associate with the male, *natural*" (282).

7. In *Rude Assignment* (1950), Lewis discusses his life as an intellectual at length. "I am," he writes, "what is described as a 'highbrow.' That is the first thing about me; it underlies, and influences, all other things that I am — all the things that it is not desirable to be." But "highbrow" is not a designation that one exactly chooses; rather, the word "was coined slightingly and damagingly to describe those who persisted in employing their critical faculties." Wyndham Lewis, *Rude Assignment* (Santa Barbara: Black Sparrow, 1984), 15, 17.

8. The ellipses are mine. The quotation can be found in Waldemar Bogoras, *The Chukchee* (New York: Johnson Reprint Corporation; reprinting the edition of New York: G. E. Stechert, 1909), 450–51. Lewis's transcription varies slightly from my edition of Bogoras; his three alterations are the substitution of "customs" for Bogoras's "manners," the omission of the word "only" from Bogoras's "interchanged only in whispers," and italicization of the concluding "shamans."

9. Lewis misremembers the title of the book: "In his *History of Moral Ideas*," he writes, "Dr. Westermarck devotes a chapter to the history of sex inversion" (289).

10. Seeking a publisher for "The Man of the World," the immense manuscript from which *The Art of Being Ruled*, as well as *The Lion and the Fox* (1927), *Time and Western Man* (1927), and *The Childermass* (1928) would eventually be derived, Lewis recommended his section on shamanism particularly to his reader's attention. In a February 2, 1925, cover letter accompanying that now lost ur-text, he advised Alec Waugh of Chapman and Hall, "I suggest if you [*sic*] reading it tomorrow, that you should start at page 13 . . . & read to p. 19. inclusive. After that the part numbered XVII & called The Shaman. It deals principally with sexual inversion, & explains the term shamanizing . . . , used frequently elsewhere" (quoted in Paul Edwards, afterword to *Time and Western Man*, by Wyndham Lewis [Santa Rosa: Black Sparrow, 1993], 483). Following the rejection of "The Man of the World" as a whole, Lewis seems to have offered some of its material to Robert

McAlmon, publisher of Contact Editions and co-partner in a marriage of convenience with H. D.'s lover Bryher; it was McAlmon who wrote back with concern that his press not gain a reputation for "propoganding [*sic*] for inversion" (quoted in Edwards, 485).

11. See, for example, Bogoras, *The Chukchee*, 415–24, esp. 420–21; Mircea Eliade, *Shamanism: Archaic Techniques of Ecstasy* (Princeton, N.J.: Princeton University Press, 1964), 27–31; and Michael Taussig, *Shamanism, Colonialism, and the Wild Man: A Study in Terror and Healing* (Chicago: University of Chicago Press, 1987), 447–48, 460–62.

12. Other ethnographers of Siberia in this period were more attracted to the idea that shamanism originated among women; evaluating the collected evidence in *Aboriginal Siberia* (1914), however, M. A. Czaplicka (to whom I will return below) found it wanting. More likely, in her view, was that shamans developed from a class of slaves, originally dressed in women's clothes in order to degrade and weaken them. M. A. Czaplicka, *Aboriginal Siberia* (Richmond, Surrey: Curzon Press, 1999), 253–55.

13. Bogoras notes not only that in the spiritual performances central to their vocation shamans "employ deceit in various forms" but also that at least some other members of the social group "are aware of the deceit" (429). In the section on the transgendered shaman, he comments that "it is difficult to find out how far auto-suggestion is responsible for the change . . . and which of these changes are merely assumed . . . in order to make an impression on the public mind" (*The Chukchee*, 451).

14. Wyndham Lewis, *Time and Western Man* (Santa Rosa: Black Sparrow, 1993), 187–88.

15. See Wyndham Lewis, *The Lion and the Fox: The Rôle of the Hero in the Plays of Shakespeare* (New York: Harper and Brothers, 1927), 153–60; also 221–27 on Falstaff's humor as an "excellent substitute" for the "*shamanizing* faculty" (224). The connection between artist and shaman would become especially significant in poetry of the 1960s and after; see, on Gary Snyder and others, Tom Henighan, "Shamans, Tribes, and the Sorcerer's Apprentices: Notes on the Discovery of the Primitive in Modern Poetry," *Dalhousie Review* 59 (1979–80): 605–20.

16. As J. G. Merquior notes in his handy summary, *Liberalism Old and New* (Boston: Twayne, 1991), liberalism "presupposes a wide *variety of values and beliefs*, unlike the moral compact alleged by conservatives or prescribed by most radical utopias," and this central tenet is entangled with the history of religious dissent. Toleration, in the vision of writers like Locke, Paley, and Voltaire, is a matter not just of justice to the individual but, more acutely, of practical benefit to society, and liberalism inherits this assumption (4, 18). By the Edwardian era, liberalism's conjoined interests in social progress (which increasingly seemed to mandate state intervention) and individual liberty were straining against each other with disruptive intensity; see on this Michael Levenson's reading of Forster's *Howards End* (1910) together with L. T. Hobhouse's *Liberalism* (1911) (Michael Levenson, *Modernism and the Fate of Individuality* [Cambridge: Cambridge University Press, 1991], 86–93). In the twenty-first century, the relation between liberalism and market-governed "neoliberalism" is much debated, but it does seem clear that neoliberalism weakens its claim to continuity with liberalism proper insofar as it pits itself against meaningful dissent.

17. Edwards, afterword, 464.

18. In *Hitler* (London: Chatto and Windus, 1931), for example, he insists that "unadulterated democracy" is "quite impossible," and that the novelty of Nazism is that "the German Nation has the chance at present of *voting* for its future tyrant," which perhaps brings it nearer "true democracy" than any other country in Europe (195). Andrew Hewitt discusses *Hitler* (and, more briefly, *The Art of Being Ruled* and *The Hitler Cult*) in his *Political Inversions: Homosexuality, Fascism, and the Modernist Imaginary* (Stanford, Calif.: Stanford University Press, 1996).

19. The stunning lacuna at the heart of Jameson's book, *Fables of Aggression: Wyndham Lewis, the Modernist as Fascist* (Berkeley: University of California Press, 1979), is that it has nothing to say about the volume in which Lewis most strongly promotes fascism as such. That Jameson had even read *The Art of Being Ruled* when he published his study is hard to imagine, given that he mentions it only once, in a list of Lewis's major polemics of the twenties and thirties; instead, he draws his impressions of Lewis's take on fascism from the more sensationally disreputable 1931 volume, *Hitler*. Under these circumstances, Jameson does fairly well: his key remark that "it is from the standpoint of" a "position of combined weakness and intelligence that Lewis' . . . polemics against the modern age are launched" is exactly to the point (121). But in missing *The Art of Being Ruled*, and in trying to tie almost everything in Lewis's writing to the intellectual's petit-bourgeois fear of communism as the completion of social leveling, Jameson is led to erase Lewis's own (proto-Althusserian) emphasis on the ideological work of state apparatuses, to obscure the degree to which fascism's appeal for Lewis lay in its putative transparency, and generally to underplay Lewis's consciousness of his own historical situation.

20. The editor of this encyclopedia was Naomi Mitchison—who was great friends with Lewis in the 1930s, in spite of their widely divergent political positions. (According to Jeffrey Meyers in *The Enemy: A Biography of Wyndham Lewis* [London: Routledge, 1980], Mitchison "did not feel he was, in any sense, a Fascist," but rather would take "cruel or violent" positions to provoke reactions in others [202].) She and Lewis even collaborated on a sort of picture book for grown-ups (words by Mitchison, illustrations by Lewis) called *Beyond this Limit* (London: Jonathan Cape, 1935).

21. A slightly different version appears in W. H. Auden, *Prose and Travel Books in Prose and Verse, 1926–1938* (Princeton, N.J.: Princeton University Press, 1996), 13; hereafter designated as *P1*. As Katherine Bucknell points out, Bronislaw Malinowski would have read this putative telepathy as a matter of custom, since he "believed there was a high level of individualism amongst the Melanesians which was not initially apparent to Western observers" (Katherine Bucknell, editor's introduction to "Auden's 'Writing' Essay," in *"The Map of All of My Youth": Early Works, Friends, and Influences*, edited by Katherine Bucknell and Nicholas Jenkins [Oxford: Clarendon, 1990], 27). A similar primitivist fantasy of the boat-society appears in *The Art of Being Ruled*, incidentally, Lewis referring at one point to "a curious unit found among the maritime Chukchee," a "little water-tight, compact group-unit, working as one man" that "must provide for its members many of the elements of ordinary happiness" (365).

22. See "Auden and Son: Environment, Evolution, Exhibition," of which this section of the present essay represents a condensation. *Paideuma* 32 (2003): 301–49.

23. W. H. Auden, *Collected Poems* (New York: Vintage, 1991), 331, 388.

24. Auden reflexively assigns highbrows the masculine pronoun; I follow that usage here precisely because it calls attention to the fact that Auden's conception was scarcely more gender-neutral than Lewis's. If Lewis continuously invokes modern femininity as inimical to the intellect, Auden largely omits women from consideration.

25. The text of *The Orators* used here is that of the second edition (1934) as presented by Edward Mendelson in EA. None of the passages quoted here varies from the first edition, though see note 33, below, on one change from first to second.

26. Peter E. Firchow, "Private Faces in Public Places: Auden's *The Orators*," PMLA 92 (1977): 253–72; John Fuller, *W. H. Auden: A Commentary* (Princeton, N.J.: Princeton University Press, 1998); Richard R. Bozorth, *Auden's Games of Knowledge: Poetry and the Meanings of Homosexuality* (New York: Columbia University Press, 2001); Edward Mendelson, *Early Auden* (New York: Farrar, 1981).

27. It seems likely that Auden also consulted an earlier essay by Layard appearing in the same journal. In "Degree-Taking Rites in South West Bay, Malekula" Layard notes that although no "pottery of any kind is made by the present inhabitants of Malekula," they do possess earthenware objects that they believe to have been made "by a race of white-skinned people called *Ambat*, who at one time sojourned in the island" (210). J. W. Layard, "Degree-Taking Rites in South West Bay, Malekula," *Journal of the Royal Anthropological Institute of Great Britain and Ireland* 58 (1928): 210. In the fifth ode in Book III of *The Orators*, Auden refers to "the tall white gods who landed from their open boat, / Skilled in the working of copper, appointing our feast-days, / Before the islands were submerged" (EA, 107). Layard would eventually publish much more of his massive collection of Malekulan notes in *Stone Men of Malekula* (London: Chatto and Windus, 1942). It must be said that there is no absolute verification that Auden read any of the essays as such. As Firchow points out, he could have received the substance of their information from Layard directly (266).

28. J. W. Layard, "Malekula: Flying Tricksters, Ghosts, Gods, and Epileptics," *Journal of the Royal Anthropological Institute of Great Britain and Ireland* 60 (1930): 504, 515, 506.

29. J. W. Layard, "Shamanism: An Analysis Based on Comparison with the Flying Tricksters of Malekula," *Journal of the Royal Anthropological Institute of Great Britain and Ireland* 60 (1930): 530.

30. The original can be found at Czaplicka, *Aboriginal Siberia*, 250.

31. Critics have noted many references to resurrection in *The Orators*, but (no doubt because Malekula has been the focus of attention) they have not remarked that some are notably linked to northern settings, as if in evocation of shamanistic Siberia: "one writes with his penis in a patch of snow 'Resurgam' " (EA, 65); "we who on the snow-line were in love with death . . . we forgot His will" (EA, 68).

32. Layard, "Malekula," 509.

33. The name is derived from Christopher Isherwood's gay uncle Henry Isherwood, who, according to Fuller, "gave him an allowance to live in Berlin and was delighted to hear stories of his sexual adventures" (*W. H. Auden*, 107). See also Auden's circa-1931 poem "Uncle Henry" (*Collected Poems*, 60). The Airman wonders about his Uncle Sam as well: "is he one too? He has the same backward-bending thumb that I have" (EA, 79).

34. See Fuller, *W. H. Auden*, 106. In EA, E's gender is specified at 83, 85, and 86; the corresponding pages in the first edition (London: Faber, 1932) are 59, 62, and 64.

35. Having noted that *The Orators* "portrays same-sex desire as a force both politically conservative and revolutionary," as by turns a meaningful transgression and "a crassly literal, bodily emulation of 'normal homosociality,'" Bozorth goes on to argue that the odes of Book III "show Auden letting go of fantasies about the inherent subversive power of homosexuality" and beginning to write "as the insider/outsider, cultivating possibilities for critique from within" (*Auden's Games*, 111–12, 134–35). Mendelson similarly closes his discussion of *The Orators* in *Early Auden* by noting that at this time Auden was discovering how poets need always to be both "a little outside" the social group (this is Auden's phrasing, in a letter) and within it (116).

36. Quoted at Fuller, *W. H. Auden*, 88.

37. For a pithy review of paranoiac imaginings of homosexual coteries in British and United States culture since the 1930s, see Gregory Woods, "The 'Conspiracy' of the 'Homintern,'" *Gay and Lesbian Review* 10, no. 3 (May–June 2003): 11–13.

38. Wyndham Lewis, *The Hitler Cult* (New York: Gordon Press, 1972), ix; W. H. Auden, *Prose, 1939–1948* (Princeton, N.J.: Princeton University Press, 2002), 102, hereafter designated as P2.

Joshua L. Miller

The Gorgeous Laughter of Filipino Modernity:
Carlos Bulosan's *The Laughter of My Father*

. . . he had become a little boy again living all the tales he had told us about a vanished race, listening to the gorgeous laughter of men in the midst of abject poverty and tyranny.
Carlos Bulosan, "How My Stories Were Written"

After such knowledge, and given the persistence of racial violence and the unavailability of legal protection, I asked myself, what else *was* there to sustain our will to persevere but laughter?
Ralph Ellison, Introduction to *Invisible Man*

The 1944 publication of Carlos Bulosan's collection of short stories, *The Laughter of My Father*, was a milestone in the literatures of Asian America and the history of United States imperialism. Bulosan was rapidly gaining notoriety as a Filipino author: he had already published stories in the *New Yorker*, *Harper's Bazaar*, and *Town and Country*, as well as a book of poems, *The Voice of Bataan* (1943), and an essay for the *Saturday Evening Post*, "Freedom from Want," specially commissioned to illustrate one of President Franklin Roosevelt's "Four Freedoms."[1] *The Laughter of My Father* was an immediate best-seller upon publication and was translated into more than a dozen languages.

Since then, however, this wartime publication by a foundational Asian American writer has been largely unavailable. Today the stories in *Laughter* are out of print and rarely discussed, even in Bulosan scholarship.[2] Why has this best-selling Asian American collection remained unpublished for six decades? Could the recovery of *Laughter* contribute to readings of Bulosan's work, not only within Asian American studies and Marxist literary criticism but also as a response to United States modernism/modernity and interwar culture? In fact, these early stories constituted Bulosan's first literary rendering of an alternative modernism, one that responded to U.S. expansionist politics in the post-1898 era and to 1940s culture more broadly.

That the book sold so well strongly suggests that it filled a specific need for U.S. readers during the late stages of World War II. Bulosan noted in a letter on May 3, 1944, that the first edition had already sold out and a second edition of 15,000 copies had been printed. In the same letter he noted that his stories were being distributed and broadcast by the Office of War Information to U.S. soldiers overseas. U.S. interest in the Philippines peaked during the war as names of Filipino cities and regions appeared regularly in newspaper accounts. Yet this very ready acceptance of *Laughter* by U.S. audiences (including the military) in the wake of the bombing of Pearl Harbor and the subsequent internment of Japanese Americans suggests, as Delfin L. Tolentino Jr. has noted, that the book "was initially well received, not because of its serious intent but because of its entertainment value."[3]

One explanation for recent critics' silence on *Laughter* is that they read this early work as a misstep: poorly written, unfortunately timed, and inadequately theorized in its narrative representation of Filipino/as. Interpretations that have found these stories patronizingly Orientalizing were reinforced by the marketing of *Laughter* in 1944 (hardcover) and 1946 (Bantam paperback) and by newspaper and magazine book reviews. Yet *Laughter* is as nuanced and subversive, if in strikingly different ways, as Bulosan's widely read masterpiece *America Is in the Heart*, which was published only two years later. In fact, the very qualities that might lead critics today to consider *Laughter* a bad narrative—that it appears simply composed, with unsympathetic and stereotypical portrayals of Filipino/as—constituted Bulosan's subversive representation of Filipino modernity: he deployed the appearance of simplicity to present a modernist treatment of collective folklore that in fact undermined readers' expectations conditioned by racism and colonialism.

In order to understand Bulosan's stories as political critique rather than comedic entertainment, one must historicize his writings as a response to interwar U.S. expansionism. I am thus arguing for an implicit comparativism that recognizes the entwined histories of the United States and the Philippines and analyzes the active role of innovative literary forms within this nexus. This comparative framework extends recent theorizations of "new modernisms" and of comparative literature in the globalized era of late capitalism[4]—for example, that of Andreas Huyssen, who has called for an interrogation of the "expanded field" of modernist studies in the context of globalization and transnational capital.[5] Huyssen suggests that scholarly "neglect" of "the modernity of the temporally and geographically 'non-modern'" should impel new work on "comparative modernisms" (HL 364). He urges comparative studies of "non-Western modernisms [that] have either been ignored as epistemologically impossible—since only the West was considered advanced enough to generate authentic modernism—or dismissed as lamentable mimicry and contamination of a more genuine local culture." In *Death of a Discipline*, Gayatri Spivak envisions a renewed, rigorous "planetary Comparative Literature" drawing on the linguistic and literary developments of the global South.[6] Shu-mei Shih has argued that the scholarly/pedagogical category of "global literature" (and its terminological predecessor, "world literature") must challenge the enduring dichotomy between Western (as modern, universal, omnipresent) and non-Western (belated, local, marginal).[7] And in *Alternative Modernities*, Dilip Parameshwar Gaonkar describes the project of globalizing the analytic category of modernity "in vernacular or cosmopolitan idioms" in order to enable a "questioning of the present" that "can provincialize Western modernity . . . and pluralize the experiences of modernity."[8] In the more capacious context of these refashionings of modernity and literary modernism, Bulosan's *The Laughter of My Father* exemplifies the importance of comparative modernist studies in reconceptualizing forgotten or systematically repressed cultural works.

The stories of *Laughter* do not conform wholly to canonical Anglo-American modernist literary techniques; rather, they respond to the historical and political trends of modernity in order to advance Filipino narrative in English. Unlike the avant-gardism of, for example, Gertrude Stein, Virginia Woolf, or Ezra Pound, Bulosan's is populist rather than elitist and folkloric rather than classical or biblical. Translation, symbolism, radical transformation, and defamiliarization — prominent tropes and formal techniques of literary modernism — activate his negotiation of Filipino folklore, contemporary urbanization, and U.S. imperialism; in Bulosan, the break with the past is driven more by a rejection of colonial narratives of power than by a need to subvert preexisting literary genres or norms. This historical rupture produces new Filipino identities through autonomous cultural forms that piece together fragments from the conflicts of modernity: postwar ennui, class struggle, intrafamilial violence, and dislocated selfhood. Regarding Bulosan through the lens of bad modernism makes clear that his work put anti-colonial rebellion, historical fracture, linguistic fragmentation, translated folklore, defamiliarization, and other elements associated with modernism into unexpected forms. Like canonical modernists, Bulosan depicted rebellion, but his rejection was less visible and less direct, because it was a refusal of a single readership and of a unitary national culture. Bulosan's translation strategies exposed cracks in U.S. colonial culture while allowing metropolitan U.S. readers mediated access to Filipino rural life, through humor, wicked satire, and revisions of folklore.[9]

One crucial way that Bulosan's Filipino modernist techniques differed from Anglo-American literary modernisms was that the traditional narrative structures he drew on and subverted were not those of realist representation but those of Filipino folklore and modern imperialism. *Laughter* portrays traditional and modern institutions at odds, colliding over marriage, prayer, legal decisions, war, and the like; in all these confrontations, rather than celebrating either traditionalism or modernization, Bulosan's stories champion spontaneous, improvisational, incomplete individual solutions. Bulosan's aesthetics are perhaps most recognizably modernist in their transitional, inconclusive, mysterious, and partially translated quality, wherein resistance to the pressure of modernization involves leaving acts and retellings liminal and unfinished.

One conclusion whose complex layering belies the apparent simplicity of the folkloric mode is that of "My Father Goes to Church." In this story, successive disasters have befallen the family and even the dubious father is willing to go to church if it will change their fortunes. The story concludes with the father's donation to the church, a live goat, which distracts the congregation with its rank smells and bleating cries. The priest angrily ejects the father from the church and the story ends without resolving, or even referring to, the story's central concern, the family's continuing misfortune:

> Father put the goat down and looked back. For a moment I thought he would say something. But he took my hand and we walked silently to our house.
>
> Father wanted to return the goat, but Mother insisted that we could find something for it. We took it to the village and let it loose in the pasture land. It played with our cows and *carabaos*. It even played with our watchdog. We found it useful.
>
> Then we heard that the priest died of overeating.
>
> "I wonder if there are goats in the Everlasting," Father said.
>
> He never went to church again. (153)

The final four lines of the story refer to four separate narrative strands, but instead of conveying certainty through narrative closure, Bulosan leaves the relation between secularity ("the priest died of overeating... [Father] never went to church again") and spirituality ("I wonder if there are goats in the Everlasting") suggestively open-ended and inconclusive.

Frequently Bulosan's sentences are terse and disconnected, and gaps appear where the child narrator does not understand adults' actions or emotions. At these junctures, the double translation (into writing and into English) of folklore's short sentences and symbolic juxtapositions meets the modernist short story's methods of (childhood) perspectivalism, interiority, and fragmentary narrative. The conclusion to "My Father Goes to Church" manifests all these literary devices, underscoring the story's multiple status as socialist folklore, translated Filipino culture, and modernist narrative. The perspectivalism of these final sentences is particularly remarkable in that Bulosan's portrayal of the young narrator's limited understanding conflicts directly with the retrospective omniscience of traditional folklore.[10]

In *The Laughter of My Father*, Bulosan's political critique is elusive — dramatically so when contrasted with the manifesto-like narrative of *America Is in the Heart*. The subtler rebellion of uncanny laughter in *Laughter*, its crossing of languages and national cultures, and its play on the "modern" and the "backward" impels broader rethinking of what qualifies as rebellion in the globally expansionist U.S. culture of the 1920s, 30s, and 40s. The

The Laughter of My Father

explicit radicalism that threw off the (political, aesthetic) shackles of history can be read usefully in conjunction with the subtler, evasive rebellion of displaced subjectivity in the colonized personae of *Laughter*.

Bulosan's thematic concerns and formal innovations parallel trends in African American literary modernism, particularly in responses to racialized minstrelsy. Scholars have read authors such as Langston Hughes, Sterling Brown, Jean Toomer, Claude McKay, and Zora Neale Hurston as shaping vernacular idioms in response to racist caricatures popularized by dialect literature and blackface minstrelsy.[11] *Laughter* can be read as performing analogous cultural work in response to similarly pernicious constructions of Filipinos and of Asian Americans more generally, and as contesting the racial binaries within which minstrelsy traditionally has been conceived. Like Hurston, who also made folktales central to interwar modernism, Bulosan played on expectations of "backwardness" and "belated modernity" by featuring characters who use the appearance of simplicity to overturn unjust power imbalances. And, like Hurston, he drew on the subversive power of laughter, depicting it as a manifestation of the uncanny, surreal, and absurd in modern life that enables, simultaneously, the expression of submission and a disarming aggressivity.[12] In *Laughter*, Bulosan sought out the most disruptive elements of laughter in an attempt to transform racial caricatures that already had become familiar in mass culture depictions of Filipino/as.

Filipinos became particularly present in the U.S. cultural psyche in the aftermath of the Filipino-American war of 1898–1902, in which active resistance to U.S. military forces belied the official narrative that Filipinos warmly welcomed the new rulers. In the following decades, minstrel-like Filipino caricatures emerged in films reenacting the Filipino-American war and its aftermath and World War II.[13] In major studio productions such as *The Real Glory* (1939), *Bataan* (1943), *Back to Bataan* (1945), *They Were Expendable* (1945), and *American Guerillas in the Philippines* (1950),[14] Filipino/as were portrayed as either inscrutable or servile, as subversively dangerous or helpless.[15] A series of popular and easily accessible short stories such as Bulosan's had the potential to unsettle these narrow conceptions of Filipino/as.

But Bulosan may have made his critique too subtle for readers and reviewers at the time. Their failure of recognition perturbed Bulosan for the rest of his life. In a letter dated April 8, 1955, he wrote that he remained frustrated that the book received what seemed to him like willful misunderstanding:

> My politico-economic ideas are embodied in all my writings. . . . Here let me remind you that *The Laughter of My Father* is *not* humor; it is satire; it is indictment against an economic system that stifled the growth of the primitive, making him decadent overnight without passing through the various stages of growth and decay. The hidden bitterness in this book is so pronounced in another series of short stories, that the publishers refrained from publishing it for the time being.[16]

What sort of satire did Bulosan have in mind? What construct of superiority was he attempting to disturb? And why do these stories continue to be read not as subversive satire filled with "hidden bitterness" but instead as self-Orientalizing minstrelsy? The laughter that haunts the stories in *The Laughter of My Father* turns out to be a surreal, absurdist, mocking form of confrontation that undermines the colonial power relations that organized U.S.-centered conceptions of modernity. But how, precisely, did the unsettling aspects of this laughter unsheathe the edge of Bulosan's satire?

The *Laughter of My Father* is a cycle of twenty-four interconnected tales portraying the narrator's family and neighbors. All the stories take place in the narrator's town on the Philippine island of Luzon, and all but three of them name the father in their titles. The folkloric repetition of the titles ("The Gift of My Father," "The Tree of My Father," "The Son of My Father"), however, only begins to hint at the complex political and economic arguments theorized within stories such as "The Politics of My Father," "The Capitalism of My Father," and "My Father Goes to Church."

Like Hurston's fiction and anthropological work, Bulosan's stories present stylized repetition (as in the formulaic titles) and surface simplicity only to subvert them. Both authors use folktales to achieve characteristically modernist ends: rebellion, critique, and (counter to expectations of folklore) anti-nostalgic reenvisioning of the past. Throughout the stories, Bulosan shifts expected constructions of backwardness in order to reorient rural Filipino modernity against the absurdities of urban aristocracies and foreign imperialists. In his stories Filipino aristocrats and colonial administrators prove to be the backward, confused, pitiable figures, while villagers deploy something like modern ingenuity. Though textual instances of laughter are less frequent than the title of the collection might imply, multivalent laughter emerges in several stories as a collectivist folk response to unjust legal and social structures. And it speaks also through its absence from other stories that detail the everyday conditions of misery and powerlessness pervading the characters' lives.

The first story of the collection, "My Father Goes to Court," is set just after the four-year-old narrator's father loses his farm in a flood that forces the family to move to a town, where they live next to a very wealthy neighbor.[17] The poor family members attempt to ignore their hunger by inhaling the sweet smells emanating from the rich family's kitchen. Bulosan describes the narrator's poor family as "healthy" because its children play outside, unlike the wealthy neighbor's children, who must remain indoors. "There was always plenty to make us laugh," the narrator relates, introducing an anecdote in which his brother fools their mother by pretending to have brought home fresh food in a sack. When his mother unties the sack, a black cat jumps out and runs away.

Similarly, in another anecdote, the narrator's sister fools both their parents into thinking she is pregnant. When the child moving in her abdomen proves to be a bullfrog, her mother faints and her father drops his lamp, nearly setting the building on fire.

> When the fire was extinguished and Mother was revived we returned to bed and tried to sleep, but Father kept on laughing so loud we could not sleep any more. Mother got up again and lighted the oil lamp; we rolled up the mats on the floor and began dancing about and laughing with all our might. We made so much noise that all our neighbors except the rich family came into the yard and joined us in loud, genuine laughter.
> It was like that for years.
> As time went on, the rich man's children became thin and anemic, while we grew even more robust and full of life.[18]

Active, strategic laughter in this passage signifies not nostalgia but class warfare. The poor family and their neighbors "began dancing about and laughing with all our might" in noisy solidarity against the aristocratic family in their midst. For the desperately poor living cheek-by-jowl with the privileged, "Laughter was our only wealth" (*LMF* 4). Bulosan literalizes the metaphorical wealth of laughter by describing how the narrator's poor family "had grown fat with laughing," while the rich family grew pale and ill. Laughter initially appears to be a symbolic substitute for material wealth, but instead it becomes a manifestation of class-based confrontation (6).

That this laughter is not spontaneous joy but rather active, strategic, collective confrontation is evident in the black cat and bullfrog anecdotes and in the story's conclusion. In the bullfrog story, the family has already returned to bed, but they are roused because "Father kept on laughing so loud we could not sleep any more." Aggrieved, the wealthy neighbor sues the narrator's father for "stealing the spirit of his wealth and food" (7). Ultimately, the father wins the case in court with a brilliant extrapolation of legal logic. If the wealthy family is suing the poor family for having stolen the spirit of their wealth by inhaling the smells of their food and listening to their lives, then, the father reasons, all he should owe them is the spirit of money, which he repays with the sound of coins jingling. The judge dismisses the case and congratulates the father with a whispered sign of identification established through this uncanny form of confrontation: "I had an uncle who died laughing" (9). The father responds by asking the judge if he would like to hear his family laugh. On the father's command, the family begins to laugh, and they are joined by the sympathetic spectators as well as the judge, who "was the loudest of all" (10). Laughter, then, is neither a sign of contentment nor a solution to the suffering of entrenched systematic poverty. In this story, Bulosan depicts it as a weapon of the underclass with the power to unsettle narrative representations of the self-satisfied aristocracy.[19] While this conclusion marks a triumph for the poor family, it is also incomplete — in keeping with Bulosan's literary strategy of depicting partial and inconclusive rebellions — since their laughter has not actually changed the material circumstances of their poverty.

The title story, which concludes the collection, provides additional examples of multivalent laughter. It also detaches the United States from its mythological status, marginalizing imperial power even as it centralizes Filipino folktale traditions and the quotidian pressures of Filipino lives.[20] Bulosan accomplishes this reversal through a seemingly simple tale about a wedding party ruined by the father's drunkenness. The story portrays a cousin's wedding that becomes an occasion for the narrator's father to abandon his farm work for nights of parties. The father, "notorious for his drinking bouts," is reminded by his son that they have to tend to their corn, but "the prospect of a jug of *basi*," a sugar cane wine, "was always too much for his self-control" (187). Having established the father as a well-intentioned alcoholic, the story plays out the unintended consequences of his actions, one of which leads to his son's exile.

The narrator, still young and rarely away from his family farm, is far less comfortable dancing and flirting than is his more experienced village cousin. Noting his son's shyness disapprovingly, the father wonders if this proves that the narrator is "the one I didn't touch," the one son to whom he neglected to transmit his virile magnetism through an "*anting-anting*, or talisman, which was what women fell for" (189). Wounded by his father's disavowal, the narrator musters enough courage to sidle up and speak with the bride. As they walk together, the bride slips and dirties her dress. When the two return to the party she has on another dress, which the drunk father, "slyly, insinuatingly," interprets as evidence of his son's sexual conquest. He loudly draws the other guests' attention to this misunderstanding: " 'Didn't the women fight for me once?' Father cried at the top of his lungs. 'Don't the women fall for my son now? I ask you! Ha-ha-ha' " (192). Days later, the bride's father reports that the appearance of impropriety forced the marriage to be cancelled and demands that the narrator marry his bereft daughter. Rather than accede to this demand, the father decides to send his son to the United States. Thus the laughter named in the story title and reiterated in the book title refers to the father's drunken mirth, which embarrasses the narrator and irredeemably shames the bride. As a result of this laughter, the narrator is uprooted and forced to leave his home for the United States. In this instance laughter again proves powerfully disruptive and antagonistic; whereas in "My Father Goes to Court," laughter is a sign of proletarian solidarity, in this story it produces intrafamily conflict.

Aside from the parents' sadness at sending their son away, the conclusion is laconically devoid of the narrator's thoughts about this life-altering moment. When the narrator's mother asks, "What shall we do?" the father replies, "There is only one way," which is to "send him to America" (193). In contrast to the weeping mother, the father is at first stoic ("We still have the girls"), then sly, telling the narrator in the final lines of the book's conclusion, "remember in America that *I* am your father. Don't forget *I touched you at birth.*" The story ends on this ambivalent note, with the mother's sadness, the father's unrepentant pride, and without a word of narratorial comment that might hint at the son's perspective on being uprooted and sent to the United States. Not only is reference to the political or rhetorical ideals and ambitions of "America" absent from this textual moment, so too is nostalgia for the Philippines.

The explicit reference to the colonial power in the last few lines of the story, which are also the last lines of the book, demonstrates this point. This melancholy resolution depicts the United States as an unfortunate and unchosen refuge from the consequences of a bullying and alcoholic father. Bulosan does not mention either economic or political opportunities as factors in this decision. The United States remains demythologized, un-romanticized, and distant from the world that Bulosan depicts. This distance is most sharply noted in the anticlimactic conclusions of this story and others.[21]

The field of reference of *Laughter* is firmly located within an autonomous local Filipino culture that is not reliant on broader colonial political or juridical institutions. For example, in "The Tree of My Father" Bulosan suggests not only that the external rule of colonialism is unnecessary but also that contact with the products of imperial "civilization" — international war, capitalist ideology, and religious persecution — is harmful rather than beneficent. The story begins with a paean to local rule:

> While I was still living in the village with Father, the Insular Government of the Philippines had nothing to do with our lives. We made our own laws and obeyed them willingly; but we did not write them down for the proper authorities to verify. These laws were handed verbally from one generation to another, and we never questioned their sources or validity. Afterward men of a new type came to our village and settled among us; but they started questioning our unwritten laws. They began a series of serious controversies over the ownership of land. (LMF 43)

Evident in this opening paragraph is this story's concern with territorial, socioeconomic, and temporal boundaries and transitions. Bulosan's narrator sets the story between an anterior time when laws were oral and voluntary and a later period when "men of a new type" used the "new written laws" to claim ownership of the land.

After this introduction, "The Tree of My Father" details the young narrator's father's response to the period of legal transition between local autonomy and bureaucratic external rule based on laws designed to aid "new settlers" in "dispossessing" residents (44). One of these newcomers "grabbed" the adjoining farm, which he was able to do because "he had a little education in English and Spanish" (44). The large bangar tree of the story title sits at the border of the two farms. The story turns on the fact that the tree is "not good for anything" and produces nothing other than a smell "like a dead person" (49). Absurdities pile up as the judge, lawyers, and police stuff cotton in their noses "in agony" as they attempt to adjudicate the disputed possession of a tree whose trunk rests on one person's land and whose branches "were all on the other side of the fence" (50). As the judge considers the inadequacy of the written law for the situation — "it had no precedent on which he could base his judgment" — a policeman's lantern drops, setting the tree on fire and rendering the entire exercise moot. The story concludes on a sober note, with the father chastising the new neighbor: "Next time pick another tree" (51). The ludicrously uncomprehending and ineffective authorities misunderstand the situation, attempt to impose legalistic definitions of land enclosure, and finally destroy the very object that had been entrusted to their judgment. This story ends without resolving any of the larger dilemmas portrayed: land-grabs through new enclosure laws, tension between oral and written traditions, juridical authority, and waning proletarian agency in an increasingly bureaucratized society. The legal problem disappears when the tree is destroyed; Bulosan carefully concludes this story too without providing resolution for structural injustices, which remain troubling. Such an open-ended conclusion highlights Bulosan's modernist tendency to fragment stories and leave them unresolved. But unlike many modernists, Bulosan gives his trope of narrative inconclusivity a class-conscious political meaning.

It is characteristic of Bulosan's portrayals that the rural characters in these stories are described as impoverished and undereducated but neither "backward" nor primitive. More often than not the rural farmers and villagers of his work prove sharper and wittier than their more comfortable counterparts in larger towns. This folkloric inversion of rural/urban is magnified when the inverted terms become Filipino/U.S. or Filipino/Western ideology and culture. In "The Capitalism of My Father," Osong, the narrator's brother, returns from the United States with "plenty of experience in selling things that did not belong to him" and "also expert in cheating and lying" (53). Although the father learns that Osong is cheating the townspeople and successfully tricks his son into giving back what he has taken, the accumulationist impulse remains intact at the end of the tale.

Even more disturbing results of contact with the Western world emerge in "The Soldiers Come Marching," which portrays the aftereffects of World War I on the narrator's town. Bulosan describes the devastating effects of postwar ennui in modernist laconic prose: "Suddenly the war came and suddenly it ended. Then my childhood was gone forever" (11). As is evident from these opening words, the story is not concerned with wartime experiences but instead with postwar depression. Of eleven soldiers from the town, only three return, and their unnarrated experiences in war have led them to paralysis: they "were always sitting on the lawn in front of the *presidencia*. They sat all day and part of the night without talking to anybody. They pulled blades of grass and looked into the sky, moving only when ants bit their ears and flies stepped on their noses" (11). This unrelenting public display of silent inertia is broken only by alcoholic binges, during which they "were always laughing and singing." This laughter and gaiety is an extension of the ex-soldiers' alienation rather than a sign of relief from it. They live hermetically sealed off from the rest of the townspeople in "a world of their own making. When a man sat among them because he was attracted by their merriment, they suddenly stopped laughing and singing" (15). In this instance, laughter is not a spontaneous expression of content but rather a marker of inclusion and exclusion. Having depicted this socially alienated dialectic of silent paralysis and detached mirth, the story concludes when the soldiers leave town, never to reappear, and a rich man whom they have tormented "goes insane and hanged himself with a rope. His tongue was sticking out when the servants found him" (18). These are the last words of the story, which is one of the bleakest portrayals of the aftereffects of the Great War in short fiction—all the more consequential since it was published in 1942, deep into the century's second world war. Like the other stories I have described, "The Soldiers Come Marching" ends with the larger systemic problems of wartime trauma and postwar alienation—particularized in the Filipino context—intact. In all these instances, though most graphically in "Soldiers," Bulosan's Marxist narrative strategy emphasizes the continuation of oppressive power relations through stories that lack resolution.

Several stories in *The Laughter of My Father* conclude on notes of uncomfortable ambiguity or painful tragedy. The third story of the collection, "My Mother's Boarders," depicts another contact zone between villagers and urban dwellers that results in unfortunate endings. When three teachers are sent to the narrator's village from "the city" to teach the increasing number of ex-soldiers' children, they bring with them stylish, provocative clothing and the music of "the jazz age" (22). In response to attention—both lascivious and envious—"the teachers just tossed their cigarettes away and laughed their healthy girlish laughter" (20). The teachers' laughter in "My Mother's Boarders" signifies their uncomfortable acknowledgment of the town's accusations and their determined defiance.

Eventually, the teachers' introduction of jazz music and dancing—which, in the town's collective judgment, culminate in alcohol abuse and youth pregnancies—leads the town council to "oust" the teachers, who "left behind them something that our town could not forget for a long time" (25). Like so many of the other stories, "Boarders" concludes ambiguously. The "something" that the "town could not forget" seems sad, but since it remains unelaborated, readers cannot know if the narrator or townspeople feel this introduction of urbanity was otherwise beneficial, profoundly disruptive, or mildly objectionable. The narrative conveys only understated, albeit pervasive, melancholy. Like most of the other stories in *Laughter*, "Boarders" includes both moments of levity and instances of laughter—which, as I have suggested, rarely are simultaneous in Bulosan's stories—but this conclusion is unremittingly somber.

The humor within these stories frequently is met with plaintive, ambiguous, and even tragic conclusions of death, exile, lost jobs, hunger, and depression. The various meanings of laughter proliferate in the stories (defiance, irony, wit, triumph, despair, withdrawal), but what it clearly does not represent is passivity, in the form of either contentment or envy. Instances of explosive laughter within the narrative contain unexpected, disjointed, even absurd moments that unsettle (rather than topple) the powerful, edu-

Joshua L. Miller   **251**

cated elites, that disrupt reading though, notably, they do not provide programmatic methods with which to counter systemic exploitation.

One of the writers with whom Bulosan is most frequently paired is Richard Wright, primarily because of the confrontational Marxism central to *America Is in the Heart*. In that work Bulosan located Wright at the genesis of his political and literary radicalism:

> I was fortunate to find work in a library and to be close to books. In later years I remembered this opportunity when I read that the American Negro writer, Richard Wright, had not been allowed to borrow books from his local library because of his color. I was beginning to understand what was going on around me, and the darkness that had covered my present life was lifting.[22]

For this reason, as well as their late 1930s Marxist identifications, the affinities between *America Is in the Heart* and *Black Boy* have been well-documented.[23] Both used fictionalized and popularized autobiographical works to articulate the stakes of mid-1940s struggles with systematic racism and colonialism.

Despite the evident parallels with Wright and the folkloric mode Bulosan shared with Hurston, the literary techniques that Bulosan employed in the stories of *Laughter* hold an even greater affinity with those of another African American writer, Ralph Ellison. Like Bulosan, Ellison sought to combat what he theorized as the associative logic of the performed yet unspoken presumptions of a racialized minstrelsy that had pervaded U.S. culture. Ellison usefully broadened the definition of minstrelsy to include cultural forms designed to confirm racist (and, in Bulosan's case, colonial) expectations. In his 1958 essay "Change the Joke and Slip the Yoke," published originally in *Partisan Review*, Ellison lamented the "Negro 'misfortune' to be caught up associatively in the negative side of this basic dualism of the white folk mind. . . . The physical hardships and indignities of slavery were benign compared with this continuing debasement of our image."[24] In folklore and popular culture, he continued, "the Negro is reduced to a negative sign that usually appears in a comedy of the grotesque and the unacceptable" in order to "veil the humanity of Negroes thus reduced to a sign" (*CRE* 103). The truly brutal consequence of the "specific rhetorical situation" of minstrelsy was the performance of "self-humiliation" that lent the audience a sense of detached superiority, "a psychological dissociation from this symbolic self-maiming" (103).

Ellison located a "symbolic self-maiming" at the core of minstrel humor: the "comic point is inseparable from the racial identity of the performer" (*CRE* 104). This analysis of the constraining legacy of minstrel comedy helps to explain the surreal, even shocking humor of Ellison's 1952 masterpiece *Invisible Man*. In order to break out of the comforting logic of racist comedy, Ellison resorted to absurdist humor in his novel, evoking laughter at the absurd situations inspired by segregation in post-slavery U.S. society.[25] He gleefully violated the dictates of African American "uplift" ideologies with the pool shark's "reverse English" backspin on Invisible Man's movements: "his mobility is dual: geographical . . . but more importantly, it is intellectual. And in keeping with the reverse English of the plot, and with the Negro American conception of blackness, his movement vertically downward . . . is a process of *rising*" (111). In this way, Ellison put "english" on his narrative, a reverse spin in which the Invisible Man's descent underground marks his highest achievement.

Similarly, Ellison posited the "reverse English" of his narrator's rhetoric as a counterpoint to the "symbolic self-maiming" of minstrel humor: "Confession, not concealment, is his mode" (104, 111). However, the figure in *Invisible Man* who does represent strategic concealment—the narrator's grandfather—attacks the foundations of the minstrel tradition as well. Ellison called the grandfather

> a weak man who knows the nature of his oppressor's weakness. There is a good deal of spite in the old man, as there comes to be in his grandson, and the strategy he advises is a kind of jiujitsu of the spirit, a denial and rejection through agreement. . . . Thus his mask of meekness conceals the wisdom of one who has learned the secret of saying the "yes" which accomplishes the expressive "no." (110)

On his deathbed, the narrator's grandfather asks the narrator to "keep up the good fight," since "our life is a war and I have been . . . a spy in the enemy's country ever since I gave up my gun back in the Reconstruction."[26] This "meekest" of men hid a subversive radical politics that he defines in his dying words: "overcome 'em with yeses, undermine 'em with grins, agree 'em to death and destruction, let 'em swaller you till they vomit or bust wide open" (*IM* 16). The "mask of meekness" that he bequeaths to his grandson is an oppositional strategy of appearing to surrender in order to conceal a deeper revolutionary spirit. Ellison's narrator remains profoundly troubled by the "constant puzzle" of how to understand "meekness as a dangerous activity" in which grins and laughter thinly conceal insurrection (16).

In the "battle royal" sequence of *Invisible Man*, Ellison produced an astonishingly layered literary representation of absurdist laughter in response to outrageous racism. As the narrator and other African American students struggle to pick up money from an electrified rug for the entertainment of the town's white male "big shots," the narrator discovers that he can "ignor[e] the shock by laughing" (*IM* 17, 27). Thus equipped to "contain the electricity," the narrator is able to sweep the coins off the rug while "laughing embarrassedly" (27). This laughter, forced from within, makes the electrocution just bearable enough to permit continued experience of the shocks. As the students struggle, one of their number falls on his sweaty back and undergoes continuous electrocution, an unforgettably searing metaphor for laughter as a survival strategy required to endure the painful shocks of everyday racism. The white audience observes this scene with "booming laughter" that attests to the entertainment value of watching the young men painfully attempting to grab the coins, and which hauntingly echoes and supplants the young men's "embarrassed laughter." The "booming laughter" continues after the electrified rug scene, repeatedly and aggressively interrupting the narrator's carefully prepared speech on Negro humility (27).

The chapter ends with the narrator accepting from the men a leather briefcase containing a letter offering "a scholarship to the state college for Negroes" (32). This resolution is immediately followed by its comic doubling in a dream in which his grandfather, who "refused to laugh" at circus clowns, watches the narrator find in his briefcase "an official envelope stamped with the state seal" containing an engraved document reading "Keep this Nigger-Boy Running" (33). At this his grandfather laughs so long and hard that the narrator reports that he "awoke with the old man's laughter ringing in [his] ears." Ellison contrasts the grandfather's impassivity in front of the clowns with the old man's laughter at the document, demonstrating that the absurdities of racial oppression can be met with laughter that is both uncomprehending and incomprehensible. The narrator himself is puzzled by this third kind of laughter, which follows the pained laughter of the electrocuted young men and the oppressive laughter of the white "big shots."[27]

Bulosan's *The Laughter of My Father* represents nothing short of an Ellisonian "reverse english," an anti-minstrel, absurdist use of folk humor, nearly a decade before the publication of *Invisible Man*. Both authors read the cultural logic of racialized literary representation and sought to undermine minstrel-based characterization through surreal comedy.[28] Ellison's strategy of depicting absurd humor in the teeth of oppression demonstrated that the situations created by de facto racism were (and are) themselves absurd, and that the only possible reaction was uncomprehending and uncompromising laughter. Bulosan's version of Ellison's "jiujitsu of the spirit" similarly subverted the racist associations of a minstrelsy nourished by colonial anxieties, but his first attempt through short stories achieved—if anything—the opposite effect.

If both Bulosan and Ellison used textual instances of unexpected laughter to combat deep-seated presumptions coded within racialized minstrelsy, why was one text hailed as a literary landmark of formal inventiveness and the other forgotten within a few years of its publication? The circumstances surrounding the publication of *The Laughter of My Father*—as evidenced by the publisher's publicity and contemporary reviewers' reception—gives strong indications for why Bulosan's work has remained marginalized for six decades and remains difficult to read today as modernist. Both the interpretations of Bulosan's story cycle advanced by the publisher (in cover art and advertisements) and reviews of the book after publication implied that it consisted of nonthreatening, self-directed ethnic humor, "simple" language and narrative structures, and "realism" in portraying Filipino/as' lived experiences.

Orientalization is especially striking on the front cover of the Bantam paperback edition: an image of a smiling, barefoot, rotund man walking carefreely next to his equally dark-skinned, grinning son. The two walk together in lockstep fashion; both have their hands inside their pockets. The son gazes admiringly up at the father, who glances out of the corner of narrow eyes down at his son. Both are clad in clean, white, baggy clothing

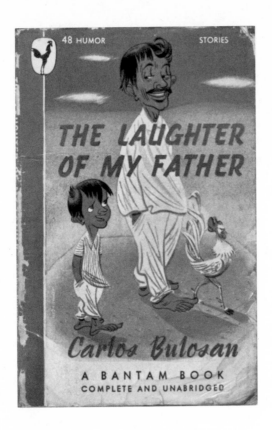

Carlos Bulosan's *The Laughter of My Father*, front cover of 1946 reprint in Bantam paperback series.

and have uneven, yet becoming hair. Striding purposefully in front of the father is a lean but regal chicken, who is also walking with the father and son. The unseen sun behind the three casts their shadows comfortably in front of them. The words of the title, "THE LAUGHTER OF MY FATHER," are literally emblazoned across the father's chest. In another intriguing detail on the Bantam cover, the flat, solid, brown earth on which these figures walk is drawn as a small rectangular area, barely extending past their shadows. Beyond this barren, sandy patch of land is the pale blue of either sky or ocean. They are thus imagined in an utterly decontextualized location, outside "civilization" and seemingly delighted in their isolation.

The cartoonish linedrawings that appear inside the Bantam edition of *Laughter* continue the associative, implicit logic of minstrelsy into which Bulosan's stories were forced. The inside cover includes a ring of six cartoon images of grinning men and overweight women in various acts of fighting a buffalo, watching a cockfight, and running from a ram. At the center of these images is a passage from "My Father Goes to Court" that I quoted above, but the passage was significantly altered without indication of this revision, appearing inside both the front and back covers without ellipses or any other textual indication that words have been removed. The unacknowledged deletions are here marked in brackets: "We [rolled up the mats on the floor and] began dancing about and laughing with all our might. We made so much noise that all our neighbors [except the rich family] came into the yard and joined us in loud, genuine laughter. It was like that for years." This invisibly edited and decontextualized quotation produces exactly the kind of exoticized, "self-maiming" representation that Ellison identified as characteristic of racialized minstrelsy. Laughter in the story signifies not a spontaneous expression of joy but a collective act of solidarity against the wealthy family, as the excised sentences make clear. The family has already gone to bed, when the father awakens them with his loud laughter. Reluctantly, they join him. In its truncated form, the passage seems to portray the Filipino/a villagers as organically (and, literally, cartoonishly) happy. Shorn of the key clause "except the rich family," the antagonism behind the communal merriment is effaced. Further, a less literal interpretation of these sentences would point out that the passage does not imply that actual laughter as a state of uninhibited joy continued uninterruptedly "for years." Instead, what extends into the future is the mutuality of the spontaneous gathering around laughter that excludes the wealthy residents.

The dark skin, wide grins, relaxed posture, and apparent contentment to laugh off suffering are all key features of racial minstrelsy, as it has been detailed by scholars of nineteenth- and twentieth-century U.S. culture. The packaging and marketing of Bulosan's book shoehorned these surprising and subversive stories into familiar ethnic stereotypes, encouraging readings of *Laughter* as self-inflicted "ethnic humor," an assimilation tale, or nostalgia for a lost history. Not surprisingly, perhaps, reviewers overlooked Bulosan's complex engagement with absurdist humor and instead took his style as simple, unironic, devoid of social commentary. This simplicity—read as comfortably nonthreatening humor and as "primitive" or "backward" writing by an Asian American writer in English—contributed to the quick success of *Laughter*. Following patronizingly glowing reviews in the *New York Times, New Yorker, Kirkus, Saturday Review of Literature*, and *Christian Science Monitor, Laughter* became a best-seller, with a second edition printed months after its original publication and republication in the popular Bantam paperbacks series two years after its initial publication.

According to its publisher, Harcourt, Brace, and Company, Bulosan's *Laughter* was a "novel about the simple, serene life in a pre-war Filipino village."[29] The back-cover copy from the Bantam edition described Bulosan as a "gifted humorist" whose "wonderfully funny stories" form "a worthy addition to the Bantam series of humorous books, which includes James Thurber's *Men, Women, and Dogs* and Sally Benson's *Meet Me in St. Louis*." In weekly advertisements, Harcourt quoted the opening of the *Times* review by Thomas Sugrue: "*Here is a new kind of humor*—new and astonishingly simple. Carlos Bulosan is a pure manifestation of the Comic Spirit."[30] The ad went on to quote the review's conclusion: "The Bulosans were a laughing family; the Filipinos are a laughing people. Here they are shown for the first time in the realism and humanness of their native peasant life. It is a joy to meet them." This was a remarkably selective interpretation of a set of stories portraying the lingering effects of U.S. colonialism: widespread hunger, domestic violence, and systematic impoverishment.[31] This reading evacuated the author's engagements with ideology, history, and collective identity in favor of "astonishingly simple" humor. The term "pure," from Sugrue's review, had several connotations in the context of Harcourt's marketing. Filipinos, according to this reading, were "a laughing people," rather than bitter, hungry, or violent, and Bulosan's stories were described as rendering accessible the "simple" humor of Filipino culture. This selective reading allowed Harcourt to position *Laughter* within the same literary tradition as James Thurber despite the spectacular dissimilarities of their linguistic styles and uses of "humor."

The publisher's need to efface any elements of ideology and radicalism was evident in its partial citation of a positive review. Harcourt eliminated most of Sugrue's actual concluding sentence: "It is a joy to meet them—and to know that they have a weapon of the spirit with which to fight the little people who rule them now."[32] This deletion of the reference to Bulosan's "weapon of the spirit" against the new rulers maintained the review's general emphasis on simplicity and nostalgic contentment, "a life serene and simple, complicated only when civilization occasionally intrudes its modern mechanisms into the drowsy imagination of the peasants."[33] According to this review, Bulosan's stories presented a fondly remembered rural childhood, devoid of the complications of "civilization" and replete with "serene" comforts. Tellingly, similar adjectives appeared in the publisher's listing of new books three days before Sugrue's review appeared: "A novel about the simple, serene life in a pre-war Filipino village on the island of Luzon."[34]

Some reviewers, however, did not even catch the "weapon of the spirit" in Bulosan's work. Clara Savage Littledale introduced readers of the *Saturday Review* to *The Laughter of My Father* as "Life with Father, but with a very different father than Clarence Day."[35] Littledale contrasts Bulosan's stories to the hit Broadway play *Life with Father* and to her only "intimate acquaintance with anyone resembling [Bulosan's] Father . . . a Filipino named Ernest who cooked for us one summer" (FSM 22).[36] Littledale's description takes "this irrepressibly bawdy book" as not merely unironic but also a "simple" and "refreshing" pre-Freudian fantasy of un-self-reflexiveness:

> No, not every father, not every family behaves with the untrammeled naturalness of this family. Nothing neurotic about them! They felt what they felt and they acted upon it. No repressions! The reader breaking out in uncontrollable laughter as he reads experiences a vast sense of relief and enjoyment at getting so near to persons who can love and hate and act as they feel with such perfect spontaneity. (22)

Even more striking than Littledale's characterization of the work as expressing "untrammeled naturalness" is her suggestion that reading this work therapeutically produces psychic healing in its beleaguered, neurotic, overly civilized U.S. readers: "anyone who is real enough himself to be able to enjoy reading about real people and who knows, as Father and his family did, that laughter is wealth" (22). This exoticized interpretation of Filipino life as geographically and temporally distant, backwardly premodern, and unthreateningly humorous is, needless to say, precisely the opposite of what I have argued the stories themselves portray.

Although I have paid close attention to the circumstances of the publication and reception of *Laughter*, I do not conclude that Bulosan was simply an unknowing victim of a craven publisher and malevolent reviewers. Such a univocal interpretation would rob the author of agency and greatly exaggerate the impact of the publisher's marketing. Bulosan chose a tragicomic folkloric mode for the stories in *Laughter*, one that was easily manipulated and misread. His awareness of his own role in the reception of *Laughter* can be seen in the hairpin turn in aesthetics that he took in his next publication.

Laughter has much more in common with Bulosan's explicitly ideological and powerful 1946 work *America Is in the Heart* than initially appears to be the case. In *Laughter*, he employs a wide range of aesthetic and formal strategies—folktale, multilingualism, translation, irony, oppositional history, polemic, and surreal/absurdist humor—that would drive the narrative methods foundational to *America Is in the Heart.*[37] Bulosan's efforts to overcome readers' misreading of *Laughter* is evident in the ways that he retooled these strategies in the more arresting autobiographical style of *America.*[38] Reading *Laughter* within Bulosan's broader political and artistic trajectories also helps explain some of the paradoxes that seem inexplicable in the later work. For example, scholars have had difficulty reconciling the apparent triumphalism in the conclusion of *America Is in the Heart* with Bulosan's otherwise consistent Marxist critique of U.S. society. By contrast, *Laughter* centralizes everyday Filipino life and marginalizes the United States in ways that suggest a more ambivalent perspective on Americanism. Taken together, *Laughter* and *America* provide a finely nuanced portrait of Filipino/a perspectives on modernity, urbanism, and assimilationist Americanism.

Bulosan's shift in narratorial strategy from folklore to polemic quickly became apparent when his publisher advertised *America Is in the Heart*. Harcourt felt obliged to present the work as a dramatic new turn for the author rather than an outgrowth of the earlier stories, since many readers would have otherwise anticipated another installment of Filipino simplicity and nonthreateningly humorous backwardness. In an ad printed in the *New York Times Book Review*, the publisher referred to the author as "best known as the author of the lovable book, THE LAUGHTER OF MY FATHER."[39] However, the ad continues:

> His big new book, a personal history of his life in the Philippines and in America, is in a different mood. You will find the same oblique humor,

the same tenderness which marked his earlier book—but this autobiography rightly shocks those not knowing the brutal, tragic discriminations against Filipinos in America. However, through all the years of struggle and abuse, Carlos Bulosan never completely lost faith in America.[40]

The care with which this advertisement narrates Bulosan's career indicates how sensitive Harcourt was to readers' investment in *Laughter* as harmless, playful humor. The publisher's attempt to frame the "different mood" of *America Is in the Heart* is striking. Despite Harcourt's efforts to link the "oblique humor" and "tenderness" of the first work to the "brutal, tragic discrimination" in the second, the comparison was forced. Giving up on ethnic humor as a selling point, Harcourt instead encouraged unambiguously assimilationist interpretations of the new work. To this end, the ad quoted from the conclusion of *America Is in the Heart* without any hint of the rhetorical repositioning of the term "America" that Bulosan's work accomplished: "no man—no one at all—could destroy my faith in America."

At the time of its publication, *Laughter* was generally interpreted as unambiguously comic, even self-mocking. But a more carefully contextualized framework for reading the work reveals an anti-exoticizing modernist darkness at its core. The stories are not comic, nor are they even tragicomic; most of them are absurdist and even anti-comic, depicting Ellisonian (if not Brechtian) laughter without humor, the laughter of the oppressed surveying the absurdity of institutionalized oppression itself.[41] The humor that Bulosan mingles with such tragedies and disappointments represents neither the levity of "astonishingly simple" people (as one *Times* reviewer suggested) nor an ethnicized Horatio Alger narrative of conclusive triumph over daunting obstacles. Instead, Bulosan's unresolved and undefined mixture of laughter and pathos, humor and ambiguity, locates Filipino modernity at the crossroads of mechanization, colonialism, folklore, and indigenous resistance.[42]

Only two years after its original publication and simultaneous with the Bantam paperback publication, Bulosan defined his artistic purpose as articulating anger, not humor: "I am an angry man. That is why I started writing." In an article he published in *The Writer* (May 1946), "I Am Not a Laughing Man," he pointed out that the underlying affective strategy of his stories was not comedy but resistant anger. The essay expressed his frustration with the strategic misreadings encouraged by his publisher and elaborated by prominent reviewers. It begins:

> I am mad.
>
> I am mad because when my book, *The Laughter of My Father*, was published by Harcourt, Brace and Company, the critics called me "the pure Comic Spirit."
>
> I am not a laughing man. I am an angry man. That is why I started writing. I guess you will have to be angry at something if you want to be a writer.[43]

Bulosan explains that his role as a writer emerged directly from painful experiences working among other Filipino migrant laborers. After sending his stories out, "*The New Yorker*, a magazine I had not read before, bought several of my stories. I was mad. What kind of publication is this that bought my stories for a fabulous sum?" After having "bought 100 back issues" to read, he finds himself too "angry with the cold" to write and starts "burning the old copies of *The New Yorker*" for warmth (OBF 140).

Bulosan thus describes his literary success as both a manifestation of his existing anger with the structural inequities of colonizing capitalism and a new source of resentment. The publication of his stories in *Laughter* made him "angry because everyone laughed reading it. I was angry when I wrote it in the back room of a cold office. But the readers did not know that" (OBF 141). He expresses frustration at being read as producing comic stories in the "self-maiming" minstrel mode, rather than the anger that his laughter (and *Laughter*) actually represented. He then describes his next publication as another attempt to narrate anger. This time instead of couching bitterness through a complex engagement with absurdist laughter, he attempts a new literary mode: "at last, in late December, my autobiography—*America Is in the Heart*—will be published to tell the world that I am not a laughing man!" (142).

In a companion essay to "I Am Not a Laughing Man" called "How My Stories Were Written," Bulosan explains his representational concerns more broadly. He defines his literary genealogy in a way that emphasizes both his ongoing engagement with narratives of Filipino/a identity and his efforts to undermine Orientalizing minstrel readings of his work. Like Ellison, Bulosan draws on collective folklore that he self-consciously revises. Bulosan's modernist folktales thus emerge in a form in which it is "impossible to determine which is fact and which is flight of the imagination" — as "folkwise stories based on the hard core of reality" (OBF 110). By describing his stories as painstakingly plotted and revised, he challenges reviewers who patronizingly read him as an "astonishingly simple" writer. In doing so he introduces a character who plays a role remarkably similar to that of the grandfather in *Invisible Man*.

Bulosan describes having heard stories just before leaving his homeland from Apo Lacay, "an old man whose age no one could remember," who inhabits a "mysterious dwelling in the mountains" and who tells innumerable folktales from generations of villagers. Apo Lacay describes his tales as rooted in a postcolonial Rousseauianism that neatly dramatizes the paradoxical modernity that Bulosan's stories portray: "The beast in the jungle with his ferocious fangs is less dangerous than man with his cultivated mind. It is the heart that counts" (113). As a result, the stories demonstrate that "laughter is the beginning of wisdom." The young narrator relates this pairing of laughter and wisdom to his emerging identity as a diasporic writer whose stories will form textual representations of home: "if the retelling of your stories will give me a little wisdom of the heart, then I shall have come home again." Apo Lacay understands this process as joint authorship — "You mean it will be your book as well as mine? Your words as well as my words, there in that faraway land" — and as a way to survive and outlast the consequences of multiple imperialisms in the Philippines:

> Then it seemed to me, watching him lost in thought, he had become a little boy again living all the *tales he had told us about a vanished race, listening to the gorgeous laughter of men in the midst of abject poverty and tyranny*. For that was the time of his childhood, in the age of great distress and calamity in the land, when the fury of an invading race impaled their hearts in the tragic cross of slavery and ignorance. (113–14, emphasis added)

Apo Lacay, as "the sole surviving witness of the cruelty and dehumanization of man by another man . . . now living in the dawn of reason and progress," embodies the "tales that were taken for laughter and the foolish words of a lonely old man who had lived far beyond his time." The essay ends with the author in the United States drawing on collective folklore and individual invention to write "stories that really belong to everyone in that valley beautiful beyond any telling of it" (114).

The old man's stories represent collective identity through strategic laughter that evokes intergenerational wisdom rather than the "laughter and foolish words of a lonely old man who had lived beyond his time." Bulosan's modernist revisions of Filipino folklore work against the notion that his stories "had lived beyond [their] time." The stories confront the backwardness myth constructed by colonialist histories of indigenous cultures and the simple, unreflective humor thought to be indicative of folklore.[44] In place of simplicity, Bulosan infuses his stories with laughter that cannot be reduced to humor, with history of "great distress and calamity" resulting from imperialism, and with literary subjects that evade even language, "beautiful beyond any telling of it" (114).

Like the Invisible Man's grandfather, who couches radical subversiveness within the meek mask of agreeable smiles and laughter, Bulosan's Apo Lacay hides tales of collective "calamity" in stories that evoke the "gorgeous laughter of men in the midst of abject poverty and tyranny." Laughter, in Bulosan's work, clearly is not passive, acquiescent, or ameliorative. Instead, it erupts at the sites of conflict; it is aggressive, resistant, and unsettling. This easily misunderstood laughter proved to be the crucial means by which Bulosan represented Filipino/a identity from within the machinery of U.S. expansionist modernity. *The Laughter of My Father* sought to challenge U.S. readers who had tacitly consented to their government's military conquest of the Philippines by playing on their expectations of a "backward" society desirous of U.S. imperial rule. Following the same logic that would lead Ellison a decade later to begin his opus on African American invisibility with the subversive grandfather, Bulosan used the unsettling, uncanny echoes of laughter to confront the violent absurdities of racism and class conflict plaguing interwar Filipinos/as.

Notes

I am very grateful for detailed readings by and ongoing conversations with Douglas Mao, Ylana and Martin Miller, Alisse Portnoy, Sarita See, and Rebecca Walkowitz. I benefited from superb research assistance by Kavita Padiyar. I would like to express my appreciation to the students at Columbia University and the University of Michigan who heard and challenged some of these ideas in early form, particularly the Columbia Ethnic Studies undergraduates in "Comparative American Multilingual Literatures" (Spring 2002) and the Michigan graduate students in "Counternarratives of Modernity" (Fall 2002).

1. Carlos Bulosan, "Freedom from Want," *Saturday Evening Post* (March 6, 1943), 15.

2. Individual stories have occasionally been anthologized. However, without the republication of the entire work or critical recontextualization of the reprinted stories, Bulosan's broader political and literary ambitions remain obscure. Among the exceptions to the critical neglect of *Laughter* is Joel Slotkin, "Igorots and Indians: Racial Hierarchies and Conceptions of the Savage in Carlos Bulosan's Fiction of the Philippines," *American Literature* 72, no. 4 (December 2000): 843–66.

3. Delfin L. Tolentino Jr., "Satire in Carlos Bulosan's *The Laughter of My Father*," *Philippine Studies* 34 (1986): 452.

4. On U.S./Pacific crossings and Asian American modernity, see David Palumbo-Liu, *Asian/American: Historical Crossings of a Racial Frontier* (Stanford, Calif.: Stanford University Press, 1999).

5. Andreas Huyssen, "High/Low in an Expanded Field," *Modernism/Modernity* 9, no. 3 (2002): 363–74. Subsequent references noted as HL.

6. Gayatri Spivak, *Death of a Discipline* (New York: Columbia University Press, 2003), 84.

7. Shu-mei Shih, "Global Literature and the Technologies of Recognition," PMLA 119, no. 1 (January 2004): 18. Subsequent references noted as GL.

8. Dilip Parameshwar Gaonkar, "On Alternative Modernities," *Alternative Modernities* (Durham, N.C.: Duke University Press, 2001), 14–15.

9. For analogous tensions in African American cinematic representations, see Jacqueline Stewart, "Negroes Laughing at Themselves? Black Spectatorship and the Performance of Urban Modernity," *Critical Inquiry* 29 (Summer 2003): 653.

10. For a canonical modernist analogue to Bulosan's complex interplay between narrator and narrative point of view, consider Henry James's treatments of perspective. In *Narratology*, Mieke Bal calls James "perhaps the most radical experimenter whose project was to demonstrate that . . . narrator and focalizer are not to be conflated" (Bal, *Narratology*, 2d ed. [Toronto: University of Toronto Press, 1997], 147). My point is that Bulosan's negotiation of oral folklore and imperial translation led him to play with similar elements of narrative, and in this way led to another literary form that we can productively read as alternatively modernist.

11. See, for example, W. T. Lhamon Jr., *Raising Cain* (Cambridge, Mass.: Harvard University Press, 1998); Peter Stanfield, " 'An Octoroon in the Kindling': American Vernacular and Blackface Minstrelsy in 1930s Hollywood," *Journal of American Studies* 31, no. 3 (1997): 407–38; Michael Paul Rogin, *Blackface, White Noise* (Berkeley: University of California Press, 1996); Eric Lott, *Love and Theft* (New York: Oxford University Press, 1993); Eric Sundquist, *To Wake the Nations* (Cambridge, Mass.: Harvard University Press, 1993); Alexander Saxton, *The Rise and Fall of the White Republic* (London: Verso, 1990), 165–82.

12. For a review of the aesthetics of laughter, see Peter Kivy, "Jokes are a Laughing Matter," *Journal of Aesthetics and Art Criticism* 61, no. 1 (Winter 2003): 8, 11–12. I am grateful to Christi Merrill for bringing this article to my attention.

13. See Robert G. Lee, *Orientals: Asian Americans in Popular Culture* (Philadelphia: Temple University Press, 2000), and Joseph D. Won, "Yellowface Minstrelsy: Asian Martial Arts and the American Popular Imaginary" (Ph.D. diss., University of Michigan, 1997).

14. I am grateful to Lincoln Faller for informative suggestions regarding this trend in World War II films.

15. Richard Slotkin, "Unit Pride: Ethnic Platoons and the Myths of American Nationality," *American Literary History* 13, no. 3 (Fall 2001): 479.

16. Carlos Bulosan, *Sound of Falling Light: Letters in Exile*, ed. Dolores S. Feria (Quezon City: University of the Philippines Press, 1960), 85.

17. Originally published in the *New Yorker* (November 13, 1943), 45–50.

18. Carlos Bulosan, *The Laughter of My Father* (New York: Harcourt Brace, 1944), 5–6. Subsequent references noted as *LMF*.

19. See Kenneth Burke on the perspectival shifts that "comic correctives" enable: "the comic frame should enable people *to be observers of themselves, while acting*. Its ultimate would not be *passiveness*, but *maximum consciousness*" (emphasis original). Kenneth Burke, "Perspective by Incongruity: Comic Correctives," *On Symbols and Society*, ed. Joseph R. Eusfield (Chicago: University of Chicago Press, 1989), 264.

20. Originally published in the *New Yorker* (December 19, 1942), 24–25.

21. Bulosan makes references to U.S. cultural movements (for example, "It was the jazz age") but they are made in passing and serve primarily to note the distance from the United States and alternative meanings in the Filipino context (*LMF*, 22).

22. Carlos Bulosan, *America Is in the Heart* (Seattle: University of Washington Press, 1973), 71.

23. Helen Jaskoski, "Carlos Bulosan's Literary Debt to Richard Wright," in *Literary Influence and African-American Writers*, ed. Tracy Mishkin (New York: Garland, 1996), 239.

24. Ralph Ellison, *Collected Essays of Ralph Ellison*, ed. John F. Callahan, (New York: Modern Library, 1995), 102. Subsequent references noted as *CRE*.

25. See Earl H. Rovit, "Ralph Ellison and the American Comic Tradition," in *Ralph Ellison: A Collection of Critical Essays*, ed. John Hersey (Englewood Cliffs, N.J.: Prentice-Hall, 1974), 151–59.

26. Ralph Ellison, *Invisible Man* (New York: Vintage, 1992), 16. Subsequent references noted as *IM*.

27. See also other scenes in which the narrator responds with laughter to painful instances of racism, for example, pages 194, 227, 257, and 311.

28. What Hortense Spillers has written of Ellison is true for Bulosan as well: "Ellison . . . had few models before him in overturning the discursive decisions that had arrested notions of 'blackness' in retrograde rhetorical behaviors." Hortense J. Spillers, *Black, White, and in Color* (Chicago: University of Chicago Press, 2003), 4–5.

29. "Books Published Today" (Advertisement), *New York Times* (April 20, 1944), 7.

30. "The Laughter of My Father" (Advertisement), *New York Times Book Review* (May 2, 1944), 17.

31. Oscar V. Campomanes and Todd S. Gernes, "Two Letters from America: Carlos Bulosan and the Act of Writing," *melus* 15, no. 3 (1988): 28.

32. Thomas Sugrue, "Laughter in the Philippines" (review of *The Laughter of My Father*), *New York Times Book Review* (April 23, 1944), 7.

33. Ibid.

34. "Books Published Today" (Advertisement), *New York Times* (April 20, 1944), 17.

35. Clara Savage Littledale, "The Way Father Stretched His Mouth" (review of *The Laughter of My Father*), *Saturday Review of Literature* 27 (June 3, 1944), 22. Subsequent references noted as FSM.

36. Michael Curtiz's film *Life with Father*, which starred William Powell, Irene Dunne, and Elizabeth Taylor, was released in 1947, three years after this review was published. Littledale was referring to Clarence Day Jr.'s memoirs, *God and My Father*, *Life with Father*, and *Life with Mother*, and the play *Life with Father*, which opened in 1939 and became the longest-running play to that point in Broadway history, running continuously for 3,224 performances from November 8, 1939, until July 12, 1947.

37. See Elaine Kim, *Asian American Literature* (Philadelphia: Temple University Press, 1982), 56–57.

38. While it would be overly schematic to suggest that Bulosan moved from a Hurstonian folkloric mode in *Laughter* to a Richard Wrightian polemical style in *America*, the infamous Hurston/Wright debate of 1937–38 on the aesthetics and politics of African American vernacular literary expression demonstrated the stakes of such different literary strategies. See Hazel Carby, "The Politics of Fiction, Anthropology, and the Folk: Zora Neale Hurston," in *New Essays on* Their Eyes Were Watching God, ed. Michael Awkward (Cambridge: Cambridge University Press, 1990), 71–93; and June Jordan, "On Richard Wright and Zora Neale Hurston: Notes Toward a Balancing of Love and Hatred," *Black World* 23, no. 10 (1974): 4–8.

39. "America Is in the Heart" (Advertisement), *New York Times Book Review* (March 10, 1946), 17.

40. Ibid.

41. L. M. Grow, "The Laughter of My Father: A Survival Kit," *melus* 20, no. 2 (1995): 43.

42. E. San Juan Jr., *From Exile to Diaspora: Versions of the Filipino Experience in the United States* (Boulder, Colo.: Westview Press, 1998), 83. Subsequent references noted as FED.

43. Carlos Bulosan, *On Becoming Filipino: Selected Writings of Carlos Bulosan*, ed. E. San Juan (Philadelphia: Temple University Press, 1995), 138. Subsequent references noted as *OBF*.

44. San Juan argues that Apo Lacay represents Bulosan's invention of "a strategy of legitimation, an originary myth . . . the fountainhead of all the stories [Bulosan] has recounted, so the author is conceived of primarily as a transmitter or conveyor of the collective wisdom and history of a people" (*FED*, 122).

The Laughter of My Father

Lisa Fluet

Hit-Man Modernism

Among the many new directions taken by modernist studies, one that has emerged from the intersection of American, film, and cultural studies emphasizes productive ways of connecting literary modernism to the heterogeneous array of media often termed "pulp fiction": hard-boiled fiction, thrillers, film noir, B-movies, graphic novels, neo-noir film.[1] Pulp seems full of contradictions: it can sound racist, sexist, and snobbish, yet gesture longingly toward populism; it looks easy to read, yet can require classroom discussion; it seems American, yet pops up in other locales; it appears strictly mid-century, yet time-travels to the here and now (suspiciously lacking historical baggage) via pastiche. Badly behaved, then, and hard to pin down, it is also notable for the way it recycles and reexamines ideas about both high modernism and popular culture, thus serving as a reliably undisciplined disciplinary object for criticism.

One implication of Paula Rabinowitz's coinage "pulp modernism," in her *Black and White and Noir* (2002), is that pulp is in fact one of modernism's ways of wandering beyond historical, categorical, and institutional boundaries and showing up, unannounced, where we least expect it. For Rabinowitz, pulp and modernism disseminate each other across the American cultural landscape in proliferating examples without hope of containment, apart from the national borders she imposes on her study. As a recycled cultural leftover, "the myriad detritus floating beyond the borders of acceptable scholarship" (18), pulp, in Rabinowitz's view, exhibits a "peculiar modernism" stemming, above all, from its "chaotic repetition" of familiar forms of American state-sponsored economic violence—against women, racial and ethnic groups, and workers (22).

In what follows, I explore the ways in which one particular character emerging through popular modernism offers an impersonal, professional intervention into private life, and paradoxically makes amends for the kinds of destabilizing violence just described—by granting a form of secure, reliable violence in the hit. My focus on the contract killer builds on recent critical consideration of noir characters—like the hard-boiled detective, the insurance agent, and the female social worker—as narrative reflections on the professional administration of social services in the United States. The hit man, however, by nature a border-crossing professional offering a consistently more violent "service," calls for an approach extended beyond American studies, to the ethically ambiguous area that theorizations of cosmopolitan identity have come to occupy.

For Fredric Jameson in *Postmodernism, or, The Cultural Logic of Late Capitalism* (1991), pulp's contemporary neo-noir manifestations call attention to our difficulties in fashioning representations of the present, difficulties that leave both high modernism and American political radicalism irrecoverably fixed in the past. We could, however, read neo-noir—as well as older pulp—a little differently. Instead of assuming that radicalism can only be a living power or something wholly repressed, we could locate the welfare state somewhere between the radical past and contemporary amnesia, as a half-remembered historical compromise between revolution and capital. And we could make use of the new attention to relations between pulp and modernism to ask whether the perpetual return of pulp is not a symptom of the welfare state, its half-remembered situation depicted through professional characters who compensate in various ways for the ambivalence that the idea of state-sponsored intervention can often raise.

Contract killers in pulp narratives share some of the "bad" qualities that have also been associated with modernism itself: illusions of formal genius wedded to lonely, cosmopolitan self-reliance; a scary attraction to formal, authoritarian control; a preference for coterie patronage of their expertise over a public sphere that will never appreciate or pay for what they do; and an ironic detachment from belief in progressive change, public accountability, and community identity.[2] At the same time, however, contract killers crucially situate this badness within scenarios of security, through the formal, deadly certainties they orchestrate, and in the consoling certainties for which they articulate an insistent need: job security, education, health care, therapy, vacation time, and other periodic, mundane sources of relief from life's anxieties that depend on the increasingly difficult-to-imagine community of the welfare state. With his reliably fatal expertise, the hit man reminds us of the half-remembered formal security that both modernism and the welfare state could conjure up, while presenting his own style of risk management in terms of a violent affective indifference to the victims of his security.

Concentrating on Graham Greene's 1936 pulp "entertainment" *A Gun for Sale*, I position Greene's late modernism in a dialogue with concerns about education, the welfare state, and working-class advancement usually reserved for postwar cultural studies. I argue that Greene's protagonist—who, like other hit men, is at once a figure of intrusive professional intervention into private life and himself the youthful, "scholarship boy" on which such intervention focuses—addresses the perceived crisis in middle-class vocation that Tyrus Miller identifies with other late-modern British authors.[3] I also argue that, in ways that come to be echoed in later hit-man narratives, *A Gun for Sale* positions the intervening femme fatale, and her brief therapeutic involvement with the contract killer, as a model for state-sponsored social work removed from the greedy acquisitiveness and manipulation of male desire usually associated with the femme fatale in pulp. I will go on to consider how modernist fascination with female interventions into the lives of angry scholarship boys—most notably in Virginia Woolf's *To the Lighthouse*—reminds us of what gendered modernity offers to affectively challenged women in the way of professional responsibility over the security of young, anxious, angry male citizens. My conclusion returns to the "wrong" feelings connecting intervening women and angry young hit men via a reconsideration of Raymond Williams's late readings of modernism and of the role that bad, recycled modernism has played in the maturity of both the hit man as character and of state-sponsored consolations to insecure young citizens.

Angry Young Hit Men

Hit men often advance from poor or obscure origins to the relative stability of white-collar life via intelligence, talent, and some form of institutional legitimation—usually conferred by the recruitment and training structures of organized crime "family" patronage, youthful gang-families, or (if they are trained as state assassins, before turning freelance) the military. This advancement from poor beginnings through these "educational" institutions to a solitary professional life in the "white-collar crime" of contract killing invites a parallel to that of the lonely scholarship boy figure of early British cultural studies.

Richard Hoggart's genealogy for this boy, in *The Uses of Literacy* (1957), positions the school as the enabling institution for his class mobility. As one of the more complex figures Hoggart introduces in this inaugural text for British cultural studies, the scholarship boy also could be said to personify the field's advancement to academic recognition, challenging the institutional preeminence of elite culture with the increased visibility of working-class culture. At the same time, both the scholarship boy and the field advance to a point from which working-class life tends to be viewed nostalgically; the boy's advancement within educational institutions testifies to his steady removal from the working-class culture he ostensibly represents, just as the field's complicated rise to institutional recognition in the twentieth century suggests some distance from its humbler origins. Thus in classically "angry" contemporary works like John Osborne's *Look Back in Anger* (1957), Kingsley Amis's *Lucky Jim* (1954), and Alan Sillitoe's *The Loneliness of the Long Distance Runner* (1959), the possibility of advancement further entails compromised personal integrity and a willed forgetfulness of personal history — an ethical dilemma that the scholarship boy feels acutely. Educational structures therefore enable his articulation of an angry, anxious critique of mainstream channels to professional success, since upward mobility, in these accounts, appears by turns hypocritical, forgetful, comical, and pointless.

Educated scholarship boys share with working-class angry young men like Sillitoe's Arthur Seaton not merely an oft-observed penchant for vocal, anti-establishment, anarchic feeling but more importantly a sense that avoiding visible class mobility, either by critiquing channels to higher professional advancement or by living for "Saturday night and Sunday morning" alone, can be a politics in itself. In their isolated distance from wholehearted belief in working-class membership, national solidarity, and white-collar achievement, angry young men tend to articulate interesting varieties of potential resistance to postwar British national identity. But the prospect of full advancement to visible professional success tends to be equated in these narratives with the loss of that isolated critical perspective. In one sense, then, the young hit man as scholarship boy both seeks secure advancement (as in Hoggart's depiction) *and* scornfully rejects the trappings of ostensible professional success (as in Osborne, Amis, and Sillitoe), since he achieves a white-collar position that remains beyond public modes of recognition and legitimation, and allows him to preserve a distanced critical perspective on traditional class mobility.

Although the postwar realism of angry young men like Osborne, Amis, and Sillitoe is frequently cast, along with the early cultural studies work of Williams and Hoggart, in reaction to the institutionalization of literary modernism, Hoggart's treatment of the alienated scholarship boy in *The Uses of Literacy* is curiously modernist. His periodic invocations of literary modernism throughout this work suggest a desire to position the scholarship boy-turned-adult intellectual that Hoggart himself became as a needed, outside authority on both elite and working-class culture. At the same time, *The Uses of Literacy* noticeably undermines the defining of literacy, and culture, solely in terms of "uses" by presenting its unfortunate conclusion to the scholarship boy's story: his too-late realization of the unmarketability of all that he has painstakingly learned. Hoggart's conclusion tacitly rebukes the youth's expectation of a market for his "brain currency" once he leaves school, so that the scholarship boy's damaged psyche and chronically anti-social status result from both well-intentioned, unironic public attempts to extend social mobility via education and the boy's own naïve belief in the scholarship system's implication of culture with the work ethic.[4] The subsequently angry scholarship boy—like Hoggart, Williams, and the other young men mentioned above—recognizes the inadequacies of such simple progressivism and ultimately learns to reject bitterly the belief that there is any better place to get to through such mobility.

Hoggart's concerns—which are shared by Williams in *Culture and Society*, another foundational cultural studies text—raise the intriguing possibility that early British cultural studies could be viewed not as a field forged in angry defiance of modernism's newly entrenched canonicity but as itself a species of late, bad modernism.[5] Cultural studies as vocalized through Hoggart and Williams echoes modernism's skeptical perspective, most closely associated with T. S. Eliot, on the democratic extension of culture to satisfy an individually utilitarian, upwardly mobile work ethic. And yet, for Hoggart and Williams, the concern shared by Eliot and Leavis for the preservation of culture against modernity and market forces fades before their own "bad" preference for potential forms of revolutionary solidarity, like working-class membership, that would ideally keep the scholarship boy from developing the unhealthy, bourgeois desire to use culture for solitary professional advancement.

Possessed of this unhealthy desire, the scholarship boy feels "physically" uprooted from the working class "through the medium of the scholarship system," yet never officially belongs with similarly declassed, successful "professionals and experts." He subsequently finds himself "no longer really belonging to any group," yet in a position to criticize both his own nostalgia for such belonging (Hoggart 238–39) and his competing desire "to be a citizen of that well-polished, prosperous, cool, book-lined and magazine-discussing world of the successful intelligent middle class" (247). As I will argue throughout, the slow emergence of the lone contract killer as a recognizable character in the twentieth century offers a unique vantage point on this dilemma (left unresolved by both modernism and cultural studies) over culture, education, advancement, and community. As scholarship boy, the young contract killer rises through institutions that instill and reward his deadly expertise to a position that parodies white-collar success, yet he still preserves a critical disdain for those who believe in such simple progress for boys like him — since he knows, unlike Hoggart's boy, that this progress cannot occur without criminality. He shares both modernism's and cultural studies' ambivalence about the utilization of culture; he knows that his own education can be very useful to him, but precisely because he need not subject his hard-won literacy (in the methods of orchestrating death) to the vicissitudes of the market. He opts instead, as many literary moderns did, for patrons who will appreciate and sponsor the formal intricacies of his knowledge work in ways the public cannot.

The class "no-place" where Hoggart's scholarship boy awkwardly finds himself bears a critical resemblance to the contract killer's perennially cosmopolitan, border-crossing "no-place." The killer, however, turns both class and national alienation into advantages, compensating for a felt lack of poise with a combination of outward coolness and metropolitan mobility characteristic of some literary moderns.[6] More significantly, however, he stages formally secure situations — hits — that should proceed inevitably to a certain outcome (the death of the target). In such orchestrations, he expresses a belief in the security created through the form of the hit, as a kind of compensation for the secure advancement promised him through education yet denied him and others like him in adult life.

Graham Greene's *A Gun for Sale* (1936) calls particular attention to the young hit man's affinities with Hoggart's sad, solitary, "anxious and uprooted" boy.[7] The novel opens with Raven, a young British contract killer, walking down a "wide Continental street" in an unnamed country en route to his assigned hit, a socialist war minister — "an old grubby man without friends, who was said to love humanity."[8] Raven's subsequent successful kill assumes greater significance than he could possibly have imagined, indifferent as he is at the novel's outset to global politics. As a result of the minister's murder, and its presumed political motivation, ultimatums are set, and it seems inevitable that England will soon enter another world war. More important for our purposes than Greene's foresight in imagining England's entry into another world conflict several years prior to 1939, however, is that *A Gun for Sale* offers a kind of meditation on three very different, "uprooted" scholarship boys, each of whom negotiates his own relationship with poor, orphan beginnings, hard-won expertise, and global effects. The first is Raven, the contract killer who almost precipitates world war; the second is the war minister who "loves humanity," opposes global militarization, and cuts army expenses in order to develop slums; and the third is Sir Marcus, the Midland steel industrialist who hires Raven to kill the minister to bring war closer and thus dramatically forwards the worldwide need for munitions.[9]

Raven's refrain of "I'm educated" throughout the novel refers directly to his abilities, learned in "the Home" he was sent to after his mother's suicide, to "understand the things I read in the papers. Like this psicko [psychology] business. And write a good hand and speak the King's English" (127). Were it not for his poorly corrected harelip, "a serious handicap in his profession" (5) and a "badge of class," of "the poverty of parents who couldn't afford a clever surgeon" (14), Raven would appear completely at ease in his hard-won professional life: "He carried an attaché case. He looked like any other youngish man going home after his work; his dark overcoat had a clerical air. He walked steadily up the street like hundreds of his kind." His harelip,

Raven believes, justifies both his detachment from the murders he commits and his strangely scornful pride over his state-administered education. His "deformity," one of many bad "breaks," keeps him perennially anxious and prevents him from capitalizing on his intelligence, as well as from having the home and the girl he seems to want. Consequently, he feels no patriotic loyalties or responsibilities toward the state that, however inadequately and grudgingly, has helped to make him the kind of professional he is—just as he has no qualms about abandoning (prior to the novel's action) his identification with the gang that trained him and served (however inadequately) as a surrogate family.

Raven only wishes, futilely as he discovers, that there might be loyalty among "his own kind": those who, like him, "didn't belong inside the legal borders" (29). The "kind" to which Raven refers—the boarding-house owner, maid, and shady surgeon who all try to betray him—inhabit the rather hyperbolically sordid fictional England traditionally termed "Greeneland" by Greene's critics. And yet, the war minister and Sir Marcus *also* can be considered Raven's "own kind," as fellow perennially dislocated scholarship boys. The humanity-loving war minister ekes out a "poor, bare, solitary" life in an untidy apartment, making him an easy target for Sir Marcus, his friend from youthful years spent in a "Home" like Raven's. Sir Marcus, bearing the markers of both the novel's ambiguous anti-Semitism and of Greene's ambivalence toward the globalizing reach of capital,

> spoke with the faintest foreign accent and it was difficult to determine whether he was Jewish or of an ancient English family. He gave the impression that very many cities had rubbed him smooth. If there was a touch of Jerusalem, there was also a touch of St. James's, if of some Central European capital, there were also marks of the most exclusive clubs in Cannes. (107)

Greene's "entertainments" are often read as meditations on a style of modernism in the manner of T. S. Eliot: "Greeneland" and *A Gun for Sale*'s Midlands look a lot like "waste lands," and Catholic iconography for each writer offers a complex symbolic subtext to the rather bleakly secular isolation and sordidness of modern life. In *Gun*, Raven, the socialist war minister, and Sir Marcus all strangely stand in as both lonely scholarship boys and sacrificial Christ figures.

Hit-Man Modernism

As James Naremore suggests, Greene's periodic anti-Semitism here also resembles Eliot's. Both "associate Jewishness not only with a dark racial otherness but also, more specifically, with modernity and American-style capitalism," as well as with cosmopolitan rootlessness, as in Sir Marcus's ambiguous origins and the "many cities" that "had rubbed him smooth."[10] Sharon Marcus acknowledges the difficulties for critical reclamation of cosmopolitanism posed by the history of nationalist thinking that attacks "internal others, such as Jews — for an unstable, rootless universality that consisted of sheer ubiquity."[11] We could link Greene directly to this history; the "unstable, rootless universality" that characterizes scholarship boys, Jews, and cosmopolitans in A Gun for Sale surrenders, in the end, to the certain "reliability" represented by Jimmy Mather, the Scotland Yard man who tracks Raven and who would immediately enlist, should the need arise. Anne Crowder, with whom both Raven and Mather are in love, loves Jimmy because "she wanted her man to be ordinary, she wanted to be able to know what he'd say next" (24). Mather, by the same token, "liked to feel that he was one of thousands more or less equal working for a concrete end — not equality of opportunity, not government by the people or by the richest or by the best, but simply to do away with crime which meant uncertainty" (38).

Mather's position in the novel suggests that "Yard men," with their straightforward efforts against the at-home immediacy of crime's "uncertainty," offer a more effectual alternative to previous efforts to "do something about" uncertainty over events in a more global, and implicitly less immediate, less material, sphere of influence. The Yard man's closeness to problems at home renders him more obviously or concretely effectual than internationalist agents like the war minister, global capitalists like Sir Marcus, and border-crossing, professional purveyors of deadly certainty like Raven. Further, when Yard men like Mather allow the predictability that they work to achieve on the job to structure how they act and what they say in their personal lives, this confusion of at-work and at-home roles seems to increase their sexual desirability, as Anne Crowder makes clear. In contrast, chronic scholarship boy bachelors like the war minister, Raven, and Sir Marcus seem to lack, and to have always lacked, such desirability, and not merely because they are perceived as untidy, ugly, and old. The war minister, "said to love humanity," has chosen an impossible group: how do you love everybody, all at once and all the time? And indeed the abstract "humanity" that receives his attention supplants a representative identification with any one group, just as Sir Marcus's cosmopolitan rootlessness supplants identification with any one of the cities which have "touched" him and Raven's "lone gunman" status would seem, rather obviously, to preclude membership in any kind of community—working-class, criminal, or professional. The unfixable nature of their professional motives and goals, the vague spheres of influence they involve themselves with, and the demarcations they draw between professional-time and down-time therefore collectively prevent their access to the smaller community that companionate love would create.

Yet Greene clearly challenges the rather banal, patriotic heroism that Mather embodies. He does so in part simply by presenting it as banal in its "rooted" ubiquity, and unquestioning of its own "concrete ends." But he also does so by presenting the goals of the less rooted three—such as the stalling of European militarization, the improvement of slums, the pursuit of capital and stock increases, the "tidy" fulfillment of professional assignments—as suggestive of greater complexity than Mather's goals. To complicate matters further, Sir Marcus's ruthless endeavors to secure a global market for Midland Steel's munitions would in fact have created new jobs for "Nottwich"'s (that is, Nottingham's) depressed economy. One of the many disconcerting images Greene leaves us with in Nottwich, after Raven's death, is of a hotel porter, formerly a steelworker, reminiscing about the better treatment he received when Midland Steel was a more active concern: "I almost feel sorry too—for the old man. I was in Midland Steel myself once. He had his moments. He used to send turkeys round at Christmas. He wasn't too bad. It's more than they do at the hotel" (173). Sir Marcus's alternate postulated origins—the "ancient English family" also present in his accent—reemerge here, in the (admittedly paternalistic) responsibility to Midlands working-class culture unwittingly accomplished through his ruthless global business dealings.

Sir Marcus also articulates, and manipulates, patriotically motivated disgust for scholarship boys like Raven, whom he represents as "fed and lodged at his country's expense" and a traitorous terror to those "able-bodied men" who would otherwise be preparing to defend their country, were they not risking their lives seeking Raven (111). But Sir Marcus's self-servingly venomous condemnation of Raven's treasonous activities also calls attention to an important connection between Raven's youthful venom and that of later, postwar angry young men. Their grudging acknowledgment that it may be good to rely periodically on the state for securities like food and housing (or education, unemployment insurance, job security, health care) tends to be matched by an angry, and necessarily critical, dismissal of the levels of soldierly gratefulness demanded of young men by the state—or by those, like Sir Marcus, also able to administer security. The hotel porter's contentment with those reliable Christmas turkeys thus serves as a parodic reminder of the "gratefulness" lacking in Raven, and in angrier young men more generally, in their refusals to devote lives preserved by the state to military service. "Why do they make soldiers out of us when we're fighting up to the hilt as it is?" as Alan Sillitoe's Arthur Seaton puts it in *Saturday Night and Sunday Morning* (1958). Seaton, a postwar update of Greene's hotel porter, echoes Raven's similar sense that he is always already "at war," rendering enlistment redundant. But he also, more importantly, poses the angry, intriguing idea that states owe citizens some unconditional securities, without their "grateful" return of military service.[12]

While there has been something that Mather and Anne Crowder could do about averting war, and securing a few years of peacetime for themselves, they cannot help the vexing situation that they, and the novel, leave behind them in the hotel porter: the seemingly irresolvable dilemma of Midlands working-class dependence on global munitions markets for job security. Greene ends with a perceived anachronism of working-class identity—presented here in the form of the hotel porter's uncritical reminiscences of Christmas turkeys and blindness to the compromised sources of such benevolence. But if Greene's modernism wearily emphasizes the impossible ethical bleakness of both the hotel porter's and Raven's situations (and allows his remaining, living protagonists to escape from having to live too close to such realities), angry young men like Sillitoe, along with Hoggart and Williams, necessarily respond to modernist abandonment with intensely realistic portrayals of the continued life of dilemmas faced by working-class communities.

The violent ends of three scholarship boys therefore signal similarly violent, abrupt ends for three versions of advancement from poverty to attempts at taking responsibility for the course of global events. Whether the purported object of one's consolatory efforts is global "humanity," steel-workers and their communities, or—in Raven's more vengeful case—others like oneself, who have had too many bad "breaks," *A Gun for Sale*, like so many of Greene's novels, raises the possibility of conscientious social service only to damn our simplistic belief in it and to shift the arena for such service to somewhere beyond this world, where "humanity" presumably has a slightly better chance of being "loved" as a whole and all the time. Mather's and Anne's hasty removal from the Midlands seems to reinforce that lesson: nothing can really be done about the more immediate predicaments of fellow countrymen, let alone those of a vague global "humanity" (which, as they know, will soon be at war anyway, for all their efforts). The only potential escape from the pangs of "pity, love, work, conscience," and, even, vengeance that drive us to seek a position of responsible service to others is the promise of the next, admittedly uncertain world, or forgetfulness— the ability to "look away" from the receding, depressed "dark countryside" of Nottwich from the train, as Anne Crowder does in the end: "It had all happened there, and they need never go back to the scene of it" (184–85).

A Gun for Sale therefore fits well with Robert Caserio's argument that "[w]hether inspired by pity, love, work, conscience, or another motive, and however diligently pursued, public responsibility is compromised, and demonstrated to be a failure, in Greene's fiction."[13] The end result of Greene's unraveling of such attempts at responsibility becomes a kind of abrupt, concluding secular blankness, where catharsis ought to be. Instead of a gesturing toward a wider social solidarity, *Gun* ends with the principal survivors safely pairing off into couples—the only "reliable," "responsible" sphere of influence, for Anne Crowder and Mather, for the hotel porter and Ruby, even for defrocked minister "Acky" (Greene's favorite) and his wife.

Social Working Girl: Employing the Femme Fatale

Yet something is wrong with this reading—or something is left out, a potential challenge to the novel's apparent surrender of public responsibility to reliably private concerns. As Caserio notes, the "absence of catharsis, the unrelieved drag of pity, the unrelieved drag of responsibility" are also the signs of an "unrelieved attachment to the world. If Greene's novels and their worlds stagger under the weight of immedicable, irreversible fear and pity, presumably it is a sign that the novels do not escape from responsibility to the world, and in the world, even if responsibility in reality exists only as heartache and yearning."[14] We can find traces of such a yearning for responsibility in Anne Crowder, who becomes Raven's sympathetic hostage as well as a betrayer paradoxically better able to articulate his betrayal than he is, and who forestalls (for a few years, anyway) the global threat initiated by his contract on the minister. More significantly, she represents a kind of therapeutic intervention for the very "anxious," angry young hit man.

Angry young men who turn to contract killing, like those who opt for more socially acceptable forms of employment, tend to view down-on-their-luck young women like Anne Crowder as the embodiment of a comfortably indifferent, nagging desire for the "better" lifestyle that would accompany white-collar success, were one willing to "sellout" and succumb to such ambitions. Yet Raven's initial sense of Anne Crowder gradually changes. Although she ultimately fulfills the femme fatale role by leading the police, and death, to him, she also assumes responsibility for what an anxious scholarship boy might really need to become less "self-conscious" and more "self-aware," in Hoggart's terms: therapy.

Raven's interest in "psicko"-logy stems from his fascination with the idea that he might tell someone "everything" about his past — his mother's death, the Home and its punishments, his many murders — "And when you've told everything it's gone" (124). Anne briefly serves a needed therapeutic function, in allowing him to tell her everything, and at the same time she articulates for Raven a sense of his place in relation to the minister he has killed. "He was poor like us," she says, leading Raven to conclude, defensively, "I didn't know the old fellow was one of us" (122, 129). She stays with Raven after discovering his role in the war minister's assassination, in spite of her repulsion, and helps him to see his position not as a lonely, self-sustaining, angry young hit man but as a part of an "us" — a tentatively forged community of men who love humanity (even if they have no reason to), women who offer therapy (even to those who don't seem deserving), and boys who still seek forgiveness (even if they have every right to stay "angry"). Not, maybe, the form of solidarity Hoggart and Williams had in mind in their criticisms of individual professional advancement, but one in which each member clearly recognizes the leap of faith that belief in community requires.[15]

Lisa Fluet

Though Mather insists that Anne has been "the biggest success," in discovering Sir Marcus's plans through Raven and effectively forestalling war, a feeling of failure dogs her efforts:

> it seemed to Anne for a few moments that this sense of failure would never die from her brain, that it would cloud a little every happiness. But she forgot it herself completely when the train drew in to London over a great viaduct under which the bright shabby streets ran off like rays of a star with their sweet shops, their Methodist chapels, their messages chalked on the paving stones. Then it was she who thought: this is safe, and wiping the glass free from steam, she pressed her face against the pane and happily and tenderly and avidly watched, like a child whose mother has died watches the family she must rear without being aware at all that the responsibility is too great. (185)

Here, Caserio's point concerning the impossibility of public responsibility in Greene seems most in evidence. In order to be happy on her return "home" to London, Anne must forget "completely" the "sense of failure" attending her endeavors with Raven. Somehow, she failed to follow through adequately on her therapeutic impulse; somehow, saving the world for "bright" and "shabby" sentiment incurred the expense of Raven's realism, and in the end demanded the sacrifice of one more anxious, angry young hit man.

But public responsibility, for Greene, tends to mean different things for men and women. While Raven bitterly resents the state's failure to be adequately responsible for him and violently seeks compensation for the social uncertainties attendant upon the stalled upward mobility of scholarship boys, Anne's concluding thought tentatively redresses the tacit assumption concerning orphaned, anxious boys underlying much of the novel's action: that angry young hit men get that way as a result of maternal irresponsibility.

"This isn't a world I'd bring children into," as Raven tells Anne earlier, "It's just their selfishness. . . . They have a good time and what do they mind if someone's born ugly? Three minutes in bed or against a wall, and then a lifetime for the one that's born. Mother love" (121). Sexual involvement, and its variable contingent outcomes, manifests itself most clearly for Raven in his mother's capacity to be "psickologically" damaging to him. He remembers her suicide, like the harelip that was never fixed, mostly for the "ugliness" of parental irresponsibility that each symbolizes. After discovering his mother's dead body, "her head nearly off — she sawn at it — with a bread knife," he blames her most for allowing him to see her: "She hadn't even thought enough of me to lock the door so as I shouldn't see" (126). "Mother love" — the "real" kind that Raven would not so bitterly disparage — presumably requires that his mother hide her need to end her own life so violently; leaving a record of her pain with him only suggests her "selfish" betrayal.

Raven's own selfishness is rather marked here, but his overt feminization of failed parental responsibility finds a measure of correction in the final image of Anne's newly assumed responsibilities. Her position "like a child whose mother has died watch[ing] the family she must rear without being aware at all that the responsibility is too great" suggests that, contrary to what Raven may think, the *option* of bringing children into the world hardly exists as a realistic choice one could make. The future responsibilities left to Anne are too great, just as the minister's were too great: in each case, the desire to act on social concern operates in a world without options or the agency presumed to attend life choices, since impossible numbers of children awaiting one's care have already been born. Being carried away by an idea of "sisterly" responsibility looks a lot like being carried away by sentimentality — but such an idea also suggests a correction to Raven's earlier criticism of being carried away by sexual desire. The very state of "being carried away," seemingly a situation of blatant irresponsibility, here looks like the only condition for imagining professional social concern. The forgetfulness of "happy and tender and avid" sentimentality thus offers a way to assume some form of consolatory social responsibility over impossible situations one did not create or earn, without the hit man's anger over whether one deserves to be saddled with such concerns, or his self-conscious anxiety over whether one can ever be professionally competent enough to complete such jobs "tidily" — Raven's favorite adverb, for the kind of impossible triumph over contingency that he seeks in contract killing.

That Anne is finally unaware of the greatness of her responsibilities also illuminates her earlier, therapeutic intervention with Raven. Then, she was only too aware of her responsibilities over him, and of the repulsion that sympathetically listening to him caused her. Their situation anticipates Hoggart's account of the place of femininity within the scholarship boy's story. But Greene also suggests a preemptive critique of Hoggart, one that, I want to suggest, returns via Anne's position in *Gun for Sale* to the complicated relations among high modernism, thrillers, and community.

Hoggart really tells two different stories about women and scholarship boys. One, the more memorable, concerns the "intimate, gentle and attractive" maternal sphere of the household where the young scholarship boy can find time to study, away from the distractions of "the world of men":

> The boy spends a large part of his time at the physical centre of the home, where the women's spirit rules, quietly getting on with his work whilst his mother gets on with her jobs. . . . With one ear he hears the women discussing their worries and ailments and hopes, and he tells them at intervals about his school and his work and what the master said. He usually receives boundless uncomprehending sympathy: he knows they do not understand, but still he tells them; he would like to link the two environments. (242)

Anxious professional adulthood finds its origins, paradoxically, in the composed, gentle shelter that the working-class kitchen, and the women within it, represents. It is hard to avoid the conflicted sense Hoggart conveys here, of an idealized, homey motherly realm that nevertheless participates in the early coddling of the scholarship boy—so that he falsely believes that what is going on with "school and his work and what the master said" truly does occupy the center of his, and everybody else's, universe. The "boundless uncomprehending sympathy" of this realm stands in significant contrast to Raven's first home with his mother; her suicide happens in the kitchen, the place where Raven expects to be safely sheltered but finds instead all that his mother refuses to hide from him—her "worries and ailments and hopes" writ large.

For all his own critique of this too-safe early environment, Hoggart still defends and celebrates this "boundless uncomprehending sympathy." And the alternative to it, when we compare his imaginary kitchen to Greene's, appears appropriately extreme. But along with this celebration of maternal placement, Hoggart also criticizes what he considers a more frequently encountered, less-than-ideal version of female feeling for the scholarship boy. This feeling hovers somewhere between knowing pity and impatient contempt, exemplified by his opening epigraph from George Eliot's *Middlemarch*:

> For my part I am very sorry for him. It is an uneasy lot at best, to be what we call highly taught and yet not to enjoy: to be present at this great spectacle of life and never to be liberated from a small hungry shivering self.[16]

He then continues his literary genealogy for the scholarship boy in his later discussion of Charles Tansley in Woolf's *To the Lighthouse*:

> He wavers between scorn and longing. He is Charles Tansley in Virginia Woolf's *To the Lighthouse*, but is probably without such good brains. Virginia Woolf often returned to him, with not so deep an understanding as one might have hoped: she gives very much the cultured middle-class spectator's view. (247)

Hoggart goes on to characterize that "view," via Woolf's diary: Woolf finds the "self-taught working-man . . . egotistic, insistent, raw, striking, and ultimately nauseating," the same critical feelings that Charles Tansley periodically raises in Mrs. Ramsay, Prue Ramsay, and Lily Briscoe—and, that Raven raises in Anne.[17] The connection between Casaubon and Charles Tansley, alternately the objects of pity, exasperation, contempt, and respect, develops in terms of how, in Hoggart's configuration, both Eliot and Woolf fail to measure up to the unreal standard of "boundless uncomprehending sympathy" for the "hungry shivering selves" of perennially ambitious, and perennially needy, intellectual males. Mr. Ramsay and Charles Tansley, along with Casaubon and scholarship boys more generally, all seek out unconditional female sympathy for the "trustful, childlike" reverence they can, periodically, safely render to it.[18] They will only enter that comforting kitchen and be "boys" again, however, if they can console themselves with the "helpful" idea, as Lily Briscoe describes, that women "can't paint, can't write," can't comprehend the throes of intellectual, and professional, work, the feelings of accomplishment intermingled with uncertainty and inadequacy that drove them—and that drive Raven as well—to seek female assurance in the first place. The scholarship boy "would like to link the two environments," the worlds of scholarship and homely maternal sympathy, but he also seems content with the fact that merely "liking" such a possibility, without any stronger feelings for it, situates such a linkage in a comfortably remote future.

Hoggart's reading of Woolf is, in one sense, very obviously unfair. In attributing to her a dismissive, "cultured middle-class spectator's view" of the scholarship boy, he pointedly ignores what can be learned from Charles Tansley's interactions with Lily and Mrs. Ramsay—namely, that scholarship boys like him thrive on a belief in the removal of lower- and upper-middle-class women from culture, on the specifically "uncomprehending" character of their sympathy. But rather than dismiss Hoggart in turn, I would argue that the implication of interdependence between the Charles Tansleys and the Mrs. Ramsays of the world actually echoes Woolf's own perspective on them. The complicated socializing intervention enacted through their relationship resists both pity and limitless, unknowing maternal sympathy and yet offers a therapeutic way out—a way for Charles Tansley to tell his story to her, and explain how he got that way. Their relationship, in fact, closely realizes Mrs. Ramsay's own secret vocational aims. Through her ability to create "sayings" and articulate a perspective through which others can "be serious" about Charles Tansley—beyond finding him merely laughable, annoying, or pitiable (197)—she does, at least in this instance, "become what with her untrained mind she greatly admired, an investigator, elucidating the social problem" (9). Her knowledgeable, at times impatient and annoyed perspective on Charles Tansley actually sounds a lot like Hoggart's own "elucidations" of the scholarship boy as a specifically "*social* problem," someone who manifests an obvious social awkwardness that calls attention to the underlying dilemma posed by the ladder of solitary educational advancement.

As Lily describes, both Mrs. Ramsay and Charles Tansley "upset the proportions of one's world" (196); both seek, through some form of outward action, to compensate for an inability to, in Charles Tansley's words, "feel it right" (11). This early, apt diagnosis of his own situation only underscores how the impossibility of summoning up the "right" feelings, untainted by what one might be tempted to conclude dismissively about other people, really afflicts everyone in the novel. Scholarship boys and aspiring "social investigators" are just that much more self-conscious about their own failure to "feel" correctly, and therefore derive a call to "do" something from that perceived affective incorrectness.

These high-modern perspectives on social work, public responsibility, and the therapeutic relations briefly forged in hopes of achieving those ends grant femininity a significant amount of interpretive agency. This in itself is not surprising, as social work's close ties to Victorian philanthropic organizations tended to make it a visibly feminine arm of welfare state intervention. What is surprising, in this comparison of Woolf and Greene, is that assuming "control of the lives and fate of large and vulnerable sections of the public,"[19] whether anxious scholarship boy, delinquent contract killer, or poverty-stricken neighbors to one's vacation home, emerges from the perceived impossibility of "feeling" rightly about those same, vulnerable publics.

The public role of British women in welfare policymaking of the inter- and postwar period has generally been linked to the extension of the private responsibilities of motherhood into issues of public concern via volunteerism, philanthropy, education, and social work.[20] Such arguments tend to take for granted that responsible being-in-public for modern women has its origins in affect, emerging from the willed transformation of at-home, maternal feelings into public feelings.[21] We expect female professionals to "feel it right," at any rate, and to temper their intervening analyses of social conditions with the right level of compassion. Yet Mrs. Ramsay's awareness that her social intervention, however well intentioned, also helps her to fortify her composed detachment from other traumatized lives prefigures Lily Briscoe's conclusion: "Half one's notions of other people were, after all, grotesque. They served private purposes of one's own" (197). Knowing that one cannot "feel it right," yet opting to act anyway—even if such actions are to a degree self-serving—thus presents a way to link ironic awareness to action, while remaining removed from the "boundless uncomprehending sympathy" presumed to accompany feminine reformist impulses.

The borderless "brotherly love" Charles Tansley advocates during wartime, like the love for humanity attributed to the socialist war minister in *A Gun for Sale*, seems doomed to irrelevance for its unlikely, homogenizing scale, its forgetful detachment from actually existing publics. Lily's ironic, concluding perspective on the ant-like, functional energy of Charles Tansley's brotherly love returns, in a sense, to the opening problem for this essay. The outpouring of scholarship boy effort, and the inherent affective wrongness Lily perceives in it, can be likened to the effort expended in contract killing. The hit man's efforts to secure the hit perfectly—so that the victim has the assurance of a certain outcome, something the angry young hit man lacks—tend to impress those touched by him with a similar sense of the dangerous implications of effortful action, the effect of this professional's apparent failure to "feel," rightly, the "client's" right to continue living. The proclaimed closeness of "brotherly love," like the briefly intimate relation between the contract killer's expertise and the body of the client, cannot help but strike its recipients hollowly—as a feeling whose effects they actually would prefer *not* to encounter in everyday life.

At the same time, contract killers share, with the women in a position to console them, the juxtaposition of "wrong" feelings to professional action. In a sense, the one source of consolation for angry young hit men, and scholarship boys in general, comes from women who have also managed to negotiate a strategic separation from "right," expected forms of affect—and this point of commonality could be one way to "link the two environments," after all.

The idea that the source of social service–oriented female professionalism lies in a willing extension of maternal feelings into the public sphere receives similar correctives in Anne Crowder's and Mrs. Ramsay's interventions with their "social problem" scholarship boys. Anne, in particular, cannot render "boundless, uncomprehending sympathy" to Raven; even her most publicly maternal imaginings, at the end of the novel, emerge from a "sisterly" sense of responsibility thrust upon her—rather than willingly chosen—and culminate in a sentimentality that we could also consider a "wrong" feeling, in its marked distance from the real conditions to which it addresses itself. Affective incorrectness, then, ties these particular modern women to the young men they encounter and attempt to help, posing the possibility that modernism's "bad" tendency to "feel it wrong" could serve as a necessary condition of the very consolations we might hope to derive from modernism.

Consolations of Contract Killing

In turning now briefly to older hit men, and to the particular consolations they seek in opting for this profession, I want to measure the development of this character against the maturing status of British cultural studies as a field, and to reconsider Raymond Williams's conclusions on modernism, thriller stars, and community in his late lecture "When Was Modernism?"

Patricia Highsmith's third Tom Ripley novel, *Ripley's Game* (1974), offers a rationale for a late career change to contract killing unique among pulp hit-man stories. Her mild-mannered killer, terminally ill British expatriate Jonathan Trevanny, becomes a hit man because he believes he will receive better health care with his new job. Ripley, snubbed by Trevanny at the novel's beginning, hears of his long-term bout with leukemia and decides to spread a rumor that his demise is hastening even more rapidly than it really is—thereby convincing Trevanny that he alone has been kept unaware of his medical fate. Everyone else "knows" he will be dead within weeks; and so Ripley convinces Trevanny that by moonlighting as a hit man for Ripley's associate Reeves Minot, he has nothing to lose, and everything to gain: a final, unequivocal medical diagnosis, better interim care, and financial stability for the family he will leave behind.

Trevanny longs for "mental ease! Simple freedom from anxiety!"—what he imagines everyone around him possesses, in their decided certainty over his fate.[22] What he gets looks more like much-needed vacations to Hamburg and Munich—away from his family and financial difficulties, tentatively enjoying the tasteful good times that a globetrotter like Reeves can show him between contracts, since he believes he is doing everything possible to secure accurate knowledge of his medical future via the "better" doctors that Ripley and Reeves provide for him. At the same time, the enduring "mental ease" of certainty that, for Trevanny, will only be achieved by the grave would of course be readily available to him, if he knew what all fans of Highsmith's most famous serial character know: people *can* be certain of their own imminent death, once they become seriously involved with Tom Ripley. But like many of Highsmith's unmoored, death-bearing protagonists, Ripley can be both a fatal harbinger and an emissary of security—making the seductive prospect of time and care for oneself, bought back from death, briefly available to those who work with him. Ripley offers welcome time *away*; as presented to Trevanny, the new professional responsibility of contract killing preserves the formal integrity of separate, scheduled hours devoted to work and recreational time, akin to the more recognizable routines of ordinary, non-murderous overnight business travel. The formal integrity of an efficiently planned professional kill thus shares with the generic reliability of serial noir fiction an aura of secure — and unreal — organization.

Ernest Hemingway's 1927 short story "The Killers" centers on a similar "business" trip for two hired killers and their planned lunch-room hit of "the Swede," Ole Andreson. But for all the implicit formal integrity of Hemingway's terse realism, probably the most unreal aspect of "The Killers" is the conclusion we are asked to draw from it: that Al and Max actually will, ultimately, succeed in killing Andreson, after the formal action of the story is over. They hardly seem worthy of the omnipotence invested in them by Andreson's pivotal, laconic observation: "There isn't anything I can do about it."[23] In acknowledging the futility of doing anything about Al and Max, however, Andreson also — suddenly — discovers that he has free time: "The only thing is, I just can't make up my mind to go out. I been in here all day," and "There ain't anything to do. After a while I'll make up my mind to go out" (287–88). He may not want to go out, as Nick Adams observes, but now, having concluded that his death will certainly be at their hands, he *can* go out — primarily because they are out already, waiting for him.

The new recruit, like Jonathan Trevanny, shares with new "clients" of hitman professionalism like Ole Andreson a profound, (literally) life-altering belief in something we might call, to echo modernism's claims to organic textual wholeness, "situational" integrity.[24] Both new killer and new client seem to derive a degree of consoling "mental ease," paradoxically, from the realization that "there isn't anything they can do" to resist the inexorable formal ordering of events involved within the organization of the hit. Hitman modernism, as I define it, balances precariously between the reinforcement of bleak futilities and consoling securities. "There isn't anything I can do" to alter the deadly formal certainty that completes itself with the contract; ceding personal responsibility over the course of events to the formal reliability of the hit suggests at once an ironic acknowledgment of the futility of personal effort *and* a belief in the concerted effort toward security of outside forces intervening into private life. At the same time, there isn't anything to be done about the insistent personal desire for consolation that recruitment can satisfy in "lone" gunmen, as my account of the scholarship boy hit man suggests. If hit men instill clients with a sense of the certain futility of active resistance—transforming Andreson into a spokesperson for the anti-progressive, ironic tendencies frequently associated with modernism—they are also the definitively engaged "do-ers" within the narratives where we encounter them, testifying to the allure of administered society's effectiveness while rather obviously enacting its violence.

Moreover, lone gunmen are frequently more attached to institutions and other persons than they at first appear. Often employed by the governing structures of organized crime, they occasionally rely on the plot equivalent of a government bailout when jobs go drastically wrong—as in the problem-solving intervention of Winston Wolfe in Quentin Tarantino's 1994 *Pulp Fiction*. And contract killers often assume responsibilities strangely akin to those of public-service-sector professionals. In *Pulp Fiction*, hit man Jules Winnfield assumes the care of "lost children" as "the shepherd" who buys Pumpkin's life back. In Jim Jarmusch's *Ghost Dog: The Way of the Samurai* (1999), Ghost Dog (the hit man) assumes an educational role in discussions with a young schoolgirl, Pearline, over the required reading she carries in her lunchbox. In Luc Besson's *The Professional* (1994), the hit man Léon intervenes unwillingly as a kind of combination social worker/foster parent for recently orphaned Mathilda, compelling her to drink milk regularly, avoid strangers, stop cursing and smoking, and—in the film's unlikelier moments—teaching her how to "clean." When placed alongside Besson's earlier film about the state education of a delinquent-turned-female assassin, *La Femme Nikita* (1990), however, *The Professional* suggests that the contract killer character has a ready capacity for playing both the representative *agent* of welfare-state responsibility (as caregiver, educator, social worker, source of needed funds) and also the youthful *object* of these forms of intervention.

The hit man therefore can maintain a lonely, critical disconnect from traditional rationales for professional life and put ironic professional self-reliance to brutally opportunistic use. And in this dual capability he shows a certain affinity with the conflicted, "bad" legacies of modernism: both defiantly disconnected and financially opportunistic, he evokes what Raymond Williams diagnosed as modernism's tendency to forget its origins as, in the late twentieth century, it became a less radical, more bourgeois version of itself. As an emblem of both beneficial and sinister models of state-sponsored security, further, he represents a postwar forgetfulness of more revolutionary programs for social transformation that, for Williams, "compromising" programs like the welfare state maintained.

Williams's concluding points from "When Was Modernism?" (1987) allow us to position both literary high modernism and late-twentieth-century contract killing narratives on the same, ultimately "heartless" continuum. "The star of the thriller" emerges in that lecture as an emblem of modernism's "bad" fate:

> What has quite rapidly happened is that Modernism quickly lost its anti-bourgeois stance, and achieved comfortable integration into the new international capitalism. . . . The painfully acquired techniques of significant *dis*connection are relocated, with the help of the special insensitivity of the trained and assured technicists, as the merely technical modes of advertising and the commercial drama. The isolated, estranged images of alienation and loss, the narrative discontinuities, have become the easy iconography of the commercials, and the lonely, bitter, sardonic and skeptical hero takes his ready-made place as star of the thriller.[25]

The canonization of high-modern authors and works signals, for Williams, a false sense of periodization (modernism ends, postmodernism remains) that ignores how much modernism is still very much with us — albeit now comfortably connected to the new international capitalism. The varied modernist iconographies of "*dis*connect" that Williams lists here become, with the help of now collectively desensitized technicists, the generic models for advertising, commercial drama, and the thriller.

For Williams, authors and works neglected by canonical modernism offer the only way out of this contemporary nonhistorical bind:

> If we are to break out of the non-historical fixity of *post*-modernism, then we must search out and counterpose an alternative tradition taken from the neglected works left in the wide margin of the century, a tradition which may address itself not to this by now exploitable because

Hit-Man Modernism

quite inhuman rewriting of the past but, for all our sakes, to a modern
future in which community may be imagined again. (35)

The post-Thatcher challenge of "imagining" a "community" for the "modern future" would lead us to "neglected works" of the twentieth century,
skirting "exploitable" modernist iconography in order to embrace the untainted "newness" that only the previously ignored can now represent.
Williams's adjectives for canonical modernism—"isolated," "estranged,"
"alienated," "experimental," "skeptical," "bitter"—are applicable to thriller
protagonists, scholarship boys, and angry young hit men, and they significantly oppose the tentative, pragmatic utopianism of the future-oriented
and community-focused welfare state.

Yet these same adjectives also delineate what Williams finds politically
transformative, and useful, in modernism prior to its canonization. For
all Williams's skepticism about "welfare socialism" and the compromised
character of the postwar "knowable community" derived from it, "When
Was Modernism?" suggests that Williams's primary antipathy is toward
certain academic and technical deployments of modernist iconography,
deployments that divest modernism of whatever subversive potential its
forms of radical disconnect once had by unthinkingly continuing the life of
"bad," community-hostile images of modernism without context, in postwar popular culture. In this essay, I have suggested how attention to a text
like *A Gun for Sale*, which links high modernism with contemporary versions of pulp, partly substantiates and partly challenges Williams's argument: it reveals how fantasies of independence can be complexly tied to
desires for security, and how failures of feeling may be surprisingly implicated in beneficial action. In closing, I want to elaborate further on these
points in relation to the finale of Greene's protagonist.

Raven longs for the tidy closure of a professional death, which seems
to him the fitting culmination of a professional life devoted to contracting
such tidiness for others. He observes that the "only problem when you were
once born was to get out of life more neatly and expeditiously than you had
entered it" (170). After he is shot, however,

> [d]eath came to him in the form of unbearable pain. It was as if he had to
> deliver this pain as a woman delivers a child, and he sobbed and moaned

in the effort. At last it came out of him and he followed his only child into a vast desolation. (170)

The desire for a neat and expeditious end to life, echoing Jonathan Trevanny's search for certainty, goes unfulfilled. What Raven gets, instead, is unbearable pain, as though the just punishment for engineering the deaths of others, and for failing to "feel" correctly mournful about them, must be spontaneous, intolerable feeling at the end. This pain is moreover a feminizing entity, for its inexorable "delivery" suggests a forceful sympathy with his mother's childbearing and childrearing conditions. He thus identifies in death with social realities that in life had caused him "psickological" damage not because he had yet experienced them himself, but because awareness of others' experience of them was unbearable. The hit man's derivation of professional authority from the certainty of death tacitly instills in him an antagonism to the symbolically untidy, inefficient contingency of being born. But in death, Raven has, in a sense, been compelled to listen to what the women keep talking about in Hoggart's kitchen. He arrives at "boundless *comprehending* sympathy" with his mother's situation, just when he can no longer be "educated" by such awareness.

Raven's "untidy" feminine death also signals the unraveling of his "tidy" professional persona. And yet, to conclude with this distinction between women and pulp male professionals risks ignoring the strategic, welfare-oriented model of professionalism that intervening, affectively challenged modern women like Anne Crowder and Mrs. Ramsay practice.[26] It is not that their femininity grants these women a symbolically redemptive hold over the giving of life, but rather that they can secure a certain professional distance with their chosen scholarship boys, in social situations somewhere between life and death where perfect affection seems impossible. Their cases suggest that one crucial way modernism allows us to imagine avenues to formal action in this world is by showing how possibilities emerge from not "feeling it right" while acknowledging that there may be no way of so feeling (or at least no way unaccompanied by pain that renders one incapable of doing anything). If Ole Andreson's insistence on the futility of action echoes Lily Briscoe's own suspicions, we could consider Hemingway's "killers," along with Jonathan Trevanny, Raven, Charles Tansley, and the women who intervene on their behalf, as insistent mediators between the predisposition to thought and the impulse to action—between the expeditious removal of the self from the world and the direct implication of the self within worldly concerns.

Notes

My thanks to Doug Mao, Bruce Robbins, and Rebecca Walkowitz for their help with this essay.

1. I am drawing here on several path-breaking works exploring relations between pulp and modernism: Michael Denning's *The Cultural Front: The Laboring of American Culture in the Twentieth Century* (New York: Verso, 1996); James Naremore's *More Than Night: Film Noir in its Contexts* (Berkeley: University of California Press, 1998); Joan Copjec's edited collection *Shades of Noir* (New York: Verso, 1993); Erin A. Smith's *Hard-Boiled: Working-Class Readers and Pulp Magazines* (Philadelphia: Temple University Press, 2000); and especially Sean McCann's *Gumshoe America: Hard-Boiled Crime Fiction and the Rise and Fall of New Deal Liberalism* (Durham, N.C.: Duke University Press, 2000). I discuss the text from which I am borrowing the term "pulp modernism," Paula Rabinowitz's *Black and White and Noir: America's Pulp Modernism* (New York: Columbia University Press, 2002), in what follows.

2. I am alluding here to a series of crucial arguments concerning the convoluted relations between modernism, professionalism, and community: David Trotter, *Paranoid Modernism: Literary Experiment, Psychosis, and the Professionalization of English Society* (New York: Oxford University Press, 2001); Lawrence Rainey, *Institutions of Modernism: Literary Elites and Public Culture* (New Haven, Conn.: Yale University Press, 1998); and Alan Sinfield, *Literature, Politics and Culture in Postwar Britain* (Berkeley: University of California Press, 1989), esp. chap. 9.

3. See Tyrus Miller, *Late Modernism: Politics, Fiction and the Arts between the World Wars* (Berkeley: University of California Press, 1999).

4. Richard Hoggart, *The Uses of Literacy: Aspects of Working-Class Life* (1957; reprint New York: Oxford University Press, 1970), 243.

5. "Another alternative to solidarity which has had some effect is the idea of individual opportunity—of the ladder. . . . Yet the ladder is a perfect example of the bourgeois idea of society, because, while undoubtedly it offers the opportunity to climb, it is a device which can only be used individually: you go up the ladder alone" (331). Raymond Williams, *Culture and Society: 1780–1950* (1958; reprint New York: Columbia University Press, 1983).

6. See Alan Liu, *The Laws of Cool: Knowledge Work and the Culture of Information* (Chicago: University of Chicago Press, 2004). In the contract killer's fusion of bohemian, border-crossing modernist mobility with the coolness of the knowledge-worker, we can see a kind of prehistory to Liu's arguments about the contemporary state of literary culture, with the late modern young hit man positioned at a series of crossroads: modernism/postmodernism, aesthetic formalism/knowledge work, awkwardness/coolness.

7. In his *Flowers in the Dustbin: Culture, Anarchy and Postwar England* (Ann Arbor: University of Michigan Press, 1993), Neil Nehring emphasizes this connection between gang-violence fictions and angry young men in Greene—focusing on their later reappearance in British punk subculture.

8. Graham Greene, *A Gun for Sale* (1936; reprint New York: Penguin, 1974), 5.

9. In focusing here on Greene, I hope to offer a reconsideration of how Greene's own vaunted style of weary cosmopolitan ennui has precluded consideration of the role his late modern and postwar fictions play in conceiving the welfare state. For a very useful counterapproach that positions Greene as a point of contrast to late-modern reimaginings of national culture, see Jed Esty's *A Shrinking Island: Modernism and National Culture in England* (Princeton, N.J.: Princeton University Press, 2004).

10. Naremore, *More Than Night*, 66.

11. Sharon Marcus, "Anne Frank and Hannah Arendt, Universalism and Pathos," in *Cosmopolitan Geographies: New Locations in Literature and Culture*, ed. Vinay Dharwadker (New York: Routledge, 2001), 90–91.

12. Alan Sillitoe, *Saturday Night and Sunday Morning* (1958; reprint New York: Penguin, 1992), 238.

13. Robert Caserio, *The Novel in England, 1900–1950: History and Theory* (New York: Twayne Publishers, 1999).

14. Ibid., 391; 399–400.

15. See Jessica Berman, *Modernist Fiction, Cosmopolitanism and the Politics of Community* (Cambridge: Cambridge University Press, 2001), for an account of international modernism's engagement with "the dual question of community and cosmopolitanism" (4)—a central concern in the approach to modernism, cosmopolitan rootlessness, and the welfare state that I am attempting to locate with the postwar contract killer.

16. George Eliot, *Middlemarch* (London: Penguin, 1994), 280.

17. See Virginia Woolf, *The Diary of Virginia Woolf*, ed. Anne Olivier Bell, vol. 2 (New York: Harcourt Brace Jovanovich, 1978), 189. In the passage Hoggart quotes, the "self-taught working man" Woolf refers to is James Joyce. Though inaccurate in terms of her depiction (Joyce was neither "self-taught" nor strictly speaking a "working man"), her impression of an "egotistic, insistent, raw, striking and ultimately nauseating" young man behind *Ulysses* invites speculation on ways in which we could connect the socially awkward intrusion of the scholarship boy into middle-class life to the analogously egotistic intrusion of *Ulysses* into modern fiction. Experimental novelistic modernism, in Joyce's case, thus arrives uninvited, like the scholarship boy.

18. Virginia Woolf, *To the Lighthouse* (1927; reprint New York: Harcourt Brace Jovanovich, 1981), 6.

19. Harold Perkin, *The Rise of Professional Society: England since 1880* (New York: Routledge, 1989), 349.

20. Denise Riley's *Am I That Name?: Feminism and the Category of "Women" in History*

(Minneapolis: University of Minnesota Press, 1988) implicates the "gendering of the 'social'" with the growing Victorian presence of women as "agents and objects of reform in unprecedented ways" (51). In attempting to situate the social work of women like Anne Crowder and Mrs. Ramsay at a strategic remove from maternal affect, my intention is not to contradict Riley's account. Rather, I would argue that the peculiar qualities of the young hit man—in particular, his closeness to the scholarship boy's unreal expectations of maternal "boundless uncomprehending sympathy" from women—suggest the necessity of conceiving a position of modernist public responsibility for women detached from maternality, in order to approach the angry, awkward, "delinquent" hit man as an "object of reform."

21. See Helen Jones, *Women in British Public Life, 1914–1950: Gender, Power and Social Policy* (London: Pearson, 2000), especially chaps. 3 and 4; see also Seth Koven, "Borderlands: Women, Voluntary Action, and Child Welfare in Britain, 1840 to 1914," in *Mothers of a New World: Maternalist Politics and the Origins of Welfare States*, ed. Seth Koven and Sonya Michel (New York: Routledge, 1993), 94–135.

22. Patricia Highsmith, *Ripley's Game* (New York: Vintage Crime/Black Lizard, 1993), 46.

23. Ernest Hemingway, "The Killers," *The Short Stories of Ernest Hemingway* (New York: Charles Scribner's Sons, 1953), 287.

24. With "situational integrity," I am invoking here Michael Szalay's consideration of Hemingway's literary formalism as an effectual engagement with the organizational complexity of the state. Belief in textual integrity, so crucial to modernist authors', and especially Hemingway's, sense of a self-reliant (and implicitly anti–New Deal) self, becomes in his formulation a way of conceiving a modernist endorsement of the welfare state. See Szalay, *New Deal Modernism: American Literature and the Invention of the Welfare State* (Durham, N.C.: Duke University Press, 2000), 82–83.

25. Raymond Williams, "When Was Modernism?" in *The Politics of Modernism: Against the New Conformists*, ed. Tony Pinkney (New York: Verso, 1989), 35.

26. In tying the femme fatale of the hit man narrative to social work, and thus to a form of professional life associated closely with the welfare state, I want to suggest an important alternative to "our common ideological notion of man's division between profession and woman," as Slavoj Žižek suggests in his arguments concerning the noir femme fatale and the hard-boiled detective. See Žižek, *Enjoy Your Symptom! Jacques Lacan in Hollywood and Out* (New York: Routledge, 1992), 165.

Lisa Fluet

Jesse Matz

Cultures of Impression

As to the others who—neglecting to ponder and to learn—pursue the impression to excess, the example of M. Cézanne can reveal to them as of now the lot which awaits them. Starting with idealization, they will arrive at that degree of unbridled romanticism where nature is merely a pretext for dreams and where the imagination becomes powerless to formulate anything but personal, subjective fantasies without any echo in general reason, because they are without control and without possible verification in reality. Jules Antoine Castagnary, "Boulevard des Capucines Exhibition: The Impressionists" (1874)

All original cultural forms, all determined languages are absorbed in advertising because it has no depth, it is instantaneous and instantaneously forgotten. Triumph of superficial form, of the smallest common denominator of all signification, degree zero of meaning, triumph of entropy over all possible tropes. The lowest form of energy of the sign. This unarticulated, instantaneous form, without a past, without a future, without the possibility of metamorphosis, has power over all the others. All current forms of activity tend toward advertising and must exhaust themselves therein. Jean Baudrillard, "Absolute Advertising, Ground-Zero Advertising" (1981)

What goes bad better than modernism? Movements slow down, dry up, but modernism has done worse, we are told, by selling out. Salvador Dali sells for Volkswagen; montage becomes an advertising format; and modernist abstraction becomes the pattern for the corporate logo. Pure abstract pictures dignify the corporate lobby; sheer modern glass becomes seedy corporate "skin"; Schoenberg's pupils go to Hollywood; Mayakovsky's futurist poetics enable Yevtushenko's "aesthetic advertising"; and modernist anomie is put on for kicks when (as Raymond Williams put it) "the lonely, bitter, sardonic and skeptical [modern] hero takes his ready made place as the star of the thriller."[1] Even modernist "estrangement" itself has become (in Fredric Jameson's account) a standard commercial pleasure. Co-optation would have been bad enough, but this is something worse: in these instances, modernism is said to welcome misappropriation, allowing its adversarial aesthetics to become just what they claimed to oppose.[2]

Len Lye's surrealist film *The Birth of the Robot* (1935) presents the alleged transformation in just six minutes. Here we see a robot making its way across the globe, through surreal deserts and wild technological landscapes, finally discovering that "Modern Worlds Need Modern Lubrication"—lubrication best supplied not by the surrealist unconscious but by Shell Oil (Figures 1-6). Lye tacked on the advertising text adventitiously, to get financial sponsorship, but he discovered a reciprocity through which modernist art would come to grease the wheels of commerce—one nicely summed up in the title of a 1944 article in *Newsweek*: "Surrealism Pays."[3] Irving Howe summed it up, too, noting in 1967 how "bracing enmity has given way to wet embraces," and Clement Greenberg feared that "an umbilical cord of gold" had stretched its way to the avant-garde from the world of capital.[4] Leslie Fiedler saw that "from a shocking anti-fashion [modernism] had gone on to become—with the help of the mass media—a widespread fashion"; Terry Eagleton noted the "devastating irony" by which "the modernist work escapes from one form of commodification only to fall prey to another," delivering itself by its own aesthetic designs into the hands of mass culture; and indeed such lamentations of modernism's "unwitting collusions" themselves became, as Bruce Robbins observed, a "new commonplace."[5] From Greenberg and his contemporaries to Williams and Jameson, from earlier critical theory to Andreas Huyssen, Lawrence Rainey, Gerald Graff, Robbins, and others, cultural criticism has wondered at the way modernism "lights up the shop windows of late capitalism with its dazzling defamiliarizations," how its styles "do not disappear but rather drift into history as empty vessels waiting to be filled with reactionary interests in need of cultural legitimation."[6]

Jesse Matz

If modernism has gone bad so thoroughly, what modernism has gone bad worse than *Impressionism*? Impressionism began in subversive energy, all color and light, a rapturous modernity fast triumphant against the bourgeois, academic, lifeless norms of institutional culture. But didn't it quickly change? Even advocates like Jules Antoine Castagnary saw what could go wrong, and after the first wild immersions in Parisian modernity, its unbridled subjectivity and unverified realities (to use Castagnary's words) began to lend themselves to other purposes. Before too long Impressionism became license to subtract out the contingencies and contexts vital to depth and meaning—enabling the promiscuous superficiality that would

Len Lye, *The Birth of the Robot*, 1935. Reproduced with permission of the Len Lye Foundation.

thenceforth quicken and spread, perhaps to become what Baudrillard, one hundred years later, would deplore: an absolute, inarticulate, instantaneous culture of impressions, the total triumph of superficial form, the exhaustion of culture. If ours is indeed a world of Impressionism gone bad, an "impressionistic" culture of distraction and fakery, of bare appearances and fleeting fantasy, we might find in those first impressions an explanation for part of our condition and even a theory of how to remedy it. At the very least, we might find a fundamental explanation of modernism's self-destructive behavior, in this first and farthest-reaching example of its notorious self-betrayal.

Jesse Matz

We might instead find, however, that consideration of the impression's example unsettles what we thought we knew about modernism. For to trace the impression's style of inattention and sensory superficiality from its origins to its bad apotheosis in impressionistic advertising is also to discover another activity of that style. It may go toward the "zero-degree," but it also goes the other way, amounting to a dynamic alternation between distraction and attention, between immediate sense and removed abstraction. In the practice and the history of Impressionist art and literature, impressions prove to involve a critical dialectic; their legacy, even into the moment of Baudrillard's "absolute advertising," proves a habit of perception that would interfere with the kind of fast practical reason through which much advertising hopes to achieve its ends. Even as it seems to go bad, Impressionism retains and in fact sharpens its original critical edge. And in this it disproves the rule about modernism, or gives us another way to explain modernism's alleged self-destruction.

The most popular form of modern art, Impressionism needs little introduction. There is little need to explain how, in Impressionism, objective reality gave way to subjective semblance, fact to feeling, stasis to change, or to describe the difference these changes made, not only to the future of the arts but to the very feel and image of modern life. What Monet, Renoir, Pissarro, and others first did to stress the instant, eschew reflective or narrative elaboration, cultivate speed and immediate felt response was so broadly adopted — as when the symbolist poets made the painters' immediacies the object of decadent aspiration; or when any number of later writers (James, Proust, Woolf, Musil), declared that "fiction *is* an impression" and dedicated modernist writing to indeterminacy, atmosphere, perspective; when Claude Debussy introduced freely moving chord progressions and did without formal cadences; and when Abel Gance, Louis Delluc, and Germaine Dulac made cinema a more flexible vehicle for feeling through superimposed imagery, point-of-view cutting, rhythmic editing, and camera mobility — that to explain Impressionism is almost to rehearse the founding conditions of modern art.[7]

It is not hard to see how this widespread Impressionism could go bad. Even if at first Impressionism worked against reification, rationalization, academicism, and elitism, and even if at first it restored art's irreverent sensuous imagination, its emphasis on the pre-rational could invite unreason, and its penchant for novelty could become a model for mass-cultural restlessness. Its interest in immediate seeing could lend itself to a purely quantitative empirics, and its subjectivism invite passivity, "fantasy and exaggeration," "self-indulgent mysticism," and, in turn, laziness or perversity.[8] Bracing skepticism often led to hedonism; the winnowing of information endorsed production of experiential commodities. And its evanescence could justify distraction. In any or all of these ways Impressionism devolved into the "impressionistic," leading from high consequence to mere diversion, insignificance, and irresponsibility.[9]

Yet there is another line of attack on Impressionism, which though less obvious is just as important, not only because it helps to explain how Impressionism could devolve beyond mere insignificance but also because it shows, eventually, what enables Impressionism's better effects and critical staying-power. According to this line of critique, Impressionism is to be faulted not for excessively immediate sensuous subjectivity but for distance, detachment, and abstraction.

This line would begin by seizing on something like the delay in Monet's process of production — on the fact that, as much as Monet may have wanted to catch the light-effects of a particular passing moment, his impressions also required longer durations. Reminiscing about the earliest motivations for his style, Monet said:

> In Algeria I spent two really charming years. I incessantly saw something new; in my moments of leisure I attempted to render what I saw. You cannot imagine to what extent I first increased my knowledge, and how much my vision gained thereby. I did not quite realize it at first. The impressions of light and color that I received there were not to classify themselves until later; they contained the germs of my future researches.[10]

Impressions did not rule out classification or research; indeed, they often compelled such extension and distinction, as they did for James and Proust. James often spoke of his impressions as "germs," too, or "seeds" that would plant themselves and then actively germinate in the soil of the imagination. He wrote that *The Princess Casamassima*, for example, was the product of impressions received on the streets but then more extensively worked up: "this fiction proceeded quite directly, during the first year of a long residence in London, from the habit and interest of walking the streets. . . . [a]nd as to do this was to receive many impressions, so the impressions worked and sought an issue, so the book after a time was born."[11] The novel may have proceeded directly from immediate impressions, but only once they worked themselves toward "issue," after a time. When James argues in "The Art of Fiction" (1881) that "a novel is in its broadest definition a personal, a direct impression of life," he is actually arguing *against* the notion (put forth by Walter Besant) that a novel ought to be a matter of direct *experience*. He is out to gain a measure of remove from experience—and to celebrate that power of imagination for what it works up apart from what is actually seen or heard.

The same longer procedure is vastly more elongated in Proust, where walking the streets conjures up impressions that have been seeking an issue for decades. At the end of *A la recherche*, when Marcel trips on the uneven paving stones outside the Guermantes mansion, impressions received long ago finally truly occur to him. Sought since the sight of the twin steeples at Martinville and even since the flavor of the madeleine, these impressions turn out to be products of extensive labor, and proof that in its first instances Impressionism took time, work, and attention. Proust's impressions (like those of James) were but provocations to write, intimations of a vocation, and even if they might have seemed to bespeak a hedonistic or passive imagination, they could not end in one.

Product of immersion in the modernities of Algeria and London, these early impressions were worked up at *leisure*. But it is just here that the second line of attack on the impression opens up. At first, the very labor of creation involved promised that Impressionism could model a redemptive mode of perception even for the masses. This was Mallarmé's hope, expressed in "The Impressionists and Edouard Manet," which equated impressionist perception with radical vision. To Mallarmé, it was "*intransigeant*"—the radically democratic product of "men placed directly in communion with the sentiment of their time" and willing "to let hand and eye do what they will, and through them reveal herself."[12] But it can be argued that the impression developed at leisure does *not* go directly from the times to the eye; instead, it has to make its way through a different sociocultural formation, thus becoming subject to radical mystification. The "extension" that made it so much more than distractions might, then, look like distraction of another kind—a remove from the primal scene of light and color, time away from communion with the sentiment of the day.

Here is a distractive state very different from what "impressionistic" tends to imply, but no less crucial. In it, the relationship between real social worlds and impressionist imaginings becomes a little obscure, as it notoriously did in the case of Paul Cézanne. Cézanne famously wanted to "make of Impressionism something solid, like the art of the museums," and this wish could well have solidified impressions enough to pass them to posterity with their contingencies intact.[13] But then Cézanne was also famously detached—working at "a distance from humanity," and turning Impressionism from an art of extensive engagement into one of timeless form. As James Rubin notes, "we should recognize the disengagement from social modernity that facilitated his aesthetic modernity": these impressions made for the museums lacked the contingency essential to their first revolutionary effects, and so they were presented to posterity as things at once too instant and too removed. Either kind of distraction might not have led Impressionism so far from its sources; together, they made for a deceptive immediacy, an emptiness of judgment, a superficial presumption—and these are the bad combinations that perhaps shape Impressionism's unwelcome legacy.

They give Impressionism what T. J. Clark calls its "complaisance at modernity," making it only very briefly *intransigeant* and "very quickly the style of the haute bourgeoisie," a style whose "dissolution into the décor of Palm Springs and Park Avenue" was "well deserved."[14] At once a leisured and a superficial distraction, Manet's "supreme indifference" vulgarized, Impressionism becomes just what Lukács disliked about modernism more generally: a dispersed, detached mode of subjective representation, elitist or precious, without responsibility to the totality of social relations. It becomes what Fredric Jameson describes in *The Political Unconscious*, an effort to revive the human sensorium, to reperceptualize the world, that ultimately amounts to a form of quiescent passivity in the realms of both perception and politics.[15] And it therefore follows the path from Castagnary to Baudrillard, always traced through a series of neo-impressionist degradations: what Walter Benjamin called Abel Gance's "invitation to a far-reaching liquidation" in the world of filmic reproductions;[16] the developments in music whereby "the delight in the moment and the gay facade becomes an excuse for absolving the listener from the thought of the whole";[17] the dynamism in twentieth-century popular art, in which instantaneous effects are less the pattern of shared modernity than the mystical vigor of the heroic auteur; the postmodern forms in which fragments are not mitigations of totality but failures of feeling; and perhaps most importantly the moment in which *advertising* reached its apotheosis in the "zero degree" Baudrillard describes.

It has become common to blame modernism for some of advertising's formal mystifications. Raymond Williams has noted influentially that "certain techniques which were once ... actual shocks" have become the "working conventions" of "deliberately disorienting" advertising styles, and Andreas Huyssen notes more specifically that "the use of visual montage, one of the major inventions of the avant-garde, has already become standard procedure in commercial advertising."[18] This recrimination ultimately implicates Impressionism — not only because montage comes out of collage, out of cubism, and, in turn, out of the impressionist revolution, but because the impression's fugitive, fleeting, intense spectacle has become advertising's key device.

Indeed it is possible to argue that the nineteenth-century triumph of Impressionism is repeated in the middle of the twentieth century to make advertising the truly effective agent of culture-industry ideology it had not yet been. This neo-impressionist transition is described in Thomas Frank's *The Conquest of Cool*, where we find that American advertising only got the entranced devotion of a broad populace when it made a key change: it abandoned a pseudo-scientific rationality in favor of the impression's freedom, lightness, speed, and suggestiveness. "In the fifties," writes Frank, "the central principle of the advertising industry was 'science': ads were to be created according to established and proven principles, after thorough research" and in a "reverence for learning" — the result of which was ads that were "hyper-rational," "technocratic," taylorized, and wordy. What replaced them, in the 1960s, were ads based in "clean minimalism" and "hip consumerism" and quick-take images.[19] Insofar as this new dynamic reworks Impressionism's complex of distractions, it implicates Impressionism in the style of mass deception that motivated the dramatic success of such revolutionary advertisements as Ed Vorkapich's 1969 Pepsi campaign, in which "rapid-fire clustering of images" drew heavily on "the technique of visual montage developed in the photographs of John Heartfield and the films of Sergei Eisenstein."[20] Heartfield, in turn, had drawn on the impression's subjective realism, its stress on the fugitive, and its penchant for dissolving association of an image's component parts. In Vorkapich's Pepsi spots, impressions finally free of authoritative vocal and narrative linkages helped revolutionize the relationship between advertising medium and corporate message; the apparent untruth of the vestigial slogan, "You've got a lot to live, and Pepsi's got a lot to give," was easily lost in the distractions provided by quick cuts among scenes of all-American iconography, here and in subsequent advertisements that would follow Vorkapich's lead.[21]

Impressionism ends up here not only because it popularized promiscuously superficial, minimal, evanescent imagery but also because it licensed such imagery through that other mode of distraction—its detachment, or decoupling from the contingencies that might have kept the impression's immediacies true to their social contexts and social responsibilities. The bad combination of "superficial form" and "complaisance at modernity" is the problem. Yet this same combination should provoke other questions, questions that may lead us to doubt whether what we have here is yet another example of modernism's readiness for co-optation. Moreover, because this case replays debates so long fundamental to the neo-Marxist critique of modernism, it may be time to ask if it still holds good. New approaches to cultural history, indebted to but pitched beyond the neo-Marxisms critical of "superficial form" and "complaisance at modernity," encourage us to revisit Impressionism with a new appreciation for its combination of effects— with insight into the way its distractions recuperate and redeem aesthetic perception.

According to Jonathan Crary in *Suspensions of Perception*, "modern distraction was *not* a disruption of stable or 'natural' kinds of sustained, value-laden perception that had existed for centuries but was an *effect*, and in many cases a constituent element, of the many attempts to produce attentiveness in human subjects."[22] It was not the violation of some naturally good attentiveness, but rather a by-product (often liberatory and very needfully relaxing) of an attentiveness produced by efforts to make perception fixed, compulsive, and productive. There is a reversal here, not unlike that at work in Benjaminian distraction, but more perpetual, because it requires us to think in terms of "regimes of reciprocal attentiveness and distraction."[23] Here, in other words, Crary describes formations in which the two reciprocally coexist, producing and counteracting each other always in the service of regimes of perceptual administration. In his account, both are products of a turn to a subjective model of perception, which Crary places around 1800 and describes as the opportunity for capitalist rationality to take instrumental control over the perceptual capacities of the human subject. Control meant compelled attention, but also regulated distraction, in various and unstable combinations. In these combinations, attention was paradoxically often a problem of savage excess, with distraction as a calming antidote; or, attention could be the mode of the automaton, or an excessive fixation on the present—desirable, but from which breaks of distraction were necessary to allow for some form of human agency. Neither is good (since both are instrumental and dehumanizing) but neither is fully bad (since each presents some sort of opportunity for mitigation of what instrumental reason enforces). This more wholly critical take on the terms of perceptual management allows for an account of nineteenth-century culture that gets past the more simply agonistic model in which attention and distraction play hero and villain. And it allows for a more incisive account of Impressionism (then and now) as a "regime of perceptual attentiveness and distraction"; it challenges us to discover exactly what sort of reciprocities impressions entailed, and exactly how they worked with or against the regimes that have been their contexts of action.

Crary's discussion of Georges Seurat can fill in the finer detail here. Seurat had a "decisive understanding of the synthetic and disintegrative processes within attention," and his "art is inseparable from an attempt to control and rationalize [the] potentially disorganizing features of perception." Seurat, in other words, knew attention for what it was—how it had been produced for perceptual management, but also how it could often exceed the bounds of managed perception. He knew, too, that art was no exception to the perceptual systems in which attention participated, and so his art always played on attention's ambivalent role within those systems. On the one hand, there is the "aspiration to a managerial control of response"; but then the work also "posits a chromatic attentiveness so self-sufficient and subjectively determined as to constitute a provisional realm of freedom for the observer." This combination is not at all what we would expect to get from painterly impressions, because there is a total chiasmus of effects. Where we might expect distraction (the encouragement of vision simply to pursue intense glimpses) we get administered attention—but then in that very attentiveness we get provisional freedom, the freedom that might have seemed the questionable benefit of distraction. Such a reciprocal mixing— similar to but crucially different from the effect of subjectivity described by Castagnary—is a turning point from which to trace the further development of the culture of the impression.

And it appears as well in Cézanne: "But the rigor and intensity of Cézanne's quest for presence disclosed to him its impossibility and opened up for him a view of the mixed and 'broken' character of a fully absorbed perception." In this "broken" perception, attention becomes distraction; and subsequently in distraction there is opportunity for provisionally free forms of attention, viable at least until regimes of attention find ways to cycle them back into administered responses.[24] This mode of broken perception breaks new ground, in Crary, for a corollary theory in which the impression partakes of the "dynamization of attention"—a dialectical process by which attention is not destroyed but produced, intensified, overwrought, resisted, and redirected.[25]

To think that impressions (then or now) always cheapen culture may therefore be to think undialectically, to revert to a deadlocked form of cultural theory too rigidly given to assessing perceptual forms for their potential for subversion or containment alone. And yet it is hardly more dialectically astute to call impressions distractions and then pit them subversively against regimes of attention. Surely more productive is to see this dynamic of distraction and attention at work within impressions themselves, and to trace this dynamic into its fuller historical and perceptual complexity. If we revisit the history of the impression now with this dynamic and dialectical sense of the way the impression participates in "modern attention," we must take a rather different view of both its "intransigence" and its "disengagement." Each of these would now appear fully produced in and through its opposite, and we would find in the impression a distractive attention or attentive distraction serving the "provisional realm of freedom" Crary sees at work in Seurat.

When Henry James masks ideological commitments through the impression's detachment, he does so, as we have seen, in an argument against that more direct model for perception that might make art too much a matter of plain experience. But he also does so in order to argue against a

Jesse Matz

model for perception that would keep writers from writing about experience not their own. In other words, the argument cuts both ways: it detaches the effete artist, and perhaps encourages his "complacence," but it also relieves the less privileged consciousness from compulsory attention to what it is permitted to know and no more. In "The Art of Fiction," James finds "chilling" those theories of the aesthetic imagination that would say, for example, that a lower-middle-class writer should limit himself to subjects appropriate to his class; against such theories James alleges the liberty of the imagination, and the power of impressions to cross class divides and translate experience from high to low. Walter Besant had said that "the novelist must write from his experience"—that "a writer whose friends and personal experiences belong to the lower middle-class should carefully avoid introducing his characters into society."[26] James counters that such a writer might in fact produce the best depictions of society, since those depictions would be full impressions rather than experiential facts. This is either a strange contradiction or an aesthetic commonplace, but one that makes perfect sense and a big aesthetic difference within the context of "regimes of attention." For James's impression then becomes a way to play attention and distraction off each other so that fiction can meet across class divides. The lower-middle-class writer can "enter society" the more his impressions fail to conform to proprieties designating what one may see, and it is only if we always equate distraction with detachment that we will miss the *intransigeance* of the impressionistic. In the last analysis, the realm of freedom James's impression opens up is one of provisional critique—as by offering, in this case, a staging ground for a lower-class incursion into high aesthetics. Here, then, critical responsibility is not only maintained but heightened, insofar as impressions entail productive failures to attend only to one's own social world.

When Virginia Woolf repeats Manet's "supreme indifference" by proving happiest to work up her impressions in subjective solitude, she also simulates Cézanne's dedication to "the mixed and broken character of fully absorbed perception." Nowhere is the dynamic chiasmus of attention and distraction more evidently productive than in Woolf's impressions, which always partake both of intense focus and subjective dissolution—both of full presence and absence of any fixity on objects themselves. In those stories and essays in which she enacts the processes of receiving and representing impressions — "The Mark on the Wall," "Mr. Bennett and Mrs. Brown," and others in which a narratorial subject both lives and dies by the subjectivity of the truths she perceives — impressions are supremely the basis for dynamically free critique. They flourish in the spaces left unmanaged by regimes of attention; they are the experimental form for enactment of insights glimpsed over the edge of a newspaper, despite the rules about looking at others on a bus, or out the window that separates the writer from the world of the living.

Such advantages are most clearly apparent, perhaps, in "An Unwritten Novel," which makes the impression's attentional dynamic a matter of theme and even plot, effectively baring the device to view. Here, Woolf's narrator regards a stranger on a train, repeatedly looking at her and looking away. In the alternation — between objective attention and subjective speculation — a story develops. The narrator gets an impression, working it up in accordance with but also despite the scopic standards set by modern transport, and, as it turns out, in error. She gets things wrong; the impression is off. And yet in the narrator's ultimate ecstasy, her delight despite her error, it becomes clear that accuracy matters less than the perceptual freedom won by this shifting among modes. The rules of looking enable it, but it becomes a visionary state far in excess of what the rules permit, a state whose adversarial value derives from the very intensity of its transpositions among permissible styles of seeing.

To appreciate this state we might return for a moment to Benjamin, who knew that reception in distraction could mean a kind of "high-speed vigilance," a "new kinetic apperception, one opened out and agitated, as it were jolted." As Howard Eiland has noted, Benjamin sought in the apperceptual changes at work in mass culture a "pedagogic function" rather than simply an impoverishment, though he was kept from finding this function by a lingering distrust of the "cult of the ephemeral" that made him unsure about endorsing mass-cultural spectacle on any terms. The case of Woolf suggests, however, how a truly impressionistic appreciation for the ephemeral might purge this distrust and reveal this "kinetic apperception" to be just what Benjamin hoped the perceptual regime of modernity might (in spite of itself) enable. In Woolf, the mutual agitations of attentional failure and success, of distraction and absorption, of concrete and abstract modes, jolt up a kinetic stimulation evocative of aesthetic perception as elaborated by Kant—one marked by propositional junctures of sense and reason, by judgments that activate a critically diverse range of human capacities.[27] Clearly, real resistance to ideological control might demand much more than any such mode of merely aesthetic perception. But if we can see how ideological imagery itself provokes this elemental resistance, activating misprision in the very combination of attention and distraction through which it would do its work, we might change our view of "the ideology of the aesthetic": *aesthesis* (as dynamic perception, rather than judgment of the beautiful or transcendence of the practical) might emerge as the pattern by which spectatorship performs what ideology demands yet in that very performance inevitably opens up chances for resistance.

What essentially motivates these aesthetic failures of attention, these productive distractions, is the broken or mixed structure of the impression itself. Whereas prior terms for perception had always ultimately committed aesthetic theory and practice to positions either subjective or objective, factual or felt, conceptual or sensational, attentive or removed, impressions found middle grounds.[28] As many studies of Impressionism's terminology have noted, the word connoted, reflected, and even forced dynamic mediations. When used by its practitioners, the term "impression" rarely refers to unmediated sensory experience; instead it tends to come up when writers or artists want to refer to some mingling of perceptual moments. Subjectively felt, impressions were nevertheless also true to life; momentary, they also lingered, and they were in a host of other ways essentially mediatory.[29] As Richard Schiff notes, for Cézanne impressions were "both a phenomenon of nature and of the artist's own being," "subjective knowledge of the self and objective knowledge of the world"; as Stephen Eisenman observes, for Manet they "elided the oppositions that compromised contemporary ideology . . . a whole rhetoric of binaries that seemed to assure political and class stability."[30] Peter Stowell sums up this synthetic tendency by calling Impressionism a mode of "subjective objectivism," and his terminology accurately reflects the impression's dialectical bearing on the perceptual binaries both essential and destructive to Western aesthetic philosophy and practice.[31]

In a sense, the impression managed to bring a certain embodied specificity to a synthesis long idealized in aesthetic theory: it joined the timeless and the momentary, the subjective and the objective, fact and feeling in a way that resisted the congealing of opposites or stabilization at one pole or the other. Incessantly dynamic, impressions were a kind of provocation to keep alive the possibility of syntheses that would have vanished had they ever become definitive. Certainly, this is evident in the work of Walter Pater, where they link body and mind—that essential aesthetic combination—precisely because they never settle on a single style of combination. Perpetually provisional, impressions (as he described them) refreshed Pater's intellect and reasoned with his sensations—though he could never (and this was just the point) precisely say how. In the famous "Preface" to *Studies in the History of the Renaissance*, impressions are what rescue Pater from hedonism: speaking of impressions mitigates the sensualism that would have dominated had Pater encouraged his acolytes to devote themselves to "sensations" alone. He does not do so; he encourages pursuit of impressions, cautioning ardent young men to pause to let their exquisite sensations mingle into thought (or experience, or sensibility) before pursuing them again. And likewise in the history of painting, impressions enabled not only glimpses of the new sudden social configurations of nineteenth-century Paris; they also invited *abstraction*, in the Post-Impressionisms of Seurat and Cézanne, and then on into Cubism and beyond.

With Cubism, impressions *became* abstractions: this is the surprising development that perhaps best portrays the impression's peculiar nature, history, and contemporary activity. It is well known that Cubism came into being, as Ortega y Gassett put it, when "Cézanne, in the midst of his impressionist tradition, discovers volume"—that Cézanne was the pivotal impressionist after whom "painting only paints ideas."[32] Yves Alain-Bois, too, has noted that "cubist semiology allowed one to turn the Cézannesque cave-in to the profit of form (no longer a matter of figures or perspectival space, but of structure)," and that "Modernism owes much to this brilliant conjuring trick."[33] Surveying representative pictures from Impressionism through Cubism shows this transformation in action. In Monet's *Bordighera, Italy* (1884), we see impressions formed through strokes of decomposition that dissolve the realist image into its primary optical components (Figure 7). In Cézanne (*Mountains in Provence* [1886–90] and then in *Le Château Noir* [1904–06]) we see those components take on shapes of their own, irrespective of perceptual configuration, squaring off into forms fit for compositions unrelated to optical science (Figures 8–9). These self-shaped impressions

Claude Monet, *Bordighera* (detail), 1884. Oil on canvas (25 ½ × 32 in.). Potter Palmer Collection, 1922.426. Photography © The Art Institute of Chicago. Reprinted with permission.

then plot the structure of the cubist grid. Cézanne's squared-off impressions intervene here because, as Clement Greenberg put it, they compel the effort both of "abstraction and of eyesight." They create a "pictorial tension the like of which had not been seen in the west since late Roman Mosaic," a "sculptural impressionism," a "vibration" which subsequently shook the impressionist canvas into cubist disarray.[34] D. H. Lawrence called it a "mysterious shiftiness," and we see it do its work across a series of pictures representative of the cubist revolution: from Braque's *Viaduct at L'Estaque* (1907) to his *Castle at La Roche-Guyon* (1909) and on to the classically cubist *Bottles and Fishes* (1910), the traces that made Monet's impressions have gone abstract (Figures 10–12). Impressionist dissolution has enabled cubist analysis.[35]

But what is critical here is the fact that the cubist grid is not a departure from the impressionist brushstroke; it follows from it. Less remarked in these pictures, though equally visible, is how it might have been no "trick"

Paul Cézanne, *Hillside in Provence*, 1886–1890. Oil on canvas. © The National Gallery, London.

Paul Cézanne, *Le Château Noir*, 1905. Oil on canvas, 74 × 94 cm. Photo: R. G. Ojeda. Musée Picasso, Paris, France. Photo Credit: Réunion des Musées Nationaux/Art Resource, NY.

Georges Braque, *Viaduct at
L'Estaque*, 1908. Oil on canvas.
Musée National d'Art Moderne,
Centre Georges Pompidou, Paris,
France. © ADAGP, Paris and DACS,
London 2005. Photo credit: CNAC/
MNAM/Dist. Réunion des Musées
Nationaux/Art Resource, NY.

Georges Braque, *Castle at La
Roche-Guyon*, 1909. Collection
Van Abbemuseum, Eindhoev, The
Netherlands. © ADAGP, Paris and
DACS, London 2005.

11

Georges Braque, *Bottles and Fishes*, 1910. © Tate, London 2005. © ADAGP, Paris and DACS, London 2005.

at all to find "volume" latent even in the midst of the impressionist tradition, in the way impressions worked both on and off the canvas. On the canvas they had already articulated nonrepresentational spaces (even if they did so at first in order to create a naturalistic view); and off the canvas they had already been coming to their creators in theory as much as vision. What emerges after Cézanne is less the trick of some discovery than a necessary self-realization on the part of the impression itself, fuller activation of its essential reciprocity. In analytic cubism — that first stage, visible in Braque, which comes before Cubism leaves Impressionism behind and moves fully into collage and abstraction — we see not a departure from the impression, but the graphic image of its attentional logic. Where we see surfaces quickly hurtling together, and yet also taking shape into things fully their own shapes; and where we are provoked to attend fully to an image dispersed into its parts, or made to feel as if our bodies were moving about an image in fact fixed and still, then we see the graphic equivalent of the provisional freedom impressions propose. Finally, impressions make their way from the field of landscape, with its experience of distance, to the world of objects at hand: the shimmering ambiguity of Monet's Bordighera gets applied to bottles and fish, putting the close object world at a perspectival distance and thereby establishing a broad alternation of perceptual styles.

Rosalind Krauss might attribute this perceptual experience to the impression's status as *index*, as the sort of material trace that achieves abstraction precisely because it is apparently but "the physical manifestation of a cause."[36] The pure and yet dialectical form of abstraction at work in the index (where primary physicality itself paradoxically entails abstraction) is what makes the impression the cause of cubism and a perpetual source of critical energy. This agitated oneness of real trace and abstract design makes for a perpetual disorientation which is also recognition of what each style of perception owes to the other. It compels viewers (and readers) to test a judgment against an alternative source of proof or justification, to cultivate a delaying indecision modeled after the way the cubist impression alternates ceaselessly between grid-stroke and rooftop. This perceptual dynamic might in turn amount to what Crary calls the "creative synthesis that exceeds the possibility of rationalization and control," the productive failure of sustained attention that would redeem the "impressionistic" and the cultures of impression devoted to it.[37]

That it also matches the classic modernist "delay" points the way toward a certain redemption of modernist advertising. Discussions of modernist art and literature often turn on the classic modernist effort to "forestall instant consumability," and thereby to resist the incursions of the marketplace.[38] But whereas treatments of this modernist delay have tended to see it at work mainly in negation (in the way modernist works obscure what they are "about" or create theatrical withholdings), this reading of the impression's legacy of provisional disorientation finds the delay in an active moment of perception itself, and thereby makes it something potentially much less available to simple co-optation. Brechtian rhythms or Futurist typographies can be domesticated for commercial use, and their adversarial postures do nothing to limit this availability once such postures become a "commercial pleasure." The impression's delay, by contrast, is a matter of

Cultures of Impression

fundamental cognitive misapprehension, which leaps to new attention at its own pace; it is a systemic frazzle which survives as such even despite the commercial system that would want to make a pleasure of it.

But even so, can such a redemption make the impression, as realized in Cézanne's cubism, a truly persistent critical force, a truly disruptive one? And what could enable it to persist as such into our culture of impressions?

We have already seen that the longer historical view has enabled Crary to reconceptualize human attention and to reach new conclusions about the relation between attention and regimes of cultural control. This longer view finds an open dynamic in what much cultural criticism has often seen as totalities or systems closed, by their very nature, to insubordination. If we turn now to a comparable reconceptualization, we will see that regimes of cultural control considered "total" in the tradition of cultural criticism likewise invite new consideration. In his recent history of the culture of advertising, Jackson Lears updates our image of the culture industry by isolating its most pernicious totalization to a narrower phase: advertising, at least, took up the project of cultural containment mainly in its mid-twentieth-century moment. Before and after, it entered into far more vulnerable engagements with precisely the form of perceptual dynamism entailed in the impression. In our first genealogy, we saw how the impression could be extended into advertising's peculiar combination of intensity and disengagement; we saw how the impression might be responsible for a commercial culture of superficial, instantaneous, irresponsible perceptual effects. Then, however, we saw how that side of the impression essentially alternates with its opposite, to model a kind of perceptual dynamism whose effects would be very different—aligned instead with a fundamental kind of aesthetic delay. It remains now to find this dynamic resistance at work in *our* culture of impressions, dominated by advertising. And with Lears's account of advertising's perceptual heritage, we will indeed see how even the impression's mass-cultural legacy is one of "mysterious shiftiness" and dynamic perceptual intervention.

Lears reminds us that there is nothing essentially reifying in advertising itself. In its earliest phases, it was very much a mode of enchantment and of animism, and even if deceptive it was not fundamentally the mode of ideological deception we often take it to be today. Only when advertising became a corporate profession, and only when a managerial culture developed with an aim to limit and restrain what had come to seem too excessively a "culture of abundance," too much a "carnivalesque atmosphere of ever-shifting surface sensations," did advertising succumb to "the dream of a market culture brought under technocratic control." Then there developed the "managerial idiom" that conformed itself and its public to "standards of bureaucratic rationality."[39] This was the moment of totalization—and, not coincidentally, the moment of *The Dialectic of the Enlightenment* and of cultural criticism's most powerful pessimism about the culture industry. The great influence of that pessimism can make us forget that advertisements do not in any simple way conform, or conform their viewers, to regimes of social control, and it can make us forget that advertising prior to the moment of "the managerial idiom" opened itself to aesthetic disorientation. The place to look for the legacy of the impression, then, would seem to be not the perceptual structure of advertisements that conform to "standards of bureaucratic rationality" but rather those that, before (and after) the moment of those standards, risked their business in order to try for the impression's perceptual dynamism.

Despite conventional wisdom, modernist forms were not comfortably co-opted by advertising. Advertisers did try to incorporate the images and styles of Impressionism, Cubism, Futurism, and Surrealism, but they found that such incorporations could only be minimal if they were not to interfere with real sales. In Lears's account, advertising flirted with modernism in order to reanimate a dying industry, but then quickly turned back to "literalist realism" once it became clear that modernism created too much ambiguity. "The influence of formalist modernism was short-lived," and it was left behind by the end of the 1930s, because of the limits it placed on direct expressivity.[40] Roland Marchand notes that the infiltration of modernist styles into advertising art raised "excited comment," but also "dismayed alarm," because of such things as "the modern artist's absorption in self-expression, and scant concern for communicating his ideas to others," which would render advertisements uselessly opaque. In the next decade there was a return to the "homely," and advertising became "Normal Rockwellish rather than Rockwell Kentish."[41] Marchand and Lears both note that advertising never really went modernist *enough*. Had it done so, it might have amounted to an insider challenge to instrumental reason, to commercial reification, and a help to what Lears sees as the suppressed potential of advertising in its relation to a culture of commodities: "a reanimation of playful relationships between people and things, against the disenchanting power of productivist rationality."[42]

A 1937 *Parnassus* article supports this point. Paul Parker's "The Modern Style in American Advertising Art" notes that "the modern style is ill-adapted to most advertising" because the images it produces "call too much attention to themselves." If "the main way of gaining attention is to eliminate distractions," modernist forms fail advertisers, who need "instant legibility." Because they see "apples [as] apples, not problems in form," advertisers would "hardly purchase the reproduction rights to a Cézanne still-life." Parker's choice of words is helpful here. When advertisers use impressions to get viewers' attention, the attention gotten ends up being a form of distraction; misdirected, it sets up a division, in which the instantaneous impression in fact forestalls instant legibility and engages a perceptual dynamic rather than commercial apprehension. Apples become problems just as Cézanne years before had hoped they would.[43]

This reassessment of the relation between advertising and "managerial culture" parallels Crary's reassessment of "attention": in both cases, regimes of cultural control are built on engagements with perceptual free play that cannot be controlled altogether. We have related this effect to Crary's history of perception; we can relate it also to Lears's narrative and end up with a parallel commercial formation in which corporate advertising gives itself over to a dialectical alternation between the attention it wants to compel and the distractions it needs to render that attention desirable and even possible. Its apparently superficial, promiscuously instantaneous impressions (the kind that form montage in Vorkapich's 1969 Pepsi campaign) fan out but aim to rein attention in; their managerial subtext, ironically, enables the dialectic whereby an otherwise "zero degree" mode of information can provoke a substantial perceptual process.

For an example that may be yet more telling, both historically and formally, let us return to another of Len Lye's modernist advertisements — this time, one for the postal service, one not surrealist but post-impressionist. *A Colour Box* (1936) is a three-minute "direct" film (one in which images are painted directly onto celluloid) made up of wild, entirely nonrepresentational sequences of color. Waves, floating spots, *fauvist* curves streak in and out of view, and a soundtrack of Cuban dance music lends further vitality to the sheer, liquid display of unrestrained chromatic energy (Figures 13–18). Absolutely without content, *A Colour Box* seems an unlikely vehicle for advertising, but as in the case of *The Birth of the Robot*, Lye financed the film by finding a commercial sponsor.[44] Here sponsorship entailed super-imposition of text advertising new lower rates at the post office. Among the psychedelics float new prices, and finally the phrase "Cheaper Parcel Post" (Figures 19–21). Like *The Birth of the Robot*, this film seems a classic example of modernism selling out. So incompatible, however, are its images and its prices that it proves a striking example of something else.

The lack of representational relationship between image and text makes *A Colour Box* a likely source of that "dismayed alarm" with which adver-tising executives often received the early combination of modernist forms and commercial messages. The film's post-impressionist effluvia might have helped to convey the new dynamism of parcels sent more cheaply, the new freedom to get messages across, but mainly the film creates a sense of dis-junction. Its direct messages seem wildly out of sync with its colors, so that the information conveyed is less the news about cheaper rates and more news about the kind of cognitive disjunction awaiting participants in the impressionist culture of advertising. The impressions never amount to a commercial message; far from it. When that message appears, and the viewer tries naturally to imagine how the prior images might support it, those images seem both to exceed and to fall short of the concept super-added. And yet, once proposed, this divergence injects itself back into the images—into that prior flood of impressions. They, too, seem to involve an interplay between concrete and abstract meanings (are the waves of color things or forms?), and the overall effect of their play of divergence is to replace narrow commercial recognition with more broadly "kinetic apper-ception." Happy to watch color-designs float across the screen, suddenly confronted with a text with a promotional message, the viewer who reads the text is compelled retroactively to reread the imagery. Did it, then, mean something too? Were those forms things, then—or does the association work the other way, and does the promotional information accede to some simpler evocation, of some epistemic liberty unrelated to any actual com-mercial pursuit? Such questions multiply, at the level of basic perception, disallowing the "instant legibility" Lye's simple impressions might have seemed to promote, generating instead a set of modernist disjunctions.

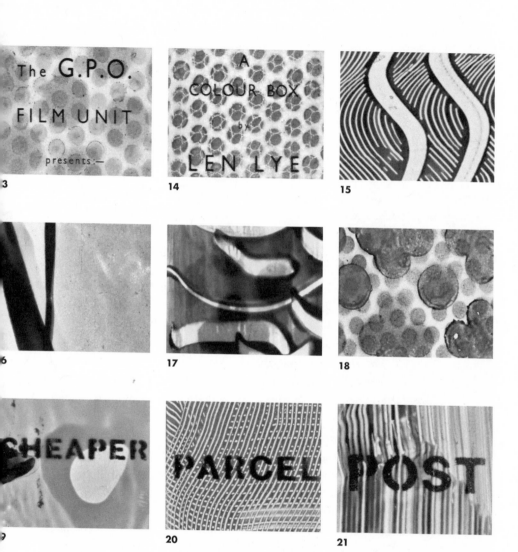

Len Lye, *A Colour Box*, 1935.
Reproduced with permission of
the Len Lye Foundation.

And it is this multiplying disjunction that is the legacy of the impression. Not the unbridled, fleeting, superficial color-display alone, but its incommensurate linkage to the text, and the way images meant to promote a meaning become the object of kinetic apperception as we try to read that meaning back into them: this is the authentic dynamic through which the impression makes its way into commercial culture. Whereas Castagnary had worried about the impression's legacy of irrational and subjective fantasy, and whereas Baudrillard has seemed to imply that we might find that legacy in the exhaustion of meaning and triumph of superficial form in advertising, Lye takes part in a different heritage, one that leads from the impressionist's dialectical efforts at perceptual immediacy and abstractive distance to these fitful encounters between free color and managed meaning. This same dialectic would persist in later years — when, as we have seen, the "managerial" approach in advertising loses ground and the pendulum swings back toward the use of modernist forms. Impressions put in the service of the commercial message always tend toward this same inadvertent ambivalence, a result that Lye's proleptic and flagrant version can help to theorize. Advertisements like Vorkapich's 1969 Pepsi campaign and its stylistic successors try to make a fleeting series of atmospheric impressions create a positive feeling for their product while also distracting away the possibility of any critical judgment against it. But this very combination of intense instants and distractive movement appears to generate a cognitive effect running counter to, or vitally supplementing, anything that could simply sell the product.

But does it really do any good? If impressionism somehow renders dialectically kinetic certain advertising efforts both to compel attention and to profit from distraction, does it therefore make any real difference — for example, to those of us who would want mass audiences to mount more critical resistance to consumer culture, or to those of us who would want to see that culture lose what might seem to be its total control over art and human values? Or to those of us who might want to cultivate modernist sensibilities against that total control? It can make a difference, if we understand it to be consumer culture's own way of cultivating the perceptual complications, delays, and misrecognitions modernism at its best tried to teach. In such cases, the critique of consumer culture could look back to modernist perceptual practice to find the pedagogical model for adversarial versions of commercial impressions. Retrospective, this possibility is forward-looking, too. As Daniel O'Hara and Alan Singer have noted in their work on "re-imagining the aesthetic within global modernity," the old utopianism that reached its furthest point in the modernist aesthetic—the "power of the aesthetic to mediate the binaries"—is "paradoxically enough both obsolete and freshly urgent."[45] It is freshly urgent because of the possibility that there is "another line of post-Kantian aesthetic speculation left undeveloped" that could justify a "new aesthetics" with "important cognitive, ethical, and political dimensions." This impressionist version of aesthetic mediation might refresh our approach to the aesthetic within global modernity by restarting the pursuit of modernist aesthesis, finding the link between politics and aesthetics in dynamics of perception and cognition (rather than in standards of taste, qualities of objects, or powers of transcendence), and calling attention to the public styles and languages through which this aesthesis operates. For even if modernism in general has not survived its co-optations, some of its specifically perceptual dynamics have been intensified by commercial forces, creating the opportunity for a neo-modernist aestheticism that would also constitute an engaged mode of refusal.

As a reminder to stress the pursuit of perceptual diversity—of aesthesis—impressionism today has other legatees, distant from the cultures of impressionist advertising but caught up in the same dynamics. In the psychology of art, for example, we have such thinkers as Michael Turner, whose theory of cognitive "blending" refits aesthesis for our times. Explaining the way human perception perpetually enacts the "blending [of] sensory experience with abstract conceptual structure," and explaining also the *fictionality* of this blending, Turner draws attention to the way our perceptions function through a dialectic necessarily and perpetually restructured by the new blends our public fictions propose.[46] His work on "the literary mind" promotes impressionist "kinetic apperception" to the role of thought itself—and encourages us to recognize the extent to which any cultural fictions might shape and reshape that dynamic. In cultural theory, the turn of mind cultivated by Arjun Appadurai also exemplifies this impressionist imagination: his *Modernity at Large* stresses the way the "work of consumption," to escape mere "social discipline," must motivate the "discipline of the imagination," where "imagination" is the free play of minds working reversals against what global capital gives them. Global capital demands ever-fresh attention to emergent commodities and achieves it by routing that attention through "fantasy and nostalgia." Critical minds take advantage of that process by routing attention through something more like a critical imagination; they make the combination of focus on commodities and licensed distraction something much more "open-ended," fashioning it into a more authentically dynamic style of judgment, one very much like the impression in the way it trades instant consumption for critical delay.[47]

Or perhaps best to celebrate the impressionist legacy we might situate it in the context of the critique that would treat it most skeptically. Adorno and Horkheimer indirectly trace the history of the impression when they refer, in *The Dialectic of Enlightenment*, to the cultural life of the "detail." In this account the detail "won its freedom" in modernism, where it ultimately became a "vehicle of protest." Thereafter the "totality of the culture industry" made the detail serve the formula, crushing its insubordination. This is Impressionism's co-optation at its worst — the darkest view to take of the impression's fate in consumer culture, and, because so comprehensive, the least open to debate. But debate reopens if the impression's "freedom" is in truth not lost to advertising but rather what we see in *A Colour Box* writ larger: that surprise of antithesis enacted by totality's very aspiration to manage the full range of perceptual life. Thus if we inhabit a culture of impressions today, we seem to have inherited the modernist dynamic whereby the detail first won its freedom. And if critics are right to say that this dynamic has been "absorbed and co-opted by Western mass mediated culture," we may, then, be surprisingly fortunate. For this absorption surely means an enrichment of that culture — and a continuance of the reverse co-optation through which modernism first violated the rules of perceptual management.[48]

Notes

1. Raymond Williams, "When Was Modernism?," *The Politics of Modernism* (London: Verso, 1989), 35.

2. For these specific complaints, see Matei Calinescu, *The Five Faces of Modernity: Modernism, Avant-Garde, Decadence, Kitsch, Postmodernism* (Durham, N.C.: Duke University Press, 1987), 231–32; Russell Berman, *Modern Culture and Critical Theory: Art, Politics, and the Legacy of the Frankfurt School* (Madison: University of Wisconsin Press,

Cultures of Impression

1989); Fredric Jameson, "Reflections in Conclusion," in *Aesthetics and Politics*, ed. Jameson (London: Verso, 1977), 196–213; Bruce Robbins, "Modernism in History, Modernism in Power," in *Modernism Reconsidered*, ed. Robert Kiely, Harvard English Studies 11 (Cambridge, Mass.: Harvard University Press, 1983), 234–35.

3. "Surrealism Pays," *Newsweek* (January 3, 1944): 57–58.

4. Irving Howe, "The Idea of the Modern," in *Literary Modernism*, ed. Howe (Greenwich, Conn.: Fawcett Publications, 1967), p. 24, qtd. in Calinescu, *Five Faces*, 121; Clement Greenberg, "Avant-Garde and Kitsch," *Art and Culture* (London: Thames and Hudson, 1973), 8.

5. Leslie Fiedler, "Death of Avant-Garde Literature," qtd. in Calinescu, *Five Faces*, 121; Terry Eagleton, "Capitalism, Modernism, and Postmodernism," *New Left Review* 152 (July/August 1985): 67; Robbins, "Modernism in History," 237.

6. "Modernism in History," 238; Benjamin H. D. Buchloh, "Figures of Authority, Ciphers of Regression: Notes on the Return of Representation in European Painting," *October* 16 (Spring 1981): 55.

7. Accounts of Impressionism as a period style include Arnold Hauser's *The Social History of Art*, vol. 4 (New York: Vintage Books, 1957–58) and Meyer Schapiro's *Impressionism: Reflections and Perceptions* (New York: George Brazilier, 1997).

8. Linda Nochlin, *The Politics of Vision: Essays on Nineteenth-Century Art and Culture* (London: Thames and Hudson, 1989), 64. Nochlin here reports Pissarro's worries, and, in her description of Pissarro's relation to Impressionism gone bad, sketches a tendency contrary to the one described here.

9. For the full range of description of this devolution, see Irving Babbitt's early indictment of the impressionist sensibility, *The New Laokoon: An Essay in the Confusion of the Arts* (Boston: Houghton Mifflin, 1910) and Fredric Jameson's account of the way the impressionist sensorium could subserve the forces of reification, *The Political Unconscious: Narrative as a Socially Symbolic Act* (Ithaca, N.Y.: Cornell University Press, 1981), 225–42.

10. Thibebauly-Sisson, "Claude Monet: An Interview," *Le Temps* (November 27, 1900), qtd. in Rewald, *History of Impressionism*, 50.

11. Henry James, "Preface to *The Princess Casamassima*," in *The Art of the Novel: Critical Prefaces by Henry James* (New York: Charles Scribner's Sons, 1946), 59.

12. T. J. Clark, *The Painting of Modern Life: Paris in the Art of Manet and His Followers* (New York: Alfred A. Knopf, 1985), 268.

13. James H. Rubin, *Impressionism* (London: Phaidon, 1999), 376.

14. Clark, *Painting of Modern Life*, 267–68.

15. See Georg Lukács, "The Ideology of Modernism," *Realism in Our Time: Literature and the Class Struggle* (New York: Harper and Row, 1962), 17–46; Fredric Jameson, *The Political Unconscious: Narrative as a Socially Symbolic Act* (Ithaca, N.Y.: Cornell University Press, 1981), 210–15.

16. Walter Benjamin, "The Work of Art in the Age of Mechanical Reproduction," *Illuminations*, ed. Hannah Arendt (New York: Harcourt Brace Jovanovich, 1968), 222.

Jesse Matz

17. Theodor Adorno, "On the Fetish Character in Music and the Regression of Listening," in *Adorno: The Culture Industry: Selected Essays on Mass Culture*, ed. J. M. Bernstein (London: Routledge, 1991), 32.

18. Williams, "The Politics of the Avant-Garde," *The Politics of Modernism*, 62; Andreas Huyssen, *After the Great Divide: Modernism, Mass Culture, Postmodernism* (Bloomington: Indiana University Press, 1986), 161.

19. Thomas Frank, *The Conquest of Cool: Business Culture, Counterculture, and the Rise of Hip Consumerism* (Chicago: University of Chicago Press, 1997), 39, 47, 53, 47.

20. Jackson Lears, *Fables of Abundance: A Cultural History of Advertising in America* (New York: Basic Books, 1994), 342–43.

21. Ibid.

22. Jonathan Crary, *Suspensions of Perception: Attention, Spectacle, and Modern Culture* (Minneapolis: University of Minnesota Press, 1999), 49.

23. Crary, *Suspensions*, 30. Here I follow Howard Eiland, whose "Reception in Distraction" (*Boundary* 2 30, no. 1 [2003]: 51–66) explores the "famous Benjaminian ambivalence" about the "new kinetic apperception" Benjamin saw "coming into being in all areas of contemporary art" and looks for ways to resolve that ambivalence into a rigorous theory of "productive distraction" (60). See below for my account of the way the dialectic of attention and distraction amounts to something productive — to what Eiland calls a "spur to new ways of perceiving."

24. Crary, *Suspensions*, 150, 152, 328.

25. Ibid., 344.

26. James, "Art of Fiction," 51.

27. Susan Buck-Morss sees this outcome as Benjamin's ultimate interest: writing about his sense of the relation between "aesthetics and anaesthetics" in the "artwork" essay, she argues, "He is demanding of art a task more difficult — that is, to *undo* the alienation of the corporeal sensorium, to *restore the instinctual power of the human bodily senses for the sake of humanity's self-preservation*, and to do this, not by avoiding the new technologies, but by *passing through* them" ("Aesthetics and Anaesthetics: Benjamin's Artwork Essay Reconsidered," *October* [Fall 1999]: 5; emphasis original).

28. The impression is not alone in staking out this mediatory position. Symbols, images, and other modernist "poememes" (to use Daniel Albright's term for the primary aesthetic units of which modernists were so fond) likewise aimed at such reconciliations (see Albright's *Quantum Poetics: Yeats, Pound, Eliot, and the Science of Modernism* [Cambridge: Cambridge University Press, 1997], 111–14).

29. See Schapiro, *Impressionism*, 21–23; William Gass, "Ford's Impressionisms," *Finding a Form* (New York: Alfred A. Knopf, 1996), 77–103; Michael Levenson, *A Genealogy of Modernism: A Study of English Literary Doctrine, 1908–1922* (Cambridge: Cambridge University Press, 1985), 105–19; and my *Literary Impressionism and Modernist Aesthetics* (Cambridge University Press, 2001).

30. Richard Schiff, "Defining 'Impressionism' and the 'Impression,'" *Cézanne and the*

End of Impressionism: A Study of the Theory, Technique, and Critical Evaluation of Modern Art (Chicago: University of Chicago Press, 1984), qtd. in *Art in Modern Culture: An Anthology of Critical Texts*, ed. Francis Frascina and Jonathan Harris (London: Phaidon, 1992), 185; Stephen Eisenman, "The Intransigent Artist *or* How the Impressionists Got Their Name," in *The New Painting: Impressionism 1874–1886*, ed. Charles S. Moffet (San Francisco: Fine Arts Museums of San Francisco, 1986), qtd. in Frascina 196.

31. H. Peter Stowell, *Literary Impressionism: James and Chekhov* (Athens: University of Georgia Press, 1980).

32. José Ortega y Gasset, "On Point of View in the Arts," *The Dehumanization of Art and Other Essays on Art, Literature, and Culture* (Princeton, N.J.: Princeton University Press, 1968), 124–25. For one of the first observations of the connection, see also Guillaume Apollinaire, "Cubism Differs" (1913), in *Manifesto: A Century of Isms*, ed. Mary Ann Caws (Lincoln: University of Nebraska Press, 2001), 124.

33. Yves-Alain Bois and Rosalind Krauss, *Formless: A User's Guide* (Cambridge: MIT Press, 1997), 28.

34. Clement Greenberg, "Cézanne" (1951), *Art and Culture*, 52, 53.

35. D. H. Lawrence, qtd. in Joseph J. Rishel, "A Century of Cézanne Criticism II: From 1907 to the Present," in *Cézanne*, ed. Françoise Cachin, Isabelle Cahn, Walter Feilchenfeldt, Henri Loyrette, Joseph J. Rishel (Philadelphia: Philadelphia Museum of Art, 1996), 57.

36. Rosalind Krauss, "Notes on the Index: Part 2," *The Originality of the Avant-Garde and Other Modernist Myths* (Cambridge: MIT Press, 1986), 211.

37. Crary, *Suspensions*, 148.

38. Eagleton, "Capitalism," 67.

39. Lears, *Fables of Abundance*, 88, 55, 139, 169.

40. Lears, *Fables of Abundance*, 169, 329. The exceptions, ironically, occur in the totalitarian cultures of this moment, as Karen Pinkus proves in her extensive survey of the modernist forms of fascist advertising in Italy, *Bodily Regimes: Italian Advertising under Fascism* (Minneapolis: University of Minnesota Press, 1995).

41. Roland Marchand, *Advertising the American Dream: Making Way for Modernity, 1920–1940* (Berkeley: University of California Press, 1985), 142, 148.

42. Lears, *Fables of Abundance*, 380.

43. Paul Parker, "The Modern Style in American Advertising Art," *Parnassus* 9, no. 4 (April 1937): 20–21.

44. Lye got commercial sponsorship through John Grierson, a producer who "agreed to promote the film if lively music and few advertising slogans were added." Thereafter Lye made a number of films for the General Post Office; see Roger Horrocks, "Len Lye's Films," in *Len Lye: A Personal Mythology*, ed. Ron Brownson (Auckland: Auckland City Art Gallery, 1980), 28.

45. Daniel O'Hara and Alan Singer, "Thinking through Art: Reimagining the Aesthetic within Global Modernity," *boundary 2* 25, no. 1 (Spring 1998): 1–5.

Jesse Matz

46. Mark Turner, *The Literary Mind: The Origins of Thought and Language* (Oxford: Oxford University Press, 1996), 112.

47. Arjun Appadurai, *Modernity at Large: Cultural Dimensions of Globalization* (Minneapolis: University of Minnesota Press, 1996), 82–83.

48. Huyssen, *After the Great Divide*, 15.

Bibliography

Adorno, Theodor W. "On the Fetish Character in Music and the Regression of Listening." In *Adorno: The Culture Industry: Selected Essays on Mass Culture*, edited by J. M. Bernstein, 26–52. London: Routledge, 1991.

———. *Minima Moralia: Reflections from a Damaged Life*. Translated by E. F. N. Jephcott. London: Unwin Brothers, 1974.

———. *Negative Dialectics*. Translated by E. B. Ashton. New York: Continuum, 1983.

———. *Notes to Literature: Volume One*. Edited by Rolf Tiedemann. Translated by Shierry Weber Nicholsen. New York: Columbia University Press, 1991.

———. *Notes to Literature: Volume Two*. Edited by Rolf Tiedemann. Translated by Shierry Weber Nicholsen. New York: Columbia University Press, 1992.

Adorno, Theodor W., and Max Horkheimer. *Dialectic of Enlightenment*. Translated by John Cumming. London: Verso, 1997.

Albright, Daniel. *Quantum Poetics: Yeats, Pound, Eliot, and the Science of Modernism*. Cambridge: Cambridge University Press, 1997.

———. *Untwisting the Serpent: Modernism in Music, Literature, and Other Arts*. Chicago: University of Chicago Press, 2000.

Althusser, Louis. "The International of Decent Feelings." In *The Spectre of Hegel: Early Writings*, translated by G. M. Goshgarian, 21–35. London: Verso, 1997.

Altieri, Charles. *The Particulars of Rapture: An Aesthetics of the Affects*. Ithaca, N.Y.: Cornell University Press, 2003.

"America Is in the Heart." *New York Times Book Review* (March 10, 1946): 17.

Anderson, Amanda. *The Powers of Distance: Cosmopolitanism and the Cultivation of Detachment*. Princeton, N.J.: Princeton University Press, 2001.

Anderson, Perry. "Modernism and Revolution." In *Marxism and the Interpretation of Culture*, edited by Cary Nelson and Lawrence Grossberg, 317–38. Chicago: University of Chicago Press, 1988.

Andréas, Bert. *Le manifeste communiste de Marx et Engels: Histoire et bibliographie, 1848–1918*. Milan: Feltrinelli, 1963.

Anscombe, G. E. M. *An Introduction to Wittgenstein's* Tractatus. London: Hutchinson, 1959.

Appadurai, Arjun. *Modernity at Large: Cultural Dimensions of Globalization*. Minneapolis: University of Minnesota Press, 1996.

Apollinaire, Guillaume. "Cubism Differs." In *Manifesto: A Century of Isms*, edited by Mary Ann Caws, 123–25. Lincoln: University of Nebraska Press, 2001.

Aptheker, Herbert. Introduction to *Dark Princess: A Romance*, by W. E. B. Du Bois. Millwood, N.Y.: Kraus-Thomason Organization Limited, 1974.

Artaud, Antonin. *Œuvres Complètes*. Paris: Gallimard, 1956.

Asholt, Wolfgang, and Fähnders, Walter, eds. *Manifeste und Proklamationen der europäischen Avantgarde (1919–1938)*. Stuttgart: Metzler, 1995.

Auden, W. H. *Collected Poems*. New York: Vintage, 1991.

———. *The English Auden: Poems, Essays, and Dramatic Writings 1927–1939*. London: Faber, 1977.

———. *Prose and Travel Books in Prose and Verse, 1926–1938*. Princeton, N.J.: Princeton University Press, 1996.

———. *Prose, 1939–1948*. Princeton, N.J.: Princeton University Press, 2002.

Bach, Evelyn. "Sheik Fantasies: Orientalism and Feminine Desire in the Desert Romance." *Hecate* 23, no. 1 (1997): 9–40.

Baker, Houston. *Modernism and the Harlem Renaissance*. Chicago: University of Chicago Press, 1989.

———. *Turning South Again: Re-Thinking Modernism, Re-Reading Booker T.* Durham, N.C.: Duke University Press, 2001.

Baker, Jean-Claude, and Chris Chase. *Josephine: The Hungry Heart*. New York: Random House, 1993.

Bakhtin, Mikhail. *Rabelais and His World*. Translated by Helene Iswolsky. Bloomington: Indiana University Press, 1984.

Bal, Mieke. *Narratology*. 2d ed. Toronto: University of Toronto Press, 1997.

Baldwin, Brooke. "The Cakewalk: A Study in Stereotype and Reality." *Journal of Social History* 15 (Winter 1981): 205–18.

Barrett, Michèle. "The Great War and Post-Modern Memory." *New Formations* 41 (August 2000): 148–57.

———. "Virginia Woolf Meets Michel Foucault." In *Imagination in Theory: Essays on Writing and Culture*. Cambridge: Polity Press, 1999.

Baudelaire, Charles. "The Painter of Modern Life." In *Selected Writings on Art and Literature*, translated and edited by P. E. Charvet, 390–435. New York: Penguin, 1992.

Baudrillard, Jean. *Simulacra and Simulation*. Translated by Sheila Faria Glaser. Ann Arbor: University of Michigan Press, 1994.

Baxter, Peter, ed. *Sternberg*. London: BFI Publishing, 1980.

———. *Just Watch! Sternberg, Paramount and America*. London: BFI Publishing, 1993.

Bearn, Gordon C. F. *Waking to Wonder: Wittgenstein's Existential Investigations*. Albany: State University of New York Press, 1997.

Beauvoir, Simone de. *The Second Sex*. New York: Vintage, 1974.

Bencherif, Osman. *The Image of Algeria in Anglo-American Writings, 1785–1962*. Lanham, Md.: University Press of America, 1997.

Benjamin, Walter. *Illuminations*. Translated by Harry Zohn. New York: Schocken, 1968.

Benstock, Shari. *Women of the Left Bank: Paris, 1900–1940*. Austin: University of Texas Press, 1986.

Berlin, Normand. *Eugene O'Neill*. New York: Grove Press, 1982.

Berman, Jessica. *Modernist Fiction, Cosmopolitanism and the Politics of Community*. Cambridge: Cambridge University Press, 2001.

Berman, Russell. *Modern Culture and Critical Theory: Art, Politics, and the Legacy of the Frankfurt School*. Madison: University of Wisconsin Press, 1989.

Bettinotti, Julia, and Marie-Françoise Truel. "Lust and Dust: Desert Fabula in Romances and Media." *Paradoxa* 3, nos. 1–2 (1997): 184–94.

Bhabha, Homi K. *The Location of Culture*. London: Routledge, 1994.

Bogaras, Waldemar. *The Chukchee*. 1909. New York: Johnson Reprint Corporation, 1970.

Bohrer, Karl Heinz. *Suddenness: On the Moment of Aesthetic Appearance*. Translated by Ruth Crowley. New York: Columbia University Press, 1994.

Bois, Yves-Alain, and Rosalind Krauss. *Formless: A User's Guide*. Cambridge, Mass.: MIT Press, 1997.

"Books Published Today." *New York Times* (April 20, 1944): 7.

Booth, Howard J., and Nigel Rigby. Introduction to *Modernism and Empire*, edited by Howard J. Booth and Nigel Rigby, 1–12. Manchester: Manchester University Press, 2000.

Bouveresse, Jacques. *Wittgenstein Reads Freud: The Myth of the Unconscious*. Translated by Carol Cosman. Princeton, N.J.: Princeton University Press, 1995.

Bozorth, Richard R. *Auden's Games of Knowledge: Poetry and the Meanings of Homosexuality*. New York: Columbia University Press, 2001.

Bradbrook, M.C. "Notes on the Style of Mrs. Woolf." *Scrutiny* 1, no. 1 (1932): 33–38.

Bradbury, Malcolm, and James McFarlane. "The Name and Nature of Modernism." In *Modernism: A Guide to European Literature 1890–1930*, edited by Malcolm Bradbury and James McFarlane, 19–55. Reprint ed. London: Penguin, 1991.

Brown, Cecil. *Stagolee Shot Billy*. Cambridge, Mass.: Harvard University Press, 2003.

Buchloh, Benjamin H. D. "Figures of Authority, Ciphers of Regression: Notes on the Return of Representation in European Painting." *October* 16 (Spring 1981): 39–69. Rep. in *Art in Modern Culture: An Anthology of Critical Texts*, edited by Francis Francina and Jonathan Harris, 222–38. London: Phaidon, 1992.

Buck-Morss, Susan. "Aesthetics and Anaesthetics: Benjamin's Artwork Essay Reconsidered." *October* (Fall 1999): 3–41.

Bucknell, Katherine. Editor's introduction to "Auden's 'Writing' Essay." In *"The Map of All of My Youth": Early Works, Friends, and Influences*, edited by Katherine Bucknell and Nicholas Jenkins, 17–34. Oxford: Clarendon, 1990.

Bulosan, Carlos. *America Is in the Heart*. Seattle: University of Washington Press, 1973.

———. "Freedom from Want." *Saturday Evening Post* (March 6, 1943): 15.

———. *The Laughter of My Father*. New York: Harcourt Brace, 1944.

———. *On Becoming Filipino: Selected Writings of Carlos Bulosan*. Edited by E. San Juan. Philadelphia: Temple University Press, 1995.

———. *Sound of Falling Light: Letters in Exile*. Edited by Dolores S. Feria. Quezon City: University of the Philippines Press, 1960.

Bürger, Peter. *The Decline of Modernism*. Cambridge: Polity Press, 1992.

Burke, Kenneth. *A Grammar of Motives*. 1954. Berkeley: University of California Press, 1969.

Butler, Judith. *Bodies that Matter: On the Discursive Limits of "Sex."* New York: Routledge, 1993.

———. "Explanation and Exoneration, or What We Can Hear." *Social Text* 72 (Fall 2002): 177–88.

Byerman, Keith. *Seizing the Word: History, Art, and the Self in the Work of W. E. B. Du Bois.* Atlanta: University of Georgia Press, 1994.

Cachin, Françoise, and Isobel Cachin, eds. *Cézanne*. Philadelphia: Philadelphia Museum of Art, 1996.

Calinescu, Matei. *The Five Faces of Modernity: Modernism, Avant-Garde, Decadence, Kitsch, Postmodernism*. Durham, N.C.: Duke University Press, 1987.

Campomanes, Oscar V., and Todd S. Gernes. "Two Letters from America: Carlos Bulosan and the Act of Writing." *melus* 15, no. 3 (1988): 15–46.

Carby, Hazel. "The Politics of Fiction, Anthropology, and the Folk: Zora Neale Hurston." In *New Essays on* Their Eyes Were Watching God, edited by Michael Awkward, 71–93. Cambridge: Cambridge University Press, 1990.

Caserio, Robert. *The Novel in England, 1900–1950: History and Theory*. New York: Twayne Publishers, 1999.

Cavell, Stanley. "Fred Astaire Asserts the Right to Praise." In *Philosophy the Day After Tomorrow*. Cambridge: Harvard University Press, 2005.

Caws, Mary Ann, ed. *Manifesto: A Century of Isms*. Lincoln: University of Nebraska Press, 2001.

Cesarani, David. "An Embattled Minority: The Jews in Britain during the First World War." In *The Politics of Marginality: Race, the Radical Right, and Minorities in Twentieth Century Britain*, edited by Tony Kushner and Kenneth Lunn, 61–81. London: Frank Cass, 1990.

Chakrabarty, Dipesh. *Provincializing Europe: Postcolonial Thought and Historical Difference*. Princeton, N.J.: Princeton University Press, 2000.

Charqus, R. D. "The Bourgeois Novel." In *Contemporary Literature and Social Revolution*. Rep. in *Virginia Woolf: The Critical Heritage*, edited by Robin Majumdar and Allen McLaurin, 342–45. London: Routledge, 1997.

Chow, Karen. "Popular Sexual Knowledges and Women's Agency in 1920s England: Marie Stopes's *Married Love* and E. M. Hull's *The Sheik*." *Feminist Review* 63 (Autumn 1999): 64–87.

Cioffi, Frank. *Wittgenstein on Freud and Frazier*. Cambridge: Cambridge University Press, 1998.

Clark, Suzanne. *Sentimental Modernism: Women Writers and the Revolution of the Word.* Bloomington: Indiana University Press, 1991.

Clark, T. J. *Farewell to an Idea: Episodes in a History of Modernism.* New Haven, Conn.: Yale University Press, 1999.

———. *The Painting of Modern Life: Paris in the Art of Manet and His Followers.* New York: Alfred A. Knopf, 1985.

Coffman, Elizabeth. "Uncanny Performances in Colonial Narratives: Josephine Baker in *Princess Tam Tam.*" *Paradoxa* 3, nos. 3–4 (1997): 379–94.

Conant, James. "The Search for Logically Alien Thought: Descartes, Kant, Frege, and the *Tractatus.*" *Philosophical Topics* 20 (1991): 115–80.

Copjec, Joan. *Shades of Noir.* New York: Verso, 1993.

Crary, Alice, and Rupert Read, eds. *The New Wittgenstein.* London: Routledge, 2000.

Crary, Jonathan. *Suspensions of Perception: Attention, Spectacle, and Modern Culture.* Minneapolis: University of Minnesota Press, 1999.

Crow, Thomas. *Modern Art in the Common Culture.* New Haven, Conn.: Yale University Press, 1998.

Cuddy-Keane, Melba. *Virginia Woolf, the Intellectual, and the Public Sphere.* Cambridge: Cambridge University Press, 2003.

Czaplicka, M.A. *Aboriginal Siberia.* 1914. Richmond, Surrey: Curzon Press, 1999.

Dante. *The Inferno.* Translated by John Ciardi. New York: Penguin, 1954.

Dasenbrock, Reed Way. "Philosophy after Joyce: Derrida and Davidson." *Philosophy and Literature* 26 (2002): 334–45.

The Day of the Jackal. Directed by Fred Zinnemann. MCA Universal Pictures, 1973.

Debord, Guy. *Comments on the Society of the Spectacle.* Translated by Malcolm Imrie. London: Verso, 1988.

Denning, Michael. *Cover Stories: Narrative and Ideology in the British Spy Thriller.* New York: Routledge and Kegan Paul, 1987.

———. *The Cultural Front: The Laboring of American Culture in the Twentieth Century.* New York: Verso, 1996.

Dettmar, Kevin J. H., and Stephen Watt, eds. *Marketing Modernisms: Self-Promotion, Canonization, Rereading.* Ann Arbor: University of Michigan Press, 1996.

Diamond, Cora. *The Realistic Spirit: Wittgenstein, Philosophy, and Mind.* Cambridge, Mass.: MIT Press, 1991.

Di Battista, Maria, and Lucy McDiarmid, eds. *High and Low Moderns: Literature and Culture, 1889–1939.* New York: Oxford University Press, 1996.

Diepeveen, Leonard. *The Difficulties of Modernism.* New York: Routledge, 2003.

Douglas, Ann. *Terrible Honesty: Mongrel Manhattan in the 1920s.* New York: Farrar, Straus and Giroux, 1995.

Dowling, Linda. *Hellenism and Homosexuality in Victorian England.* Ithaca, N.Y.: Cornell University Press, 1994.

Du Bois, W. E. B. "The Criteria of Negro Art." Pages 993–1002 in *Writings.* New York: Library of America, 1986.

———. *Dark Princess: A Romance.* Jackson: University of Mississippi Press, 1995.

Dummett, Michael. *Frege and Other Philosophers.* Oxford: Clarendon, 1991.

Eagleton, Terry. "Capitalism, Modernism, and Postmodernism." *New Left Review* 152 (July/August 1985): 60–73.

———. "Capitalism, Modernism, and Postmodernism." In *Art in Modern Culture: An Anthology of Critical Texts*, edited by Francis Francina and Jonathan Harris, 91–100. London: Phaidon, 1992.

———. *Exiles and Émigrés.* New York: Schocken, 1970.

Edwards, Paul. Afterword to *Time and Western Man*, by Wyndham Lewis. Santa Rosa, Calif.: Black Sparrow, 1993.

Eisenman, Stephen. "The Intransigent Artist *or* How the Impressionists Got Their Name." In *The New Painting: Impressionism 1874–1886*, edited by Charles S. Moffet, 51–59. San Francisco: Fine Arts Museum of San Francisco, 1986.

Eliade, Mircea. *Shamanism: Archaic Techniques of Ecstasy.* Princeton, N.J.: Princeton University Press, 1964.

Eliot, George. *Middlemarch.* London: Penguin, 1994.

Eliot, T. S. "Professional, Or . . ." *The Egoist* (April 1918): 61.

———. "Tradition and the Individual Talent." Pages 37–44 in *Selected Essays: 1917–1932.* New York: Harcourt, Brace, 1932.

Elliott, Bridget, and Jo-Ann Wallace. *Women Artists and Writers: Modernist (Im)positionings.* London: Routledge, 1994.

Ellison, Ralph. *Collected Essays of Ralph Ellison.* Edited by John F. Callahan. New York: Modern Library, 1995.

———. *Invisible Man.* New York: Vintage, 1992.

Engels, Friedrich. "Preface to the German Edition of 1883." In *Birth of the Communist Manifesto*, edited by Dirk J. Struik, 129–30. New York: International Publishers, 1971.

Esty, Jed. *A Shrinking Island: Modernism and National Culture in England.* Princeton, N.J.: Princeton University Press, 2004.

Fabre, Geneviève. "Pinkster Carnival: 1776–1811: An African-American Celebration." In *Feasts and Celebrations in Northern American Ethnic Communities*, edited by Ramón Gutiérrez and Geneviève Fabre, 13–29. Albuquerque: University of New Mexico Press, 1995.

Feldman, Jessica. *Gender on the Divide: The Dandy in Modernist Literature.* Ithaca, N.Y.: Cornell University Press, 1993.

Felski, Rita. *Doing Time: Feminist Theory and Postmodern Culture.* New York: New York University Press, 2000.

———. *The Gender of Modernity.* Cambridge, Mass.: Harvard University Press, 1995.

Fenn, Elizabeth. " 'A Perfect Equality Seemed to Reign': Slave Society and Jonkonnu." *North Carolina Historical Review* 65 (April 1988): 127–53.

Fiedler, Leslie. "Death of Avant-Garde Literature." *Collected Essays of Leslie Fiedler.* Vol. 2. New York: Stein and Day, 1971.

Fillin-Yeh, Ellen, ed. *Dandies: Fashion and Finesse in Art and Culture*. New York: New York University Press, 2001.

Finch, Henry Le Roy. *Wittgenstein — The Early Philosophy: An Exposition of the* Tractatus. New York: Humanities Press, 1971.

Firchow, Peter E. "Private Faces in Public Places: Auden's *The Orators*." PMLA 92 (1977): 253–72.

Fischer, Michael. "Wittgenstein as a Modernist Philosopher." *Philosophy and Literature* 17 (1993): 279–85.

Fitzgerald, F. Scott. *The Crack-Up*. Edited by Edmund Wilson. New York: New Directions, 1945.

FitzGerald, Michael. *Making Modernism: Picasso and the Creation of the Market for Twentieth-Century Art*. New York: Farrar, Straus and Giroux, 1995.

Forster, E. M. "Visions." *Daily News* (July 31, 1919): 2. Rep. in *Virginia Woolf: The Critical Heritage*, edited by Robin Majumdar and Allen McLaurin, 69. London: Routledge, 1997.

Forsyth, Frederick. *The Day of the Jackal*. New York: Viking Press, 1971.

Foster, Helen Bradley. *"New Raiments of Self": African American Clothing in the Antebellum South*. New York: Berg, 1997.

Foucault, Michel. *The History of Sexuality*. Vol. 1. Translated by Robert Hurley. New York: Vintage, 1978.

Frank, Thomas. *The Conquest of Cool: Business Culture, Counterculture, and the Rise of Hip Consumerism*. Chicago: University of Chicago Press, 1997.

Frascina, Francis, and Jonathan Harris. *Art in Modern Culture: An Anthology of Critical Texts*. London: Phaidon, 1992.

Friedlander, Eli. *Signs of Sense: Reading Wittgenstein's* Tractatus. Cambridge, Mass.: Harvard University Press, 2001.

Friedman, Susan Stanford. "Definitional Excursions: The Meanings of Modern/ Modernity/ Modernism." *Modernism/Modernity* 8 (2001): 493–513.

———. "Geopolitical Literacy: Internationalizing Feminism at 'Home' — The Case of Virginia Woolf." Pages 107–31 in *Mappings: Feminism and the Cultural Geographies of Encounter*. Princeton, N.J.: Princeton University Press, 1998.

Fuller, John. *W. H. Auden: A Commentary*. Princeton, N.J.: Princeton University Press, 1998.

Fussell, Paul. *The Great War and Modern Memory*. London: Oxford University Press, 1975.

Gaonkar, Dilip Parameshwar, ed. *Alternative Modernities*. Durham, N.C.: Duke University Press, 2001.

Garelick, Rhonda. *Rising Star: Dandyism, Gender, and Performance in the Fin de Siècle*. Princeton, N.J.: Princeton University Press, 1998.

Gass, William. "Ford's Impressionisms." Pages 73–103 in *Finding a Form*. New York: Alfred A. Knopf, 1996.

Gates, Henry Louis, Jr., and Karen C. C. Dalton, eds. *Josephine Baker and La Revue Nègre: Paul Colin's Lithographs of* Le Tumulte Noir *in Paris, 1927*. New York: Henry Abrams, 1998.

Geist, Anthony L., and José B. Monléon. "Introduction: Modernism and Its Margins: Rescripting Hispanic Modernism." In *Modernism and Its Margins: Reinscribing Cultural Modernity from Spain and Latin America*, edited by Anthony L. Geist and José B. Monléon, xvii–xxxv. New York: Garland, 1999.

Gibson, John, and Wolfgang Huemer. *The Literary Wittgenstein*. London: Routledge, 2004.

Gikandi, Simon. *Writing in Limbo: Modernism and Caribbean Literature*. Ithaca, N.Y.: Cornell University Press, 1992.

Gilbert, Sandra, and Susan Gubar. Introduction to *The Female Imagination and the Modernist Aesthetic*, edited by Sandra Gilbert and Susan Gubar. New York: Gordon and Breach, 1986.

———. *No Man's Land: The Place of the Woman Writer in the Twentieth Century*. New Haven, Conn.: Yale University Press, 1988.

Gilroy, Paul. *Against Race: Imagining Political Culture beyond the Color Line*. Cambridge, Mass.: Harvard University Press, 2000.

———. *The Black Atlantic: Modernity and Double Consciousness*. Cambridge, Mass.: Harvard University Press, 1993.

Glick, Elisa. "Harlem's Queer Dandy: African American Modernism and the Artifice of Blackness." *MFS: Modern Fiction Studies* 49, no. 3 (Fall 2003): 414–42.

Glock, Hans-Johann, ed. *Wittgenstein: A Critical Reader*. Oxford: Blackwell, 2001.

Graves, Robert, and Alan Hodge. *The Long Week End: A Social History of Great Britain, 1918–1939*. New York: Macmillan, 1941.

Greenberg, Clement. "Avant-Garde and Kitsch." Pages 3–21 in *Art and Culture*. London: Thames and Hudson, 1977.

———. "Cézanne." Pages 50–58 in *Art and Culture*. London: Thames and Hudson, 1977.

———. *The Collected Essays and Criticism*. Vol. 1. Chicago: University of Chicago Press, 1986.

Greene, Graham. *A Gun for Sale*. 1936. New York: Penguin, 1974.

Grosse Pointe Blank. Written by Tom Jankewicz et al. Directed by George Armitage. Hollywood Pictures, 1997.

Grow, L. M. "The Laughter of My Father: A Survival Kit." *melus* 20, no. 2 (1995): 35–46.

Guetti, James. *Wittgenstein and the Grammar of Literary Experience*. Athens: University of Georgia Press, 1993.

Guha, Ranajit. *History at the Limit of World-History*. New York: Columbia University Press, 2002.

Gumbrecht, Hans Ulrich. *In 1926: Living at the Edge of Time*. Cambridge, Mass.: Harvard University Press, 1997.

Habermas, Jürgen. "Modernity—An Incomplete Project." In *Postmodernism: A Reader*, edited by Thomas Docherty. New York: Columbia University Press, 1993.

———. *The Philosophical Discourse of Modernity: Twelve Lectures*. Translated by Frederick G. Lawrence. Cambridge, Mass.: MIT Press, 1987.

Hacker, P. M. S. *Wittgenstein's Place in Twentieth-Century Analytic Philosophy*. Oxford: Blackwell, 1996.

Hammond, Bryan, and Patrick O'Connor. *Josephine Baker*. London: Jonathan Cape, 1988.

Hansen, Miriam. "Pleasure, Ambivalence, Identification: Valentino and Female Spectatorship." *Cinema Journal* 25, no. 4 (1986): 6–32.

Hauser, Arnold. *The Social History of Art*. New York: Vintage Books, 1957–58.

Hejinian, Lyn. "Barbarism." Pages 318–36 in *The Language of Inquiry*. Berkeley: University of California Press, 2000.

Heller, Scott. "New Life for Modernism." *Chronicle of Higher Education* 46, no. 11 (November 5, 1999): A21-A22.

Hemingway, Ernest. "The Killers." Pages 279–89 in *The Short Stories of Ernest Hemingway*. New York: Charles Scribner's Sons, 1953.

Henighan, Tom. "Shamans, Tribes, and the Sorcerer's Apprentices: Notes on the Discovery of the Primitive in Modern Poetry." *Dalhousie Review* 59 (1979–80): 605–20.

Hewitt, Andrew. *Political Inversions: Homosexuality, Fascism, and the Modernist Imaginary*. Stanford, Calif.: Stanford University Press, 1996.

Highsmith, Patricia. *Ripley's Game*. New York: Vintage Crime/Black Lizard, 1993.

Hisama, Ellie M. *Gendering Musical Modernism: The Music of Ruth Crawford, Marion Bauer, and Miriam Gideon*. Cambridge: Cambridge University Press, 2001.

Hitler, Adolf. *Mein Kampf*. Translated by Ralph Manheim. Boston: Houghton Mifflin, 1960.

Hobsbawn, Eric J. *Age of Revolution: Europe 1789–1848*. London: Weidenfeld and Nicholson, 1962.

Hoggart, Richard. *The Uses of Literacy: Aspects of Working-Class Life*. 1957. New York: Oxford University Press, 1970.

Horrocks, Roger. "Len Lye's Films." In *Len Lye: A Personal Mythology*, edited by Ron Brownson, 25–31. Auckland: Auckland City Art Gallery, 1980.

Horsley, Lee. *Fictions of Power in English Literature: 1900–1950*. London: Longman, 1995.

Howe, Irving. *Literary Modernisms*. Greenwich, Conn.: Fawcett Publications, 1967.

Hughes, Robert. *The Shock of the New*. New York: Alfred A. Knopf, 1981.

Hull, E. M. *The Sheik*. London: Virago Books, 1996.

———. *The Sons of the Sheik*. New York: Dell, 1925.

———. "Why I Wrote 'The Sheik.'" *Movie Weekly* (November 19, 1921): 3.

Hutcheon, Linda. *A Theory of Parody: The Teachings of Twentieth Century Art Forms*. Urbana: University of Illinois Press, 2000.

Huyssen, Andreas. *After the Great Divide: Modernism, Mass Culture, Postmodernism*. Bloomington: Indiana University Press, 1986.

———. "High/Low in an Expanded Field." *Modernism/Modernity* 9, no. 3 (2002): 363–74.

Jacobs, Lea. *The Wages of Sin: Censorship and the Fallen Woman Film, 1928–1942*. Berkeley: University of California Press, 1995.

James, Henry. "The Art of Fiction." Pages 39–48 in *Henry James: Literary Criticism*. Vol. 1. New York: Library of America, 1984.

———. Preface to *The Princess Casamassima*. *The Art of the Novel: Critical Prefaces by Henry James*. New York: Charles Scribner and Sons, 1946.

James, William. *The Varieties of Religious Experience: A Study in Human Nature*. 1902. Edited by Martin E. Murray. New York: Penguin, 1982.

Jameson, Fredric. *Fables of Aggression: Wyndham Lewis, the Modernist as Fascist*. Berkeley: University of California Press, 1979.

———. *The Political Unconscious: Narrative as a Socially Symbolic Act*. Ithaca, N.Y.: Cornell University Press, 1981.

———. *Postmodernism, or The Cultural Logic of Late Capitalism*. Durham, N.C.: Duke University Press, 1991.

———. "Reflections in Conclusion." In *Aesthetics and Politics*, edited by Fredric Jameson, 196–213. London: Verso, 1977.

———. *A Singular Modernity: Essay on the Ontology of the Present*. London: Verso, 2002.

———. "The Vanishing Mediator; or, Max Weber as Storyteller." Pages 3–34 in *The Ideologies of Theory: Essays 1971–1986*. Vol. 2. Minneapolis: University of Minnesota Press, 1989.

Janik, Allan. *Wittgenstein's Vienna Revisited*. New Brunswick, N.J.: Transaction, 2001.

Jaskoski, Helen. "Carlos Bulosan's Literary Debt to Richard Wright." In *Literary Influence and African-American Writers*, edited by Tracy Mishkin, 231–41. New York: Garland, 1996.

Johnson, James Weldon. *Black Manhattan*. New York: De Capo Press, 1991.

Jones, Helen. *Women in British Public Life, 1914–1950: Gender, Power and Social Policy*. London: Pearson, 2000.

Jordan, June. "On Richard Wright and Zora Neale Hurston: Notes Toward a Balancing of Love and Hatred." *Black World* 23, no. 10 (1974): 4–8.

Joyce, James. *A Portrait of the Artist as a Young Man*. New York: Penguin, 2003.

Kadlec, David. "Pound, BLAST, and Syndicalism." *ELH* 60, no. 2 (1993): 1015–31.

Kaplan, E. Ann. "Fetishism and the Repression of Motherhood in Von Sternberg's *Blonde Venus* (1932)." In *Women and Film: Both Sides of the Camera*, edited by E. Ann Kaplan. New York: Methuen, 1983.

Keeley, Edmund, and Philip Sherrard, eds. and trans. *The Dark Crystal: An Anthology of Modern Greek Poetry*. Athens: Denise Harvey, 1981.

Kenner, Hugh. "The Making of the Modernist Canon." *Chicago Review* 34, no. 2 (Spring 1984): 49–61.

———. *Wyndham Lewis*. Norfolk, Conn.: New Directions, 1954.

Kermode, Frank. *D. H. Lawrence*. New York: Viking, 1973.

Kessler, Harry. *Berlin in Lights: The Diaries of Count Harry Kessler: 1918–1937*. New York: Grove, 1999.

Khalip, Jacques. "Pater's Sadness." *Raritan* 20, no. 2 (Fall 2000): 136–58.

Kim, Elaine. *Asian American Literature*. Philadelphia: Temple University Press, 1982.

Kivy, Peter. "Jokes Are a Laughing Matter." *Journal of Aesthetics and Art Criticism* 61, no. 1 (Winter 2003): 5–15.

Knight, Arthur. *Disintegrating the Musical: Black Performance and American Musical Film*. Durham, N.C.: Duke University Press, 2002.

———. "Star Dances: African-American Constructions of Stardom, 1925–1960." In *Classic Hollywood, Classic Whiteness*, edited by Daniel Bernardi, 386–414. Minneapolis: University of Minnesota Press, 2001.

Koch, Gertrud. "Exorcised: Marlene Dietrich and German Nationalism." In *Women and Film: A Sight and Sound Reader*, edited by Pam Cook and Philip Dodd, 10–15. London: Scarlet, n.d.

Koselleck, Reinhard. *Vergangene Zukunft: Zur Semantik geschichtlicher Zeiten*. Frankfurt am Main: Suhrkamp, 1979.

Koven, Seth. "Borderlands: Women, Voluntary Action, and Child Welfare in Britain, 1840 to 1914." In *Mothers of a New World: Maternalist Politics and the Origins of Welfare States*, edited by Seth Koven and Sonya Michel, 94–135. New York: Routledge, 1993.

Kracauer, Siegfried. "The Little Shopgirls Go to the Movies." In *The Mass Ornament: Weimar Essays*. Edited and translated by Thomas Y. Levin, 291–304. Cambridge, Mass.: Harvard University Press, 1995.

Krauss, Rosalind. "Notes on the Index: Part 2." Pages 210–20 in *The Originality of the Avant-Garde and Other Modernist Myths*. Cambridge, Mass.: MIT Press, 1986.

———. *"A Voyage on the North Sea": Art in the Age of the Post-Medium Condition*. London: Thames and Hudson, 1999.

Lamos, Colleen. *Deviant Modernism: Sexual and Textual Errancy in T. S. Eliot, James Joyce, and Marcel Proust*. Cambridge: Cambridge University Press, 1998.

Lash, Scott. *Another Modernity, A Different Rationality*. Oxford: Blackwell, 1999.

"The Laughter of My Father." *New York Times Book Review* (May 2, 1944): 17.

Lawrence, D. H. *Aaron's Rod*. Edited by Mara Kalnis. Cambridge: Cambridge University Press, 1988.

———. *The Complete Short Stories*. 3 Vols. New York: Penguin Books, 1981.

———. *Kangaroo*. New York: Penguin Books, 1980.

———. *Lady Chatterley's Lover*. Edited by Michael Squires. London: Penguin Books, 1993.

———. *The Plumed Serpent*. Edited by L. D. Clark and Virginia Crosswhite Hyde. London: Penguin Books, 1995.

———. *Selected Literary Criticism*. Edited by Anthony Beal. London: Heinemann, 1973.

Layard, J. W. "Degree-Taking Rites in South West Bay, Malekula." *Journal of the Royal Anthropological Institute of Great Britain and Ireland* 58 (1928): 139–223.

———. "Malekula: Flying Tricksters, Ghosts, Gods, and Epileptics." *Journal of the Royal Anthropological Institute of Great Britain and Ireland* 60 (1930): 501–24.

———. "Shamanism: An Analysis Based on Comparison with the Flying Tricksters of Malekula." *Journal of the Royal Anthropological Institute of Great Britain and Ireland* 60 (1930): 525–50.

———. *Stone Men of Malekula*. London: Chatto and Windus, 1942.

Lears, Jackson. *Fables of Abundance: A Cultural History of Advertising in America*. New York: Basic Books, 1994.

Leavis, F. R. *D. H. Lawrence: Novelist*. New York: Alfred A. Knopf, 1956.

Bibliography

Leavis, Q. D. "Caterpillars of the Commonwealth Unite!" *Scrutiny* 7, no. 1 (1938): 203–14.

———. *Fiction and the Reading Public*. London: Penguin Books, 1979.

Lee, Robert G. *Orientals: Asian Americans in Popular Culture*. Philadelphia: Temple University Press, 2000.

Levenson, Michael. *Modernism and the Fate of Individuality*. Cambridge: Cambridge University Press, 1991.

Levin, Harry. "What Was Modernism?" *Massachusetts Review* 1, no. 4 (August 1960): 609–30.

Lewis, Barbara. "Daddy Blue: The Evolution of the Dark Daddy." In *Inside the Minstrel Mask: Readings in Nineteenth-Century Blackface Minstrelsy*, edited by Annemarie Bean, James V. Hatch, and Brooks McNamara, 257–74. Hanover, N.H.: University Press of New England, 1996.

Lewis, David Levering. *When Harlem Was in Vogue*. New York: Penguin Books, 1997.

Lewis, Reina. *Gendering Orientalism: Race, Femininity and Representation*. London: Routledge, 1996.

Lewis, Wyndham. *The Apes of God*. London: The Arthur Press, 1930.

———. *The Art of Being Ruled*. Edited by Reed Way Dasenbrock. Santa Rosa, Calif.: Black Sparrow Press, 1989.

———. *Blast 1*. Foreword by Bradford Morrow. Santa Rosa, Calif.: Black Sparrow Press, 1997.

———. *The Childermass*. London: Chatto and Windus, 1928.

———. *Hitler*. London: Chatto and Windus, 1931.

———. *The Hitler Cult*. New York: Gordon Press, 1972.

———. *The Lion and the Fox: The Rôle of the Hero in the Plays of Shakespeare*. New York: Harper and Brothers, 1927.

———. *Men without Art*. 1934. Edited by Seamus Cooney. Santa Rosa, Calif.: Black Sparrow Press, 1987.

———. *The Revenge for Love*. 1937. Chicago: H. Regnery, 1952.

———. *Time and Western Man*. Edited by Paul Edwards. Santa Rosa, Calif.: Black Sparrow Press, 1993.

Lewis, Wyndham, and Naomi Mitchison. *Beyond this Limit*. London: Jonathan Cape, 1935.

Lezra, Jacques. "Unrelated Passions." *differences: A Journal of Feminist Cultural Studies* 14, no. 1 (2003): 74–87.

Lhamon, W. T., Jr. *Raising Cain*. Cambridge, Mass.: Harvard University Press, 1998.

Littledale, Clara Savage. "The Way Father Stretched His Mouth." Review of *The Laughter of My Father*. *Saturday Review of Literature* 27 (June 3, 1944): 22.

Liu, Alan. *The Laws of Cool: Knowledge Work and the Culture of Information*. Chicago: University of Chicago Press, 2004.

Locke, Alain. "The Legacy of the Ancestral Arts." In *The New Negro*, edited by Alain Locke, 254–67. New York: Atheneum, 1992.

———. "The New Negro." In *The New Negro*, edited by Alain Locke, 3–16. New York: Atheneum, 1992.

Lott, Eric. *Love and Theft: Blackface Minstrelsy and the American Working Class.* New York: Oxford University Press, 1993.

Luckhardt, C. G. *Wittgenstein: Sources and Perspectives.* Ithaca, N.Y.: Cornell University Press, 1979.

Lukács, Georg. "The Ideology of Modernism." Pages 17–46 in *Realism in Our Time: Literature and the Class Struggle.* New York: Harper and Row, 1962.

The Lustful Turk. Ware, Hertfordshire: Wordsworth Editions, 1995.

Lyon, Janet. "Josephine Baker's Hothouse." In *Modernism, Inc.: Body, Memory, Capital,* edited by Jani Scandura and Michael Thurston. New York: New York University Press, 2001.

———. *Manifestoes: Provocations of the Modern.* Ithaca, N.Y.: Cornell University Press, 1999.

Lyotard, Jean-François. *Lessons on the Analytic of the Sublime.* Translated by Elizabeth Rottenberg. Stanford, Calif.: Stanford University Press, 1994.

Mahar, Willam. *Behind the Burnt Cork Mask: Early Blackface Minstrelsy and Antebellum Popular Culture.* Urbana: University of Illinois Press, 1999.

Mao, Douglas. "Auden and Son: Environment, Evolution, Exhibition." *Paideuma* 32 (2003): 301–49.

———. *Solid Objects: Modernism and the Test of Production.* Princeton, N.J.: Princeton University Press, 1998.

Marchand, Roland. *Advertising the American Dream: Making Way for Modernity, 1920–1940.* Berkeley: University of California Press, 1985.

Marchetti, Gina. *Romance and the "Yellow Peril."* Berkeley: University of California Press, 1993.

Marcus, Sharon. "Anne Frank and Hannah Arendt, Universalism and Pathos." In *Cosmopolitan Geographies: New Locations in Literature and Culture*, edited by Vinay Dharwhadker, 89–132. New York: Routledge, 2001.

Marcus, Steven. *The Other Victorians.* New York: Basic Books, 1966.

Marcuse, Herbert. *Eros and Civilization: A Philosophical Inquiry into Freud.* Boston: Beacon Press, 1966.

Marinetti, F. T. "Fondazione e Manifesto del Futurismo." In *Teoria e Invenzione Futurista*, edited by Luciano De Maria. Milan: Mondadori, 1968.

Martin, Wendy. " 'Remembering the Jungle': Josephine Baker and Modernist Parody." In *Prehistories of the Future: The Primitivist Project and the Culture of Modernism*, edited by Elazeur Barler and Ronald Bush. Stanford, Calif.: Stanford University Press, 1995.

Marx, William, ed. *Les arrière-gardes au XXe siècle: L'autre face de la modernité esthétique.* Paris: Presses Universitaires de France, 2004.

Matz, Jesse. *Literary Impressionism and Modernist Aesthetics.* Cambridge: Cambridge University Press, 2001.

McCann, Sean. *Gumshoe America: Hard-Boiled Crime Fiction and the Rise and Fall of New Deal Liberalism.* Durham, N.C.: Duke University Press, 2000.

McGuinness, Brian, and G. H. von Wright, eds. *Ludwig Wittgenstein: Cambridge Letters*

(Correspondence with Russell, Keynes, Moore, Ramsey and Sraffa). Oxford: Blackwell, 1995.

Melman, Billie. *Women and the Popular Imagination in the Twenties: Flappers and Nymphs*. London: Palgrave Macmillan, 1988.

Menand, Louis. *Discovering Modernism: T. S. Eliot and His Context*. New York: Oxford University Press, 1987.

Mendelson, Edward. *Early Auden*. New York: Farrar, Straus and Giroux, 1981.

Menninghaus, Winfried. *In Praise of Nonsense: Kant and Bluebeard*. Translated by Henry Pickford. Stanford, Calif.: Stanford University Press, 1999.

Merquior, J. G. *Liberalism Old and New*. Boston: Twayne, 1991.

Meyer, Stefan G. *The Experimental Arabic Novel: Postcolonial Literary Modernism in the Levant*. Albany: State University of New York Press, 2001.

Meyers, Jeffrey. *The Enemy: A Biography of Wyndham Lewis*. London: Routledge, 1980.

Miller, Monica. "Figuring the Black Dandy: Negro Art, Black Bodies, and African-Diasporic Ambitions." Ph.D. diss., Harvard University, 2000.

———. "W. E. B. Du Bois and the Dandy as Diasporic Race Man." *Callaloo* 26 no. 3 (2003): 738–65.

Miller, Tyrus. *Late Modernism: Politics, Fiction and the Arts between the Wars*. Berkeley: University of California Press, 1999.

Mitchell, Timothy, ed. *Questions of Modernity*. Minneapolis: University of Minnesota Press, 2000.

Modleski, Tania. *Loving with a Vengeance: Mass-Produced Fantasies for Women*. Hamden, Conn.: Archon Books, 1982.

Moers, Ellen. *The Dandy: Brummell to Beerbohm*. New York: Viking Press, 1960.

Moretti, Franco. *Modern Epic: The World-System from Goethe to García Márquez*. Translated by Quintin Hoare. New York: Verso, 1996.

Morrisson, Mark S. *The Public Face of Modernism: Little Magazines, Audiences, and Reception, 1905–1920*. Madison: University of Wisconsin Press, 2001.

Morton, A. V. "In the Garden of Allah." *Daily Express* (January 23, 1924): 5.

Moten, Fred. "The New International of Decent Feelings." *Social Text* 72 (Fall 2002): 189–99.

Naremore, James. *More than Night: Film Noir in its Contexts*. Berkeley: University of California Press, 1998.

Naremore, James, and Patrick Brantlinger. *Modernity and Mass Culture*. Bloomington: Indiana University Press, 1991.

Nash, Gary. *Forging Freedom: The Formation of Philadelphia's Black Community, 1720–1840*. Cambridge, Mass.: Harvard University Press, 1988.

Nealon, Christopher. *Foundlings: Lesbian and Gay Historical Emotion before Stonewall*. Durham, N.C.: Duke University Press, 2001.

Nehring, Neil. *Flowers in the Dustbin: Culture, Anarchy and Postwar England*. Ann Arbor: University of Michigan Press, 1993.

Nelson, Cary. *Repression and Recovery: Modern American Poetry and the Politics of Cultural Memory, 1910–1945*. Madison: University of Wisconsin Press, 1989.

Nichols, Bill. *Ideology and the Image: Social Representation in the Cinema and Other Media.* Bloomington: Indiana University Press, 1981.

Nietzsche, Friedrich. "Der Fall Wagner." *Richard Wagner in Bayreuth, Der Fall Wagner, Nietzsche contra Wagner.* Stuttgart: Reclam, 1991.

Noble, Marianne. *The Masochistic Pleasures of Sentimental Literature.* Princeton, N.J.: Princeton University Press, 2000.

Nochlin, Linda. *The Politics of Vision: Essays on Nineteenth-Century Art and Society.* London: Thames and Hudson, 1989.

North, Michael. *The Dialect of Modernism: Race, Language, and Twentieth-Century Literature.* Oxford: Oxford University Press, 1994.

North, Michael. *Reading 1922: A Return to the Scene of the Modern.* Oxford: Oxford University Press, 1999.

Nussbaum, Martha. "Patriotism and Cosmopolitanism?" In *Respondents, For Love of Country: Debating the Limits of Patriotism*, edited by Joshua Cohen, 2–20. Boston: Beacon Press, 1996.

O'Hara, Daniel, and Alan Singer. "Thinking through Art: Reimagining the Aesthetic Within Global Modernity." *boundary 2* 25, no. 1 (Spring 1998): 1–5.

Ortega y Gasset, José. "On Point of View in the Arts." *The Dehumanization of Art and Other Essays on Art, Literature, and Culture*, 105–30. Princeton, N.J.: Princeton University Press, 1968.

———. *The Revolt of the Masses.* Edited by Kenneth Moore. Translated by Anthony Kerrigan. Notre Dame: University of Notre Dame Press, 1985.

Orwell, George. "Good Bad Books." *The Collected Essays, Journalism and Letters of George Orwell: In Front of Your Nose: 1945–1950.* Vol. 4. Edited by Sonia Orwell and Ian Angus, 37–41. London: Penguin Books, 1968.

Ostrow, Matthew. *Wittgenstein's Tractatus: A Dialectical Interpretation.* Cambridge: Cambridge University Press, 2002.

Palmer, Jerry. *Thrillers: Genesis and Structure of a Popular Genre.* London: E. Arnold, 1978.

Palumbo-Liu, David. *Asian/American: Historical Crossings of a Racial Frontier.* Stanford, Calif.: Stanford University Press, 1999.

Parker, Paul. "The Modern Style in American Advertising Art." *Parnassus* 9, no. 4 (April 1937): 20–23.

Pater, Walter. *The Renaissance: Studies in Art and Poetry.* Oxford: Oxford University Press, 1998.

———. *Studies in the History of the Renaissance.* London: Macmillan, 1873.

Pease, Allison. *Modernism, Mass Culture, and the Aesthetics of Obscenity.* Cambridge: Cambridge University Press, 2000.

Peppis, Paul. *Literature, Politics, and the English Avant-Garde: Nation and Empire, 1909–1918.* Cambridge: Cambridge University Press, 2000.

Perkin, Harold. *The Rise of Professional Society: England since 1880.* New York: Routledge, 1989.

Perloff, Marjorie. *The Futurist Moment: Avant-Garde, Avant-Guerre, and the Language of Rupture*. Chicago: University of Chicago Press, 1986.

———. *Twenty-First-Century Modernism: The "New" Poetics*. Malden, Mass.: Blackwell, 2002.

———. *Wittgenstein's Ladder: Poetic Language and the Strangeness of the Ordinary*. Chicago: University of Chicago Press, 1996.

Piersen, William D. *Black Yankees: The Development of Afro-American Subculture in Eighteenth Century New England*. Amherst: University of Massachusetts Press, 1988.

Pinkus, Karen. *Bodily Regimes: Italian Advertising under Fascism*. Minneapolis: University of Minnesota Press, 1995.

Pippin, Robert. *Modernism as a Philosophical Problem: On the Dissatisfactions of European High Culture*. Oxford: Blackwell, 1991.

Platt, Oliver H. "Negro Governors." *Papers of the New England Historical Society* 6 (1900): 315–35.

Posnock, Ross. *Color and Culture: Black Writers and the Making of the Modern Intellectual*. Cambridge, Mass.: Harvard University Press, 1998.

Pound, Ezra. *Jefferson and/or Mussolini: Fascism as I Have Seen It*. New York: Liveright, 1936.

Powell, Richard J. "Sartor Africanus." In *Dandies: Fashion and Finesse in Art and Culture*, edited by Susan Fillin-Yeh, 217–42. New York: New York University Press, 2001.

Quinones, Ricardo. *Mapping Literary Modernism: Time and Development*. Princeton, N.J.: Princeton University Press, 1985.

Rabinowitz, Paula. *Black and White and Noir: America's Pulp Modernism*. New York: Columbia University Press, 2002.

Rainey, Lawrence. *Institutions of Modernism: Literary Elites and Public Culture*. New Haven, Conn.: Yale University Press, 1998.

Raub, Patricia. "Issues of Passion and Power in E. M. Hull's *The Sheik*." *Women's Studies* 21 (1992): 119–28.

Reck, Erich H., ed. *From Frege to Wittgenstein: Perspectives on Early Analytic Philosophy*. Oxford: Oxford University Press, 2002.

Reidy, Joseph P. " 'Negro Election Day' and Black Community Life in New England, 1750–1860." *Marxist Perspectives* 1, no. 3 (1978): 102–17.

Rewald, John. *The History of Impressionism*. Vol. 1. New York: Museum of Modern Art, 1961.

Riding, Laura, and Robert Graves. *A Survey of Modernist Poetry*. London: William Heinemann, 1929.

Riley, Denise. *Am I That Name? Feminism and the Category of "Women" in History*. Minneapolis: University of Minnesota Press, 1988.

Riva, Maria. *Marlene Dietrich*. New York: Alfred A. Knopf, 1993.

Robbins, Bruce. "Modernism in History, Modernism in Power." In *Modernism Reconsidered*, edited by Robert Kiely, 229–45. Harvard English Studies 11. Cambridge, Mass.: Harvard University Press, 1983.

———. "The Village of the Liberal Managerial Class." In *Cosmopolitan Geographies: New*

Locations in Literature and Culture, edited by Vinay Dharwadker, 15–32. New York: Routledge, 2001.

Rogin, Michael Paul. *Blackface, White Noise: Jewish Immigrants in the Hollywood Melting Pot*. Berkeley: University of California Press, 1996.

Rose, Phyllis. *Jazz Cleopatra: Josephine Baker in Her Time*. New York: Doubleday, 1989.

Rovit, Earl H. "Ralph Ellison and the American Comic Tradition." In *Ralph Ellison: A Collection of Critical Essays*, edited by John Hersey, 151–59. Englewood Cliffs, N.J.: Prentice-Hall, 1974.

Rubin, James H. *Impressionism*. London: Phaidon, 1999.

Rudd, Anthony. *Expressing the World: Skepticism, Wittgenstein, and Heidegger*. Chicago: Open Court, 2003.

Ryder, Rowland. *Edith Cavell*. London: Hamish Hamilton, 1975.

Said, Edward. "Heroism and Humanism." *Al-Ahram Weekly On-line* 463 (January 6–12, 2000).

San Juan, E., Jr. *From Exile to Diaspora: Versions of the Filipino Experience in the United States*. Boulder, Colo.: Westview Press, 1998.

Saxton, Alexander. *The Rise and Fall of the White Republic*. London: Verso, 1990.

Schapiro, Meyer. *Impressionism: Reflections and Perceptions*. New York: George Brazilier, 1997.

Schiff, Richard. *Cézanne and the End of Impressionism: A Study of the Theory, Technique, and Critical Evaluation of Modern Art*. Chicago: University of Chicago Press, 1984.

Schnapp, Jeffrey, ed. *A Primer of Italian Fascism*. Translated by Jeffrey Schnapp, Olivia E. Sears, and Maria G. Stampino. Lincoln: University of Nebraska Press, 2000.

Schulte-Sasse, Jochen. Foreword to *Theory of the Avant-Garde*, by Peter Bürger. Translated by Michael Shaw. Minneapolis: University of Minnesota Press, 1984.

Scott, Bonnie Kime, ed. *The Gender of Modernism*. Bloomington: Indiana University Press, 1990.

Sedgwick, Eve Kosofsky. *Touching Feeling: Affect, Pedagogy, Performativity*. Durham, N.C.: Duke University Press, 2003.

Sedgwick, Eve Kosofsky, and Andrew Parker, eds. *Performance and Performativity*. New York: Routledge, 1995.

Shelton, Jane. "The New England Negro: A Remnant." *Harper's Magazine* 88, no. 526 (1894): 533–38.

Sherry, Vincent. *Ezra Pound, Wyndham Lewis, and Radical Modernism*. Oxford: Oxford University Press, 1993.

Shih, Shu-mei. "Global Literature and the Technologies of Recognition." *PMLA* 119, no. 1 (January 2004): 16–30.

Shklovsky, Victor. "Art as Technique." 1917. Rep. in *Russian Formalist Criticism: Four Essays*. Lincoln: University of Nebraska Press, 1965.

Sillitoe, Alan. *Saturday Night and Sunday Morning*. 1958. New York: Penguin Books, 1992.

Silver, Brenda R. *Virginia Woolf Icon*. Chicago: University of Chicago Press, 1999.

Simpson, Hilary. *D. H. Lawrence and Feminism*. DeKalb: Northern Illinois University Press, 1982.

Sinfield, Alan. *Literature, Politics and Culture in Postwar Britain*. Berkeley: University of California Press, 1989.

Slemon, Stephen. "Modernism's Last Post." In *Past the Last Post*, edited by Ian Adam and Helen Tiffin, 1–11. Calgary: University of Calgary Press, 1990.

Slotkin, Joel. "Igorots and Indians: Racial Hierarchies and Conceptions of the Savage in Carlos Bulosan's Fiction of the Philippines." *American Literature* 72, no. 4 (2000): 843–66.

Slotkin, Richard. "Unit Pride: Ethnic Platoons and the Myths of American Nationality." *American Literary History* 13, no. 3 (Fall 2001): 469–98.

Smith, Erin A. *Hard-Boiled: Working-Class Readers and Pulp Magazines*. Philadelphia: Temple University Press, 2000.

Smith, Stan. "Re-Righting Lefty: Wyndham and Wystan in the Thirties." *Wyndham Lewis Annual* 9–10 (2002–3): 34–45.

Smitherman, Geneva. *Black Talk: Words and Phrases from the Hood to the Amen Corner*. Boston: Houghton Mifflin, 1994.

Snitow, Ann. "Mass Market Romance: Pornography for Women is Different." In *Powers of Desire: The Politics of Sexuality*, edited by Ann Snitow, Christine Stansell, and Sharon Thompson, 258–75. New York: Monthly Review Press, 1983.

Somigli, Luca. *Legitimizing the Artist: Manifesto Writing and European Modernism 1885–1915*. Toronto: University of Toronto Press, 2003.

Sorel, Georges. *Reflections on Violence*. Translated by T. E. Hulme. New York: B. W. Huebsch, 1914.

Speller, Irene. "How I Was Loved by a Sheik!" *My Story Weekly* (October 15, 22, 29 and November 5, 1927).

Spillers, Hortense. *Black, White, and in Color*. Chicago: University of Chicago Press, 2003.

Spivak, Gayatri. *A Critique of Postcolonial Reason: Toward a History of the Vanishing Present*. Cambridge, Mass.: Harvard University Press, 1999.

———. *Death of a Discipline*. New York: Columbia University Press, 2003.

Stanfield, Peter. " 'An Octoroon in the Kindling': American Vernacular and Blackface Minstrelsy in 1930s Hollywood." *Journal of American Studies* 31, no. 3 (1997): 407–38.

Stanton, Domna. *The Aristocrat as Art: A Study of the honnête homme and the Dandy in Seventeenth and Nineteenth Century France*. New York: Columbia University Press, 1980.

Staten, Henry. *Wittgenstein and Derrida*. Lincoln: University of Nebraska Press, 1984.

Steedman, Carolyn. *Landscape for a Good Woman: A Story of Two Lives*. New Brunswick, N.J.: Rutgers University Press, 1986.

Sternberg, Josef von. *Fun in a Chinese Laundry*. New York: Macmillan, 1965.

Stewart, Jacqueline. "Negros Laughing at Themselves? Black Spectatorship and the Performance of Urban Modernity." *Critical Inquiry* 29 (Summer 2003): 650–77.

Stowell, Peter. *Literary Impressionism: James and Chekhov*. Athens: University of Georgia Press, 1980.

Strychacz, Thomas. *Modernism, Mass Culture and Professionalism*. Cambridge: Cambridge University Press, 1993.

Studlar, Gaylyn. *In the Realm of Pleasure: Von Sternberg, Dietrich, and the Masochistic Aesthetic*. Chicago: University of Illinois Press, 1988.

———. " 'Out-Salomeing Salome': Dance, the New Woman, and Fan Magazine Orientalism." In *Visions of the East: Orientalism in Film*, edited by Matthew Bernstein and Gaylyn Studlar, 90–129. New Brunswick, N.J.: Rutgers University Press, 1998.

———. *This Mad Masquerade: Stardom and Masculinity in the Jazz Age*. New York: Columbia University Press, 1996.

Sugrue, Thomas. "Laughter in the Philippines." Review of *The Laughter of My Father. New York Times Book Review* (April 23, 1944): 7.

Sundquist, Eric. *To Wake the Nations*. Cambridge, Mass.: Harvard University Press, 1993.

"Surrealism Pays." *Newsweek* (January 3, 1944): 57–58.

Sutto, Walter. *The Dial: Pound, Thayer, Watson and The Dial: A Story in Letters*. Gainesville: University of Florida Press, 1994.

Szalay, Michael. *New Deal Modernism: American Literature and the Invention of the Welfare State*. Durham, N.C.: Duke University Press, 2000.

Tate, Claudia. Introduction to *Dark Princess: A Romance*, by W. E. B. Du Bois. Jackson: University of Mississippi Press, 1995.

Taussig, Michael. *Shamanism, Colonialism, and the Wild Man: A Study in Terror and Healing*. Chicago: University of Chicago Press, 1987.

Taylor, Clyde. " 'Salt Peanuts': Sound and Sense in African/American Oral/Musical Creativity." *Callaloo* 5 (1982): 1–11.

Terada, Rei. *Feeling in Theory: Emotion after the "Death of the Subject."* Cambridge, Mass.: Harvard University Press, 2001.

The Third Man. Written by Graham Greene and Alexander Korda. Directed by Carol Reed. Produced by Alexander Korda and David O. Selznick. Rialto Pictures, 1949.

Thormählen, Marianne. Introduction to *Rethinking Modernism*, edited by Marianne Thormählen. Houndmills: Palgrave Macmillan, 2003.

Thurman, Wallace. *Infants of the Spring*. Boston: Northeastern University Press, 1992.

Times Literary Supplement, London. Review of *The Sheik* (November 6, 1919): 633.

Tolentino, Delfin L., Jr. "Satire in Carlos Bulosan's *The Laughter of My Father*." *Philippine Studies* 34 (1986): 452–61.

Tompkins, Jane. *Sensational Designs: The Cultural Work of American Fiction, 1790–1860*. New York: Oxford University Press, 1985.

Torgovnick, Marianna. *Gone Primitive: Savage Intellectuals, Modern Lives*. Chicago: University of Chicago Press, 1990.

Trilling, Lionel. *Beyond Culture*. New York: Harcourt, 1965.

Trotsky, Leon. *Literature and Revolution*. Ann Arbor: University of Michigan Press, 1960.

Trotter, David. *The English Novel in History: 1895–1920*. London: Routledge, 1993.

———. *Paranoid Modernism: Literary Experiment, Psychosis, and the Professionalization of English Society*. New York: Oxford University Press, 2001.

Tucker, Paul. " 'Reanimate Greek': Pater and Ruskin on Botticelli." In *Walter Pater: Transparencies of Desire*, edited by Laurel Brake, Lesley Higgins, and Carolyn Williams. Greensboro, N.C.: Macmillan Heinemann ELT, 2002.

Tuma, Keith. "Wyndham Lewis, *Blast*, and Popular Culture." *ELH* 54, no. 2 (1987): 403–19.

Turner, Mark. *The Literary Mind: The Origins of Thought and Language*. Oxford: Oxford University Press, 1996.

Turner, Victor. *The Ritual Process: Structure and Anti-Structure*. New York: Aldine Publishing, 1969.

Wade, Melvon. " 'Shining in Borrowed Plummage': Affirmation of Community in the Black Coronation Festivals of New England (c. 1750–c. 1850)." *Western Folklore* 40, no. 3 (1981): 211–31.

Washington, Booker T. *Up from Slavery*. Edited by William L. Andrews. New York: W. W. Norton, 1996.

Weber, Max. *The Protestant Ethic and the Spirit of Capitalism*. Translated by Talcott Parsons. 1920. New York: Routledge, 1996.

Wexler, Joyce. *Who Paid for Modernism? Art, Money, and the Fiction of Conrad, Joyce, and Lawrence*. Fayetteville: University of Arkansas Press, 1997.

White, Graham, and Shane White. *Stylin': African American Expressive Culture from its Beginnings to the Zoot Suit*. Ithaca, N.Y.: Cornell University Press, 1998.

White, Shane. *Somewhat More Independent: The End of Slavery in New York City, 1770–1810*. Athens: University of Georgia Press, 1991.

Wicke, Jennifer. *Advertising Fictions: Literature, Advertisement and Social Reading*. New York: Columbia University Press, 1988.

———. "Appreciation, Depreciation: Modernism's Speculative Bubble." *Modernism/Modernity* 8, no. 3 (September 2001): 389–403.

Williams, Raymond. *Culture and Society: 1780–1950*. New York: Columbia University Press, 1958.

———. *The Politics of Modernism: Against the New Conformists*. Edited by Tony Pinkney. London: Verso, 1989.

Williams-Meyers, A. J. "Pinkster Carnival: Africanisms in the Hudson Valley." *Afro-Americans in New York Life and History* 9, no. 1 (1985): 7–18.

Willison, Ian, Warwick Gould, and Warren Chernaik, eds. *Modernist Writers and the Marketplace*. New York: St. Martin's, 1996.

Wilson, Edmund. *Axel's Castle: A Study in the Imaginative Literature of 1870–1930*. Reprint ed. New York: W. W. Norton, 1984.

Wittgenstein, Ludwig. *Briefe an Ludwig von Ficker*. Edited by G. H. von Wright. Salzburg: Otto Müller, 1969.

———. *Culture and Value*. Edited by G. H. von Wright. Translated by Peter Winch. Chicago: University of Chicago Press, 1984.

———. *Notebooks: 1914–1916*. 2d ed. Edited by G. H. von Wright and G. E. M. Anscombe. Translated by G. E. M. Anscombe. Chicago: University of Chicago Press, 1979.

———. *Philosophical Investigations*. Rev. 3rd ed. Translated by G. E. M. Anscombe. Malden, Mass.: Blackwell, 2001.

———. *Philosophical Remarks*. Translated by Raymond Hargreaves and Roger White. Oxford: Blackwell, 1975.

———. *Tractatus Logico-Philosophicus*. Translated by D. F. Pears and B. F. McGuinness. London: Routledge and Kegan Paul, 1974.

———. *Werkausgabe Band 1 (Tractatus logico-philosophicus, Tagebücher 1914–1916, Philosophische Untersuchungen)*. Frankfurt am Main: Suhrkamp, 1984.

———. *Zettel*. Edited by G. E. M. Anscombe and G. H. von Wright. Translated by G. E. M. Anscombe. Berkeley: University of California Press, 1970.

Won, Joseph D. "Yellowface Minstrelsy: Asian Martial Arts and the American Popular Imaginary." Ph.D. diss., University of Michigan, 1997.

Woods, Gregory. "The 'Conspiracy' of the 'Homintern.' " *Gay and Lesbian Review* 10, no. 3 (May-June 2003): 11–13.

Woolf, Leonard. *Beginning Again: An Autobiography of the Years 1911 to 1918*. London: Hogarth Press, 1972.

Woolf, Leonard, and Virginia Woolf. *Two Stories*. London: Hogarth Press, 1917.

Woolf, Virginia. *The Diary of Virginia Woolf*. Vol. 2. Edited by Anne Olivier Bell. New York: Harcourt, 1978.

———. "The Mark on the Wall." 1921. Pages 83–89 in *The Complete Shorter Fiction of Virginia Woolf*. 2d ed. Edited by Susan Dick. New York: Harcourt, 1989.

———. "Modern Fiction." 1925. Pages 103–10 in *Collected Essays*. Vol. 2. New York: Harcourt, 1967.

———. *Mrs. Dalloway*. 1925. New York: Harcourt, 1981.

———. *A Room of One's Own*. London: Hogarth, 1929.

———. *Three Guineas*. London: Hogarth, 1938.

———. *To the Lighthouse*. 1927. New York: Harcourt, 1981.

———. "An Unwritten Novel." Pages 12–23 in *A Haunted House and Other Short Stories*. London: Hogarth Press, 1944.

———. *The Voyage Out*. London: Duckworth, 1915.

———. *The Years*. Edited by Hermione Lee. Oxford: Oxford University Press, 1992.

Yeats, W. B., ed. *The Oxford Book of Modern Verse, 1892–1935*. New York: Oxford University Press, 1936.

Yeazell, Ruth Bernard. *Harems of the Mind: Passages of Western Art and Literature*. New Haven, Conn.: Yale University Press, 2000.

Yegenoglu, Meyda. *Colonial Fantasies: Towards a Feminist Reading of Orientalism*. Cambridge: Cambridge University Press, 1998.

Yúdice, George. "Rethinking the Theory of the Avant-Garde from the Periphery." In *Modernism and Its Margins: Reinscribing Cultural Modernity from Spain and Latin America*, edited by Anthony L. Geist and José B. Monléon, 52–80. New York: Garland, 1999.

Žižek, Slavoj. *Enjoy Your Symptom! Jacques Lacan in Hollywood and Out.* New York: Routledge, 1992.

Zucker, Carole. *The Idea of the Image: Josef von Sternberg's Dietrich Films.* London: Associated University Press, 1988.

Zwerdling, Alex. *Virginia Woolf and the Real World.* Berkeley: University of California Press, 1986.

Notes on Contributors

Lisa Fluet is an assistant professor of twentieth-century British literature at Boston College. She is completing her book *Expertise: The New Class Character in the Twentieth Century*.

Laura Frost is an associate professor of English at Yale, where she teaches twentieth-century British and comparative literature and gender studies. She is the author of *Sex Drives: Fantasies of Fascism in Literary Modernism*. She is currently at work on a book on modernism and pleasure, and a project on narrative and September 11.

Michael LeMahieu is a visiting assistant professor of English at Clemson University, where he teaches twentieth-century American and British literature. He is working on a book about post–World War II American fiction and the philosophy of language.

Heather K. Love teaches twentieth-century literature and gender studies at the University of Pennsylvania. She has published on modernist, queer, and transgender topics in GLQ, *New Literary History, Feminist Theory, Postmodern Culture,* and *Transition*. She is finishing a book titled "Feeling Backward: Loss and the Politics of Queer History."

Douglas Mao is an associate professor in the English Department at Cornell, and the author of *Solid Objects: Modernism and the Test of Production*. He is currently at work on a book about human development and aesthetic environments in late-nineteenth- and early twentieth-century literature.

Jesse Matz is an associate professor of English at Kenyon College. The author of *Literary Impressionism and Modernist Aesthetics* and *The Modern Novel: A Short Introduction*, he is currently at work on two projects: one on the legacies of Impressionism in various "impressionist cultures," and one on contemporary cultural uses for narrative temporality.

Joshua L. Miller is an assistant professor of English language and literature at the University of Michigan. His articles consider race and ethnicity, language, and genre in twentieth-century literature, photography, and film. He is currently completing a book on modernism and interwar language politics in the United States.

Monica L. Miller is an assistant professor of English at Barnard College, where she specializes in African American literature and cultural studies. She is currently completing a cultural history of the black dandy titled "Slaves to Fashion: Black Dandyism in the Atlantic Diaspora."

Sianne Ngai is an assistant professor of English at Stanford University. She is the author of *Ugly Feelings*, on the aesthetics of minor emotions in the administered world. She is currently at work on a second book on modernist poetry and consumer aesthetics, tentatively called "The Cuteness of the Avant-Garde."

Martin Puchner, an associate professor of English and comparative literature at Columbia University, is the author of *Stage Fright: Modernism, Anti-Theatricality, and Drama* and *Poetry of the Revolution: Marx, Manifestos, and the Avant-Gardes*. He has edited, co-edited, or written introductions to several books, including *Against Theatre: Creative Destructions on the Modernist Stage* and *The Communist Manifesto and Other Writings*. He is co-editor of the forthcoming two-volume *Norton Anthology of Drama*.

Rebecca L. Walkowitz, an assistant professor of English at the University of Wisconsin-Madison, is the author of *Cosmopolitan Style: Modernism Beyond the Nation* and a co-editor of five books in the field of literary and cultural studies, including *The Turn to Ethics* and *Secret Agents*.

Index

bad modernism (*continued*)
postwar culture and, 293; in reading film, 151–53, 173–74; reverse discourse and, 24–25; Wittgenstein and, 71, 88–89; Woolf and, 141–42

badness: artistic behavior and, 2–4, 14; black American vernacular speech and, 24–25; defined, 19, 23–24, 42n11; domestication of, 4–5; as evaluation, 15, 44–45, 62–64; as failure of apprehension, 15, 121; genre fiction and, 97–98, 102–6, 111, 115; liberalism and, 207–8, 228–32; manifestos and, 50; political subjectivity and, 40; social domination and, 25, 41n5

Baker, Houston, 179–80, 194, 201n12, 202n21

Baker, Josephine: as "Black Venus," 149, 150–51, 170–71; *Blonde Venus* as inverted portrait of, 149, 152–53, 157–58, 162–65, 172–73; Chez Joséphine and, 150, 151; dance as abstracting movement and, 169–170; *danse sauvage* and, 149, 150; Dietrich and, 145, 147, 177n33; failed repatriation of, 167; as floating signifier for otherness, 166–67; in *La Sirène des Tropiques*, 174n3, 176n15; modernism and, 165–66, 170–71, 176n13; primitivism and, 150, 156, 170; in *Princess Tam-Tam*, 166–67; in *Shuffle Along*, 149, 170; in *Zou Zou*, 154–55

Bakhtin, Mikhail, 189, 203n35

Bal, Mieke, 265n10

Barrett, Michèle, 123–24, 137–38, 143n13

Baudelaire, Charles, 150, 185

Baudrillard, Jean, 301, 305, 324; absolute advertising and, 302, 306

Beauvoir, Simone de, 208–9

Bencherif, Osman, 98

Benjamin, Walter, 47, 141, 305, 307, 311, 328n23, 328n27

Bergson, Henri, 61, 227

Berlin Wall, 5

Besant, Walter, 304, 310

Besson, Luc, 291

Bhabha, Homi K., 39

black dandy: blackface and, 187–91; black imaginary and, 181, 201n12; black modern identity and, 180–81, 196–97; black modernism and, 191, 200–201; as critique of hierarchies, 182; Du Bois and, 192–97; Harlem Renaissance and, 187–88, 191, 198–200; as modernism's other, 184; mulatto modernism and, 181, 194, 200; Washington as, 180, 201n12

blackface, 155–56; dandyism and, 187–91

black modernism: H. Baker on, 179–80; black dandy as sign of, 181, 191, 196, 200–201; cosmopolitanism and, 195; innovation in, 22–23; modernism and, 181, 185, 200; as mulatto phenomenon, 181, 194, 200

Black Venus: Baudelaire on, 150; as spectral figure in *Blonde Venus*, 152, 158, 161, 165; traditions of, 162–63. *See also* Baker, Josephine; *Blonde Venus*

Blake, Eubie, 149, 170

Blast, 45–46, 66n28; avant-garde and, 52, 66n30; individualism and, 54–55; manifesto modernism and, 55, 56, 66n29; rear-guardism and, 58, 63–64; Sorel and, 59; women's suffrage and, 52–53

Blonde Venus (Sternberg), 147, 149, 163, 174n5; badness of, 152; black performance excluded from, 159–61, 163; Black Venus inverted in, 149, 151, 157, 162–63, 165; critical readings of, 148–49; Dietrich in, 152–56, 174n6; distortion in, 152–53, 157–58; gender in, 148, 175n8; homage and parody in, 155–56, 161–63, 165–66, 171–74; "Hot Voodoo" in, 153–59, 163; inversion in, 156–57, 163–64; as portrait-of-the-artist film, 147–48, 175n9; racial roleplaying in, 155–56, 164–65. *See also* Dietrich, Marlene

Gikandi, Simon, 9

Gilpin, Charles, 159

Gorris, Marleen, 131–32, 144n26

Graves, Robert, 4, 96

Greenberg, Clement, 4, 5, 176n16, 299, 314

Greene, Graham: cosmopolitanism and, 277–78, 296n9; public responsibility and, 279–84, 287–88, 293–95; scholarship boy and, 271, 275–76, 278–79

Gubar, Susan, 8

Gumbrecht, Hans, 170

Gun for Sale, A (Greene), 271, 275–84, 287–88, 293–95

Habermas, Jürgen, 71–72, 93n44; Wittgenstein and, 68, 70, 74, 86–87

Harlem: black modern identity and, 180, 186; dandyism and, 187–88; Johnson on, 185, 187; Locke on, 187

Harlem Renaissance: H. Baker on, 179; black dandy and, 188, 191, 201n13; Locke and, 197–98; modernism and, 181, 192; New Negro aesthetic and, 182; success and failure of, 201n1; Thurman's satire of, 199–200

Heartfield, John, 306–7

Heidegger, Martin, 68, 72, 75

Heine, Heinrich, 30–31, 42n18

Hejinian, Lyn, 144n31

Hemingway, Ernest, 44, 60, 150, 297n24; "The Killers," 290–91, 294

Hichens, Robert, 116n9

high modernism: black Americans and, 23; Lewis and, 44, 60, 63; Lucifer as emblem of, 22; manifestos and, 49–50; popular culture and, 7; public responsibility and, 287; rethinking of, 20; *Tractatus* and, 69; Williams on, 292–93

Highsmith, Patricia, 289–90

Hitler, Adolf: Baker and, 167; Lewis on, 44; *Mein Kampf*, 58, 111; propaganda and, 66n43; Woolf on, 122

hit-man, 270–72, 281–84, 289–91. *See also* Greene, Graham; Hemingway, Ernest

Hobsbawm, Eric, 48

Hodge, Alan, 96

Hogarth Press, 125, 143nn17–18, 220

Hoggart, Richard: community and, 281; *The Uses of Literacy* and scholarship boy, 272–74, 296n17; on women and scholarship boys, 284–286, 294

homosexuality: Auden and, 222–25, 236n33, 237n35; Foucault on, 24; identity and, 41n8; Lewis and, 208–14; Pater and, 26, 29, 31–32, 33

Horkheimer, Max, 320, 326

Horsley, Lee, 111, 114

Howe, Irving, 3, 4, 299

"How I Was Loved by a Sheik!" (Speller), 94–95

Hughes, Langston, 150, 196–97, 199, 243

Hughes, Robert, 4–5

Hull, E. M.: eroticism and, 95–96, 98, 108, 110; genre fiction and, 97–98; imperialism and, 107; Orientalism and, 95, 98, 100–101; pornography and, 111–13. *See also* *Sheik, The*

Hulme, T. E., 59

Hurley, Harold, 160

Hurston, Zora Neale, 199, 243, 244, 252, 267n38

Hutcheon, Linda, 147, 161–62

Huyssen, Andreas, 5, 183, 240, 299, 306

Imagism, 51, 52. *See also* Pound, Ezra

imperialism, 8–9, 119; Baker and, 170; Bulosan and, 238, 240–41, 246–49, 264; Joyce and, 21; Lawrence and, 107; Woolf and, 121, 129, 139–42

Impressionism, 298–326; advertising and, 306–7, 320–24; Cubism and, 313–17; as modernism gone bad, 300–303, 327n8; theories of impression and, 303–13, 317–26

58, 60–61, 67n50, 217, 227; on women and feminism, 233n6, 236n24; on Woolf, 122. *See also Blast*

Lezra, Jacques, 93n49, 121

liberalism: Auden and Lewis on, 207–8, 214–17, 220, 226–32; Merquior on, 234n16

Little Review, 51

Littledale, Clara Savage, 259

Liu, Alan, 295n6

Locke, Alain, 196, 200; dandyism and, 188, 192, 198–99; Harlem Renaissance and, 197; *The New Negro*, 187, 192

Loos, Adolf, 172, 178n44

Lukács, Georg, 305

Lustful Turk, The (anonymous), 112

Lye, Len, 299, 321–324, 329n44

Lyon, Janet, 51; on Baker, 170, 176n13; on feminist manifestos, 53; on Pound, 52, 66n35

Lyotard, Jean-François, 92n28

Mackenzie, Andreas, 152, 178n39

Malinowski, Bronislaw, 235n21

Mallarmé, Stéphane, 59, 304

Manet, Edouard, 310, 312

manifesto: *Blast* and, 51, 52–54; collective movements and, 54–55; critiques of, 49–51, 52, 65n16, 65n17; defining features of, 48; Futurism and, 48–50; Harlem Renaissance and, 192; history of, 47–48; moralism and, 62; playful use of, 55–56; politics and, 53, 57–58

Mao, Douglas, 66n32

Marchand, Roland, 320

Marcus, Sharon, 277

Marcuse, Herbert, 37–38

Marinetti, F. T., 65n21, 65n26; *Blast* and, 52; fascism and, 57–58, 60; Futurism and, 47, 65n18; manifestos and, 48, 50–51, 58; masculinity and, 53; Vorticism and, 56

"Mark on the Wall, The" (Woolf), 124–25, 126–31, 132, 143n18, 311

Martin, Wendy, 170

Marx, Karl, 19, 57, 58. *See also Communist Manifesto*

Marxism: Bulosan and, 239, 250–51, 252, 260; Hitler on, 58; Lewis on, 62; modernist critics and, 5; Sorel and, 57; Wright and, 252, 267n38

masculinity, 208–14, 217–18

mass culture. *See* popular culture

Mayakovsky, Vladimir, 299

McFarlane, James, 3

Melford, George, 95, 115n4, 116n10

Melman, Billie, 101, 111, 115n4, 115n5

Men of 1914, 19, 44

Mendelson, Edward, 221, 237n35

Menninghaus, Winifred, 91n22

Mercure de France, 65n22

Merquior, J. G., 234n16

Meyer, Stefan G., 9

Miller, Tyrus, 61, 271

Milton, John, 22

minstrelsy: Bulosan and, 243–44, 252–57, 262; dandyism and, 190–91, 194–95

Mitchison, Naomi, 235n20

modernism: death of, 5; defined, 2–16; "dominant" vs. "marginal," 23, 41n5; early retrospectives of, 4–5; failure in, 25; gender and, 8, 183–84; "mulatto," 180, 181, 194, 197, 200; politics of, 206; as response to victimization, 23; tradition vs., 6, 19; transgression and, 20–21. *See also* avant-garde; bad modernism; black modernism; British modernism; high modernism; rear-guard modernism

modernismo, 9

modernity: African Americans and, 181, 185, 201; Filipino identity and, 241–44; Impressionism and, 305–7, 324–26; modernist language and, 111; Parisian, 300; Wittgenstein and, 70–74, 77–78, 87–89, 92n33

Moers, Ellen, 182

Monet, Claude, 302, 303, 313, 314, 318

Monléon, José B., 9

Moran, Maureen, 30

Moréas, Jean, 48

Morton, H. V., 98

Mosley, Oswald, 113

Moten, Fred, 120

Mrs. Dalloway (Woolf): critical heroism in, 132–41; euphemism in, 132, 136–37; evasion in, 133–40; film version of, 131–32, 144n26; gender in, 133–37, 140; imperialism in, 139–40; parataxis in, 135, 137–38

"mulatto" modernism, 180, 181, 194, 197, 200

Mussolini, Benito: action-speech and, 66n43; communism and, 58; Lewis and, 216; revolution and, 60; Sorel and, 57; time and, 61

My Story Weekly, 94–95

Naremore, James, 277

Negro Election Day, 189–90

Nehring, Neil, 296n7

neo-Marxism, 307

New Yorker, 262

Nichols, Bill, 152, 163, 164, 176n19

Nietzsche, Friedrich: art and, 63; manifestos and, 57; transvaluation of all values and, 19, 45; Wittgenstein and, 68

Noble, Marianne, 118n35

nonsense, in Wittgenstein, 71–89, 91n19, 91n22, 92n33, 92n39

North, Michael: *The Dialect of Modernism*, 152, 156; on *Tractatus*, 69–70, 77–78

O'Hara, Daniel, 325

O'Neill, Eugene, 159

Orators, The (Auden), 220–30, 231; "Address for a Prize Day," 221, 225–226; "The Journal of an Airman," 221, 224–227

Orientalism: Baker and, 166–67; Bulosan and, 239, 243–44, 255–59, 263; *The Sheik* and, 95, 98, 100–101

Orphic/Narcissistic tradition, 37–39

Ortega y Gasset, José, 59, 313

Osborne, John, 272, 273

Oxford English Dictionary, 42n11

Paramount Studios, 145; *Blonde Venus* and, 148, 171; Sternberg-Dietrich films and, 147, 152, 165

Parker, Paul, 321

parody, 147, 155–56, 161–63, 165–66, 171–74

Pater, Walter: aestheticism and, 27, 62; "Apollo in Picardy," 42n12; on Botticelli, 32–35; disappearing subject and, 28–30; images of expectation and, 43n20; impressions and, 313; Marcuse and, 38; marginalized sexual identity of, 25, 29–30; politics of refusal and, 26, 32, 40; queerness and, 26, 27–28, 35–36; victim as hero and, 30–31

patriotism: Butler on, 119–20; Woolf and, 11–12

Pease, Allison, 113

Pepsi campaign, 306, 307, 321, 324

performativity: dandyism and, 180–81, 187–88; gender and, 209; queer, 27–28, 37

Perloff, Marjorie: on Futurism, 49; on modernism, 6–7; on *Tractatus*, 69–70, 80–81, 92n29

Picasso, Pablo: appropriation and, 161; Baker and, 172; portraiture and, 173, 175n9; racial roleplaying and, 164

Pinkney, Tony, 173

Pinkster (festival), 189–90

Pissarro, Camille, 302, 327n8

popular culture: Baker and, 150; critiques of, 102–5; as mass movement, 59; pornographic representation and, 113

positivism: modernism vs., 11; Wittgenstein and logical, 68, 83

postcolonialism, 8–9

Post-Impressionism, 313

postmodernism, 6, 15

Pound, Ezra, 60, 165, 179; "ABC's," 52; avant-garde and, 240; *The Dial* and, 65n22; fascism and, 58; *Hugh Selwyn Mauberley*, 161; manifestos and, 51–52, 54, 55, 66n35; Marinetti and, 65n21, 65n26; racial role-playing and, 164; Radio Rome and, 58. *See also Blast*

praise, 145–47, 157, 170–74

primitivism: Auden and, 217–19, 235n21; Baker and, 150–51; in *Blonde Venus*, 153–56, 159, 163–65, 170; Bulosan and, 244, 249, 257–59, 263; Hull and, 104; Lawrence and, 106–10; Lewis and, 212–14, 217–18, 235n21; modernism and, 230–32

professionalism, hit-man and, 270–80, 284, 287–95

Prometheus, 37–38

Proust, Marcel, 44, 60, 61, 105, 221; impressions in works of, 303, 304

pulp fiction, 269–71. *See also* Greene, Graham; hit-man

Pulp Fiction (Tarantino), 291

queerness: Auden and, 220, 225–27, 229; black dandy and, 201n13; performativity and, 27–28, 37; politics of refusal and, 26, 39–40; as term, 24; texts and readers, 42n15. *See also* Pater, Walter

Rabinowitz, Paula, 269

race: black dandy and, 179–205; *Blonde Venus* and, 152; Lawrence and, 107; modernism and, 179–80; stereotyping in *The Sheik* and, 95, 98, 100–101. *See also* Baker, Josephine; Bulosan, Carlos

Rainey, Lawrence, 77, 51, 65n21, 65n26, 299

Raub, Patricia, 111

rear-guard modernism, 64n4; Lewis and, 45–46, 58–60, 61–64; satire and, 56, 61; strategies of, 57

Renoir, Pierre-Auguste, 302

revolution: art and, 53; modernity and, 48, 58; rear-guardism and, 45–48, 57, 60; time and, 61

Revue Nègre, 149–50, 151, 163, 170. *See also* Baker, Josephine

Riding, Laura, 4

Rigby, Nigel, 8–9

Riley, Denise, 296n20

Ripley's Game (Highsmith), 289–90

Robbins, Bruce, 119, 299

Robeson, Paul, 159

Rogin, Michael, 156

Rubin, James, 305

Russell, Bertrand, 55, 58, 61, 62; *Tractatus* and, 76, 78, 92n29; Wittgenstein and, 68, 69, 70, 85–86, 89

Sade, Marquis de, 111

Said, Edward, 9, 121

San Juan, E., Jr., 268n44

satire: in Bulosan, 244; as rear-guard style, 56, 61–64

Sauvage, Marcel, 151

Schiele, Egon, 147, 175n9

Schiff, Richard, 312

Schoenberg, Arnold, 299

scholarship boy, 271, 272–74, 296n17; in Greene, 275–79; women and, 284, 296n20; in Woolf, 285–86

Schulberg, B. P., 147–48

Second World War, 125; Baker and, 167, 177n33; Dietrich and, 177n33; internationalism and, 120; Philippines and, 239, 243

Sedgwick, Eve Kosofsky, 27–28, 37

Seurat, Georges, 308, 313

sexuality: alternative tradition of, 37; Hull and, 98; Lawrence and, 96–98; modernism and, 115; pornographic representations and, 113. *See also* homosexuality; queerness

Douglas Mao is an associate professor of English
at Cornell University.

Rebecca L. Walkowitz is an assistant professor of
English at the University of Wisconsin, Madison.

Library of Congress Cataloging-in-Publication Data
Bad modernisms / edited by Douglas Mao and
Rebecca L. Walkowitz.
p. cm.
Includes bibliographical references (p.) and
index.
ISBN 0-8223-3784-3 (cloth : acid-free paper) —
ISBN 0-8223-3797-5 (pbk. : acid-free paper)
1. English literature — 20th century — History
and criticism. 2. Modernism (Literature) —
English-speaking countries. 3. American
literature — 20th century — History and
criticism. I. Mao, Douglas, 1966– II. Walkowitz,
Rebecca L., 1970–
PR478.M6B33 2006
820.9′112 — dc22
2005028235